Why We Left a Cult

Why We Left a Cult

Six People Tell Their Stories

Latayne C. Scott

BAKER BOOK HOUSE
Grand Rapids, Michigan 49516

Published by Baker Book House
P. O. Box 6287, Grand Rapids, Michigan 49516-6287

Printed in the United States of America

ISBN: 0-8010-8338-9

For my two precious children:
my strong, witty son, Ryan,
and my sweet, sensitive daughter, Celeste.
You are the joy of my life
and my hope for the cause of Christ
in the future.

Contents

Preface

Loving, concerned Christians who are active in sharing their faith with the lost often draw an invisible line in their minds. They will cross over the lines of denomination, of status, of race, of economic background, even the line of personal likes and dislikes, to teach the gospel to someone. But one line often remains—few will cross the line of a cult.

Many times, trying to reach a cult member with Bible truth is like going to another country, one in which the language is similar but has strange meanings attached to familiar words. There is a feeling of culture shock for the Christian who tries to enter into the thought world of the cult member because there is sometimes no firm base for communication or commonality. An acute awareness of conflict and implied judgment quickly surfaces in such a situation—for the Christian, who is convinced that he or she knows the only way to heaven, and equally for the cult member, who will certainly believe the same of the cult's doctrines. Many hardy Christians emerge from such a situation convinced that the gap is unbridgeable. Some even end up converted to the cult rather than leading the cult member out.

Even when cult members are helped to see that they have been taught error, it doesn't automatically follow in their minds that they should embrace the brand of thinking endorsed by the person who led them out. *Out of the frying pan, perhaps into the fire to be burned again,* they think. And being burned once is enough for anyone.

The Christian, meanwhile, is left disoriented and bewildered by the entire process. What kind of hold could this group have on a person, to continue to influence him or her even after the person left the cult? A phrase in our contemporary culture describes such a phenomenon. We speak of someone being "zapped." The inherent image is that of something like lightning, which originates "out there," comes down precipitously, striking without warning (and sometimes seemingly without reason).

In using this analogy to describe the cultic effect on the human personality, I recently learned something from my teenage daughter, Celeste, who was preparing a science-fair project on lightning. I had always thought that lightning originated in the sky and fired down to earth (for reasons I never understood). I now know that lightning is actually the explosive "connection" between opposite electrical charges in the clouds and on the earth. Similarly, what we see as the zapping by a cult is the result of a connection between the very powerful elements of a human personality and a supercharged system of thought.

It would be easy and convenient to make sweeping generalizations about what makes a person vulnerable to a cult. However, I have found in my own experience as a former member of the cult known as Mormonism that there are as many reasons for joining a cult as there are individual personalities. When I am asked why I became a Mormon, I always answer that I wanted to please God, and I became convinced that the Mormon church was the only earthly organization that could help me do that.

In my book *Ex-Mormons: Why We Left* (also published as *Why We Left Mormonism*) I interviewed seven people who, like myself, had once been Mormons but who had left the Church of Jesus Christ of Latter-day Saints. Our reasons for being Mormons as well as for leaving Mormonism were as varied as our backgrounds—leading me to conclude that there is no one "magic formula" for extracting all people from the considerable hold of Mormonism.

Choosing seven people to participate with me in that book was relatively easy, because my ministry as a writer and a speaker had brought me into contact with many people who have left the Mormon church and become faithful Christians. But when I embarked on the project of using that same basic format to write a book that focused on other cults, I found there were several problems inherent to the task.

First, I had to decide which cults I would examine. One source I consulted estimated that there are over five thousand religious cults in the United States. I decided to focus on those termed "Christian cults" because of their appeal to and reliance on the terminology and tradition of biblical teachings. I selected four groups I believed would be most relevant to readers: Jehovah's Witnesses, Christian Scientists, New Age believers, and World-wide Church of God (Herbert W. Armstrong's movement.) However, after many conversations with ex-members of the Armstrong group, I find I must agree with the assessment of the *Christian Research Journal* that such astounding changes have taken place in both the doctrines and practices of that group (accompanied by a significant decline in membership) that they can no longer be accurately viewed as a cult. While, of course, many cultic groups (most notably and overtly the Mormon church) have tried vigorously through an image-changing campaign in the media to be accepted as "another Christian church," the Worldwide Church of God seems to be doing it through repenting and changing instead of publicity and advertising. Only time will prove the group's sincerity. Meanwhile, I am fascinated with the prospect that a cult, as a group, can turn to God.

I decided to pursue only the remaining three cults on my list and found that just making the initial contacts with prospective participants was complicated. I made scores of telephone calls and wrote numerous letters, trying to find just the "right" people. My preliminary requirement was that a participant had to have been actively involved in the cult, been "out" for at least three years, and now be an active member of a mainstream local Christian church. In other words, I was looking for two things in my ex-cult members: validity and stability.

I found this combination (accompanied, of course, by willingness to participate in my project) to be a rare thing indeed. To find such people, I had to rely on the recommendations of those whose judgment and expertise I trusted, such as the Christian Research Institute and various other ministries that specialize in cults. I believe that the end result—the participants who were finally chosen—is the product of my fervent prayer and the petitioning of many others who interceded for us all.

I am deeply humbled by the wisdom that these people have to share. The strength of what they have to say is due partly to their diversity. There are two men and four women. They range in age from late thirties to nearly seventy years of age. Three were "born into" cults; three were converted. Two live on the East Coast, three on the West Coast, and one lives in Arizona. Three of the people are involved in full-time ministry—speaking, writing, counseling—to members and ex-members of the cult that they left. The other three are "regular" folks who either hold full-time secular jobs or are retired. They are active within a local congregation and often speak to groups about their experiences as cult members.

Once I had prayerfully selected these six people, I asked them to sign an informal statement: "I am a mature, committed Christian." At that time I gave them the opportunity to decline without explanation my invitation to participate in this book if they were struggling with any sort of problem that, if known to others, could compromise the effectiveness of their testimonies. I also asked each participant to excuse himself or herself from giving a testimony if unable to affirm active participation in a church that would be recognized as "mainstream." I found I had to be precise in my requirements. I was amazed when one person I had contacted identified herself as a mature, committed Christian, yet said she had not attended worship services for years. Though the story of her cultic involvement was fascinating, I explained to her that I would not be able to use her testimony because readers of a book such as this would want to know not only how to get someone out of a cult, but how to help that person become a functioning part of the body of Christ.

I sent each of the six participants a set of blank cassette tapes and a list of questions. These questions covered three main areas of information: (1) the participant's background and extent of involvement with the cult; (2) his or her "point of departure"— the factors leading up to leaving the cult; and (3) advice to Christians who are trying to reach cult members with the gospel.

I encouraged the participants to tell as much as they could about family background, pertinent childhood experiences, and any involvement in churches before becoming a cult member. This was an attempt to show in individual cases what might have "prepared the soil" for the cultic seed to take root. (However, it is incorrect to say that all members of cults became affiliated because of certain supposed personality quirks: a substantial percentage of cult members were *born* into association with the group. Looking for any "cause" other than birth circumstances in these cases is unproductive.)

Each participant was asked to be as specific as possible about his or her "point of departure." I have found in the many times that I have spoken on my experiences as a Mormon that the most common question I am asked has to do with the specifics of what "put me over the edge" in making a decision to leave Mormonism. People's interest in this seems to me to be symptomatic of our culture, which encourages us to cut through the fat, go for the jugular, get to the good stuff, cut to the chase. However, I would caution that such turning-point experiences must, like Scripture, be viewed in context.

In the first part of the book, the accounts of each participant's background and subsequent conversion to Christ have been dealt with in the third person. I begin each person's testimony with a vignette that illustrates something of the flavor of his or her story. In the complete narrative that follows, I have tried to use the participants' own terminology in describing their conversion, whether it be "accepting the Lord," "praying the sinner's prayer," or submitting to biblical baptism. The second portion of this book is a kind of round-table discussion of various issues that are of interest to Christians who deal with cults. This is the same format that I used in *Ex-Mormons* and would be familiar to anyone who watches panel discussions and talk shows on television. How hard it is to escape our culture!

In the question-and-answer section, I asked the participants how their views of God, the Bible, and earthly leadership have changed since becoming Christians, and I think some of their answers may surprise you. In addition, they gave some specific and challenging insights into how we as Christians can meet the needs of people who come out of cults into the body of Christ. One area of particular interest, I believe, is their responses to the question, "What would you tell parents that could help them protect their children from cultist indoctrination?"

The participants' varied answers reflect their diverse personalities and experiences, but if you have a friend who is involved in a cult, perhaps you will see similarities to someone within these pages. I also asked each participant to define some terms specific to his or her cult, and these definitions appear in a glossary at the back of this book.

In an effort to keep the material readable, the participants and I have tried to keep documentation to a minimum. Even scriptural notations have been used sparingly, for two reasons: to maintain an uninterrupted narrative flow and also to minimize the possibility of making the mistake that cultists want us to make—accepting what someone tells us *about* a Scripture without looking it up in its context. So use your concordance!

All in all, this is not a book of information, but a source of insights into how people are attracted to cults, why they leave them, and what helps an ex-cult member become a mature Christian.

Back in the late seventies, when I wrote my first book on the cultic experience (*The Mormon Mirage*), I shared from my heart the cost and the joys of leaving Mormonism. In *Ex-Mormons: Why We Left*, I shared a little and listened a lot. In this book, I have listened and learned a lot in the process. I know that cults, like lightning, are only momentary disturbances in God's grand scheme, because for all their blinding power, they will someday be exposed by Jesus as the perversions of his gospel that they are. But, also like lightning, they can be devastating in their annihilation of lives and souls and relationships.

The call is for mature Christians to be the lightning rods that diffuse the destructive power of cults. We must equip ourselves with the knowledge of Satan's wily schemes, standing high and visible in the crashing storm, firmly upheld by the power of God's might. It is my fervent prayer that this book will be an instrument of that power.

Introduction

The Archipelago of the Cults

In a recent conversation with a close spiritual mentor, I mentioned this book and made an off-the-cuff remark about "us ex-cultists." My friend was shocked and told me so—he never thinks of me as an "ex-cultist."

"Well, I spent ten years as a faithful Mormon," I responded. "And we would both agree that it is a cult, right?"

He fidgeted for a while before he replied. "Oh, yes, Mormonism is a cult—but when I think of a *cultist*, I think of someone who wears a robe and burns incense or acts strange."

My friend's reaction is not a bit unusual. In fact, I imagine that if you were to ask an average Christian to define a cult, about the best he or she would come up with would be the conclusion that cultists "are not like us."

In trying to define a cult, you can't say that the major cultic groups don't use the Bible. In fact, some of them study it more rigorously than a lot of Christians do, and they often base distinctive doctrines on specific Bible passages or phrases. Many of them have the name "Christ" or "God" in their group's name. And, as for dedication and fervor, they often put most Christians to shame.

Yet, they are *not* like us. Sometimes we feel that difference more than know it. On the other hand, unless we are able to identify exactly why they are not like us, we have no basis other than personal preference and background on which to condemn their teachings. For a Christian, the standard against which we judge error must always be the Bible, not our feelings.

For many years, when I was speaking on Mormonism, I used a handy little definition from the Utah Christian Tract Society (now known as "Mormonism Researched"). A "Christian" cult, according to this organization, is a group whose doctrines deify man, humanize God, ostracize the Scriptures, and provide a different view of salvation.

Mormonism, for example, fits this definition quite well. Mormons believe they will become gods, like their god who once was a man. They claim that the Bible is mistranslated and thus inferior to their own writings, and that where you spend eternity is not based solely on the sacrifice of Christ (that only provides resurrection) but on whether or not you live their ordinances faithfully.

While that four-part definition of a cult has served me well for many years, I have garnered some other characteristics of cults through observation and reading what others have written about them. Few cults will encompass all these features, but all share most of them.

I believe this is because the cults are like an archipelago, literally defined as a group of islands in a sea. Islands that are close to each other geographically are connected beneath the surface of the water—none of them just floats independently of the others. One may appear to have a flat, sandy terrain, while its neighbor a few miles away may have craggy cliffs that jut high above the waterline. But the islands all share a common base beneath the surface. It is that which connects and unites them that shows their common origin.

Similarly, neither do cults just float around in the sea of truth independently of each other! They all have a common heretical base, which reflects their origins in the mind of the great liar, Satan. Here are some of the characteristics of that base:

1. A redefinition of God, either as a former human or an impersonal force.

2. A redefinition of Jesus, either as merely human, or as just an illustration of the "Christ principle," or as one of many prophets or holy men, or as the brother of Lucifer or Michael the archangel.

3. A redefinition of the Holy Spirit, either as a force without personality or as a commodity to which only the cult has access.

4. Rejection of the biblical doctrine of the Trinity by claiming that God, Jesus, and the Spirit are totally separate, or that one or more of them is either inferior to or absent from the others.

5. Elevation of man to godhood, either by his earning that status or by his "becoming one with" God.

6. Devaluation of the Bible, either by claiming that it must be translated or interpreted only by the group or by ranking it below other writings of the cult.

7. A claim to exclusive revelation and guidance from God.

8. A proclivity toward prophetic predictions, most of which do not happen when or how the group predicted.

9. Use of biblical terms with "new" meanings, derived neither from context, original language sources, nor historical usage.

10. A flexible theology that changes according to circumstances.

11. A charismatic founder and/or leadership that can and often does place itself above the teachings it imposes on the group.

12. A claim to "new truth," or unique revelation hidden from the world until brought forth by the group or a leader of the group.

13. The claim that pleasing God and going to heaven are achievable only by being a member of the cult.

14. Measurement of salvation by works.

15. Overt rejection of orthodox or mainstream Christianity and other churches.

16. Strictly regulated and harsh treatment of apostates.

17. A connection between the group and either national or world government in the future.

18. Male-female dualism (teachings about a "mother god" or that the organization or leader is "mother" to Father God).
19. Use of deceased persons as "spirit guides."
20. Teaching that death is illusory or neutral in nature, or that the soul is reborn into a different form or body in new lives.
21. Use of mind-control techniques by leaders.
22. Use of special ritualistic ceremonies, mantras, or "high doctrines" for the elite.
23. Extreme dependence on subjective feelings or personal experience as "proof" of the validity of the group's doctrine.
24. Use of altered states of consciousness achieved through fasting, drugs, meditation, or other techniques to receive "revelation."
25. Use of Bible terminology or verses out of context as the basis for nontraditional teachings or practices.
26. Emphasis on authority and connection to the past, which is disavowed when these would make the cult look bad in the eyes of outsiders.
27. Repressive "discipling" techniques that require submission to others in such tangible matters as activities and dress, as well as in such "spiritual" matters as amount of time spent in prayer.
28. Claims to special knowledge about the second coming or end of the world.
29. Aberrations of New Testament teachings on monogamy and chastity: forbidding marriage, advocating polygamy, or allowing unfettered sexual freedom.
30. The teaching or implication that group leadership is "the church" and that members thereof are merely a substructure.

Of course, the most accurate way to define a cult might be to tell what it is *not*. A cult is not biblical Christianity, which may be loosely defined as the way that people for two thousand years have agreed on such basic concepts as acknowledgment of the Oneness of God the Father, his divine Son Jesus Christ, and the Holy Spirit who indwells believers; an identifiable point of salvation by grace through faith, followed by a life commensurate with gratitude for that salvation; and belief in the Bible as God's Word to all people of all ages.

Perhaps you, like I, may rankle a bit at the mention of the word *tradition*, because we Christians pride ourselves on relying on God's Word, not just the heritage of past practices and thinking. But consider this perceptive insight about "tradition" from theologian Clark H. Pinnock in *The Use of The Bible in Theology/Evangelical Options* (John Knox Press, 1985; edited by Robert K. Johnston):

> When I confront heretical teachers who advance their novelties in the name of some lost-sight-of exegetical insight (and which of them does not?), the creeds of the church universal, though not infallible, both provide temporary respite by alerting me to the time-honored convictions of multitudes of believing persons before my time and make me pause before accepting innovations. Tradition has a way of buying time for me while a proper exegetical response is worked out. The burden of defending the faith is not one we have to carry alone but one which is shared by countless others living and dead. . . .
>
> The biblical faith is never found apart from tradition. It does not exist in pure essence free of historical forms and fallibilities. But the essence and the forms are not identical and must not be equated. The Bible represents within the flow of history the norm and criterion for determining what is permanent and what is changing, what is legitimate and what is not. Tradition never mirrors purely and perfectly the truth of the gospel, and it always needs to be monitored by God's Word. Tradition is a wonderful servant but a poor master. It serves the church in many ways. But it does not share the same plane with Scripture.

We might summarize what Pinnock said by agreeing that while tradition helps protect us from error, that tradition is only valid inasmuch as it accurately reflects Scripture. For the Christian who wants to evaluate and deal with a cult, there is a preliminary step that must precede all action: The Christian must know what he (or she) personally believes and be able to satisfy both himself and any opponent that the basis for this belief is not found solely in personal experience or preferences—it must be from the Bible and must fit in context with all other biblical doctrines.

Meanwhile, our heritage of Christian belief—tradition, if you will—serves the purpose of alerting us to error, which in turn can be properly assessed only against the standard of truth of the Bible. Therefore, Christians who see cultic doctrine as "strange" are only reacting to the clash of such doctrine to their own background and echo what even the most cult-ignorant of us feels deep in our heart: The cults ultimately "are not like us."

That is why it is vitally important to listen to the words of the people within the pages of this book. Because they know exactly where those crucial differences lie, they can help you chart the perilous course between the reefs of the archipelago of the cults.

PART ONE

Personal Testimonies
and Points of Departure

1

David Reed

We often speak of the visible scars that people bear as a result of their experiences. The apostle Paul, for example, spoke in 2 Corinthians and in Galatians of bearing in his own body evidence of his association with Jesus. If you were to look carefully into David Reed's mouth, you would find evidence of his devotion to a different master—the Watchtower organization of the Jehovah's Witnesses. Because David fervently believed Watchtower teachings that Armageddon would take place around 1975 and reasoned that time was short, he had his dentist pull his ailing teeth rather than do expensive dental work. Today, there are still spaces in David's mouth that remind him of just how much he was willing to sacrifice for the Watchtower Society.

Like many children of the "baby-boomer" generation, David Reed came from parents whose religious backgrounds differed and who at first didn't regularly attend church. Then, for a while, young David and his little sister attended a Baptist church where his mother was baptized, but all he recalls of that church is a few Bible stories. About the time David entered the seventh grade, he and his sister and mother became active in a Unitarian church in nearby Milton, Massachusetts. With its large white building and towering steeple and church bell, it looked on the outside like a traditional New England church.

"The eighth-grade Sunday school class there had a very important impact on me," David recalls. As part of the curriculum of studying other religions, the class would attend other churches every other Sunday and on alternate weeks studied the doctrines of the church they would visit next.

As a result of this study, David concluded like Karl Marx that religion was "the opiate of the people," and that its function was to make money, exert power over mankind, and give comforting "answers" to questions that, in David's mind, really had no answers. David now attributes part of this conclusion to the Unitarian teachings, which rejected the doctrine of the Trinity and claimed instead that there was only one God—in the singular sense—and that Jesus was not divine.

By the time David entered high school, he was a confirmed atheist who believed that organized religion was contrary to both science and common sense. A Seventh-day Adventist neighbor, knowing of his interest in astronomy, once gave David a book describing a "hole" in the Orion nebula through which Jesus would return. David's arguments that space itself was by definition the absence of matter, and that it therefore couldn't have a hole in it, fell on deaf ears. He was told that he just needed to "have more faith."

"I had other reasons for wanting to believe there wasn't a God and that I wasn't responsible to anyone for my actions," David says. "After all, if you believe you are descended from an ape, then there are no moral standards—and no reasons to feel guilty."

David was not stupid—he attended Harvard on a National Merit Scholarship. By the time he was twenty-two and met Paul, a co-worker who was a Jehovah's Witness, arguing about religion had become an intellectual exercise. But when David would ask Paul questions about religion, he would give him logical responses, answers he would reinforce to David by looking up Scripture verses.

"Without sermonizing, without pressure—and almost without my knowing what was happening—this man had me in a weekly Bible study," David recalls. The logical, organized method of study, along with David's awakening understanding of what he termed the "dead-end thinking of atheism" combined to sharpen his awareness of, and need for, God.

At his friend's urging, he began to read Watchtower books, which characteristically began by teaching ideas with which any reader could easily agree, and which then gradually and subtly introduced more "eccentric" doctrines. David began to attend all the Watchtower Society meetings, to advance as a Witness, and finally was baptized by them in the spring of 1969.

He soon became a full-time "pioneer" minister, devoting the required hundred hours a month to knocking on doors and talking to people about the *Watchtower* magazine. He met Penni, a bright psychology/sociology major at Western Michigan University, herself a "pioneer" from a devout Jehovah's Witnesses family. They married in 1971.

Though David and Penni were not able to continue the pace of "pioneering" (most "pioneers" are supported by parents or some other outside source of income), they still zealously devoted about thirty hours a month to the preaching work. Keeping secular employment to a minimum, they lived frugally in a three-room apartment, eschewing "luxuries" like dental work. David became an elder as soon as he qualified, serving in that capacity for eight years.

During their thirteen years together in the organization, David and Penni continually sought ways to serve the Watchtower Society, reasoning that being a Witness was the same as being a servant of God. To them, the Society was the organization that connected them to God, his way of communicating and dealing with people, so they happily cooperated with its agenda. They studied with dozens of people, ultimately leading some thirty people to become baptized, active Jehovah's Witnesses.

When David and Penni left the Jehovah's Witnesses organization, David likened it to leaving an apartment building that was on fire. "Do you escape through the nearest exit?" he asked himself. "Or do you pound on doors to wake the neighbors and help them escape, too?" He concluded that he had an obligation to the family and friends he had led into that "burning building," and he began to warn people of the urgent danger. Today, he continues in this role as speaker, author of several standard works on the Watchtower organization, and editor of the quarterly, *Comments from the Friends*.

David's exit from the Watchtower Society, though visceral, was by no means sudden or impulsive. In fact, he can identify several cumulative factors that led to that decision. The first incident involved, surprisingly enough, a copy of the Catholic version of *The Living Bible*, entitled *The Way*.

Another Witness had brought this book to a Kingdom Hall meeting, excited because this paraphrased version of the Bible seemed to vindicate their own teaching that "the LORD" should be referred to in the Old Testament as Jehovah. David and Penni overcame the fears they had been taught to have about demons lurking in Christian bookstores and went to a local store to buy their own copy.

They took the Bible home and began reading it and comparing it to *The New World Translation*, the Watchtower's official version. About that time, another event took place that also encouraged their Bible reading. David and Penni attended a very large convention of Witnesses at the Providence, Rhode Island, Civic Center where almost twenty thousand people were in attendance. Outside the building, a handful of picketers held up signs. One of them caught David's eye: "Read the Bible, not the Watchtower."

Though they had no sympathy for the people picketing, David and Penni did decide to begin reading both the Bible and the *Watchtower* with the aim of becoming better Jehovah's Witnesses. (A later calculation revealed that their yearly reading assignments required them to read over three thousand pages of Watchtower literature, as compared to only two *hundred* pages of Bible text.)

As they began to fulfill their new resolve to read the Bible, a transformation took place in their thinking. "We began to see Jesus," David remembers, "and to see him not just in the sense of a theological definition, but as our example, the one whom Christians should follow."

David took special note of how Jesus related to the people around him. He noticed that Jesus condemned the scribes and Pharisees for following traditions that they put above the Word of God. In his door-to-door tracting, David would confront Catholics with the Scripture: "These people honor me with their lips, but their hearts are far removed from me. . . . their teachings are but rules" (Matt. 15:8–9).

Meanwhile, in his capacity as an elder among Jehovah's Witnesses, David found himself doing exactly the same thing, as he counseled people according to Watchtower standards of dress. He says, "You couldn't wear either tapered or flared trousers. Women couldn't wear pants to meetings. I would tell men that they had to trim their hair to a 1950s-style haircut and wear sideburns no longer than to the ear. There were all sorts of rules I was enforcing that I knew were not in the Bible. It finally hit me one day that *I* was teaching commands of men as doctrines, because I was telling people that they couldn't please God unless they did what I told them to do."

This realization shook David. He remembered how many young men he had invited to his Kingdom Hall who had been making progress in their studies, but who would terminate their study over the haircut issue. Feeling that the problem lay in local leadership and not necessarily with the Watchtower Society, David decided to follow the example of Jesus when he refused to be bound by man-made commands. If an elder had longer hair, David reasoned, it would not be such an issue for other young men who came looking for truth. So he let his own hair grow—just a little, perhaps half an inch—over his ears and collar.

"That started World War Three in the Kingdom Hall," David recalls. "They instigated judicial hearings, prosecuting me, bringing forth witnesses. When I appealed one of their decisions, they brought forth a committee of older businessmen from Rhode Island for several consecutive weekends. Witnesses were called and interrogated in meetings that went on for hours. And all this over half an inch of hair—an 'untheocratic haircut.' The higher the issue went in the Watchtower organization, the more questions I had about what I was seeing—circuit overseers and district overseers disagreeing over silly issues—organization men, not godly men."

In the meantime, the Watchtower Society itself was in the process of reversing its prior stance on the treatment of "disfellowshiped" members. In 1972, they had liberalized what had historically been a very strident policy against ex-members. As of 1972, Witnesses were instructed to treat disfellowshiped members kindly and allowed to have such people in their homes, especially if they were relatives. But, in the midst of David's haircut troubles, the Society went back to the older and harsh way of treating such people. Even saying "hello" to such a person was forbidden. This change was called "a new truth," and the cover of the September 15, 1981, *Watchtower* magazine announced it with a question: "When God speaks, do you listen?"

David recognized this not as "a new truth" but as a policy reversal designed to isolate dissenters. He thought that if the organization he had wholeheartedly supported as "Jehovah's mouthpiece" could be so arbitrary with these matters, perhaps other teachings could be wrong, too.

"It began to occur to me that some things I'd believed couldn't be supported by the Bible—the belief that Jesus had returned invisibly in 1914, that 1935 was the end of the heavenly calling and people who came to God after that would have a future of a life in the earthly paradise. I began to speak up on things like this."

In his position as "service overseer" in the congregation, David was responsible for motivating people in house-to-house field service. One of the members related that another leader had advised him to stop reading the Bible, that it would confuse him, and he should "just stick to *The Watchtower*." David was upset by this, and the following Thursday night when he was supposed to address the congregation in Kingdom Hall on his assigned topic of the Book of Zechariah, he told the group that if they had to make a choice between reading the Scripture text or reading *The Watchtower* commentary on it, they should read the Bible.

"I told them that the Bible was inspired of God, and that *The Watchtower* was written by men, who made mistakes and often had to go back and correct them, whereas the Bible never needed 'correcting.'"

David, who had been a frequent speaker in congregations throughout eastern Massachusetts and Rhode Island, never again was able to speak from the platform at a Kingdom Hall. Though he and Penni were able to speak about the importance of the Bible from their seats at the Sunday-morning Watchtower question-and-answer sessions, that, too, soon ended, since they were consistently refused the microphone.

David and Penni were faced with a dilemma. They felt a responsibility to their friends, especially those they had led into the Jehovah's Witnesses organization. But, if they were to be disfellowshiped, the "new truth" ruling meant that no one, not even their close relatives in the church, would be able to speak to them. So they began very quietly to share what they had found with close friends and family. David began also to produce a newsletter, which he called, "Comments from the Friends."

David chose a pen name, Bill Tyndale, Jr., hoping that newsletter readers would see a parallel between his inability to use his real name and the fact that centuries earlier, William Tyndale had to deal with an ecclesiastical authority that likewise did not allow open dissent. The issues the newsletter examined were not major points of doctrine but were challenges to the church to think about the implications of "less Bible reading," or "new truths." Still, the project was one that had to be done in secret.

David explains: "Penni and I went to the public library and looked up addresses of Kingdom Halls across the United States;

we sent newsletters to them, as well as to individuals we knew. Because we had neighbors who were Witnesses, we would bundle up the thousand-or-so newsletters in brown paper bags and take them out to the car at night. Then we would drive across the state line to Rhode Island, or in the other direction to Connecticut, and mail them so that they would not have a local postmark. I even mailed batches to postmasters in Bethlehem, Pennsylvania, and to Truth or Consequences, New Mexico, hoping that those postmarks would cause people to think."

Because of the different postmarks, the Watchtower officials concluded that there was a widespread organization they called "the Tyndale Movement." They interrogated dissident Witnesses across the country about their supposed involvement with what was in reality the work of one man on an old manual typewriter.

One evening, David and Penni had a very unusual study with a woman whom they had been teaching. Rather than leading her to the Watchtower Society and its doctrines, they encouraged her to look to the Bible as the source of truth and to Jesus Christ as her leader and example. When they returned home from the study around nine o'clock, they were unable to park near their home because there were so many cars there. As they walked in the darkness, two men dressed in trenchcoats (really!) suddenly got out of one of the parked cars. When they stepped into the light, David recognized them as two Jehovah's Witnesses elders.

Their question was as abrupt as their appearance: "Are you going to continue publishing that newsletter?"

"Well, why?" David responded. "What's wrong with it? What was in it that you disagreed with?"

"We don't want to discuss that with you," one of the men answered. "We just want to know whether you're going to publish another issue."

"You'll find out when you get the next one in the mail," was David's reply, and the men left. David later learned that his actions had been reported to the other elders by two of his friends, and he knew that another trial would soon follow. After the exhausting thirty-hour hearings concerning his "nontheocratic haircut," David refused to attend any more hearings. It was at that point that he and Penni were officially disfellowshiped, in absentia, for publishing the newsletter.

The Reeds immediately began to hold meetings at their apartment on Sunday mornings, and as many as fifteen people who had been associated with the Jehovah's Witnesses attended. David and Penni realized the importance of making a commitment to Jesus Christ and began to try to find out what that meant.

For a Jehovah's Witness, the idea of being "born again" is fraught with fear. According to official doctrine, the "anointed class" of 144,000 people were the only ones who would have that privilege. Unfortunately, most of those people had already lived and died in earlier centuries, and of the remaining 9,000, many were the present Watchtower leaders. Definitely, then, only very special Witnesses now alive would be "born again," and anyone outside the Watchtower organization who claimed to be spiritually reborn might be viewed as possessed by a demon who pretended to be the Holy Spirit. (Only those who emphasize being "filled with the Spirit" are seen this way—Jehovah's Witnesses do not view all born-again believers as demon-possessed.)

Very early one morning, David was alone and reading his Bible. He turned to Luke 11 and read the read the words of Jesus: "Ask and it will be given to you; seek and you will find; knock and the door will be opened to you. For everyone who asks receives; he who seeks finds; and to him who knocks the door will be opened. Which of you fathers, if your son asks for a fish, will give him a snake instead? Or if he asks for an egg, will give him a scorpion? If you then, though you are evil, know how to give good gifts to your children, how much more will your Father in heaven give the Holy Spirit to them who ask him!" (vv. 9–13).

So David prayed, asking for God's Spirit and confessing that he was a sinner who had been following men instead of God's Son, whom he acknowledged as his only hope of salvation. After the prayer, he waited quietly with his eyes closed, savoring the feeling of peace he felt.

Later in the morning, as he was driving to work, David again began to pray, as was his custom. To his surprise, when he opened his mouth, he did not address God in his usual way—"Jehovah God"—as he had been taught. Instead, without any planning or premeditation on the matter, David addressed him as "Father."

"I stopped short and asked myself, why did I say that? And then it hit me immediately that this was a fulfillment of what the Bible said in Romans 8 and in Galatians 4 about God's sending the Spirit of his Son into our hearts, crying, 'Abba, Father.' I knew that God had really answered my prayer by accepting me as his child and sending his Spirit into my heart."

Later that day, David was driving home after a very stressful time at work. His job had been especially taxing—phone calls, multiple demands on his time and energy, and other matters that made the prayer of that morning seem very distant. He felt physically depleted, and his eyelid was twitching from the stress. He asked God to heal him emotionally and physically, so he could share the spiritual discoveries of the morning with Penni. Immediately the vibrations ceased, and he felt a real peace that was underscored when Penni, with whom he had had no chance to talk all day, said, "You know, David, I think we should be calling God 'Father' when we pray."

That same morning, she, too, had experienced for herself something like David had. This commonality was the foundation for the life they would embark on from that day forward, a life of sharing with others that the way out of the burning "Watchtower" is through just one Door, Jesus Christ.

2

Joan Cetnar

One of the most beautiful farms in Pennsylvania stretches for five hundred acres on lush, fertile soil. Like the Watchtower organization that its owners espouse, it flourishes year after year. Less than half a mile away is the home of Joan and Bill Cetnar, two people who left both that farm and the Jehovah's Witnesses. Joan's parents still live on the farm and serve in the organization, but they have no fellowship with their daughter.

When Joan passes her parents on the road, they will not speak. The farm, a mute testimony of the earthly inheritance Joan will never have, provides a stark contrast to something that is more real in her mind than the farm's furrows and timbers—her heavenly hope. Instead of receiving a transitory legacy, Joan bequeaths a richer and more lasting one to us, her Christian family: her testimony.

Though Joan Cetnar's parents were young children during the years of 1914 through 1918, during which the Jehovah's Witnesses' prophecies of the end of the world failed, their faith never flagged. Joan's mother, in fact, actively distributed the 1920 book *Millions Now Living Will Never Die* and was apparently nonplused in 1925 when a third prophecy—of the resurrections of Abraham, Isaac, and Jacob—never materialized.

Joan's father was the "congregational servant" in the Kingdom Hall in Brodheadsville, Pennsylvania, when it was established in the early 1930s. Joan, a fourth-generation Jehovah's Witness, recalls that during her childhood she participated actively in promulgating Watchtower doctrine—on street corners, in Bible studies, and in door-to-door tracting. She was taught early by her parents to answer the incredulous objections of those who said that the Watchtower Society had often before predicted the end of this world. "No, we didn't!" young Joan would reply, and she grew up believing what she said.

Yet, Joan's home was a curious mixture of strict adherence to Watchtower Society policies and inexplicable leniency. On the one hand, her parents circumvented the state law that required schoolchildren to have Watchtower-forbidden smallpox vaccinations by taking her to a sanitarium in Camden, New Jersey, where she was given an acid burn on her thigh to simulate vaccination and a forged inoculation certificate so she could enroll in public school. And she and other Witness children attended a school whose administration excused them from saluting the flag and participating in activities connected with such holidays as Christmas and Easter.

On the other hand, Joan's father—though in close contact with Bethel headquarters, which forbade birthday celebrations—allowed Joan to have a cake and party every year until she was in the ninth grade. These parties were often attended by Society officials from Bethel, the Watchtower Society's headquarters.

Such inconsistencies were not recognized by Joan, who decided at age thirteen that she wanted to dedicate her life to God and to the Watchtower Society, which she believed was God's organization on earth. After her graduation at age sixteen as valedictorian of her high school, she set about making her dream of "becoming part of the Bethel family" a reality. After secretarial training, Joan attended a district assembly where she told the head of the Watchtower Society, President Knorr, of her desire to work full-time for the organization.

Joan knew that a position such as she had requested was usually granted only to young women who had labored at the Staten Island cannery for a summer and who had served as "pioneers," distributing tracts and teaching lessons for at least a hundred hours a month for two or three years. Her parents' close association with the Society, however, smoothed the way for immediate placement at headquarters.

She also knew that the position she wanted would involve considerable sacrifice on her part. She would have to commit to a stay of at least three years, during which time she could not marry. Though Joan would be provided room and board, she would be paid only fourteen dollars a month. Even in the 1950s, that was very little money, but she was cheered by her belief that everyone at Bethel—even President Knorr—was paid the same salary.

Joan joyfully accepted assignment to housekeeping duties at Bethel, a job that lasted about eight months. Then she was given a desk in the correspondence department, where she was responsible for routing mail received from one region of the country to the appropriate departments within the Society. She occasionally even answered such correspondence, signing it with the "Watchtower Bible and Tract Society" rubber stamp and her desk code letters.

Several months later, Joan was crushed to receive news of what she considered a demotion—work downstairs in the magazine department. "I couldn't understand why my overseer, Harley Miller, had not come to me and lovingly told me how I had proved unworthy. Because I had known Max Larson, the 'factory servant,' from childhood, I asked him about it. He told me that my removal was because of a facial expression I had made to Harley Miller that showed a lack of respect for him. I learned later that he had never wanted me in the correspondence department from the beginning and that this was a good excuse for my removal. This was my first experience at the hands of God's 'loving' organization, and I was shocked."

Other things began to bother Joan. She was aghast at the dining-room tirades that President Knorr, who sat at the head of the table at each meal, broadcast with his microphone at any hapless employee who had crossed him. And she began to wonder how the president, supposedly on the same salary that she received, could afford the Cadillac he owned and could travel worldwide and entertain visitors lavishly at expensive restaurants and Broadway shows.

Amidst all this mental turmoil, Joan met handsome young Bill Cetnar, a gung ho Watchtower employee who had been taught by his parents from childhood that the Society was never to be questioned, for it was not only "God's theocratic organization on earth," but also God's only channel for Bible understanding. Bill had begun full-time "pioneer" service in 1947 at the age of eighteen and had come to Bethel in 1950. There his responsibility was a great one—he served in a department where he had jurisdiction over one-third of the United States in matters of organizing congregations, approving circuit assemblies, and appointing servants. This "service department" also acted as a court of appeals in disfellowshiping cases.

One of Bill's most important duties involved answering letters on doctrinal issues. Most often this was just a matter of sending out form letters, but Bill felt unable to agree with Watchtower policy on "the crime of vaccinations," which at that time stated that inoculations were equated with the biblically forbidden practice of eating blood. (The Society later reversed itself and said that "God changed His mind," stating that decisions on vaccinations were the province of individual decision, but Bill's failure to yield had already been noticed.)

He, like Joan, saw things at Bethel that shook his faith. For example, a famous apostate, Anton Koerber, bought his way back into the graces of the Society and its president with extravagant gifts, and Koerber boasted about it to Bill. On the other hand, Bill saw humble Watchtower employees publicly humiliated, ousted, and abandoned when they became a financial liability to the organization.

Bill and Joan became more and more aware of the abuses of power that surrounded them. Joan felt she needed time away from Bethel, a chance to think things over. Bill had served eight and a half years at the Society, Joan four. By that time, sickened by disillusionment, they decided to talk to Joan's parents about what they had seen and heard in those years at headquarters. They were told to be patient, that with time "everything would work out."

Joan wasn't so sure. Bill had been warned before leaving Bethel that if he let any of his feelings about blood transfusions be known to "rank and file" Witnesses, he would be disfellow-shiped. And Joan's parents had told her sternly that it was dangerous to her soul to go counter to what they regarded as God's mouthpiece on earth.

"I made up my mind to disagree with the organization," Joan recalls, "and it is a difficult thing, when you are under that kind of mind control, to make a conscious decision like that." She concluded that the changes in "truth," as well as the behavior of the leaders of the Watchtower Society, could mean only one thing: Men, not God, were making the pronouncements from the Watchtower. If they could be wrong on something like blood transfusions, Joan thought, they could be wrong on other things.

The transfusion question seemed vitally important to Bill and Joan because it truly dealt with irrevocable, life-or-death issues. Bill in particular wrestled with his conscience. He reasoned that if he counseled someone to refuse a transfusion, and that person died, Bill himself would feel responsible if the Watchtower later reversed itself on transfusions (as it had, within his own memory, reversed itself on vaccinations in 1952.)

Bill and Joan resigned from headquarters and were married in September 1958. At the ceremony, the sermon was preached by their good friend Colin Quackenbush, former editor of *Awake* magazine. Bill was offered the position of district or circuit servant, but he turned them down. Although he, like Joan, wanted time to think things over, away from the pressures of headquarters, he ruefully admitted, "All I have been trained to do is preach." His new father-in-law suggested that he work on his farm. For four years, Bill did just that, and he and Joan lived harmoniously in the same home with her parents.

Bill and Joan gradually eased back into Witness work. Bill finally agreed to be Ministry School servant, then Bible-study servant in the local congregation. Joan's dream was that moving to the country would allow them to be "happy JW's again." Things went along fairly smoothly, at least outwardly, but Joan's "decision to disagree" continued to grow inside her.

"I did not question Witness doctrine at that time," Joan recalls. "I felt I could prove what I believed from the Bible. But my experiences at Bethel had given me serious doubts about the claims of authority of the organization and hierarchy of the Watchtower."

It was in the midst of these doubts that the Watchtower did one of its doctrinal flip-flops. Before Joan had left the headquarters, she had had grave misgivings about the Society teaching that when John 3:16 speaks of God's loving "the world," it means that he loves just the "new world society"—the Jehovah's Witnesses.

Hard as that was for Joan to deal with, it was even harder to accept the "new truth" that the Society announced after she got married, saying that God indeed loved the whole world. While Joan was pleased that the new doctrine was biblically true, she was greatly distressed that the organization couldn't make up its mind on something so basic. "For four years, I put these doubts and questions in the back of my mind, trying to make a go of it," she remembers. "I thought if I got away from headquarters, the doubts would eventually go away, and I could be content again."

However, Bill and Joan discovered a cache of old Watchtower publications in the basement of her parents' house. Instead of strengthening her faith, these multiplied years of issues painted a picture of a history of doctrinal conflicts, contradictions, and changes.

Bill's moment of truth came when the grandparents of a young child who needed a blood transfusion put Bill on the spot with the question, "What would you do in our situation?" Bill's reply—that he would let the doctor decide—was based on several factors. First of all, while Bill could never condone the drinking of blood, he knew that Jesus was more concerned about what came out of a person rather than what went into him (Mark 7:14). He also knew that even Jesus had been willing on occasion to test important laws—like Sabbath laws—against human need.

Bill's response to the transfusion question soon became public knowledge and drew sharp criticism from church officials. Suddenly, Bill was being taken to task for questioning the Watchtower ban on transfusions, and Joan was confused. She knew that just a few years earlier her Witness grandfather, William Kimmel, who was identified as one of the 144,000 "anointed class," had received a blood transfusion to save his life. Even more significantly, Joan's own father, presiding minister Carl Howell, and her uncle Hayden Howell had not only donated some of the blood but had encouraged neighbors to give also. Now her father was among the most vocal in indicting Bill!

Her father's response—that he hadn't been sure at the time of Watchtower doctrine—didn't hold water with Joan because she knew he had called on Bethel officials many times to settle far less weighty matters. As she began to think of other times her parents had hedged on issues, she was sick at heart with disappointment and disillusionment.

Not long thereafter, a letter from the Society arrived for Bill, requesting his presence at a church hearing on the transfusion issue. As a result, he was disfellowshiped, and Joan's father asked him to leave his home, saying, "You know you can't stay here anymore. You have done enough damage already."

The "damage" was indeed substantial, for many people who had known and respected Bill began to leave the Kingdom Hall, confiding in him that they had had the same questions but had been afraid to voice their thoughts as he had done.

Meanwhile, Joan was caught between the pressure of Witness relatives and friends, who urged her to remain faithful to the organization, and her loyalty to and agreement with her husband. "Although I was not told to leave Bill, it was indicated that if I did, my three small children and I would be 'cared for,'"

Joan remembers. "I couldn't leave my husband, because I didn't have any reason to reject the position he took. In fact, I suspected that many things were wrong with the doctrines we were expected to believe as Jehovah's Witnesses. But at that point I didn't have a concrete basis for those feelings."

It was an emotional moment for Joan when, three months later, she and Bill and their children drove past the Kingdom Hall where she had worshiped all her life. With all their belongings in a rented trailer, they were leaving for California, where Bill had been promised a job with his brother Leo.

In California, Bill learned quickly from his brother, who was a painting contractor, and soon became an apprentice instructor himself. Meanwhile, Leo was learning from Bill, too—about why the Cetnars had left Pennsylvania and the JW organization. Though he was a Witness himself, Leo had long had his own doubts, and he left the Society after a few discussions with Bill. Phyllis, Leo's wife, made her final break with the Witnesses when she was advised from Bethel headquarters that she had violated the law of God when she had permitted *her dog* to have a blood transfusion! Incredulous, a friend wrote to headquarters, asking what would happen if her pet were to eat a mouse without draining the blood. The reply came back: "You must keep your animals under control."

In 1963, Joan's parents came to California and tried to get her to change her mind about the Watchtower Society. "By this time," Joan says, "I had been able to sort out my thoughts more carefully, and my parents' attempts were unsuccessful. They left after this and have not been in our home since."

Joan's disfellowshiping from the Society occurred some time later, after she attended a talk that Bill gave about the Witnesses and blood transfusion, presented at the First Christian Church in Santa Ana. The local JW congregational servant and a circuit servant came to her home to ask her if she agreed with what her husband had said. Her statement that she *did* was followed not long afterward by notice that she was to be disfellowshiped without a trial by the judicial committee of her former Kingdom Hall in Pennsylvania, where her father still served as congregational servant. On her request for a local hearing, a judicial committee in Santa Ana acted as proxy, and the action was finalized. This procedure—a man presiding over his daughter's excommunication—made headlines in the *Orange County Register*.

After her final break with the Witnesses, Joan realized that she was sorely lacking in Bible knowledge. She began to read the Bible both alone and with the aid of materials that contrasted biblical truth with Witness doctrine. "We were amazed to find out how badly we had been deceived as Witnesses," Joan says now. "I came to realize that although I had studied Watchtower literature carefully, I really wasn't much of a student of the Bible. In fact, I had never really been allowed to come to any conclusions from the Bible on my own. I had given control of my thinking on the Bible to the Watchtower Society."

One Scripture that was particularly convicting to Joan was Luke 21:8, where Jesus spoke about people who would come in his name, claiming, "I am he!" and, "The time is at hand!" Joan looked up the phrase, "I am" in a Bible encyclopedia (the word *he* in this passage does not appear in the original Greek) and learned that this "I am" referred to taking on the incommunicable name of God, *Yahweh* (less accurately rendered, *Jehovah*). Connecting this fact with the knowledge that one of the first books published by the JW movement was entitled *The Time Is at Hand* seemed to Joan to have an unmistakable message when she read the entire verse from Luke: "And he [Jesus] said, 'take heed that you are not led astray; for many will come in my name, saying, "I am *he*!" and, "The time is at hand!" *Do not go after them*'" (RSV, italics added).

Joan recognizes that there was a time after she left the JW organization and was able to speak publicly about its false nature, yet was not a Christian herself. She remembers with fondness the juncture at which she realized that it had not been an organization, but a *person* who had died for her. "This was a matter between Jesus Christ and me. I realized that he cared for *me* and that it was his blood that was shed for my sins. I needed to trust him completely. I asked this loving Savior to come into my life and be my Lord and my God."

It was at this time that Joan and Bill and their three children were baptized in the Pacific Ocean. That marked the beginning of a new life for them, one in which Joan joyfully relates that God has met their every need—spiritual, physical, and material.

3

Carolyn Poole

> Carolyn Poole began to feel the stirrings of some personal power in Christian Science at a very early age. She had these feelings confirmed when she lost a ring, her most-prized personal possession, on the school playground. She prayed, or "knew the truth," according to Christian Science terminology, and was vindicated in her belief when the ring was found and returned to her.
>
> How little Carolyn suspected at the time that her real most-valued asset, her soul, was at that time lost—and would remain so until she came to the knowledge of the truth about her Savior, Jesus Christ. Today she is active in helping other Christian Scientists find that same truth through her ministry, "The Christian Way."

Carolyn Poole's roots in the Christian Science movement go back to the year 1909, when her grandfather, who was dying of tuberculosis, joined the Church of Christ Scientist. His membership papers and those of his wife were signed by John V. Dittimore, one of the last men appointed to the church's board of trustees by its founder, Mary Baker Eddy, before she died.

Carolyn's mother married outside the faith and gave birth to Carolyn's brother eight years before Carolyn was born. Her parents divorced when Carolyn was four years old, and both children attended Christian Science Sunday school faithfully. A family friend and faithful devotée of the religion, Mrs. Carter, who was her Sunday-school teacher and influenced her spiritual development, often commented to the young girl's mother that Carolyn had the best understanding of Christian Science of anyone in her class, and the most perceptive answers to questions.

Carolyn was a normal child with the usual childhood interests, but her religion was something that she turned to even as a youngster, especially when she was fearful. One of these times was when she contracted the mumps, and her mother's distress was not only at the illness, but at the fact that she would be unable to pay for any medical care. Though her mother attended a Christian Science church regularly, she was not "legalistic," as Carolyn terms it, for she would use simple remedies such as laxatives or applying salt water to infections when needed. This time, however, her mother cautioned: "You just can't get sick—we can't afford it."

When the swelling on one side of her face diminished, Carolyn disobeyed her mother's admonition not to play outside in the rain, and soon thereafter the other side of her face began to swell. Little Carolyn immediately went into the house and began the process that Christian Scientists refer to as "knowing the truth"—that is, assuring herself that she wasn't sick, that she was perfect, as taught in Christian Science. When she went to the mirror a few minutes later, the swelling had completely disappeared, and from that moment onward Carolyn believed she had received an incontrovertible Christian Science "demonstration." While quite young, Carolyn was also able to use Christian Science philosophy to comfort an adult Scientist who was grieving over the death of a sister.

Carolyn grew to be afraid of doctors and medical care, believing the Christian Science teaching that thinking that one was sick would actually cause sickness. This led to a memorably bad experience when her mother took her to a doctor for a smallpox vaccination when Carolyn was fourteen years old. After the inoculation, Carolyn fainted three times—not because of the medical procedure, but because she was so fearful that she was giving in to what Mrs. Eddy termed "mortal mind error." As a faithful Scientist, Carolyn had been taught that seeking medical help was not only futile, because all disease is illusionary, but that it was a sign of faithlessness. Such a conflict of thoughts—having to have a vaccination as state law required, yet thereby going against what she had been taught in church— literally overwhelmed her.

But, in other ways, her religion was a refuge to her. "It was almost like a special secret I had," Carolyn recalls. "It was something that I knew I had experienced, a place I could go when I had a problem. It was almost like another world or dimension, because other people didn't even know it existed. But it was real for me."

By the time that Carolyn and her mother moved to Hollywood, California, during her high school years, both of them had stopped attending church regularly, except for occasional visits to the Christian Science church attended by many of the movie stars, including Ginger Rogers. Though Carolyn continued to believe in Christian Science, it was not a big part of her daily thought world. Carolyn now believes it was this kind of private practice of her religion that caused her to be quite nonthreatening to tall, slim, handsome young Richard Poole, whom she met in September 1941 while working in Hollywood. It was love at first sight for Carolyn, and when she told Dick that she was Christian Scientist, he was unperturbed. "I'm not interested in religion," he told her flatly. "Besides, I've got relatives that are Christian Scientists, and they've done all right."

During their whirlwind courtship of eleven months, Carolyn and Dick did not attend church at all. When World War II began, Dick joined the air force. They were married outside the military post in Rantoul, Illinois, then stationed in Salt Lake City, Utah, before Dick was sent overseas. In Dick's absence, Carolyn attended a Christian Science church and wrote to tell him that she was "knowing the truth" that he would be kept safe while they were apart.

"I didn't know at the time how angry that made him," Carolyn remembers, "but when he came back he told me that he felt I had no right to be thinking such things when people all around him were dying. You see, Mrs. Eddy said that God's work was complete, and everything is perfect, and we shouldn't pray to change his mind, but just try to 'know the truth' of what was already an accomplished fact. This seemed very unfair to Dick—that others died while he had a wife who could protect him in prayer."

When Dick returned home after two and a half years, he seemed like a virtual stranger to Carolyn. Because she felt their marriage was shaky, she went for support to a Christian Science practitioner, paying her, as is the custom, for a mental treatment. What the practitioner told Carolyn was of little help. "I'm so tired of you people who marry out of the faith," the practitioner said. "You don't marry a Christian Scientist—and then you have all these troubles."

The ensuing years brought many happy experiences for the couple, but also some difficult times. When Carolyn became pregnant with their first child, her old fears of doctors and medicine resurfaced, and she again began to study Christian Science. A practitioner began to give her treatments, and even though she had a difficult labor and delivery, Carolyn began to rely more and more on her religion. Shortly after the baby was born, she formally joined the Christian Scientist Church.

"It isn't easy to join the church," Carolyn states. "You have to be interviewed by a membership board and be able to affirm that you do not go to doctors or take medicine or drink or smoke. You are also supposed to have a fairly thorough knowledge of Christian Science doctrine and be committed to reading daily lessons. But I was unable to answer one significant question: 'What is the difference between Jesus and Christ?' Although they let me join because I was able to tell them about how I had been raised in the religion and about the healings I had had, they told me to go home and research the answer to the question about Jesus and Christ and memorize the definitions that Mrs. Eddy gave."

Carolyn intended to research and memorize as she had been told, but soon thereafter a new priority dominated her mind: a second pregnancy. With the help of her practitioner and Dick, who read her passages from *Science and Health*, Carolyn again went through the labor-and-delivery process. This time, though, was different.

Carolyn explains: "The passages that are supposed to be read during childbirth include a section that says, 'This truth [meaning Christian Science] removes properly whatever is offensive.' The implication for me was that my baby was offensive and needed to be removed. Furthermore, I could feel no joy in the beginning of this new life, because as a Christian Scientist I had to believe that all existence was just an endless circle without beginning or end." Pain, too, was supposed to be just an illusion, and even though Carolyn tried to "know the truth" about it, her labor contractions became so intense that she quit praying and begged for sedation.

After her babies were born, Carolyn loved her children deeply and became very involved in child-rearing, an active social life, and working on her college degree. Eventually she lost interest in religion and wrote a letter resigning from the Christian Scientist Church.

Before she earned her degree, one of her professors suggested that she might enjoy attending the local Unitarian church, which Dick consented to attend with her, thinking that it was, in his words, "less kooky" than Christian Science. However, when Carolyn asked the pastor why God was never mentioned, he assured her not to worry, that she would still be welcome there if she believed in God—they "didn't mind."

It was while Carolyn was attending UCLA that she had her first formal exposure to hypnosis during a meeting on campus. Though Christian Science forbade any contact with hypnosis, Carolyn reasoned that the great emphasis that her religion put on the mind had a definite connection with the principles of hypnosis. She volunteered to be a subject and went slightly "under" on the first attempt. Returning home, out of curiosity she persuaded a neighbor to let her hypnotize him. When he went "under" almost immediately, she became frightened and resolved to never do it again.

During this time, Carolyn's growing need to know God remained unsatisfied, in spite of her attendance at Unitarian, Religious Science, Presbyterian, and Community churches. She and her husband moved to Long Beach, where she earned her degree from Long Beach University.

Dick began a new business in the small desert town of Mojave in 1958. It was there that Carolyn met an intelligent, refined Christian Scientist named Russ Wilson, who worked in Dick's office. His perception of her distress led him to tell her, "You need to work on 'the thought of home.'" To a Christian Scientist, that meant a return to the church. Through his influence, Carolyn again began a daily regimen of studying Christian Science and attending related meetings.

By 1969, she had settled into a routine of sorts. Their two daughters had by then graduated from high school and left home. Carolyn joined a branch Christian Science church, as well as the Mother Church, and served on various Christian Science committees and even as president of the executive board. Dick began attending church with her, and they both noticed that this seemed to help him fight a depression over some difficult business problems.

Carolyn applied for "class instruction," a once-in-a-lifetime privilege for a dedicated Christian Scientist. After an interview with her prospective teacher, she rented a motel room in San Diego for the intensive two-week session. The information she received and notes she took were so secretive that she had to commit to never sharing them with anyone. In fact, she was told to leave instructions that her notes were to be mailed back to her class in case of her death.

Two major events happened in Carolyn's life that she believes precipitated her decision to leave the church and the thought world to which she was once so dedicated. The first of these events occurred in 1969. Carolyn read in the local newspaper that Billy Graham was coming to lead a great crusade at the Anaheim Stadium. She was curious about the famous evangelist and thought idly that it would be great to be able to tell her grandchildren that she had met such a man. Because she was unable to convince any of her friends or family to accompany her, she went alone.

"I'm not sure exactly why I did it," she recalls, "but at the end of the service I went forward and received prayer. I was standing so close to Mr. Graham that I could see the pancake makeup on him that they had applied for television. It occurred to me that someone I knew might see me on TV, and I became very embarrassed. After one of the attendants wrote down my name and address, I went quickly back up to my seat.

"Then," relates Carolyn, "I had a frightening experience. I felt a swirling light, a mass of power that came and stood right next to me. It told me that I would be dead before the night was over. I was struck with fear and confusion. Mrs. Eddy had said there was no such thing as evil power, because all power comes from God. But the message was clear—I had gone over into the wrong realm by being at that crusade. I said, 'God, forgive me. I'll never come to anything like this again.'" Immediately, Carolyn adds, the overpowering feeling left her, and she went home.

After that, Carolyn threw herself even more wholeheartedly into Christian Science. When her teenage daughter, who was studying Eastern religions at Long Beach State University, pointed out the similarities between Hinduism and Christian Science, Carolyn was nonplused. "Mrs. Eddy brought us this truth," she told her daughter, "and it really doesn't matter where she got it."

Nonetheless, Carolyn had a great curiosity about the Bible that accompanied her devoted study of the words of Mary Baker Eddy. She had read the first five books of the Bible, struggling through the archaic King James language without any study aids and then abandoning it. But her desire to know what the Bible meant remained strong, and when she learned that there was a Christian Scientist who advertised that she was a Bible scholar and had tapes for sale, Carolyn decided to buy the taped classes for herself and other Christian Scientists to study.

She presented her proposal to the membership, and at first they agreed to the idea. Later, however, they stipulated that such a study must take place in an official "reading room" and not in a private home. The class never materialized.

Meanwhile, Carolyn faithfully attended the highly formalized Wednesday-night meetings, where she and the few others present would give testimonies about the goodness of God and their experiences of healings and "demonstrations," which they attributed to Mrs. Eddy's writings. Because Carolyn's total immersion in the church had left her with virtually no personal contacts except Christian Scientists, this filled her need for fellowship. All in all, she termed herself a very devoted—and contented—Christian Scientist.

One day, as Carolyn sat in her home, reading her Bible after completing the obligatory daily lesson study from Mrs. Eddy's writings, there was a knock at her door. There stood two neighbor women (whom Carolyn later learned had been quite separately prompted to action by God), inviting her to a home Bible study.

"I was surprised," Carolyn recalls, "because though I knew that such studies must exist, I had never met anyone who attended one. That, combined with my inability to get my own church to sponsor a study, made me swallow my fear of being taken in by some strange religion. Though I told them that I was a Christian Scientist, they didn't mind at all. They said the study would be nondenominational, so I said I'd come."

Her practitioner disparaged the idea when Carolyn told her about the women's invitation, and Carolyn herself still had fresh memories of her unsettling experience at the Billy Graham crusade. Nonetheless, she went to the first study at a home just around the corner from her own.

"The women were so sweet, and it was obvious to me that they loved God," says Carolyn. "But I was disappointed in the study for several reasons. First of all, I wanted something on a college level, with lots of facts and notetaking for later study. And it also seemed that they were saying the same things that I believed as a Christian Scientist except that they used different words." Those women treated Carolyn with "great respect and love," and she completed the entire five-week session with them.

The following summer, Carolyn attended several Christian Women's luncheons, though the testimonies offered there of how some of the women had found Jesus "slid past me," she remembers. When she began attending a fall Bible class, she told the women that she enjoyed it but was planning to take a real-estate course and would be unable to return. Yet, by the next week, the ties of love she had felt there drew her back, and she returned for class after class until she had finished the whole session.

It was during this fall Bible class that Carolyn experienced a very vivid dream, which she related to her Bible study group. In it, she was standing on the landing of a staircase that was filled with people, all of whom were completely silent, as she was. She was aware of an atmosphere of waiting—for the return of Jesus.

"Up until that time, Jesus was to me just a man, an Exemplar, as Mary Baker Eddy termed him. He was just a human. But in my dream I felt the greatest feeling of love for him, and great joy in the thought that he was coming back. When I told the women in my Bible study about my dream, one woman said, 'You were dreaming of the second coming of Jesus.'"

The Bible class had been studying about Jesus' second coming and had read of how he will return with angels, on the Mount of Olives. Carolyn went to the writings of Mary Baker Eddy to find out all she could about this second coming. She was surprised to learn that Mrs. Eddy had said that the second coming of Jesus had already occurred; she equated that event with her own discovery of Christian Science.

While Carolyn was still mulling over this contradiction, she and her husband discovered another. While reading, as was their custom, a daily chapter from the Bible, they encountered Matthew 23:10 in the Good News Bible (Today's English Version), which they used for their morning devotional time. It contained a warning from Jesus against applying the title "Leader" to anyone but himself. This bothered both of them, for one of the most common titles Mrs. Eddy had appropriated for herself was "Leader"—and she had even specified in her writings that she alone could be referred to by that title with a capital "L." And yet only Jesus was "Leader," according to this text.

This conflict stirred Dick to a new interest in Bible study, and he began to read it with a fresh intensity. Meanwhile, Carolyn's questions at her Bible study took on greater importance. In the spring, she began a third Bible study with these women, this time allowing it to be held in her own home. She began to wonder why Mrs. Eddy had said in the Christian Science *Church Manual* that she was the only Leader. It disturbed Carolyn to realize that she had been taught to refer to Mrs. Eddy as "revered Leader"—when the Bible attributed reverence only to God. She began to see similarities between the Gnostic heresies, which John's epistles were written against, and her own Christian Science teachings. The reality of hell, completely denied by Christian Science doctrine, became a personal truth for her. And the verse about all having sinned and come short of God's glory (Rom. 3:23) particularly convicted her, especially when the women explained that the only way back to God was through Jesus.

One day in her study with the women's group, a classic biblical question was posed: "Who do men say that I am?" Carolyn remembered from her Christian Science teachings the tenet that Jesus and Christ were not the same.

When Carolyn learned of Peter's confession, "You are the Christ, the Son of the Living God" (Matt. 16:16) and the response of Thomas, who exclaimed, "My Lord and my God!" (John 20:28), she realized that she had reached a crossroads in her faith journey.

In a vividly remembered episode, Carolyn visualized herself standing before Jesus, and his asking her, "Who do *you* say that I am?" She realized that she could only respond, "I don't know who you are." She tried to reconcile Christian Science teaching—that the God who is "spirit" could have nothing to do with any material thing—with the fact that the Bible taught that Jesus, a material being, *was* God. Though all her life she had believed the teaching of John 1:1 that Jesus was God, she had never seen the implications of John 1:14, which clearly stated that the Word, Jesus, did indeed become living flesh.

Yet Carolyn made a momentous mental decision: to believe in Jesus as God. In some ways, the implications of this decision terrified her, because it seemed impossible for God, who is Spirit, to be in the flesh. But she knew that the Bible clearly stated it—Jesus was God!

At this time, however, she was serving as vice-president of the executive board at her Christian Science church and actively participating in its program. "It was like leading a double life," she recalls. "I was unable to share any of my thoughts with my practitioner or anyone there."

On May 19, 1976, she shared her agony with the trusted little group of Bible-study women. "I'm leaving Christian Science," she sobbed.

The women were delighted. "We've been praying for you!" one of them exclaimed.

Carolyn was shocked. She had been taught in Christian Science that you couldn't pray for anyone without first asking his or her permission, and also that only one person at a time (usually a practitioner) could pray for another. And now she found that all these women and many more "behind the scenes" had been interceding for months in her behalf before the throne of the very real Jesus.

With the supportive help of this group of women, Carolyn wrote a letter to Christian Science headquarters, telling them that she had at last discovered the Jesus of Scripture. He had become her new, lifelong Leader.

4

Elaine Dallas

After a lifetime of striving to demonstrate the "Christ, Truth" of her religion, Elaine Dallas began at the half-century mark of her life to begin to investigate the first part of the title she had borne since birth: Christian Scientist. She began to examine the doctrines in the textbook of her religion, *Science and Health with Key to the Scriptures*, written by its "Discoverer and Founder," Mary Baker Eddy, and to compare these doctrines to the Bible.

The spiritual battle that ensued inside Elaine did not cease until a year and a half later, when a clear Victor emerged.

Elaine Betty Dallas was born, in her own words, "straight into Christian Science." Her roots in that religion went back to her grandparents on her father's side of the family, and to her great-grandparents on her mother's.

Her maternal grandmother was instrumental in beginning the first Christian Science church in La Crosse, Wisconsin, and became its first Reader. Elaine's father recalled the beginnings of the Christian Science movement in his own farm community of Troy Center, Wisconsin, as being like a tidal wave that swept almost everyone in their little town along in its influence, his own family included.

With such strong pioneer roots, it is no surprise that Elaine's parents met through a Christian Science organization in college. Their marriage produced two children, Elaine and a son, whom they raised in their strongly held faith. Though both children were started in Christian Science Sunday school at age three, Elaine's brother never seemed to relate to the religion, while she accepted it wholeheartedly and unquestioningly. Its doctrines were more than just sterile teachings to her, and they influenced her response to many of life's situations.

Elaine's mother, as a loyal Christian Scientist, continually applied Mrs. Eddy's doctrines to her daughter's upbringing. Elaine recalls that when she was involved in childhood mishaps—skinning her knee, for instance—her mother would declare, "There are no accidents in Divine Mind." During times of illness, her mother would assure her that "God is all—there is no sickness."

"I remember wondering why everyone else could not see that Christian Science was the truth," Elaine says. "It was so logical. How could they say it wasn't true? It wasn't until much later in life that I realized that the basic premise of Christian Science—'God is All'—produced unscriptural conclusions."

Elaine was convinced from childhood on that any doubts about Christian Science that might arise in her mind were to be attributed to her own lack of understanding of her own religion, not to any fault in the doctrines thereof. For Elaine, Christian Science was just what its founder adamantly claimed: "unerring and Divine." In 1943, at the age of sixteen, Elaine became a member of the Mother Church, and continued to attend Sunday school until she was twenty years old.

Elaine met Bill Dallas, her future husband, in 1947. After their marriage in 1948, he, too, wholeheartedly embraced Christian Science. Though Bill was not raised in Christian Science, his mother was open to and studied many of the Mind Science movements, including Christian Science, Science of Mind, and Unity School of Christianity, and eventually the "I Am" movement. His father was involved in the Hindu "self-realization" movement brought to the United States by Swami Yoganada—a movement Bill and Elaine would later see as amazingly similar to Christian Science.

Elaine and Bill were blessed with two sons, whom they naturally raised in Christian Science, starting each boy in Sunday school at age three.

Years passed, and in 1978 Elaine recognized a strong growing desire to read the Bible. "Through the years I had read a great deal *from* the Bible in the Christian Science Lesson-Sermons, but I had never read the whole Bible on its own, word for word. So I decided to do so, starting with the New Testament. Every evening, when my day's work was done and I was ready for bed, I would read."

Her daily reading progressed through the Gospels and Acts, but by the time she began to read Paul's epistles, she found the wording of her King James version so difficult to understand that she became frustrated. She remembered reading some quotations in *The Christian Science Sentinel* that were from the more modern New English Bible, so she bought her own copy and continued her reading in that version. During the next year, she completed the rest of the Bible, skipping only parts of Leviticus and other sections in the Old Testament that dealt with the law.

"As I read," she remembers, "I noticed some places that did not seem to fit with what I had been taught in Christian Science, but I simply dismissed them." Her childhood philosophy—Christian Science is perfect; it is always right—endured.

Just as Elaine finished reading through the Bible, she and Bill learned of a Christian Science tour to Israel. An unexpected bequest from a deceased relative's estate provided the exact amount of money for the tour, and they left for Israel in the fall of 1979 on this excursion, which took them "from Dan to Beer-sheba" and emphasized the archaeological sites of the Bible. This experience was the first of many others that would change Elaine's thinking and, indeed, her life. She explains, "After we returned home, my interest in the Bible increased. Having been in the very places where events that I had read about in the Bible actually happened, the Bible began to come alive to me."

As Elaine began to reread the New Testament and portions of the Old, she began to notice discrepancies between Christian Science doctrines and what the Bible was saying. One particular area of variance was between Mrs. Eddy's teachings that the Holy Spirit *cannot* be "in" man and the Bible's repeated teachings that the Holy Spirit can and does dwell in a believer. "Such differences bothered me some, but I shrugged them off," says Elaine. "I felt that I just needed to understand Christian Science better and then there would be no problem."

One morning in January 1980, while Elaine was turning her radio dial, searching for a newscast, she discovered a local Christian radio station, KFIA. For the entire morning, as if in a new world, she listened, entranced, to Bible teachings on Genesis, Acts, and Daniel. The next morning she listened again, and continued in fascination every morning thereafter. She began to take notes on what she heard, keeping them on a clipboard. Each evening when Bill came home, she would follow him from room to room, sharing her new discoveries in Scripture.

Bill was far from an eager participant in Elaine's enthusiasm. "I just can't agree with that," was his stock answer to her daily reports. Elaine began to believe that if her husband could only hear some of the programs for himself, perhaps he would understand better, so one day she tape-recorded one of her favorite programs.

"I waited until he'd gotten in the shower one morning, and then I put the tape player in the bathroom and started it. He seemed to be listening, so I did the same thing for several days. It wasn't long before he was asking me, 'Well, what program am I going to hear today?' As he began to see what I was seeing, his objections began to fade away."

One of Elaine's most rewarding discoveries about the Bible was the richness of the Hebrew and Greek languages in which the Scriptures were originally written. Until that time, Elaine had depended on Mrs. Eddy's redefinition of scriptural terms to determine their meanings. Though Mrs. Eddy had claimed that these redefinitions came directly from God, Elaine realized that they changed the original intent of the relevant passages.

Through Christian radio, she learned of two newer Bible translations: the New American Standard Bible and the New International Version. In the hope that these would help her understand biblical passages better, she visited a local Christian bookstore. Being in the midst of so many books on Bible study was an overwhelming experience. When a clerk offered help, Elaine found herself telling this woman that she was a Christian Scientist but was disturbed at finding that her religion seemed to disagree with the Bible.

What the clerk began to tell Elaine was familiar to her. She had already heard it several times on the Christian radio programs and had summarily dismissed it as "too foolish to consider." The woman explained that salvation was a gift—unearned and offered to anyone who is willing to accept it. She told Elaine that she, too, could receive the forgiveness of her sins and eternal life through faith in Jesus Christ's death and resurrection. Then, after the clerk told her that God loved her and wanted her to have eternal life, she asked Elaine if she would like to pray with her and accept that gift of salvation.

Elaine recalls, "All that I had learned in Christian Science screamed inside me, 'No!' I found myself being propelled backwards as I said, 'Oh, no—NO!' There was no way I was going to do anything like that."

Undismayed, the clerk offered Elaine a little pamphlet entitled, "The Four Spiritual Laws." Elaine completed her purchase of the two Bible versions she had come for, along with a massive volume of *Strong's Exhaustive Concordance*, which contained Hebrew and Greek dictionaries with cross-references. She returned home and put the clerk's little pamphlet away, unread.

For months afterward, Elaine would spread out the four versions of the Bible on the kitchen table. With the help of the concordance and its Greek and Hebrew dictionaries, she would meticulously examine Bible passages from her weekly Christian Science lessons, paying particular attention to the original meanings of words as she looked them up.

What she found was very unsettling. She began to discover that many of the Christian Science teachings to which she had so firmly held were not only unsubstantiated by the Scriptures, but were actually in direct contradiction to them. Most shocking of all, though, was the new way that she was seeing Jesus Christ in the Bible.

"I was beginning to see a different picture of the man, Jesus of Nazareth, from that which I had been taught all my life in Christian Science. I had come across Scripture after Scripture revealing his true identity, but I refused to believe it because of what Mrs. Eddy had taught about the concept of God as an impersonal 'All.'"

Elaine began to turn the spotlight of her investigation onto her daily Christian Science Lesson-Sermon readings. Instead of just reading the fragmentary passages from Scripture, she began to look up entire passages and try to see the context. "As I did this," she recalls, "I discovered that many, if not most, of the selected Bible passages did not correlate with or corroborate Mrs. Eddy's teachings in that Lesson at all. In fact, many of them had nothing whatsoever to do with what was being discussed in the Lesson. Gradually, as the weeks went by, this making the Bible appear to be saying what Mrs. Eddy said in *Science and Health* became so offensive to me that I finally stopped reading the weekly Lesson-Sermons."

She and her husband continued to attend the Christian Science church. However, Elaine found that she could no longer read the Lesson to Bill as he ate breakfast, which she had done for years. "I can't read this anymore," she told him one morning. "If you want to go on reading it, okay—but I can't."

One Sunday morning at church, she was shocked to hear a passage from Daniel that used the word *man* (which Elaine knew from her study referred to the individual Daniel) twisted and applied to all mankind. Like all her Christian Science friends, she didn't bring a Bible to church, but she verified her assessment when she returned home.

The mental war that had been raging inside Elaine came to the surface at last. Although she had been praying earnestly that God would show her the truth about Christian Science, she now realized that she had been denying what she had been seeing, mentally blocking out the fact that there were discrepancies in Mrs. Eddy's teachings about the Bible—falling back unconsciously to her old childhood belief that since Christian Science was perfect, she must be at fault for questioning it.

The incident at church had brought Elaine to a mental and spiritual turning point. She reflects, "That part of me that had wanted to quit all this studying, and go back to simply believing Mrs. Eddy without question, became much less intense, while the other part of me that *had* to find out where God's truth lay became really dominant."

Because she began to wonder if other Bible passages had been taken out of context by Mrs. Eddy, Elaine bought paperback copies of both *Science and Health* and the King James Bible. Using *The Concordance to the Writings of Mary Baker Eddy* as a guide, she cross-referenced and marked every single Bible quote in Mrs. Eddy's writings. She made four astounding discoveries. First of all, she found by looking at the marked passages in her Bible that Mrs. Eddy had only dealt with a very small percentage of the Bible; it was not the comprehensive treatment that Elaine had been led to believe. Second, nearly all the Bible quotations used by Mrs. Eddy were incomplete sentences—at times, no more than a word or two—and often deleted conjunctions such as "but" or "therefore," which tied them to previous thoughts. Third, Elaine was disturbed to find that many of Mrs. Eddy's Bible quotations of thought fragments had been wrenched out of their original contexts. They often were begun by Mrs. Eddy with a capital letter and ended with a period, as if these quotations were within themselves complete thoughts from the text. Finally, she found that the practice of taking scriptural passages out of context and misapplying them was the rule, not the exception, in Mrs. Eddy's writings.

Elaine says, "As the many months of studying the Scriptures and listening to the Bible studies on the radio went by, I gradually became aware of the good news of salvation that God was offering to me. I am amazed now," she adds, "to realize that I never saw this Scripture truth while first reading the Bible from cover to cover. I know now that this was because then I was reading God's Word through Mrs. Eddy's redefined words and concepts. This put a veil over my eyes, so to speak, hiding God's true message of salvation so that I could not see it."

One redefined word alone, Elaine realized, changed the whole message of the Scriptures—the word *Christ*. Mary Baker Eddy had taught that Jesus of Nazareth was *not* the Christ, nor was he God manifest in the flesh. She separated Jesus from Christ and taught that Jesus simply "expressed" Christ, which she defined as "the divine manifestation of God, which comes to the flesh to destroy incarnate error" (*Science and Health* 583:10–11). *Anyone*, Mrs. Eddy taught, can "express" or "demonstrate" Christ.

Elaine recognized with horror that this was "a different gospel," which Paul had warned about in Galatians 1:6. She realized that if Christian Science was incompatible with the Scriptures and one of them were to be believed, *the other must be denied*.

"Sitting at my kitchen table with all my various Bibles and concordances and dictionaries and notes before me, it was as if the balance of scales had tipped solidly," remembers Elaine of a fateful morning in May 1981. "I suddenly realized with great finality that Christian Science is false. Christian Science is not the truth of God's Word—it is a falsification of his Word."

Elaine felt limp, but she knew her moment of decision had come. She immediately and deliberately made the choice to follow God in his Word, the Bible. She was filled with joy as she searched for the still-unread pamphlet that had been given to her months before by the clerk in the Christian bookstore. Elaine recalls, "I had never even opened it before, because I knew in my heart what was in it and that it would give me the gospel of salvation through Jesus Christ's death and resurrection. I had refused to believe this as being true for me personally. But now I opened it and read it completely."

Elaine remembered from her Bible reading about praying in our "inner rooms" (Luke 12:3) and bowing our knees to Jesus.

So she went into a private place, knelt, and confessed aloud to the Lord Jesus that she was a sinner and that she wanted to accept him—the Word made flesh—as her own Lord and Savior. Then she thanked him for forgiving her sins and asked him to take control of her life.

She returned to the kitchen and resumed her studies. In looking back at the fact that she didn't immediately "feel different," Elaine has concluded that the following months brought her several gradual, yet inestimable, gifts of peace. The first was in the form of her growing realization that being free of Christian Science meant being released from what it taught was an essential requirement for salvation—that of "demonstrating" that the material world was not real.

"What a relief to be freed from this unrealistic, impossible requirement!" she says. "I felt a great load being lifted off me, and for the first time in my life I felt free to enjoy and savor life as it actually is!"

The most profound gift of all, though, was a deep inner joy and peace beyond anything Elaine had ever known. She now had the Holy Spirit dwelling in her—and a secure future with God for all eternity.

Not long after this experience, Elaine's joy was doubled when her husband, Bill, also accepted Jesus. In the ten years that have passed since that time, Elaine has continued in a methodical and probing way to examine and dispute the claims of Christian Science so that she can help others to see the truth of the Bible.

5

Irene Guthrie

When Irene Guthrie was heavily involved in classes in the occult and preparing herself to serve as a "good witch" practicing white magic, she wrote a story that she hoped one day to publish. The main characters in this story were the astrological constellations familiar to most of us as the twelve "signs" of the zodiac. These characters—such as the bull, the crab, the twins—met together in order to reveal each one's individual personality and what it represented in the universe. Irene entitled her story, "The Gathering."

Nine years later, a very different Irene Guthrie was listening to a recording of a radio broadcast in which she had been the guest speaker, telling people about the upcoming National Day of Prayer. As founder and president of Arizona's National Prayer Day Rally, she heard herself describing the upcoming event as "the gathering." With a start, as she remembered the story she had written so long ago when she was so far from God, she marveled at how God had changed her and graced her to bring together supernatural forces in a very different way from what she ever would have imagined.

The early life of Irene Guthrie is a textbook illustration of the sociological theories that children tend to duplicate their parents' life-styles. Irene's mother, of Polish background, had an unstable home life, leaving it at age fifteen to marry and later divorce a man by whom she had two children. She subsequently married Irene's father, a man of Ukrainian heritage who, like her first husband, was a heavy drinker. Irene's father died of cirrhosis of the liver in 1958, when Irene was seven. By that time, her mother had divorced Irene's father, remarried her first husband, and was in the process of divorcing him again. Soon afterward she met the man who would eventually become her third husband and moved in with him.

When Irene's grandmother heard of the new living arrangements, she invited Irene to come to live with her. Before Irene moved, however, there occurred some traumatic events that had a profound effect on her. "I became a victim of molestation by my cousin," Irene says, "and that memorable incident of sexual abuse while I was a child, along with some that I did not remember until much later, brought about a spirit of sexual harlotry that remained with me until salvation occurred in my life."

Indeed, the ensuing years were rough ones for Irene. Even though her grandmother gave her the love and acceptance Irene so much needed, she also introduced destructive elements into her life. They attended a Catholic church, but only "going through the motions," Irene remembers. She had no personal knowledge of Jesus. Young Irene was encouraged to drink liquor at an early age. Furthermore, her grandmother's practices of reading tea leaves, telling fortunes, and interpreting dreams led Irene into a world that she identifies with the "familiar spirit" that would characterize her early life.

When Irene was fourteen, her mother married the man with whom she had been living. His three boys, who had also been living with them, had left by the time that Irene finally moved in when she was in the tenth grade. The earlier separation from her mother, however, had resulted in what Irene calls "a spirit of rejection" that she felt deeply. Even when she did make the move to her mother's house, she was frightened by the drinking, arguments, and violence she found there.

Irene moved in with her older, now-married half-sister when she was sixteen. She had stopped attending church and began searching for the love and attention she had never received from her father. She began to become sexually active, sometimes with older men. By the time Irene began attending Briarwood School for Women, a college in Southington, Connecticut, she was dabbling in the occult by using a ouija board and attempting to hold seances.

In 1969 she met a young man named John and became pregnant by him. Not believing that the twins she was carrying were his, he refused to marry her until two months after their sons were born.

The occult continued to play an important part in Irene's life. During her pregnancy, she had attempted to ascertain the sex of her children by dangling a needle and thread over her wrist, relying on a superstition that the way the needle moved would indicate whether the child would be a boy or a girl.

John's drinking problems and emotional problems, a legacy from his own father, were evident in the marriage, so Irene again found herself living in a world of alcoholism and suspicion. Their marriage survived a serious accident in which Irene and John were struck by a hit-and-run driver while riding a motorcycle, but it could not endure the violence inside the four walls of their home. By 1976, having decided that their twin boys needed stability more than they needed the harmful presence of their father, she divorced John.

Irene sought this stability by moving to a nearby town. However, she became heavily involved in the murky world of drugs, and took marijuana, "speed," cocaine, and even once experimented with a hallucinogenic substance. Once, while high on drugs, Irene sustained substantial injuries in a car accident in which her head hit the windshield of her prized 1973 Monte Carlo.

"I spent more time in the bars than I did with my boys," Irene recalls. "I had a mother-in-law who was a convenient babysitter, while I was out looking for a good time, love, and for someone to turn to in my distress."

In May 1977, Irene had an experience that she identifies as a crossroads in her life. "I was resting on my bed when suddenly a vision appeared before me. I was in a trancelike state (see Acts 10:10). In this vision before me were two figures—Jesus on the left and Satan on the right. Praise God, I immediately ignored Satan once I saw him and looked to Jesus, asking him in my mind if there was something he wanted to tell me. At once Satan fled. I had made a choice—Jesus was saying to me, 'Choose this day which way thou shalt go.'"

The tenor of the next two years of Irene's life, however, would belie that experience. The following month, at the behest of barroom friends, she enrolled in an astrology class at a school for parapsychology in Bristol, Connecticut, called Alpha Logics. By definition, astrology is a form of fortune-telling that is done by reading the stars and charting horoscopes. Irene's childhood memories of her grandmother's reading of tea leaves and other forms of divination prepared her to wholeheartedly accept what she was taught. "I pursued this class with all my being," she says. "I was determined to become proficient in astrology."

In the midst of her studies, Irene experienced a series of events that she identifies as visions. The first one involved a panoramic view of a battlefield, with soldiers headed by one whose whole being was so bright that she could not identify the facial features. Immediately afterward, she saw another scene, that of a map of the old world and the Queen of the Nile, Nefertiti. In looking back, she believes that in the first vision she was "called into the army of the Lord" and, in the second, shown in contrast what she would experience in the world of the occult.

Irene continued in classes about the supernatural, learning all the New Age techniques. Though this philosophy has surfaced throughout world history, Irene states, its most recent manifestation is marked by the age-old teaching that each man is his own god. Eastern mysticism was integrated in the thought that "all is one," and "one is all." It flatly denied the existence of individual sin and the correlative need for repentance and remission of sin. If you are your own god, how can you be sinful or unholy?

Her astrology instructor, Frank, was a dynamic teacher and mesmerizing personality who taught his classes with a large Bible sitting in the corner of the room. In her course of studies, Irene learned about astral projection (out-of-the-body experiences), clairvoyance (discerning objects imperceptible to the senses), astrology charts, intuitive healing, pyramidology, and meditation techniques that were heavily influenced by Buddhism and Hinduism.

Many of Irene's daily experiences seemed to confirm what she was being taught. Once, while she was in class, for instance, she "saw" a group of spirit beings behind her instructor at the chalkboard. She decided to use her knowledge in a practical way and opted for "white witchcraft." A book she read on this subject identified the universal cosmic energy that most people call "God" as female in character, closely tied to the ancient Roman fertility deity, Diana. The practice of white witchcraft, she learned, focused on the cycles of seasons, the worship of nature, and the idea of reincarnation.

In her practice as a white witch, Irene would dream about people and then enjoy the surprise on their faces when they admitted that she had perceived something true (but hidden) about them. She claimed she had the ability to diagnose the physical illnesses of others by describing her sensations of illness in her own body.

Drugs continued to be an important part of Irene's life. Along with witchcraft, her life-style was characterized by substance abuse, rock music, and the "night life" of bars. She was still searching for Mr. Right, and in March of 1978, she found him. "It was love at first sight," says Irene of meeting Mike Guthrie. They soon began living together, and Mike brought a new dimension of love, acceptance, and stability to her life and that of her twin sons.

One night as she was in the public library doing research for her astrology class, Irene recalls hearing a voice say, "Arizona." She dismissed the thought from her mind, only to be interrupted a few minutes later by the same word: "Arizona." She excitedly told Mike that they were to move to Arizona, and they began preparations.

A hairdresser friend of Irene's, who also dabbled in the occult, told Irene that she had dreamt that Irene had bought a Bible. Irene went to a local department store, purchased a King James Bible, and began reading it along with her book on white witchcraft. Like many people unfamiliar with Scripture, she began reading with an agenda. In this case, she wanted to find the part in the Bible where the world would be destroyed by fire, because her grandmother had taught her that this would happen in the year 2000. As she read, two things happened.

Irene's first efforts at reading the Bible met with what she regards as demonic opposition. "Severe pains rose up in my chest and I thought I was going to die," she recalls. Under a doctor's care, she recovered from this attack, but something else began to change as she read the Bible. She found that she was spending much more time in God's Word and less and less in her witchcraft books.

Mike and Irene finished the preparations for their move and arrived in Phoenix, Arizona, in late June 1979. There Irene discovered a local Christian television station, KPAZ, and felt the spiritual void in her life begin to fill as she listened and watched.

"I found out the truth from the Bible about astrology and other such activities," says Irene. "It took me by surprise when I found out what happened to witches in the Old Testament days—they were stoned to death! And I found out what it was that I had needed in my life all along. It was Jesus Christ. In July 1979, I said the sinner's prayer and accepted Jesus as my Lord and Savior."

Mike was skeptical of this "new religious kick," putting it in the same category as the astrology classes to which Irene had also been so devoted. But he could not deny some of the changes that had come about in Irene's life. Her desires to drink alcohol and use drugs disappeared. Even her long-time habit of cigarette smoking, though more difficult for her to abandon, was eventually conquered.

Irene's spiritual growth was not matched by stability in some other areas of her life, however. In October 1979, Mike was involved in a car accident that totaled the family car and left him with chronic back problems. In a two-year period starting that December, Irene lost seven jobs, but in November 1981, she found work with the state of Arizona, by which she is still employed.

Her newfound interest in the Bible led Irene to implore the Lord's help in making another area of her life pleasing to him. She asked the Lord to supply their need for a wedding so that she and Mike could be married. By faith she picked a date and was amazed and grateful when Mike "coincidentally" selected the same date. On October 25, 1980, they were married in a Catholic church.

For the next two years, Irene's boys went to Catholic school, and the entire family attended Catholic services. Then, Irene states, "One day my eyes were opened to understanding spiritual principles as contrasted to religious tradition, and I knew I could no longer participate in the Catholic mass." In April 1981, Irene visited a Baptist church and made a public profession of faith; a month later, she and her boys were baptized. The following February, she sought the baptism of the Holy Spirit in a charismatic church. "There was no immediate manifestation of my receiving the baptism," she says, "and I was very distracted by others speaking in tongues and falling on the floor! I later realized it was a matter of my getting alone with God, when—alone in my bathroom—I uttered those first baby words in tongues."

Mike, however, was slower in his spiritual growth. It was not until over a year later that he made his public profession of faith in Jesus Christ, after which he and Irene embarked on a project she refers to as "church shopping." They finally settled on a nondenominational Bible church she characterizes as "full gospel in nature," and they attended that church for four years.

"During the time that we were there, the Lord launched me into a street ministry for a season," Irene says. During lunch-hour breaks from her job at the Arizona state-capitol complex, she and two other Christian women would go to surrounding homes, sharing the gospel, ministering to the sick, and praying with and for the downtrodden and brokenhearted homeless people of that area.

"With my partners, Barbara and Nancy, I trod ground around the capitol area to take back territory that Satan had stolen. We laid hands on the buildings being used for the devil's work and cursed the finances. Later we saw these places shut down—no longer operating. What an exhilarating feeling it is to go back to work after experiencing the wonder-working power of the Lord. We saw God reap his harvest—healing the sick and providing miracles we had prayed for. That season in my life was not only encouraging for purposes of ministry, but it made me stronger and stronger as I entered into enemy territory, knowing that God's grace and power would sustain me and keep me safe in every way."

In 1985, Irene attended a conference that she believes changed her life and her ministry. Along with 2,500 other believers at the Morris Cerullo 24th World Conference, she received an individual anointing for what she identified as a certain purpose. That purpose became clear to her the next month, when she attended a luncheon where she believed she would receive the answer to her request for guidance in this special purpose.

"There the Lord birthed in my spirit the idea for the National Prayer Day Rally of Arizona," Irene explains. "I knelt on the floor by my chair, and the anointing of God fell upon me. I accepted my orders to 'go and gather.'"

Since that time, Irene has been actively "gathering" as she ministers to people who are trying to understand both the will of God and its evil counterpart, the New Age movement, in which she was once so intensely involved. Though this system of thought is harmful to so many, Irene sees the good that God has brought in her life even through the deception she experienced. Like Joseph in the Old Testament, she says, "God intended it for good to accomplish what is now being done, the saving of many lives" (Gen. 50:20).

6

Will Baron

Will Baron uses an unusual word when he speaks of his salvation experience—he describes it as being "rescued."

Such a term brings to mind images of fiery crash scenes or violent storms at sea. And, indeed, such images are appropriate for a man like Will. At the culmination of his devotion to the New Age movement, he was at the point of physical and financial exhaustion, being driven by demonic forces in a seaside "witnessing ministry" that set him on a collision course with hell.

Will Baron was born in 1949 into a Christian family. His father was a lay preacher for a small congregation near Manchester, England, and during Will's childhood the family attended church regularly. Will says that as a young boy, he believed without question that Jesus Christ was the Son of God and that the Bible was God's Word.

However, England in the 1950s was in the midst of a decline into secularism. Will recalls that few of his childhood friends and their families attended church. In fact, he cannot remember anyone his age even discussing religion except as the butt of a joke all the years he was in school.

Will adapted to the atheistic values around him. At about age nine, he felt what he terms a "spirit of adventurism" that manifested itself in several ways. He began to experiment with cigarettes and alcohol, often stealing liquor from his uncle's pantry and replacing it with water. He also began to use profanity and would amuse his friends with vulgar jokes.

By the time Will graduated from high school, Christianity had become empty and meaningless to him. When he left home to attend a university, he not only ceased attending church, but his "adventurism" was manifested in outright rebellion against the values and mores of his parents and the educational system in which he was involved.

There are several factors to which Will attributes this. In some ways he was very typical of English youth of that day and reflected a national trend toward secularization. In addition, his journey through adolescence took its toll, and he battled with what he terms irrational fears, which subsequently developed into claustrophobia and panic attacks. Will's spiritual interests, instead of being centered on the faith of his family, focused instead on unexplained phenomena and psychic powers.

Will periodically visited theaters showing horror movies, including those dealing with satanic activities, all of which he regarded at the time as "mere entertainment." While he still retained a conscious belief in God, he had concluded that Bible teachings about a devil were "utter nonsense." This conclusion was bolstered by a high school philosophy teacher, Mr. Harding, who taught the theories of Sigmund Freud on this subject— that Satan was a purely mythical symbolic representation of man's own destructive impulses. Will's interest in what is now termed "paranormal phenomena" was also sparked when he was in high school, where a geography teacher would often speak of such things as mental telepathy, unidentified flying objects, and extrasensory perception.

The completion of Will's university training brought some major life-style changes. He embarked on a "frenzied pursuit of exciting pastimes" that led the once-withdrawn adolescent into involvement with everything from motorcycle gangs to mountaineering, in a wild attempt to "fully experience life." As the novelty of each activity faded, however, it was replaced by a growing emptiness. In his search for happiness, Will moved for a few months to Toronto, Canada, but found that this change only increased his depression.

Then Will returned to his fascination with psychology, checking out books on Freudian and Jungian theories from his local library. It was there that he came into contact with a book that, in his words, "stimulated a series of changes that resulted in my switching careers, living on a different continent, and becoming fully immersed in a satanic cult." This book, *Stress Disease* by psychotherapist Peter Blythe, introduced Will to the term "New Age" and to mystical healing, psychic surgery, and other metaphysical ideas.

A London-based organization, Health for the New Age, was mentioned in this book, and Will made an appointment to meet with its founder, Colonel Marcus McCausland. Will was still having problems with phobias and irrational fears, and he hoped that McCausland could direct him to someone who would help him with a new technique known as "primal therapy." Due to a dream Will had had when he was in his late teens—about the nervous breakdown his mother suffered as a result of war trauma—he believed that this technique would help him regress to his childhood, deal with the events that transpired there, and thus rid himself of their psychological effects.

Through McCausland's organization, Will heard about an "alternative psychology center" named Atlantis, a small, hippie-style commune in southern Ireland. He paid the required fee, quit his job, and became involved for several months in this community, which was housed in a former hotel painted with psychedelic colors and astrological symbols. Will divided his time between helping with farming and gardening chores and receiving "primal therapy"—an intense regression technique that involved deep breathing and screaming outbursts of emotion. Although the therapists were also engrossed in doing astrological charts and psychic readings in their leisure time, Will was more interested in the apparent success of the therapy than in the mystical realms being investigated by the therapists. He spent six months in this commune and another four months in a sister-commune in central London before concluding that these people were, in his words, "dilettantes." His experiences in these centers, along with other personal counseling, encounter groups, "human potential" seminars, and "group process" workshops left him little better than before in regard to his problems. Will next decided to move to Los Angeles, where in 1979 he enrolled in a psychological institution called The Center for Feeling Therapy, which was founded by professors from the University of California at Irvine. The therapy offered there was designed to deal with the increasing failures of the "primal scream" therapy: after initial improvement, patients tended to slip back into former patterns as if no true healing had taken place. When malpractice attorneys closed the center after Will had attended it for a year, he felt "lost and depressed."

One day while Will was at work in his engineering office, he distinctly heard a voice deep in his mind. "What about your soul?" the voice asked. In an attempt to answer that question for himself, Will then began a search for a shaman—someone with special psychic power to probe into his psyche and help him manifest his "destiny potential." Will had been profoundly influenced while at Atlantis by the writings of Carlos Castanedas, who claimed to have been an apprentice to Mexican brujos, or sorcerers, and had written of them as people able to channel profound cosmic power and wisdom.

His search led him to a psychic fair, where he met a woman who called herself Muriel Isis. Will was impressed by her master's degree from a prestigious California university and her state certification as a counselor. Fashionably dressed and in her mid-sixties, Muriel impressed him even further at their first appointment by accurately telling Will interesting and intricate details about himself and his parents, his friends, and work associates.

Will began attending classes at Muriel's "The Lighted Way" metaphysical center, which was located in the affluent Pacific

Palisades area. It offered classes in astrology, Egyptian tarot, numerology, psychosynthesis, and Eastern meditation. There Will was taught that he must develop his "higher self" to contact God and become at one with his "divine consciousness." Under Muriel's tutelage, he learned in meditation to channel a spirit "master" named Djwhal Khul and his "fellow brother, the Master Jesus," and a master known as "Lord Maitreya."

The apparent accuracy of the insights of Muriel and others at the center into Will's past and current relationships completely convinced him that he had finally found the source of power for which he had been searching. He began to hear an inner voice that directed his life. First it told him to break up with a girlfriend. Later, it directed him to junk his car, even specifying the make and model of the car he was to buy to replace it.

In his book, *Deceived by the New Age*, Will describes the effect of this guidance on his life. "I came to believe," he states, "that if I aligned my life to the voice of the higher self, 'God' would bless me. I strove to develop a faith that would allow me to hand my life over to the will of 'God' expressed to me through the higher self. I believed that by so doing, I would come into the abundance and joy of the New Age and would experience both a material blessing and an abundance of happiness as I fulfilled by destiny plan."

On the morning of October 30, 1981, after a year at The Lighted Way, Will underwent a visionary, blinding-light experience in which a being, which he first thought was Jesus Christ, appeared to him. Djwhal Khul, purportedly a high-ranking member of the "White Brotherhood of Masters," had chosen Will to be a personal disciple, and promised him "a very, very rigorous training."

Will embarked on an intensive reading of the twenty-five books written by Alice Bailey, who was once a devout Christian and wife of an Episcopal priest but had been heavily influenced by the metaphysical Theosophical Society. She claimed that her books had been dictated verbatim to her by Djwhal Khul. According to these books (published by the Lucis—formerly Lucifer—Trust), Djwhal Khul, once the abbot of a Tibetan lamasery, attained immortality and has lived in his physical body for almost four hundred years, directing the minds of other mortals in his role as an "ascended master." This "ascension" is also referred to as "mastership" or "Christhood." According to New Age teachings, others who have undergone numerous incarnations and finally attained this standing include Buddha and Jesus Christ, and this hierarchy, or "White Brotherhood," is presided over by their leader, Lord Maitreya.

According to Djwhal Khul, a New World religion that integrated Christianity and Eastern religions would bring about world harmony. The being known as "the Master Jesus" would telepathically transmit ideas into the minds of leaders of Christian churches to direct them toward this New Age religion.

Will continued to receive instructions "from an inner voice." He was directed to move from his house in Los Angeles to the city of Torrance, and he was told in advance of the fact that someone at his work would leave and that he would be promoted. He maintained a rigorous schedule of meditation and communion with his spirit guides. When Muriel Isis suddenly suspended Sunday-morning services at The Lighted Way, Will obeyed a mental impression that he should attend a nearby Lutheran church. Finally, Muriel "channeled" a message that he was to sell his possessions and move back to England.

Soon after his arrival in England, Will was told by his "inner voice of meditation" to visit Findhorn, which has been described as "the Vatican City of the New Age Movement." Begun in 1962, this northern Scottish retreat center has hosted thousands of guests in its palatial eighty-seven-room hotel and been the site of many international conferences. Its avowed purpose is to train people to "attune to the 'Christ' within and to use it to guide their lives."

Will's two-day visit stretched into two months as he worked for the publications department in helping to produce New Age magazines, books, and brochures. At Findhorn, Will met many people who professed what they termed "New Age Christianity," including a former Jesuit priest, a seminary professor, several psychologists, and some former Bible teachers. Will soon began to perceive himself as a type of priest. He had embraced a vow of celibacy and now saw himself as a New Age monk, renouncing worldly aspirations and devoting himself to a life of humble service to humanity.

However, shortly after he had been accepted as a "full member of the community," Will received from his spirit guide a startling revelation that he must return to Los Angeles. When he met again with Muriel back in the United States, she told him that the command to return had been a test of his obedience. Furthermore, she told him that she had begun receiving instructions from "the Father" and would be revamping The Lighted Way's curriculum. When she said she would need six thousand dollars for the project, Will immediately drained his savings account and gave Muriel all the money he had—five hundred dollars.

Over the following two-week period, Will was oppressed by uneasy feelings after receiving psychic instructions to contribute more money. He sent Muriel another five hundred dollars, postdating a check against his salary. His feeling of relief lasted only until he received another, stronger mental impression to borrow a thousand dollars against his credit card. Again he sent the money, and a few days later was told to do the same. This pattern of instruction was repeated with increasing force until Will had sent the entire six thousand dollars Muriel had said she would need for her project. He had reached the limit of his credit line and his endurance when the "supernatural" appeals for money finally ceased.

The reason behind Muriel's monetary requirements was revealed when she announced that she had been instructed to start using the Bible as "the main reference book" for studies at the center. She attributed the widespread changes she was about to begin to the visitation to her hotel room of a powerful being who identified himself as "Jesus Christ." Muriel urged class members to begin watching television evangelists, especially Kenneth Copeland.

A few weeks later, Will heard an inner voice compel him to attend a Copeland convention being held in Anaheim. He attended on two nights, feeling bored and enduring the long evening only by engaging himself in occult meditation visualizations, incantations, and invocations. The third night, however, he was amazed to hear Copeland announce that Jesus Christ would soon begin to appear in physical form in churches. This concurred exactly with The Lighted Way teachings that many of the "ascended masters" would soon begin to show themselves physically to their followers, a process termed "externalization."

The Lighted Way itself became more and more Christian in appearance. Muriel announced one morning that Djwhal Khul had "fallen" from his position to such an extent that Muriel identified him with "Satan." She instructed class members to devote themselves to the "most powerful Master," Jesus Christ, and even changed the name of The Lighted Way to reflect this metamorphosis. It was now The New Lighted Way, "a New Age Christian Church." Meditation, the Lord's Prayer, hymns, and asking for help in Jesus' name became the norm. Muriel herself was transformed into "the Reverend Muriel Isis," conducting Sunday-morning worship services that Will attended from 1985 through 1987.

Having previously spent five years of very different metaphysical training at this center (at which he had become the senior board member), Will at first felt betrayed. Later, though, he came to accept the changes when the inner voice purporting to be his "higher self" said that he was to "adopt a conventional religion." Reverend Muriel urged her followers to submit to the being she identified as Jesus, and Will, like many others now prayed to this being and accepted salvation from him. Finally, prompted by a message channeled by Muriel, he threw all his occultic literature into a dumpster. As Will devoted himself to Eastern-style meditation and reading the Bible, he concluded that many of the Scripture writers had simply been unenlightened about various "truths," such as reincarnation and channeling, concepts still advocated by Muriel.

It was into this ambiance that the most startling intrusion of the spirit world occurred in Will's life. He was suddenly awakened from sleep in the middle of the night by what he first thought was an earthquake. A new being he identified as "Jesus" spoke clearly to him. "I heard it with some sort of inner ear," Will recalls. "It was quite different from the voice of my 'higher self,' which was like someone else's intelligent thinking superimposed upon my own. This voice was much more powerful."

Not long after that, Will had a vivid dream in which he was presented with a pendant, a small wooden cross on a chain. Like his mentor Muriel, he believed that he had been initiated into the Melchizedek priesthood. He purchased a cross like the one he had seen in his dream and, following the urging of the new voice he began to hear, went to another Kenneth Copeland convention, where he responded to an altar call for those who wanted to enter into Christian ministry.

The "master" whose voice Will was obeying proved to be a strident entity who insisted that he go to a local shopping mall and preach. Will, whose shyness and inexperience made such a thought terrifying, resisted the increasing frequency of urgent demands to go to the mall, stand there with a Bible, and tell strangers that "Jesus Christ" would appear on the earth in fifteen years. Then the inner voice began to scold and reprimand Will for his disobedience, telling him that he must "die to self," "take up his cross," and obey without question. He was subsequently commanded to take his "ministry" to the dilapidated boardwalk area of Venice, beachfront habitat of hoboes, punk rockers, street musicians, and crowds of tourists.

There he set up an easel with a message he had received in meditation. It portrayed a familiar picture of Jesus with a printed message above it: "IF YOU ARE WAITING FOR THIS MAN TO COME, YOU ARE WASTING YOUR TIME." Below the picture was printed: "BECAUSE I CAN TELL YOU WHERE HE IS!"

Not surprisingly, Will's poster generated a lot of interest. He would tell interested passersby that "Jesus" had spoken with him and had healed him, and that such power was available to anyone who would meditate on this being, whose presence existed inside every human.

"I stayed at the beach all afternoon, witnessing to all kinds of people—Christians, Hindus, atheists, agnostics, and New Agers," Will states in his book, *Deceived by the New Age*. "For each type of person, I was careful to tailor my basic message to be acceptable for their individual background. The witnessing turned out to be a successful venture."

Will wrote, had printed, and distributed brochures about this New Age "Jesus" and his accessibility through Eastern-style meditation. Soon he was spending every weekend, all day Saturday and Sunday, witnessing on the beach. During the week, after work each day, inner voices would command him to go to local shopping malls and talk to strangers who were willing to listen. He would tell them that he was a born-again Christian. Advocating a personal relationship with "Jesus" such as he had, Will would tell others that this charismatic, miracle-working being would soon appear and unite all world religions.

This life-style began to take a toll on Will's health and nerves, yet the incessant inner voice became more demanding and menacing, accusing Will of a lack of humility and obedience. At its insistence, Will was baptized at Peach Apostolic Church and was "coerced" by the church staff there to receive "the gift of the Holy Spirit" by repeating "Thank you, Jesus" over and over until he "spoke in tongues." This experience, Will recalls, "felt like the channeling I had done in The Lighted Way channeling groups—but this time it was in a language I didn't understand."

Will's "Jesus" gave him the mission task to "infiltrate" local Christian churches, and he noticed that they seemed to fall into two classes. In some of them, such as Christ's Community Church, he found little resistance to his teachings. In fact, they had printed in their worship program "The Great Invocation," the most important occult prayer of the New Age movement. But in other churches he noticed a disturbing contrast: a happy, relaxed attitude of the pastors that was jarringly different from the stress he saw in himself and in Muriel, who continued to receive the donations forcefully demanded of Will by his "Jesus." By this point, Will was thousands of dollars in debt.

It was at this time that two factors made him reassess his position. The first emerged as he began reading Christian books about the New Age. One in particular angered him: *Out on a Broken Limb* by F. LaGard Smith, which countered Shirley MacLaine's New Age teachings. "But it put me in a tight corner," Will recalls, "because I could see with my own eyes the difference between the teachings of the Bible and our New Age 'Christianity.' I also became aware of the peace which Christians had, compared to the tension which filled my own life and that of Muriel."

In direct opposition to the emphatic inner voice, Will went one evening to a revival meeting presented by Reinhard Bonnke, who has sometimes been described as "the Billy Graham of Africa." Will was incensed at the evangelist's insistence that salvation was through the blood of Jesus. Will's agitation against this "fundamentalist doctrine" was so obvious that a woman sitting next to him asked him about it. When he told her that he was a New Age Christian, she told him that she, too, had once been involved with that movement. "But that was before I came to the Lord," she said humbly and sweetly. "Do you mind if I pray for you right now?" She took his hand and worded an earnest prayer that God would reveal his truth to Will.

Although Will was pleased to have extra "prayer support," he dismissed the hint that he needed the truth of fundamentalist Christianity. A couple of weeks later, when he was reading a biography of Ellen G. White, he was shocked to read her description of Satan. She depicted him as a once-kingly being whose face was now marked by anxiety, hatred, and deceit. Will suddenly realized that this, not the Jesus of the Bible, was the entity who had been dominating his life.

"It's him, my master," he said aloud. "I have been a follower of Satan all these years."

Will's turn to the real Jesus was very different from his days of slavery to Satan. He realized that God's salvation was a free gift. Instead of going to Christian churches to teach them New Age "truth," he knew he had to go and confess his sins as a repentant prodigal. He began to recognize the power that the persistent prayers of his godly parents and others had finally had in his life. After six months of intensive Bible study under the guidance of Pastor Siegfried Neuendorff, he finalized his commitment to the authentic Jesus Christ with a baptism that was very different from the one he had undergone before.

"As I entered the water, no voices hounded me to do their work. I spent the entire day filled with the simple joy of peace in the Lord. I was experiencing salvation by grace—salvation by faith in what Jesus had done for me."

PART TWO

Identifying Factors Involved in Leaving the Cult and Effective Nurture of Ex-Cultists

7

Personal Costs and Compensations

At what personal costs did you leave the cult?
What effect did this have on family and friends?
What seemed to compensate for these costs to yourself and to others?

David Reed

Some of our friends followed us out of the Jehovah's Witnesses, but we left most of them behind. Many of Penni's friends would call and say something like "Good-bye. I'm never going to talk to you again." Penni says it was like waking up one morning and finding that all your friends have died, so you'll never hear their voices again.

My mother and my sister, whom I had led into the Watchtower Society, had been disfellowshiped years before, when—as new converts—they became subject to a "new truth" that smoking was grounds for disfellowshiping. As good Witnesses, we had at the time cut off communication with them. We thank God that they did not hold this against us when we went to them and apologized after we left.

Just before the public announcement that we were going to be thrown out, Penni and I went to see her parents, who had been Witnesses for many, many years. If they were to follow the current Watchtower teachings, they would have had to show us the door and tell us never to come back, so we were very afraid of their reaction. To our great surprise and relief, they both said they were glad that we were leaving! They told us that *they* had wanted to leave for years, but were afraid that we would cut them off and have nothing more to do with them.

That illustrates the kind of fear experienced by those whom I refer to as "underground Jehovah's Witnesses." I am in close contact with many such people, some of them in high positions, such as elders and "ministerial servants" who no longer believe *The Watchtower* to be the truth, but who know that if they just step out of the Kingdom Hall and speak freely of their feelings, they will lose their families. Those who work for other Witnesses would lose their jobs, and young people living with Witness relatives would be evicted. I compare such people with Nicodemus or Joseph of Arimathea, who both were "secret" disciples of Christ.

We naturally admire courage, but we can also respect a person who doesn't want to lose all contact with his or her spouse and children. These people need and deserve much support and prayer, and work with such "undergrounds" is a primary focus of my ministry. I tell them that we, too, faced such fears. But the compensation for such costs (of friends, especially) is that we now know Jesus Christ, and knowing him is worth all that we have given up or will ever give up.

Joan Cetnar

I feel that I personally lost fellowship with immediate and extended members of my family, as well as with many friends. Though we live only a half-mile from my parents, for instance, we often pass them on the road and they will not speak to us or recognize us. It has been twenty-five years now, years in which there have been weddings, new babies born, and other events that we would love to share with them. All we can do now, though, is pray for them, hoping they will let God touch their hearts and let them know just how deeply they have been deceived.

God has truly compensated by giving us a loving "family" of Christian friends. There were first of all the believers who helped us in the early years by answering our questions on doctrine and showing us Christian love. As our speaking ministry developed and we received substantial radio and television exposure, we were brought into contact with many other ex-Witnesses. We realized that others needed a support system, too. So, in 1979, we had our first convention in Pennsylvania, and it continues annually with the name, "Witnesses Now For Jesus."

I guess there was also a financial cost. When we drove away from Pennsylvania, we had all our belongings in a station wagon and rented trailer. We left behind all hope of ever having the farm that we had lived on and worked on for so long. But God blessed us abundantly. Bill worked as a stockbroker and financial planner and was able to provide for us well. In addition, his profession allowed him the freedom to spend as much time as he needed for counseling people who were leaving the Jehovah's Witness movement. It has truly been a fulfillment of Mark 10:29, which promises that "there is no one who has left house or brothers or sisters or mother or father or children *or lands* . . . for the gospel, who will not receive a hundredfold . . ." (NASB, italics added)—and that's certainly been true for us!

Carolyn Poole

Until I became a Christian, all my friends were Christian Scientists. I didn't make it a secret that I was studying the Bible with that little women's group—in fact, I had even invited my church's clerk to see how it was being conducted. But, after I resigned from the Christian Science church and it became known, I was immediately dropped, even by friends I had had for twenty-five or thirty years in the church. The church clerk, whom I really liked, reacted by coming right away to my house to pick up my key to the church building.

Because I felt that I owed friends like this a more complete explanation of my actions, I wrote each a letter, telling them that I loved and appreciated them, but that I had left the church because I had discovered the real Jesus. When one of the women called me a short while later, she refused to discuss the issue of Jesus. She told me that she and her friends had discussed my situation and decided that the reason I had been unhappy with the church was that I was a city girl and had never been happy in the small town where I lived. They knew, also, that I had been through several crises involving my mother's death and problems with my daughters, and they thought these problems had caused me to be discontent. I tried to assure her that these things were not my reasons for leaving, but I think her mind was already made up.

However, whereas I lost my lifelong friends, my decision for Christ has brought me even closer to my very best friend, my husband.

When I first left the Christian Science church, I was so gung ho about my decision that I was watching Christian television every morning and evening and attending a Baptist church. Richard was attending with me, too, and enjoying it, but that church told me that they didn't want me to join it until my husband did—and he was quite resistant to the idea.

Both Richard and I enjoyed evangelist Pat Robertson's preaching very much, so one Sunday we went to where he was preaching. To my great joy, Richard accepted Jesus one evening, though he didn't tell me about it until later. We both joined the Baptist church and were baptized together. Since that time, he has been a sincere, dedicated follower of Jesus, reading his Bible regularly and backing me solidly in my ministry to Christian Scientists.

Elaine Dallas

I certainly did pay a price for leaving Christian Science, first of all with my friends. They still talk to me when we happen to meet, but there is now an impenetrable barrier between us.

My greatest heartache, however, is over my immediate family and relatives. Of our two sons, one is still a very staunch Christian Scientist, while the other is now saved. What a feeling of joy the latter one brings, but my heart will remain heavy until the other son and his family escape the bondage of Christian Science and receive God's gift of eternal life.

After I left Christian Science, I sent a long letter to all my relatives who were still Christian Scientists, explaining and documenting why I had left the church. In it I included the "good news" of God's gift of salvation.

I received mixed reactions. Several became angry and hostile, while others indicated that this was nice for me if it made me happy. One uncle, to whom I later sent a taped version of my testimony, tried lovingly to bring me back into Christian Science. He sent me all kinds of materials, and I agreed to read these if he would read material I sent him. He agreed, and for some six years we exchanged letters and had many lively discussions on the phone. But he could never see past Mrs. Eddy's teachings. He passed away a while ago, and my hope is that before he died he just might have accepted Jesus as his Lord and Savior and that I'll have the joy of seeing him when I get to heaven.

Another uncle read my long letter and did not resent it. Several years later, after a number of letters and phone calls, he prayed to accept God's gift of salvation over the phone with me, some three thousand miles away. What joy!

There was a time when I felt prompted by the Holy Spirit to witness to a Christian Science friend whom I had known and loved for many years, but I procrastinated. I kept feeling I had plenty of time. I learned a painful lesson, though, about ignoring these promptings when my friend suddenly passed away before I "got around" to talking to her. We never know if a loved one will be here tomorrow—we really only have today.

I need to mention my mother and father. My mother, who was a very loyal Christian Scientist, died two years before I was saved, so I was never able to show her God's true salvation in the Bible. However, my father was still living after I was saved, and I had the joy and privilege of showing him in the Scriptures God's wonderful gift of forgiveness of sins and eternal life. When he saw how the doctrines of Christian Science had so shockingly perverted this wonderful truth, he joyfully prayed to accept God's loving gift. I praise God for this! Two years later, when he died at the age of eighty-four, I experienced one of the blessings of salvation—the peace it gives us when a saved loved one dies. Though I miss him very much, I have great joy in knowing that he is now with our Lord Jesus and that I will see him when my life on this earth is also over.

I contrast this with my feelings after my mother died. At the time of her death, I was still a Christian Scientist, and I grieved deeply for her. Through Christian Science, I had no assurance as to her future and whether I would ever see her again. Christian Science gives a superficial kind of peace by denying that a loved one has died, but that's as far as it goes.

According to Mrs. Eddy's teachings, if a person has not before the point of his or her death attained salvation through making the "final demonstration" that All is God, Spirit—and that matter, sin, sickness, and death have no existence—that person will have to live another material life like this one. If "salvation" has not been attained during this "plane of existence," death will occur again, and this process will continue until "perfection" has finally been reached. This, of course, is the doctrine of reincarnation, though this term is never used in Christian Science.

These teachings of Mrs. Eddy gave me no comfort at all. My mother obviously hadn't come anywhere near making such a "demonstration." I didn't know where she was after she died, and I didn't know if I would ever see her again. According to Mrs. Eddy, we can never see our loved ones again unless and until we each individually "demonstrate" deathless perfection (*Miscellaneous Writings* 42:1–23; *Science and Health* 82:9–28). Thus, there was no joy in my heart as I thought about my mother. When I contrast this with the deep wonderful peace and joy and anticipation that I felt when my father died, and which I still feel now—well, there's just no comparison.

Irene Guthrie

About one year after entering the New Age School, at the halfway point of my New Age education, I was still searching for answers to my big question: "What is going to happen in the future?" Even when I began reading the Bible, I was looking for information about the end of the world.

But Satan knew that if I discovered the truth about the New Age movement by reading the Bible, that truth would set me free. In my testimony I told of the experience of having excruciating chest pains while reading the Bible. At the emergency room, they said that it was just a bad case of heartburn. I now know better—it is part of the cost of leaving the New Age movement.

The material cost was next. I lost seven jobs in Phoenix after accepting Christ and renouncing the occult. But I must say that the Lord has blessed me seven times over since then, especially financially.

There was also an emotional cost in that when I first became a Christian, my husband thought I was crazy. He felt that I had laid down my obsession with the occult and taken up a new one, and that this one, too, would pass.

I believe that Satan exacted a cost from those I loved, too. Three months after I accepted Christ, Mike was involved in a car accident, rear-ended by a driver on drugs who was traveling eighty-five miles an hour. Mike walked away from the car, but his whiplash and back injuries and subsequent insurance settlement troubles were very hard on him.

As for the effect that my Christianity had on family and friends, you would have thought I had contracted a terrible disease. It seemed that having a witch in the family was okay and nonthreatening, but having a Jesus freak around was not acceptable! With my new life-style, changed attitude, and unquenchable thirst to know Jesus, family and old friends no longer enjoyed my company. All I wanted to do was talk about Jesus and what he had done for me. This caused a great deal of heartache between Mike and me at first, because my desires for worldly activities changed long before his did.

I learned the hard way from this how *not* to win your family to Christ. I was too zealous and overbearing. I lacked wisdom and patience. But, with Jesus' help, we overcame the difficulties. Jesus broke down the barriers.

There were many compensations for the costs involved. No longer did the phrase "New Age" eclipse the real meaning of the "newness" of my life. Spiritually, I gained eternal life—my name was written in the Lamb's Book of Life. I had gained a new heart, and if nothing else were given me, this was enough to compensate for all I went through.

Though I felt that Satan tried repeatedly to kill me, I also keenly felt God's protection. Fear and oppression were gone, and this had a positive effect on my physical well-being. And I had gained a new body that was free from drugs and alcohol and promiscuity. God supplied all our physical and financial needs.

I also received a new mind. I had very deep emotional scars from the physical and emotional abuse I experienced as a child and the violence of my first marriage. One of the effects of my new mental attitude was my ability to forgive my mother for having abandoned me to my grandparents. I realized that we had both suffered similar traumas, but that *I* had Jesus, which gave me compassion and understanding toward her.

My relationship to my children began to change. I had once been very neglectful of them. When I repented to them, we all learned together—and continue to learn—what the real meaning of love is.

In addition, the Lord has given me new friends and a whole new family, the family of God, including the people I have helped lead to the Lord.

Will Baron

The pastor who first helped me with Bible study after my "rescue" showed me from Scripture that I should expect opposition from Satan. One of the most surprising places where this showed up was at my work.

I was working at a small company, and its founder and owner was a decidedly secular man of Deist sentiment. As long as I was involved with the New Age movement, I never tried to convince him to accept my beliefs, and we got along very well. As soon as I became a Christian and he learned of it, our relationship went sour. He was no longer friendly toward me, and it became very difficult for us to work together or relate to one another.

However, that seems a very slight cost when compared to the tremendous freedom I have felt since I found the true Jesus. My last four years as a New Ager was an absolute nightmare. I was devoting almost every spare moment to witnessing to strangers on the beach and in malls. Though I put on a big smile, inside I was full of tension and fear, wondering what I would be forced to do next—what embarrassing or uncomfortable thing would be required of me. In the long term, Satan's power is not an energy of peace. It is full of unhappiness, stress, strain, and anxiety—and ultimately misery and death. What a relief to be freed from all that! My parents were delighted to hear I had left the New Age movement—they had been praying for that for over fifteen years.

I had few friends in the movement. The New Age discipleship path is a very lonely one. At our church we would attend classes, but we never had any social interaction outside of church activity. Most of us were instructed to infiltrate local Christian churches, so when The Lighted Way closed after Muriel moved to Dallas, we lost touch with each other.

After my rescue from the New Age, I made contact with several of my former acquaintances. One of them did not want to listen to me when I told him that the New Age was satanic. Another said she had become a Christian, but I know she was practicing meditation, which makes me doubt that she made a clean break. A third friend, one I had known since my stay at Atlantis, left the New Age but said he wasn't interested in Jesus Christ. It seems he wanted to continue his promiscuous lifestyle. I have basically withdrawn from my relationship with him, though I still pray for him.

8

Opposition from the Cult

What techniques were used by friends and family and church officials to discourage or prevent your leaving the organization?

David Reed

Of course, the threat of not ever being able to talk to a faithful Witness again was something that made us give very serious thought to what a decision to leave would mean. I knew that our actions would burn all bridges between us and most of the people I had known and loved, and even converted to the organization.

One of the most frightening things that happened to us occurred just before our church trial for publishing the newsletter. One night I received a phone call from someone who said he was going to "come over and take care of" me if I continued to publish the newsletter. This was followed, a few days later, by two messages left on our telephone answering machine. One said, "David, you're going to die." The second one said, "David, I'm going to kill you." It was mainly due to such threats that we decided not to attend the trial.

Joan Cetnar

When we began to question the truth of Watchtower teachings, we were warned that this was God's organization, and to question it was to question God. We were given strong doses of fear of the wrath of Jah at Armageddon, when we would be "forever annihilated." Our only hope, they told us, was to be faithful to Jah's organization. This caused real mental anguish.

When we found proof that the Watchtower organization was actually proclaiming a false prophet, the words of Deuteronomy 18:21–22 were a great comfort to us: "And if you say in your heart, 'How may we know the word which the LORD has not spoken?'—when a prophet speaks in the name of the LORD, if the word does not come to pass or come true, that is a word which the LORD has not spoken; the prophet has spoken it presumptuously, you need not be afraid of him" (RSV).

During the time of Bill's disfellowshiping and my being expelled, I was contacted by members of my family and Watchtower officials who tried to influence me not to follow my husband's lead. I was made to feel completely responsible for the eternal welfare of myself, our children, and my wayward husband. I was intimidated and made to feel that a young woman had no right to question the "truth" that men like my grandfather had believed all their lives. "Who do you think you are?" I was asked.

Fear of losing all family and friends is one of the main controlling techniques used by the Watchtower organization.

Carolyn Poole

When I first began having doubts about Christian Science, I wrote to a practitioner I knew in San Diego and asked him to "know the truth" for me about what I should do. He wrote me back, saying that he would pray for me, but that I shouldn't leave, that Christian Science was changing, and it needed me.

Once I had made my decision to leave Christian Science and had shared it with my Bible-study group, I wrote three short notes about how important Jesus had become to me and that therefore I was leaving the church. I sent one to the Mother Church in Boston, one to my branch church, and one to the man who had been my class instructor.

I received a hostile response from my instructor. He called me, indignant that I was causing "a black mark" on his record. "If you have any questions about Jesus," he sternly admonished me, "you call me. I will tell you what's what."

At first my husband was not happy about my decision either. It saddened him to see me going through the mental turmoil I was experiencing, and he hated to give up the comfortable routine of the Christian Science life we led.

The Mother Church responded to my letter by writing me that they were holding my resignation and would not accept it because they wanted me to take more time to consider. It wasn't until two months later that they finally accepted my resignation.

All of this is very much in line with Mary Baker Eddy's own teachings about leaving her church. In her writings are very explicit threats of suffering for anyone who thinks of doing so.

Elaine Dallas

Actually, at the time I was making my decision, no one from the church opposed it in any way—because no one knew about it except my husband.

When we announced that we were leaving Christian Science, we sent our letters of resignation to the Mother Church in Boston and to our local branch church. Within a few weeks I received a long-distance phone call from a spokeswoman from the Mother Church. She was very pleasant and strongly encouraged me to return to Christian Science. Although I didn't know as much about the Bible then as I do now, the Lord brought to my mind the very words and Scriptures I needed to refute her statements of Mrs. Eddy's words. We went back and forth for nearly ten minutes: she quoted Mrs. Eddy, and I quoted the Bible. She finally relented and said she could see I could not be persuaded, to which I heartily agreed. She then asked to speak to my husband. After he told her that he felt the same way I did, she politely ended the conversation.

The phone call we got from our local branch church was equally pleasant. However, here there was no real attempt to convince us to come back. The person who called just said that they were very sorry that we were leaving the church, and that if we ever wanted to return, we would be most welcome. I think that is very characteristic of how most Christian Scientists handle things—they're generally very pleasant and genteel.

Irene Guthrie

The relationships I had established in the New Age school in Connecticut were more acquaintances than friendships. I really had no time to spend with these people outside class because I was working full-time and had two small children. That is probably why it was easy for me to leave the New Age movement without any interference, at least from a human standpoint.

Moving to Arizona cut more ties. My class teacher assumed that I would make the contacts he suggested with New Age people in Scottsdale. But, outside of phone calls to just a few close friends and relatives, I lost touch with most people in Connecticut. Even family members "backed off" from me when I started witnessing about Jesus.

After we arrived in Arizona and began attending the Catholic church, I began to understand that the New Age movement had a lot in common with Catholicism. One incident stands out in my memory. On November 1, at an All Saints' Day Mass, the priest who was officiating began calling out the names of dearly departed saints. I was immediately uncomfortable—I felt as if I were back in New England in the New Age school, performing necromancy by calling on the dead! A precious Baptist lady at my work, Gloria Lee, opened my understanding of the conflict between the Scriptures and Catholic doctrine. When I went to my priest to ask about these things, the answers he gave me disappointed me because they seemed to be nonscriptural. I knew I had to leave Catholicism, too, but here again, we had no opposition from church leaders. In fact, I have no recollection of anyone calling or visiting us with questions about our departure.

Will Baron

The opposition I experienced was not from people in the New Age movement. When I left, I had been involved in a one-man beach ministry, witnessing to strangers. I really had no contact with other New Agers.

I did undergo a direct assault by demons, however. Within a week of ceasing meditation, I would be awakened in the night by my bed shaking violently. I could still hear voices in my mind, telling me that they had power over me and would kill me. They taunted and intimidated me by saying that I had no chance to survive, that I was wasting my time in Christianity.

When that happened, I would get out of bed and onto my knees and ask God in Jesus' name to help me. Then I would feel great peace.

When I began to write my book about my experiences in the New Age, the attacks began again. They harassed me as before, but they also used more subtle techniques. One was sexual temptation—obsessive fantasies and fornicational urges toward women I knew at church. But I did what the Bible says—I persisted in resisting the devil, and he fled from me. But it was a very, very difficult time for me.

9

Mistakes Made by Christians in Witnessing

What mistakes did Christians make when they tried to influence you to accept Christ?

David Reed

I would have to say, unfortunately, that during the thirteen years in which I was spending many hours a month for the Watchtower Society, going house to house and talking to thousands of people—I could count on my hands the number of times that any Christian made a sincere effort to share the gospel with me. Of that small number who tried, most had no idea of what would be effective, and some actually strengthened my faith in my Jehovah's Witness beliefs.

I encountered only two people in those thirteen years who witnessed effectively to me, and they did it by showing me Watchtower literature that exposed errors in the organization's doctrine.

With Scripture alone, it is very, very difficult to reach a Jehovah's Witness, because he will look at the Bible through Watchtower-colored glasses. Talking about the Trinity, for example, is almost always ineffective, because we were taught that this doctrine was a pagan belief originated by Satan.

Of course, you can't put God in a box and say that he can't use Scripture and the Holy Spirit to reach someone's heart. But it is my experience that the heart must first be softened by a general awareness that the organization that gave the Witness his view of Scripture and doctrine *might* be flawed.

Joan Cetnar

To be honest, I cannot remember anyone who ever really tried to talk to me about Christ. There were people who said they were Christians and then slammed the door in my face, or who wanted to argue about why Witnesses wouldn't salute the flag. Considering all the doors I knocked on, I recall plenty of arguments about the Trinity and other doctrines, but no one ever talked to me about being born again or about accepting Jesus as my personal Savior and having that assurance of salvation.

I believe that many Christians think it is their duty to argue about doctrine, but most don't realize they are dealing with a closed and blinded mind. Jehovah's Witnesses believe that the Bible cannot be read or understood by itself, that it is only understood with the help of Watchtower literature. It would never occur to them to ask the Holy Spirit to help them understand, because they believe that the Holy Spirit deals only with the men who write the publications, not with other individuals.

So, before Christians can discuss doctrinal subjects effectively, the closed mind of the Jehovah's Witness must be opened by asking questions regarding the authority of the Watchtower organization.

Carolyn Poole

My brother became a Baptist in early adulthood. When he came to visit my mother and me, he would not make a big issue of religion except in a very loving way, gently making fun of Christian Science doctrine about God's being "All in All." He didn't try to tell me anything about the reality of Jesus or who he was. He did take my two little girls to Sunday school with him, and he once asked permission to have his pastor come over and talk to me. But after he began a confusing discourse about Lazarus and hell and eternal damnation, I stopped him short. Since I believed that God was a God of love who would never permit anything like hell, I was incensed that he would talk to me about such a thing or teach my children about it. So I forbade them ever to go back to that church.

While growing up, I never heard any non-Christian Scientist say anything about my religion except to tell the same story about some little boy who had appendicitis and whose parents were Christian Scientists and refused medical care for their child, who died. That story had absolutely no effect on me, because I was convinced that my religion was a healing one, and that staying in it offered me protection.

Even at points where I was disillusioned with Christian Science and was attending other churches, no one ever talked to me directly about how Jesus was not correctly taught in Christian Science. As a matter of fact, my family and I attended a Presbyterian church in Lancaster, California, where the pastor *never* talked about Jesus. To this day, I have my doubts about whether that man was saved himself at that point.

I have counseled with many people who have left the Christian Science church, and most of us have had similar experiences. Christians would tell you about how refusing to go to a doctor was wrong, but they never took the time to sit down with you and show you in the Gospels who Jesus is.

Elaine Dallas

With the exception of the woman at the Christian bookstore, no one witnessed to me during the time I was discovering the nonscriptural nature of Christian Science. All that I learned came from the Bible, from Christian radio, and from the books I had acquired.

Irene Guthrie

There were two major mistakes that well-meaning Christians made in witnessing to me. Ironically, they were the same mistakes that I later made when I, as a new Christian, was witnessing.

The first mistake was overzealousness. I ran into Christians who were outspokenly anti-Catholic or anti-New Age, when their emphasis should have been on witnessing to me through sound doctrine and their own life-styles. One person was a busybody and always obsessed with the evils of the New Age, but she neglected to keep her house clean. Although I knew very little about Christianity, I could see that this lady was very worldly.

The other mistake was made by people who were more concerned with influencing me to become a member of their own denomination than with helping me to grow in Christ. It seemed like they relished the self-satisfaction of conquest when they "won another Catholic to Christianity." The tendency of many Christians is to convert a new Christian to active membership in the denomination where he or she made a public profession of Christ. But I believe the proselytizer should allow the Holy Spirit to guide the newborn on the narrow path—that's what I wound up doing, anyway.

Will Baron

Part of the problem with my childhood was that I grew up in the very secular culture of England in the 1950s and 1960s. In spite of the church's teachings about God, I simply didn't believe in the reality of Satan. In retrospect, I believe that although the church in general certainly emphasized the socially acceptable moral teachings of Christianity, it failed to teach about the existence and power of Satan and his demonic angels. This subject matter is very biblical, but culturally frowned on. Even when as a New Ager I was witnessing in Lutheran, Anglican, Pentecostal, and other churches, or out in public, no one opposed my introduction of New Age concepts into Christian terminology or teachings. Unfortunately, many Christians today are not sufficiently grounded in fundamental Bible doctrines to be able to confront those who have been deceived.

However, by the time I was rescued from the New Age, I was so happy and so enthusiastic that if there were any mistakes made by Christians toward me, I simply didn't realize it! I was so relieved to learn that salvation was not earned by obsessive work. I could see in others that Satan was tempting and deceiving them, too, but that just gave me greater encouragement to witness to them and help them avoid backsliding.

10

"What I Miss"

What do you miss about your association with the cult?

What changes could individual Christians and the church body institute to make the transition to Christianity easier for ex-cultists?

What lacks do you see in Christianity as it is practiced today?

David Reed

It was very, very comfortable being in an organization where you knew how everyone thought—because to stay in it, everyone had to think the same way! I didn't say it was *good*—but it was comfortable. You could be relaxed in any Kingdom Hall anywhere in the world.

Being a Christian gives me more freedom, of course, and such freedom always results in differences. To me, some disagreement within the church body is infinitely more healthy than the lockstep conformity I had known.

One area where Jehovah's Witnesses and many other cults excel is in the realm of study. Though they don't do much that we would consider worship, Witnesses spend many hours a week in teaching situations, whereas it seems to me that many Christians regard Sunday school as something only for children, and they don't take advantage of the opportunity to study the Bible in groups. In-depth study is the reason that Jehovah's Witnesses are able to argue so persuasively.

Of course, effective arguing should never be our focus for Bible study. If we could put more emphasis on learning the basis of our own beliefs, we wouldn't be so vulnerable to cult indoctrination or to any teachings that would take us away from the body of Christ and into splinter groups that could become cults.

Joan Cetnar

There's nothing I really miss about the Jehovah's Witness organization except the association with my family members, who are still in the organization. Though it has been twenty-five years, and I can't say I really know them personally anymore, I still miss them.

As to changes that individuals or churches could make—I don't think any major changes are necessary. There are enough good Christian churches out there for an ex-Witness to attend. The Holy Spirit can, I believe, guide such a person to where he or she would be most comfortable.

The only thing I see lacking in modern Christianity is that there is not enough good Bible study in the churches. When people come out of the Jehovah's Witnesses, they are accustomed to spending many hours a week studying doctrine, so they need guidance to learn *true* doctrine.

There is also a need for more holiness among believers, being obedient to the Father's commands as admonished in 1 Peter 1:14–15. Also, Jehovah's Witnesses coming out of the cult should be able to see God's unconditional love being practiced in the body of believers.

Carolyn Poole

I really miss the *culture* of the Christian Science church. First of all, it is more than just a religion; it is a way of life and a way of thought. And it is a very refined way of life, where people try hard to be courteous to one another and display good manners.

I also miss the Christian Scientist's way of handling money. Many Christian Scientists are quite wealthy, and you will rarely see one of their churches in a poor section of town. As such, it attracts upper-class, moneyed people. The "intellectual" qualities of Christian Science are attractive to many such people. They immediately see the logic in some of the teachings—recognizing, for instance, that a great many illnesses have their cause in the mind. Combine the fact that many Christian Scientists are wealthy with the fact that they earnestly believe in what they are doing, and you will know why they don't preach tithing or ask for money. Yet many of their people are very generous with their donations.

Another thing I have really missed since becoming a Christian is the inspiring testimonies that are such an important part of Christian Science assemblies. Telling what God has done for you is a good way to strengthen others, and most Christian churches don't provide an opportunity for that.

Elaine Dallas

I so miss past friendships—we had some very good Christian Science friends who are now very distant. And I especially miss the closeness that I used to have with some of my relatives. I don't know if that breach will ever be healed, but it seems for now that the door is closed. We are praying that the Lord will open those hearts.

Our first year after being saved was an interesting one—we visited all kinds of churches in our area. Looking back, I am really glad we gave ourselves time to do that. With some churches, my husband and I felt led *not* to return, while others we visited several times. We finally narrowed it down to two choices.

For nearly ten years now, we have been attending the church we eventually chose. Two things influenced our choice. First and most important was the fact that God's whole Word was being faithfully preached from the pulpit. After having been deceived and misled for so many years by a Bible-twisting religion, we wanted a church that was true to God's Word. Second, we found the people to be very friendly—one couple in particular took us under their wing and made sure we were included in all that the church had to offer. We are very grateful to them.

I think that it would be very helpful for churches to offer classes for new Christians. There is so much to learn and, for those of us who have come out of a cult, there is so much to *unlearn*. At first, Bill and I felt intimidated in church classes because others knew the Bible so well, and we knew so little. Also, words and terms that seem natural to established Christians are quite foreign to new Christians.

Bible Study Fellowship, a worldwide organization devoted to a deep study of the Bible, was a wonderful blessing to me. The wife of one of my husband's co-workers invited me to join. We had not yet settled on a church home, and I was in great need of Bible instruction.

One of the great things I learned from BSF was how to pray. You see, in Christian Science, one doesn't pray by asking God, as the Scriptures tell us to do, but by holding in one's mind the thought that "God is All"—all is perfect, and therefore there can be no pain or sickness or whatever the problem happens to be. Until I learned how to pray biblically, I was in a kind of scary no-man's-land: I knew Christian Science "prayer" was wrong, but I didn't yet know how to pray correctly. When problems and troubles came along, as they always do, I found myself being drawn back to the security I had always felt in Christian Science, where I could handle my problems by simply "knowing" that they weren't real.

Another thing that meant so much to me in BSF, in addition to the wonderful Bible instruction, was the love and friendship the women in the class gave me right from the start. An experience I will never forget happened as I was leaving my first class. I was walking out with one of the women and happened to mention that I had just been saved out of Christian Science. She looked at me, threw her arms around me, and said, "Hallelujah! Thank the Lord!"

I had never experienced Christian love like that before. In Christian Science, although the people are very pleasant, my experience has been that they tend to be a little aloof and more "into themselves." Also, during times of illness, accident, or bereavement, there is seldom an outward expression of concern or empathy, because to do so would be to "make a reality" of the situation—which would counteract the efforts being made to "know" their unreality.

Although Christian Scientists are possibly some of the most sincere and dedicated religious people and make their faith a part of every waking hour, their insistence on mentally denying any sickness or evil around them makes them seem uncaring, especially to outsiders. On my tour of Israel, for instance, one Christian Science man walked ahead of his handicapped wife while she struggled to walk and keep her balance. He obviously believed he was "helping" her by not making a reality of her troubles by acknowledging them. In another case I remember vividly, our newly elected First Reader was absent one morning, and someone else took his place. After four or five Sundays of the First Reader's absence, we asked a practitioner friend in the church where he had been. "Oh, he passed on," was her casual answer. No announcement of the death was ever made, nor was the man ever mentioned in our presence again. The same situation occurred when the husband of one of our best friends, someone we socialized with, passed on. It was weeks before this dear friend mentioned his death—and that, only when we asked about him.

As to the lacks that I feel exist in Christianity today, I guess I cringe when I see some of the television programs that call themselves Christian. I find myself hoping that no non-Christian will watch them and get a distorted view of what Christianity is all about. There's something about the coiffed hair and phony hype of some of the televangelists, and the fact that they are always haranguing for money, that makes me glad that *I* didn't see this kind of television before I was saved.

Irene Guthrie

That first question sounds strange when you know that New Age is an evil lie. But, as in any cult, there are certain things that are attractive enough to trap people into joining the New Age network. I miss the movement's:

1. *Love and acceptance.* These folks lure you into their fold with open arms. They take you just as you are. Of course, it is a phony love most of the time, but if you feel good about yourself, you can accept others under the "I'm okay/You're okay" umbrella. In fact, *I never experienced rejection* in the company of New Age believers.

2. *Unity.* There was no fighting or bickering. There was no disagreeing on anything—everyone was truly in one "occord" (occult accord.)

3. *Lack of competition.* There was no jealousy. Everyone had his or her own talent, which came, of course, from a supernatural force. But I never remember anyone saying, "I wish I could do that," or anyone coming across as "superior" just because he or she could tell you your future better than you could draw up your own astrology chart. In addition, no one tried to influence you to take on a particular gift or talent. You were allowed to "flow" with what came naturally from your spirit guide or from the spirit world.

Here are the changes that I believe that individuals and churches could institute to make the transition for New Agers to Christianity easier:

1. Take the pressure off baby Christians to become members of a church or to do church work. Instead, offer good, solid new-believers' classes that emphasize the sovereignty of God and assurance of salvation. It is critical that they start out on a solid foundation.

2. Through Christian love, understanding, and patience, offer follow-up and discipleship for new Christians in the importance of loving one another according to Bible standards. Be sensitive to individual needs, taking into consideration a person's health, family situation, and work schedule.

3. Emphasize salvation through grace, not works, so that the new believer doesn't fall into a trap of guilt. Many churches push new Christians into works, then wonder why they feel no different than when in the cult, which measured loyalty by legal-

istic rituals. Instead, allow them the freedom to express loyalty to Christ and his body by the direction of the Holy Spirit.

4. In accordance with 1 Timothy 3:6, never place novices in a position of spiritual leadership until they have had a chance to grow in the Lord. Sound doctrine and godly motives must precede ministry. Only when godly attributes begin to show in their lives as well as in their relationships with God, family, and others, should they be trained for leadership.

5. Allow the Holy Spirit to bestow gifts on new believers as he wills (1 Cor. 12:11), teaching the novice to focus on Jesus as the Giver rather than on the gifts. This helps eliminate jealousy and allows God to receive the glory—not the pastor or teacher who consecrated the use of the gifts by the new believer by the laying on of hands.

I see lacks in today's Christianity in the following areas:

1. *Truth.* There is a lack of sound doctrine, which stems from the fact that seminaries and Bible colleges have been led astray by liberal theologians. For the sake of unity, the church has compromised the gospel so much that even Jesus' words no longer have the meaning or impact he intended when he spoke of "entering in at the narrow gate" (Matt. 7:13).

2. *Balance.* Christendom is dominated by extremes. Overemphasis in one area (such as missions, holiness, social issues, gifts of the Spirit, etc.) keeps us from having a full, balanced gospel and leads to a "pick and choose" religion.

3. *The Berean way of life*—where people do not accept anything they are taught without searching it out for themselves in the Bible. Christians need to be taught *how* to study Scripture with the tools we have available: a good Bible translation, concordances, dictionaries, lexicons, etc.

4. *Nurturing/discipling.* Newborn Christians need "incubator care," an atmosphere that allows them to grow and develop under the Holy Spirit's guidance without the pressures of leadership. They should not be manipulated to develop talents that fill the needs of the local church.

5. *Knowledge of the New Age and other cults.* The church loses Christians to cults because it doesn't show them how to rec-

ognize error. I have actually seen witches come into Christian congregations (especially charismatic ones, where tongues-speaking is done aloud) and heard them do incantations without any opposition from church leaders. As such persons infiltrate nurseries and Sunday school teaching positions, sowing seeds of discord and New Age philosophies, they split a church before it knows what is happening. The Lord has said: "My people are destroyed for lack of knowledge" (Hosea 4:6 RSV).

6. *Order.* First Corinthians includes standards for the church, but I see many abuses, especially in full-gospel/charismatic churches. Other churches, for example, are ignoring what God said about ministry by ordaining men who are sexually immoral.

7. *Godly standards.* Lately it is difficult to tell the difference between Christians and "the world." They listen to the same music (even New Age music), watch the same television programs and movies, play the same games, and wear the same clothing and jewelry (often with New Age symbols on them.) On the other hand, holiness should not be legalistically defined, but should be a normal characteristic of the everyday Christian life-style.

Will Baron

As a New Ager, I could freely be part of this world. New Age teaches that everything is part of God—a doctrine correctly labeled as pantheism. New Agers believe that people who are not spiritually minded are "compelled" to be worldly in order to balance out certain energies from past lives and may in future lifetimes become more spiritual. Meanwhile, someone who is obsessed with making money, or with sex, is viewed with an attitude that says, "That's fine—that's just their karma, and they have to exercise their creativity."

Christianity, of course, calls on us to look to entirely different ethical standards. It is our Christian duty to be *different* from the rest of the world—to take care of the poor, for example, and to keep ourselves from sexual immorality. We know that we are *not* the world—we can be in it, but not of it.

I'm shocked to see so much of the New Age in Christian churches, however. It's one thing to see worldliness on billboards and in newspapers and magazines, but quite another to see Christians embracing satanic things without even knowing it. For instance, I read that 56 percent of Methodist clergy don't even believe in the existence of Satan. I was stunned once to attend a camp meeting in my own Seventh-day Adventist church where a speaker had all two thousand people in the audience involved in mystical meditation! I stormed out in shock and anger until I realized that this was a great opportunity for me to warn these unsuspecting people about the infiltration of New Age practices.

11

Changed View of God and the Bible

How has your view of God and his Word changed since leaving the cult?

David Reed

My view of God changed as I was beginning to leave the Witnesses. Then I began to realize that he was not the legalistic God that the Watchtower organization presented him to be, but that he was a God of love. I realized that God wanted us to follow him personally, rather than through an organizational relationship. Before, I had just read about him in books, and since they were Watchtower literature, much of that was erroneous. But, as my prayers became less mechanical and I saw my prayers being answered, it was a wonderful time—kind of like a honeymoon with God—a relationship that has grown stronger with time.

Up until 1953, *The Watchtower* taught that God dwelt on the star Alcyone in the Pleiades constellation, but softened this in 1981 by saying that his "spirit body has a place where he resides, and so he could not be at any other place at the same time."

Now I realize, of course, that "heaven and the highest heaven, cannot contain" God (1 Kings 8:27).

Probably the biggest change in my thinking occurred when I actually experienced my adoption as a child of God, as Jesus explained in John 3. I had never believed that I could be "born again," as it describes, because all of the 144,000 slots had already been filled, according to Watchtower doctrine. When I found that I *could* be born again, and that God would be my Father, I was overjoyed.

However, my view of the Bible has remained basically unchanged. As a Jehovah's Witness, I always viewed the Bible as my ultimate authority, as I do today. I think that is what allowed me ultimately to see that the Watchtower was wrong, because I could see how it differed from the Bible.

Although I believe our personal relationship with God supplements the Bible, I know it can never take the place of his written Word. God gave us the Bible for a reason, and we should not expect that through our relationship with him, he will personally provide us with answers that he has already provided in the Bible.

Joan Cetnar

The Jehovah's Witnesses' view of God is so limited. Their Jehovah is not omniscient, he is not omnipresent, and he is confined to only the Father. He must rely on his angels to keep track of the events going on in his universe.

Once you really come to know God, you realize just how great he is. When I read Scripture now, I am in awe of his greatness—his boundless power and love. I have trusted in God for so much, and he has done so many beautiful things in my life, that my view of him is unlimited.

As a Jehovah's Witness, I was taught that Jehovah only answered my prayers inasmuch as I was a part of the organization. I would not "trouble" him with personal concerns, but only as they related to the organization. So when I came into a personal relationship with God, it was such a joy to trust him with *any* concerns I might have, such as which job my husband,

Bill, should take, where we should live, the sickness of my child, and our future in a ministry. In reverence, we watched his mighty, loving hand on our lives. My love grows daily for this almighty God who cares so personally for me.

In some ways, my view of the Bible has not changed, because I always did believe that it was God's Word. But my faith has grown stronger with the realization that when I was taught "truths" by the *Watchtower* that didn't fit with the Bible, it was the Bible that was reliable. This has made me appreciate the Word of God even more, especially now that I am able to read it with the help of the Holy Spirit for understanding.

With all the reading of Watchtower literature that I was required to do, I was never able to read the Bible alone and give it the attention it deserves. And, of course, reading "outside" literature was frowned upon, even if you could find the time to do it. Now that I'm a Christian, my faith has also been strengthened by reading church history. As Jehovah's Witnesses, we were taught that the doctrines of Christendom were not taught by Jesus and the early Christians, but were formulated at the Council of Nicea in A.D. 325. It has been a comfort to me to learn that, on the contrary, Witness doctrine is the aberration—the departure from Christ's original doctrine—not the reverse.

Carolyn Poole

Christian Science teaches a very impersonal God. Since I have become a Christian, I have found that God has personality traits, ones we can identify with, such as jealousy. Of course, I don't mean that he is human, just that he is far from being the vague cosmic force I once believed. I would never have taken my problems to the God of Christian Science, because their God doesn't recognize the existence of evil. In addition, Mrs. Eddy taught that prayer cannot change anything, because God has completed his work. According to her, the task of the believer was to just align one's mind with the understanding that "all is perfect."

Because Jesus has a very minor place in Christian Science theology, he is not talked about very much. I have found that it is difficult to engage a Christian Scientist in discussion about him. I was always puzzled about why the Bible said that Jesus was both the Son of God and the Son of man. But then I realized that he was the only person in history whose body was not formed by the union of an egg with a human sperm; and thus he was both God and man. That is a thought very foreign to the Christian Scientist mind, but essential for a Christian.

My view of the importance of the Bible has changed tremendously, too. As a Christian Scientist, I just accepted what Mary Baker Eddy said about the Bible, instead of reading it for myself. A good example of this is where she said, "Jesus is not God, as he himself declared" (*Science and Health*, published by the Trustees under the Will of Mary Baker Eddy, Boston; page 361). Had I taken the time to read the Bible, I would have known that Jesus never made any such statement! Instead, I just took her word for it.

The daily readings, or Lessons, of a Christian Scientist have you reading a passage from the Bible and then a passage from *Science and Health* that may or may not be related to the Scripture passage. The implication is that the Bible needs to be explained, and Mary Baker Eddy made it clear that she was the "revelator" who could do this. Since Christian Scientists study only from the King James Version, many are discouraged from trying to read it alone. Even when I tried to read through the Bible on my own, I gave up after the first five books of the Old Testament.

I remember what my practitioner said when I proposed a Bible study for myself and other Christian Scientists. She stipulated that such a study could not take place in a private home, but instead should be in the Reading Room. One of the church members warned me, "You can't study the Bible without *Science and Health* to go with it." She and others would say, "Christian Science is the perfect and final revelation."

Although memorization of Scripture is not emphasized in Christian Science, you *are* expected to memorize definitions and long passages from Mrs. Eddy's writings. I also spent a lot of time reading testimonies of other Christian Scientists from the

Christian Science Sentinel and the *Christian Science Journal*, as well as "authorized" books on the life of Mary Baker Eddy.

I can see how the emphasis on study carried over into my life as a young Christian. Because I wanted facts in my Bible study, taking notes and looking things up were important to me.

Elaine Dallas

My view of God has changed radically. In fact, I have learned that the God of Christian Science is not the God of the Bible, because Christian Science actually teaches an impersonal, pantheistic-type God.

In pantheism, God is All, the totality of existence—*pan* meaning "all," and *theos* meaning "God." Mrs. Eddy teaches that "God is All," but she denies that this is pantheism simply by redefining the word. According to her, pantheism means the "belief" that God is in or of matter (*Science and Health* 27:18–21), and that matter has intelligence (*Science and Health* 129:11–12). This is a good example of how she changed the meaning of any word she chose so it would fit into her own ideas.

In Christian Science, God is an impersonal "All." Mrs. Eddy herself even refers to God as an "it." She defines God as "Principle; Mind; Soul; Spirit; Life; Truth; Love; all substance; intelligence" (*Science and Health* 587:6–8). According to her, God is the only Mind, the only Soul and the only Spirit that exists; man has no individual mind, soul, or spirit of his own—he exists only as the "reflection" of God. In addition, she teaches that God has created, and is still creating, everything out of himself—creation being the "emanation" of God's "infinite self-containment"—and that nothing exists outside of God.

You can see how vastly different the impersonal God of Christian Science is from the personal God of the Bible. According to the Scriptures, God is a living spiritual being who created everything out of nothing—not out of himself—and who is separate from, yet sovereign over, all that he created.

Mrs. Eddy confirms this unbridgeable difference between what she herself calls "the Christian Science God" and the "Lord God" of the Bible by teaching that the Lord God is not the true

God. According to her, the LORD God is merely a "Jewish tribal deity," a "tribal god," a "heathen conception," a "finite deity," a "man-projected God," a "pagan Jew's . . . misconception of Deity" *from* which, she says, we turn "with sickened sense."

Mrs. Eddy's teachings about God were so strongly instilled in me that the scriptural truth of God's being made flesh and dwelling among men as the man Jesus of Nazareth was at first impossible for me to accept. According to everything I had believed all my life, nothing could be further from the truth. How could I accept that God, infinite "All," could be confined in something finite, particularly when that something was unreal and a lie, and that God had no consciousness of it? Thus, the incarnation of God was the last and most difficult Scripture truth for me to believe and accept.

My view of the Bible has changed tremendously also. Mrs. Eddy claimed that the Bible was her only authority—that all her Christian Science doctrines came from the Scriptures. However, she quietly elevated her book, *Science and Health with Key to the Scriptures*, above the Bible. She did this in a number of subtle ways. One of them is by implying that because the Bible is a translation, its reliability is suspect—whereas her own book is the untranslated revelation of Christian Science and therefore reliable. She also accused the Bible of being filled with hundreds of thousands of mistakes, while she said that the Christian Science contained in her book was "unerring," "irrefutable," "Divine," and "eternal."

I realize that in all my years as a Christian Scientist, I seldom turned to the Bible for help, but relied instead on *Science and Health*. Mrs. Eddy's words gave me the assurance that all was well. I generally referred to the Bible only for reading the selected passages given in our weekly Lessons.

The Bible was not really that important to me, and I suspect that this may be true for most Christian Scientists. In the Wednesday evening Testimony Meetings, for instance, I recall that most of the gratitude expressed was to "our revered Leader" and her writings, rather than to God and his Word.

Irene Guthrie

Because I had started out as a Roman Catholic with a very dim and "religious" view of God, it was easy to slide into the horrendous error of New Age thinking about him. I was taught that God was an impersonal force that had no bearing on my behavior with the exception of the phenomena that was manifested through me. I was my own God, and a poor, pitiful god at that! I was headed for destruction by indulging in drugs, alcohol, and promiscuity, which were the forerunners to my practicing witchcraft. I was self-centered—after all, when you are God, you are very arrogant and self-confident, and you do things that you wouldn't ordinarily do if you had a sound mind and a healthy, wholesome conscience.

Once I was exposed to the gospel, it became clear to me by the grace of God that I had been living a lie. God became to me a real, personal, living, factual God—a God who could love and accept me just as I was. This God could protect me from paranoia and fear, from drugs and demonic influences. He was a Savior who could deliver me from my sinful self by drawing me to repentance.

What a wonderful relief to know that I was not God! I no longer had the weight on my shoulders of being in charge of my life, because I knew I had made a mess of it. Suddenly the word *holy*, which was used to describe God in my childhood religious training, took on new meaning. My behavior became proportionate to my understanding of this holy God, who required the same holiness from me. The born-again experience taught me that God had the power to change me from the inside out.

My view of the Bible has changed radically, too. When I was young I was ignorant of it—it was just a holy book to be associated with religious relics and icons found in monasteries. When my astrology teacher referred to a huge Bible he kept in his classroom and told us that he himself was a reincarnation of the apostle Paul (telling us details from Paul's shipwreck experience), I had no way to prove or disprove his story, because I did not know what the Bible was all about. In my mind, having that Bible on a table gave credibility to my teacher and to his "past life" insights. As a matter of fact, many other New Agers today claim to "channel" Bible characters.

I have learned that ignorance of the Bible is not bliss. When my psychic hairdresser told me that she had a dream that I purchased a Bible, I took it as a "sign" and went out and bought one. As I sat with my white witchcraft book in one hand and the Bible in the other, I realized that only one of these could be the blueprint for my life and win my heart. When I read the Bible, I would experience peace; when I read the witchcraft book, I would experience fear.

I then found that I couldn't perform the step-by-step rituals the witchcraft book required—spells, incantations, and so on— particularly when it told me to set up an altar in front of a mirror, stand naked, and summon spirits there. I know now that I was unable to do these things because the Holy Spirit of God kept me from them.

I began to spend hours and hours, devoting time to searching God's Word. My view of life changed when I discovered that the Bible had the answers to life's most perplexing questions: Who is God? Who am I? Why am I here, and where am I going? How can I relate to a holy God? Through it, God entered my heart and saw the longing I had to fill the void that could only be filled by Jesus.

The Bible became my book of life—no longer a dead relic sitting on a table, to be interpreted solely by the adepts of a religious system. It has the explanations for questions about living a good life. It has saved me lots of money on doctor and counseling bills, and it will supernaturally change your life and keep you fit for the kingdom of God.

Will Baron

In my book, I refer to my teenage years as a time when God "disappeared" from my life. It wasn't that I wasn't attending church or hearing about him there, it was that I simply never thought about him or the role he should have in my life. I didn't feel any need for a relationship with Jesus, yet I believed that if

I were to die, I would go to heaven. Devotional religion was something I categorized as belonging to my parents, not to me.

It didn't take much for me to come to believe that everything *was* God—that the whole world and everything in it was God, including me. This of course is pantheism, which is just Hindu philosophy adapted for Western culture. Satan just "repackaged" this Hinduism, getting rid of all its fearful, repulsive deities, then gave this pantheistic "god" of everything the same name as that of the Father Most High of our Judeo-Christian tradition.

I remember that when I was involved in my "witnessing ministry," I would be careful to ask people what religion they were before I would start talking. If they said they were Christians, I would use Bible terminology. If they were New Agers, I would tell them that I had learned that "Jesus" had more power than the Hindu guru I had formerly served, and that "Jesus" was head of all gurus and masters.

Of course, I went into the New Age as just an ordinary guy looking for better health, self-esteem, and peace. I became a slave, literally, to demons who bore the name of "Jesus," who tortured me with demands of what I should do for them.

My focus now is very different. I am overwhelmed by the reality of a Savior who has done everything *for me*. I know that Jesus is God's Son and is literally God in human flesh.

That truth was there all the time for me in the Bible. As a New Ager, I studied the Bible a lot, but I had been taught in school that there were subjects outside the Bible's domain, like psychology and paranormal events, things to which the Bible simply didn't apply. I never learned first to judge things by the Bible's standards of truth.

When I became involved with the New Age, I was taught that there were many scriptures. We were told that Hindu writings, the sayings of Buddha, the Koran were all from God. And we believed that messages channeled through New Age prophets were also from God.

I remember meeting an elderly man on the beach who told me how much he enjoyed the Bible. "Reading the Bible is good,"

I told him, "but it has its limitations. It does not tell you what God wants to communicate with you right now. The only way to know God's will for you right now is to meditate."

Even though we read the Bible at The Lighted Way center, Muriel constantly "interpreted" it for us. In reading 1 Corinthians 15, for instance, she told us that the resurrection spoken of there was a transformation process that New Agers would undergo, which would make their current bodies immortal so they could live eternally on this earth. She claimed to be undergoing this very process and that she would eventually reach the equivalent of age twenty-eight.

In my own Bible readings, I could never see the truths that were there because I was constantly twisting the meanings of words and ideas to make them harmonize with my already-existing metaphysical beliefs. Even when I read something that flatly contradicted what I believed—such as the verse in Hebrews about men being appointed once to die and then to face judgment—I just explained it away in my mind by reasoning that the writer of that verse just hadn't obtained a full knowledge, like I had.

I know now that the Bible is both inerrant and trustworthy. I read it just as it is written, without trying to twist things or read esoteric hidden meanings in its truths.

12

The Role of Demonic Elements

What were you taught and what did you believe about the influence of the demonic in today's world?

Looking back, can you identify experiences or teachings that you would now evaluate as being demonic or satanic?

David Reed

I had Witness friends who were so afraid of demons that if there was sickness in any member of their household, they would begin going through things they had purchased at yard sales and would throw out knickknacks and break vases. My friends thought that sickness could be related to the fact that such objects might have been owned previously by someone who was "demonized," and that the demon could have entered their house with the object. But I can't say that such behavior was a big part of my life or thinking.

Like most Witnesses, I associated demonic activity most strongly with Christian churches. Once I offered a Watchtower magazine to a Catholic gentleman when I called on his home, and he agreed to read it if I took one of his Catholic periodicals. But when I got home I left it in the car because I was afraid a

demon might be attached to it, and I didn't want to risk bringing it into my house.

When I would go to the door of someone who claimed to be
"filled with the Spirit," I would leave quickly. I can remember
discussing such situations afterwards with other Jehovah's Witnesses. "You could tell that person was possessed by demons,"
we would say. "You could see it in their eyes." We believed that
any Christian who claimed to have spiritual experiences or gifts
of the Spirit was (a) a fake or (b) possessed by demonic spirits
instead of God's Spirit because such people were outside of
God's organization.

Looking back, I would say that the Watchtower Society itself
has had demonic influence. For several years the society cited
The New Testament (1937) by Johannes Greber in support of
unusual translation renderings in the *New World Translation*,
which is the official version used by Witnesses. However, when
the 1980 edition of Greber's version stated in a foreword that
Greber's wife, a spirit medium, was instrumental in producing
his work, the Watchtower organization announced it was "ceasing to use" Greber's book. They had known about this connection with spirits for years, as noted in a 1956 *Watchtower* article.

I believe now that though there is a common demonic direction given to all pseudo-Christian cults, most of the deception
involved is due to the fact that *people* are misleading other
people. Any false religion that leads us away from God is at its
source demonic, but most of the agents in the deception, I
believe, are human beings.

Joan Cetnar

Witnesses' doctrine teaches to avoid the demonic, and they
warn people against such influence. However, they would not
define "demonic" the way a Christian does. For instance, we
were taught that demonic influence could be brought into a
home by means of a cross. Jehovah's Witnesses are taught that
the cross is a heathen symbol used in sex worship. People who
were studying with a Witness were often told that they had to
get rid of any crucifixes in their homes, even the cross that might

be imprinted on the front of a Bible, if they were to rid the house of demonic influence.

In addition, we were warned against such occultic practices as fortune-telling, so it was a surprise to me to learn after I had left the organization that in 1915 the signs of the zodiac were used in a public address to "prove" that Christ would return in 1874. I also learned that the first president, C. T. Russell, had been very involved in pyramidology and phrenology—he wrote in *The Watchtower* (3/15/1913) that the shape of your head indicated whether or not you loved God.

And, of course, for years the Watchtower Society supported its translation of John 1:1 ("and the Word was *a* god") with a similar translation done by Johannes Greber, a spiritist who "received" his translation of the New Testament with the aid of spirits. His wife, a spirit medium, also helped convey answers to Greber from these messengers. It is most disturbing to know that the doctrines I held as "truth" were the same doctrines communicated to Greber while he was acting as a medium. The demon contacted by Greber said such things as: Jesus Christ is not God but rather a created being; Michael is a god; Christ's body was not resurrected; there is no eternal hell; and the Christian church of today is not preaching the gospel. As anyone familiar with Jehovah's Witness doctrine will immediately recognize, these are all Watchtower Society tenets!

Jesus said that there would be wolves in sheep's clothing— people who would look Christian, but not be Christians. I have to conclude that even sincere Witnesses can fit that description, because not only can some of their teachings deprive you of your physical life (refusing a vital transfusion, for instance), but their doctrine can lead you so far astray as to deprive you of *eternal* life. It is Satan's goal to steal and kill and destroy (John 10:10). So, in that sense also, the Watchtower Society is a work of Satan.

In the book my husband and I wrote, *Questions for Jehovah's Witnesses Who Love the Truth*, we have included many photocopies of documents that prove the Jehovah's Witness doctrine's connection with the occult. (It is available through our ministry. The address is R.D. #3, Kunkletown, PA 18058.)

Carolyn Poole

I would have to say that any system of thought that totally denies Jesus, as Christian Science does, must at least be thought of as having demonic power behind it. I'm not sure about some of the healings that I heard about in Christian Science—some Christians would say that they were demonic, but I'm not willing to go that far. What I will say is that I am convinced that God was leading me even while I was in Christian Science, and because I wanted to be obedient to God, he honored my desire. He protected my life and allowed me time to come to a knowledge of the truth.

Although many Christian Scientists teach that evil is just a state of mind and not a reality, they nonetheless live in a state of fear. One of the earliest treatments I gave was to an elderly woman who was frightened to stay alone at night after a near relative died.

My experiences with hypnosis made it clear to me that much of Christian Science is closely related to hypnosis. I can remember thinking many times that the kind of power that reading Mrs. Eddy's words exerted over me reminded me of the feelings I had had while under a hypnotic trance. I entrusted my mind to her, and repeated the same things over and over again.

After I left Christian Science, I learned some interesting things about the process that Mary Baker Eddy said occurred when she was writing *Science and Health*. She described herself as "a scribe under orders" and said that she would write all day long, the pages falling to the floor as she finished. This is very similar to occultic descriptions of automatic writing.

There is a very famous picture of Mrs. Eddy, which she herself commissioned and which appears in the famous Christian Science book, *Christ and Christmas* (1983, published by the Trustees under the Will of Mary Baker Eddy). It portrays her with a halo, standing above Jesus and handing him a scroll of Christian Science. Another picture portrays her sitting in the attic room where she spent three years writing *Science and Health*. On the floor near her is a talking serpent. I believe that this is a true representation of the origin of her writings.

I do believe I had several experiences that involved demonic elements while I was a Christian Scientist. As I mentioned in my testimony, I had my first such frightening encounter at the Billy Graham Crusade I attended in 1969. Then, years later—at the time I was in the process of leaving Christian Science and writing letters to let church officials know of my decision— something similar happened: I felt a tremendous, inexplicable heat on my back and heard a voice telling me not to mail those letters, that they would hurt my friends.

The most overt experience of this type happened after I had become a Christian and had been asked by Dr. Walter Martin to address one of his classes on my reasons for leaving Christian Science. I was in my room in a high-rise hotel, kneeling and praying beside my bed, when I distinctly heard a man's voice tell me to get up and go to the veranda and jump. I was so frightened that I didn't know what to do. Then the command came again, this time angrily: "I told you to go and jump out." Because I was a new Christian and didn't know how to handle this, I just did the only thing I knew to do—I jumped into the bed and opened my Bible. As soon as I began to read, that presence left me.

Elaine Dallas

Mrs. Eddy uses the terms devil and serpent more often than the term *Satan*. Her definition of devil is "Evil, a lie . . . a belief in sin, sickness, and death." She further states that "the devil saith: I am life and intelligence in matter . . . I am mind—a wicked mind, self-made or created by a tribal god. . . ." (*Science and Health* 584:17–22). (It's interesting that she refers to the LORD God as "a tribal god"!)

Actually, Mrs. Eddy views the devil in the same way she views matter, sin, sickness, and death—they are altogether unreal, untrue, a lie, and nothing but a false belief that "Christ, Truth" must destroy.

As I am learning more about the New Age movement (which is in reality age-old occultism dressed up in new terms), I find that Mrs. Eddy's "system of Mind-healing" is disturbingly similar to what New Agers today call "visualization."

I have learned that visualization is basically the ancient occultic mind-over-matter technique where change in the material world is brought about through the power of the mind. It is a technique that has been used in witchcraft for thousands of years, wherein images held in the mind are used as a means of healing diseases and otherwise manipulating the physical world.

In their book *The Seduction of Christianity* (Harvest House: 1985), Hunt and McMahon quote practicing occultists in their definitive study of visualization: "For the Egyptian followers of Hermes, who believed that everything is mind, disease was thought to be cured by visualizing perfect health. Paracelsus, a Swiss alchemist and physician of the sixteenth century, believed that 'the power of the imagination is a great factor in medicine. It may produce diseases in man, and it may cure them.'"

Mrs. Eddy states in her textbook, *Science and Health*, that "Mind, not matter, is causation. A material body only expresses a material and mortal mind. A mortal man possesses this body, and he makes it harmonious or discordant according to the *images of thought impressed upon it*. You embrace your body in your thought, and you should delineate upon it thoughts of health, not of sickness" (p. 208, italics added). She also states, "Hold thought steadfastly to the enduring, the good, and the true, and you will bring these into your experience proportionally to their occupancy of your thoughts" (p. 261).

Hunt and McMahon tie shamanistic visualization to something called "mental alchemy," an attempt to create or manipulate the supposedly-illusory physical world. Mrs. Eddy similarly teaches that the entire physical universe is an illusion. She speaks of a process in Christian Science she calls "chemicalization," whereby material "error" is transformed into a spiritual "higher manifestation."

Hunt and McMahon state that "the whole idea of visualizing a vivid image in the mind in order to produce an effect in the physical world is not just missing from the Bible, but is present in all occultic literature as far back as we can go (and is in fact one of the most basic shamanistic devices)."

After I came out of Christian Science, I was amazed to learn that this "system" of healing was not Mrs. Eddy's original "discovery"—she learned her healing theory from a "healer" named Phineas Quimby. Although Mrs. Eddy and the Christian Science church vehemently deny this fact, it has been thoroughly documented.

Irene Guthrie

With my religious background as a Catholic, I had no real knowledge of the demonic element. Subconsciously I believed there was a devil—a personality my grandmother described as someone who tried to get people to do bad things. But I never took him seriously.

That's just the way he wanted it! He kept me blinded to the truth and purposed to kill me so that he would become the victor of my soul. In the New Age center, there was never any discussion of the demonic. Instead, we were taught the division of white and black witchcraft, yin (female principle) and yang (male principle), or the occultic force of good/evil.

In the school I attended, Alpha Logics, we practiced only white witchcraft—to do only good to people, never evil. We had spirit guides who were the source of our psychic information. Whether we learned about acupressure, acupuncture, past life regressions, psychic healings, reflexology, automatic writing (journaling), palmistry, biofeedback, astrology charts, or any other sort of divination, each person's source was his or her individual spirit guide.

A spirit guide could be anyone you chose—depending, I suppose, on your religious background. My spirit guide was "Jesus." I would see him in vision form; he looked like any typical religious picture. Little did I know at the time that my spirit guide was only counterfeiting the real Jesus. The real Jesus was aware of these activities and was protecting me from even deeper occultic activity, but I know that he is not the "Jesus" that gave me the occultic powers I manifested during those months.

Looking back, I can absolutely identify all my experiences in the New Age as being demonically inspired. Listed below are some of the occultic techniques we learned about. I am grateful to Berit Kjos for his definitions which I have used from his book *Your Child and the New Age* (Victor Books: 1990).

1. *Hypnosis*. A sleeplike state in which a subject surrenders his mind and body into the hands of another. The teacher I had in the New Age center was no different from a sorcerer in using mind-control techniques. I realized this years later, when I read *Hypnosis and the Christian* by Martin and Deidre Bobgan (Bethany House: 1984). As this book showed me, my teacher used repetition, deception, stimulation of the imagination, and suggestions. He programmed us to believe what he was teaching, and through affirmations, I was hooked.

We participated in *hypnotic regression*, too. Each time we went to a class, we were brought deeper into the lies of Satan and further from any truth we may have once known about God. I believe many of the same techniques are being used today in Christian churches, out of ignorance, and that they are having the same destructive results in the body of Christ.

2. *Automatic writing*, or *journaling*, whereby a spirit entity writes a message by moving the medium's hand and pen. Under such an influence, I was led to believe that in a past life I had lived in England and that my hairdresser had been my sister. This practice depends on the theory of reincarnation, which the Bible strictly denies in Hebrews 9:27.

Sad to say, this type of activity is going on in Christian churches, using the Bible. Many people think it is of God because the Bible is involved, but an occult technique cannot change just because the tool being used is the Bible.

3. *Altered states of consciousness*. These mental states, ranging from near-normal to deep-trance, are induced by such spiritual exercises as meditation, guided imagery, hypnosis, or mind-

altering drugs. The purpose is to relax and experience oneness with all things, connect with "higher self," or channel "spirit guides." Through such states, I believed that God was the higher self inside me, and I could therefore proclaim myself as God. Little did I know how I was blaspheming the true God of the ages.

4. *Divination*. I believed that I could gain special spiritual insights and see into the future by palmistry, tarot cards, numerology, astrology, use of a Ouija board, communing with my higher self, and self-hypnosis.

Even in my college days, I had experimented with a Ouija board and had gone to my father's grave to try to contact him. (Thank goodness it was only a one-way conversation!) The practice of trying to contact the dead, or necromancy, I now know to be forbidden in Deuteronomy 18:11. I believe what it says in *Unger's Bible Dictionary*—that neither ancient nor modern spiritism can have communion with the spirits of departed dead (as the medium's fear in 1 Samuel 28 shows). What spiritistic mediums *can* do, however, is to impersonate the spirits of the dead and give superhuman knowledge by reason of their superior powers as evil spirit beings.

5. *Meditation*. As practiced in the New Age, meditation has Hindu roots and involves a disciplined focus on a certain mantra or theme such as self. Its purpose is to relax, attain higher states of consciousness, and connect with the cosmic mind. I would practice meditation during class exercises and at night before bedtime. My focus became so inner-directed that it became hard for me to perform outward responsibilities. For instance, instead of paying bills, I would spend money on myself (as in these God-forbidden occultic classes.)

I now understand that I am to meditate on Jesus Christ, not on myself. And all Christians, of course, need to meditate on the Word of God (Ps. 1:1–3; 63:6).

6. *Astrology*, which *Unger's Bible Dictionary* describes as "the ancient art of divination by consulting the planets and stars . . . particularly the signs of the zodiac in relation to observed human events and making deductions and predictions on this basis." My first class in the New Age school was on astrology.

I was obsessed with "knowing the future," and through this class I was introduced to a host of other practices that trapped me as a servant of Satan.

I no longer rely on stars, wizards, and prophetesses, but instead consult God for my daily decisions. I didn't know that I had my answers all along in the Word of God. And my future, like that of all people, was clearly laid out—either heaven or hell.

7. *Clairvoyance and clairaudience.* These refer to the power to see and hear beyond the natural ability of the human eye and ear. One evening during a class, I suddenly saw half a dozen figures behind our teacher Frank along the wall, outlines of beings in light form. I didn't say anything to anyone in the class until much later, when another woman acknowledged that she had seen the same thing I did. I remember other times: lying in bed and hearing voices in my head, or being home alone in the shower and hearing someone talking to me. I began to experience visions early in the morning when I awakened from sleep—visions that were so clear and so real to me that I still can recall them in detail.

Praise God that now I worship him in spirit and in truth, and any experience that I have now is through the gifting of the Holy Spirit working in my life, severally as he wills.

8. *Parapsychology.* This field of study is concerned with the investigation of evidence for paranormal psychological phenomena, such as telepathy, clairvoyance, and psychokinesis. It was the other area in which I was heavily involved in the New Age school. I practiced mental telepathy with people I encountered and was so accurate (using my spirit guide as my source of information) in telling a certain co-worker about his activities that I had dreamt about that he was convinced I was a witch. In another incident, I told another co-worker at the hospital where I was employed about the nature of a pain in his leg (a pain I could feel in my *own* leg.)

I no longer have to pride myself on my powers as a white witch, but instead can boast in the Lord. If perchance I am given information as revealed to me by the Spirit of God, let it be for the purpose of praying and ministering to God's people.

9. *Healing workshops.* One type of these involves the techniques of "scanning" an ill person by passing one's hands over the patient and then transferring energy from the healer to the patient. A couple of years after I was saved, I attended a large Christian church in Phoenix that had invited a well-known healing pastor/evangelist for a seminar. I was appalled when he used the same techniques I had been taught in my New Age workshops. When I asked one of the seminar counselors if the New Age practices were just a counterfeiting of the New Testament practice of laying on of hands, he said he didn't know. However, I know that the scanning/therapeutic-touch techniques are not biblical.

Another technique for inner healing that I was taught in the New Age center involved hypnotic regression into one's past. I remember one "forgiveness" workshop I attended. Through visualization and guided imagery, with the help of my spirit guide ("Jesus," in my case), I was to forgive the person who had hurt me most in the past, with the help of the one who had loved me the most. This practice is widely used in the body of Christ today, and some church leaders refuse to accept the fact that it is occultic.

Reflexology, a foot massage based on the belief that illness can be diagnosed and treated by the connection of certain zones of the foot to all other areas of the body, is also an occultic technique that is practiced by many Christians, who apparently have no idea that it is tied to the occult.

Will Baron

When I was involved in the New Age, I never doubted that the being who was leading my life was the true Jesus. I never suspected that I was a slave to demons who were masquerading as angels of light. My confidence in the New Age path and in my spirit guides had been building for years—after reading the Alice Bailey books, having "secret" things about myself and my family revealed through channeling, and being taught about messages and visitations, I was a candidate for total possession. Nothing could shake my faith in the authenticity of my spirit guide. I was blinded by "counterfeit miracles, signs, and wonders" (2 Thess. 2:9).

The devil has scored a major publicity victory by inspiring the media to represent him as a loathsome, fictitious being having the form of an ugly beast. If people do not stand firmly behind the truth of the Bible as the inerrant Word of God, they are easily led astray when Satan appears in his shining angelic form. They automatically think that the great being of light in front of them is Jesus Christ—or at least one of God's great angels—no matter what unbiblical ideas the false messenger begins to propound.

Satan is very smart. He teaches *some* truth—certain New Age teachings about health and ecology are being accepted by science. But, of course, the theology of the New Age is *totally demonic*.

13

Current Religious Life

Where do you now worship?
How do you feel about Christians of other denominations?

David Reed

Penni and I began attending the First Baptist Church in North Abington, Massachusetts, shortly after we left the Watchtower organization in 1982. Later I served as a deacon. I think we were drawn there because we felt a lot of freedom in the American Baptist denomination. As ex-Jehovah's Witnesses, we were allowed to slowly develop our doctrinal thinking, without being pressured because we were "different." We have since moved quite a distance from that church and are now affiliated with Trinity Baptist Church in Brockton.

I see Christians of other denominations as my brothers and sisters. My ministry takes me to all different types of churches, and I feel comfortable fellowshiping there. Of course, some people attend churches for the wrong reasons: social, family, even sinister reasons. But that's been true since Corinth and Galatia!

Joan Cetnar

We now worship at a local independent church called Middlecreek Christian Church. It used to be a mainline denominational church, but they became independent in an effort to remain truer to Bible teachings. It is a fellowship where Jesus is lifted up, and the Bible is taught as the inerrant Word of God. We are out on the road speaking quite a bit, but we are always happy to return there to our church "home."

I believe that someone who knows Jesus as his or her personal Savior is a Christian, regardless of denomination. I think God's main concern about denominations is that they not divide the body of Christ. If we are united in Christ, with our eyes on him, we can concentrate on central doctrines of Christianity that all believers agree on. It will better equip Christians to oppose cults and those who worship Satan if we aren't sidetracked by disagreeing about nonessential, peripheral issues.

I love worshiping and fellowshiping with folks in different denominational churches as we present seminars to them. There is a kinship in Christ that is just beautiful.

Carolyn Poole

My husband and I recently began attending St. Paul's Episcopal Church, and we love it. We are taking weekly classes preparatory to joining. Our number-one reason for liking it is the friendliness of everyone there. I think I feel at home with them because they are a little more conservative and intellectual than people from some other churches we have attended. (This is probably a reflection of my Christian Science upbringing—for the most part, I believe that when a person becomes a Christian, he or she doesn't change personality or identity.) This church has somewhat more formality and ritualism than others, and it is an "old" religion in that we weekly repeat the Nicene Creed. I admire the way they draw children into the rituals of the service, too. It is a very active church with a lot of things to do.

I believe that all Christian churches meet a need and are fine as long as the basic teachings are biblically sound and as long as Jesus Christ is Lord. With my job as director of a ministry to Christian Scientists—The Christian Way—I do not judge or get involved in what I call peripheral issues. But I take a dim view of churches that preach a social gospel, or where one never hears the salvation message, or where the truth about the existence of hell is not taught.

Elaine Dallas

We worship at a nondenominational church that teaches fundamental doctrines of the Bible. We feel really blessed to have found this church. While we were visiting other churches, which we did for nearly a year after leaving Christian Science, we found that so many of them did not teach the whole counsel of God. We believe that God protected us as we were making our decision about where to attend.

So many denominations are falling away from the truth. They no longer consider the Bible to be the inerrant Word of God as they once did, but leave it up to the individual to decide what "speaks to me" to be the truth. That's a hopeless quicksand, with no clear truth defined.

I'm so glad that there are still churches that are faithfully preaching the whole Word of God. However, I recognize that this falling away from the faith was prophesied to happen "in the last days."

Irene Guthrie

I worship at Calvary Community in Phoenix, Arizona, which is affiliated with Calvary Chapels (Chuck Smith). I praise God for this balanced fellowship and for a shepherd graced with discernment and a blessed teaching ability. He is honest and unafraid to speak the truth in love. In a day when many churches are compromising the gospel by preaching another Jesus, another gospel, it is refreshing to be among those who want sound doctrine. The grace of God is truly with us, and people are led here every week. The congregation grows steadily in numbers as the Lord adds to it.

I know there are Christians in other denominations. But I believe that according to their hearts' desires, God may lead them out of major denominations to join Bible-believing churches where Jesus is preached.

Personally, I don't think God had denominations in mind when he started the church (as recorded in the Book of Acts). The Lord has one church, not a denomination; one body, not several denominations; and one doctrine and faith. If a denomination is keeping an individual from trusting in, relying on, and adhering to God's Word, in my opinion it becomes a "demon nation," working against the kingdom of God. I believe all believers must come out from denominations and be separate unto Christ, obeying his Word at any cost.

Will Baron

I am now a member of the Seventh-day Adventists, attending a congregation in Norwalk, California. It was the pastor of this church who lent me the book about Ellen G. White that opened my eyes to the reality of Satan and helped me see that this was the being I had been serving.

I believe that members of other denominations are my fellow brothers and sisters in Christ, but I am apprehensive that the deception of the New Age is infiltrating many Christian churches, including my own. We have a tremendous task ahead of us in alerting people about this deception.

14

Changed Attitudes
Toward Leaders

How has your view of earthly church leadership changed since you left the cult?

David Reed

Naturally, I no longer see any group as being "God's organization on earth" in the sense of being successors to the twelve apostles who have authority over Christians.

I think that what we call church leadership falls into two categories. There is organizational leadership in the church, and there is moral leadership. Someone who is a moral leader, who speaks and teaches by proclaiming the Word of God, may not have an organizational position. He or she may be more important, and more biblically oriented than an organizational leader.

I have a lot of mistrust, in fact, of Christian organizations in general. Sometimes their leadership exercises such control over people that it reminds me of the Watchtower Society. Because organizations tend to concentrate on power and money, they attract people who want prestige. On the other hand, I know of many fine church organizations that are made up mostly of strong Christians who are working hard to proclaim the Word of God.

The important thing is focus. If we see Jesus Christ as our leader—in daily life as well as in church matters—we won't get hung up on petty things. Buildings and liturgies sometimes obscure him. Going to church is a fine opportunity to learn and help and strengthen others, but it is not the way to salvation. It is Jesus Christ who saves us—the church is just where we gather together.

Joan Cetnar

When Bill was working at Bethel for Watchtower, he questioned the process by which a group of men on an editorial committee could at first argue and then come to agreement about a doctrinal matter. He knew that by the time a statement was published by the presses that were on Bethel's sixth floor, many on the committee would have had to "pad" their differences so as not to lose position or be considered heretical. In 1952, President Knorr said, "Brothers, you can argue all you want about it, but when it gets off the sixth floor, *it is the truth*."

Many Witnesses have blind, unswerving faith in their leaders and in the statements they make. In our book, *Questions For Jehovah's Witnesses Who Love the Truth*, Bill and I have documented the fact that in World War II over two thousand Witnesses stood before Hitler's firing squads with perfect assurance from their leaders that God would stop the bullets. This tragedy along with the death of five "protected Jonadabs" who refused to take cover during an air raid, shattered the illusion of protection that many German Witnesses had.

Of course, I didn't know of these incidents as I was growing up. But I was disturbed by the fact that the Watchtower president, who was supposed to be "sacrificing" like the rest of Bethel employees, was living in sumptuous quarters and entertaining like a millionaire.

Now, when I look at church leaders, I realize that because they are only humans who can make mistakes, I do not have to look to them for the "last word" on what is true. I have a great deal of respect for the majority of Christian pastors because of the time they have invested in going to school and studying the Bible. But I also believe that along with their teaching, we have the Holy Spirit to teach us individually. So I never hesitate to question a minister of the gospel if I feel his interpretation is not correct—but I always do it with respect.

Carolyn Poole

As my testimony shows, it was this issue that began to open my eyes to the error of Christian Science. I read in the Bible that Jesus said to call no one "leader" except Christ, the Messiah (Matt. 23:10 NASB). We cannot have two masters, each being the only leader.

As much as Mary Baker Eddy denied using the word *miracle* and also denied that Jesus was the Christ, she still made herself out to be equal to him. There are apocryphal stories of how she raised her own secretary from the dead, for instance. And she had many followers who believed so strongly in her that they installed a telephone in her tomb so that she could call for help when she herself was resurrected.

I don't think I can overemphasize the influence that Mrs. Eddy had on my life when I was a Christian Scientist. Whenever I was faced with a decision, I would ask myself, "What would Mary Baker Eddy say?"

Once you have regarded an earthly leader with the kind of awe with which Christian Scientists view Mary Baker Eddy, it makes it difficult to have a balanced view of church leaders, even after you become a Christian. As a new Christian, I viewed my pastors with a kind of hero worship, so it was devastating to me when some I knew well fell. It was a hard lesson for me, but I learned that human beings *will* fall, and that we should *all* keep our eyes on Jesus, who will never disappoint us.

Elaine Dallas

Christian Science is a woman-originated religion. Mary Baker Eddy, its "Discoverer and Founder," is regarded by her followers with a reverence that borders on worship.

Mrs. Eddy held herself up so very high—seemingly above Jesus Christ. She said that her teachings on Christian Science were the *"final* revelation," which of course implies that *she* (not Jesus) had the final truth. She said of Jesus that "He expressed the highest form of divinity, which a fleshly form could express in that age" (*Science and Health* 332:29–30), implying that "higher" forms of divinity would be expressed in later ages.

I was shocked to realize as I analyzed Mrs. Eddy's Bible quotes that she usurped for herself a command Jesus reserved for himself alone. In the *Church Manual*, under the section "Relations and Duties of Members to Pastor Emeritus [Mrs. Eddy]" she stipulated that if she were to need household help, the board should immediately appoint someone to the task, and that this person should "go immediately in obedience to the call." The Scripture that she used to enforce this edict was Matthew 10:37—"He that loveth father or mother more than Me is not worthy of Me." I find myself aghast at her usurpation of Jesus Christ's words for herself!

Irene Guthrie

While I was in the New Age movement, I had no respect for church authority, mainly because of the experience I had had at the age of eighteen. Pregnant out of wedlock, I went to a priest for counsel, reaching out for God in the only way I knew, which was through the mediation of a priest.

He told me not to marry the father, because he came from a troublesome family, and that I should give the baby up for adoption. Later, out in the parking lot, I had a chat with the Lord and told him that I couldn't give up my child. I didn't go back to church for eleven years.

Now I have a respect for and understand the position of church leadership as laid out in orderly fashion in the Bible in 1 Corinthians 12:28. I am able to seek godly counsel when I need it from these gifted saints, ordained especially by God.

Will Baron

I never watched them on television, but I view such people as the Bakkers and Jimmy Swaggart as a great tragedy. We know that church leaders are not without error.

But we are not to look just toward our earthly leaders. We are to look to Jesus Christ, and my view of *him* has not changed in the five years that I have been a Christian. Church leaders are always going to have their weak points; they are always going to be tempted like everyone else. But praise the Lord that Jesus was tempted but had total victory over temptation. Through our repentance, his righteousness is imparted to us—and that makes us righteous. It is through his grace that we have the strength to overcome temptation in our own lives.

15

Advice for Concerned Christians

Based on your own experiences what advice would you give to a Christian who is trying to influence a cult member toward Christ?

David Reed

Since I've written four books on this subject, it may be a little hard to answer that question in a few words! But there is a basic fact that anyone can put into practice when dealing with a cult member. If you want to reach a Jehovah's Witness—whether he or she be a neighbor, a friend, or the stranger at your door—you must introduce that person to Jesus Christ through your own conduct and your own love. This is more effective than any doctrinal or organizational argument you can put into words or down on paper.

Don't push the person you are trying to influence. Jesus, the Good Shepherd, taught us how to be shepherds, too. You know, there is a difference between a shepherd and a cowboy. A cowboy gets behind and shoots guns and cracks whips and stampedes the cows. The Watchtower organization certainly exercises "cowboy" tactics! A shepherd, on the other hand, goes ahead of the sheep, and they follow because they want to.

I sometimes hear Christians talk about being in control of a conversation with a Jehovah's Witness. I really advise against such bullying, especially if you have a strong personality yourself. It is more important to make the truth appealing to a Jehovah's Witness, especially by showing how wonderful our own relationship with Christ is.

Jehovah's Witnesses and other cult members are lacking something, and they feel that lack. I remember working house-to-house with a very respected woman who had been a Pioneer, a full-time worker, for many years and who was at that time in her seventies. She confided in me that she didn't believe she would survive Armageddon, that she knew she wasn't good enough. We both knew she was doing all she possibly could, but I couldn't find anything in Witness doctrine to say to her to encourage her.

As a Christian, I know that none of us is "good enough" to get to heaven on our own. But I have the joy of knowing that my goodness isn't what will earn heaven—it is only on account of the fact that Jesus died for me that I have the hope of heaven.

What will lead someone to Christ is his love and knowing him as a person. That love shines out of us more brightly than any doctrinal arguments.

Joan Cetnar

Be patient. Be prepared to spend time teaching and helping him or her, and do not expect instant results. Start by being a friend to that individual. Jehovah's Witnesses have been taught that the only people they can trust are inside the Watchtower organization, that anyone outside is under the devil's power and thus cannot be trusted. This means that you must be sincere and that all you do must be done out of love. If what you say and do is not done out of love, it is better not done at all.

In such a situation, *pray* for the Spirit's direction in order to know when and how to approach the Witness. Also, there are several tactics that Witnesses have been trained to use that you must be aware of. For example, when you begin to discuss a subject that makes a Witness uncomfortable, the Witness will change the subject to something he or she is comfortable with. Remember, these people are under mind control; they have given their thinking processes over to the Watchtower organization on certain subjects. They automatically look to the Society for the last word on such matters as the nature of God, eternity, and the Bible. So a Witness will be more likely to think about what you are teaching if it is presented in the form of questions, instead of the flat statements he or she has been trained to counter with answers prepared by the Watchtower Society.

Be aware that a Jehovah's Witness is allowed to lie. In the Watchtower publication, "Insights Into The Scripture," a lie is defined as "speaking an untruth to someone who deserves to know the truth." Therefore, if a Witness believes that you don't deserve to know the truth, he or she will feel justified in telling you a lie. Witnesses call this "theocratic war strategy."

Christians should know *why* they believe what they believe, and know *where* in Scripture it is taught. This enables you to give a defense. Of course, a Christian must learn something about what his or her Jehovah's Witness friend believes, so as to effectively present information that will help change that person's mind.

Most assuredly, the Christian's exemplary life and conduct will be a powerful testimony to his or her faith in Jesus and to the indwelling of the Holy Spirit.

Carolyn Poole

In conjunction with my ministry to former Christian Scientists, I conducted a survey to find out which were the most important elements involved in helping someone leave that organization. Not surprisingly, prayer topped the list. But even though a Christian should intercede continually for a Christian Science friend, it is not a good idea to tell him or her that you are doing so. This kind of prayer is frightening and threatening to Christian Scientists and will often drive them away. That is because Christian Scientists are afraid of someone else's thinking hurting their own thinking. For instance, I remember feeling like a piece of meat being pulled on by two dogs when the women of my Bible study told me they had been praying for me. It was as if I were being torn apart inside, although I also felt grateful and privileged that they would do that for me.

Many Christian Scientists really love God, insofar as they understand him. They are sincere in that love and honest about expressing it. Therefore, it does no good to attack their character or judgment.

It is always good to invite a Christian Scientist to special events at church, especially anything that will fill their need for deeper Bible study from a nondenominational perspective.

I believe that the nature of Christian Science is such that the older a person becomes, the more difficult it is for him or her to leave it. However, I know of several instances where a Christian Scientist appeared to have accepted Jesus just before death, so I know it is possible. My mother, for example, seemed to reject Christian Science just before her death, but because I didn't know Jesus at the time, I couldn't be much help to her.

One of my greatest needs when I was struggling with Christian Science was to be able to speak to someone else who understood from his or her own experience what I was suffering. I had never met someone who had given up Christian Science for Jesus. This decision involved not only changing the way I thought— it also involved changing the way I acted. For example, it is difficult for an ex-Christian Scientist to go to a doctor. It would have been much easier if someone who had been through the same thing could have helped me handle such feelings.

Elaine Dallas

It has been my experience that most Christian Scientists refuse to hear or read anything that disagrees with, or exposes as untrue, what they have been taught in Christian Science. They read only "authorized literature" and listen only to "authorized" lecturers and practitioners, all of which have been approved by the Mother Church.

They are thereby unwittingly trapping themselves *through fear* (although they will vehemently deny this)—fear of allow-

ing to enter their minds even one thought that might damage
their unquestioning radical faith in Mrs. Eddy's Christian Science teachings. They have been taught that without this radical faith they cannot "demonstrate" healings. Even beyond this,
their very "salvation" is at stake. If they allow the slightest doubt
to enter their minds about the validity of the "truths" of Christian Science, this would defeat their "final demonstration" of
the "allness" of God and the "nothingness" of matter, sin, sickness, death, and evil—two tenets Mrs. Eddy required for "salvation" in Christian Science. Unfortunately, the longer Christian Scientists allow themselves to be controlled by Mrs. Eddy's
metaphysical belief system, the less they seem able to think independently and objectively.

Giving the Scripture's gospel of salvation to a Christian Scientist is almost like pouring water on a duck's back. It won't
mean a thing to them, because Christian Science teachings have
inoculated them against ever believing these Bible truths.

For instance, they cannot believe that Jesus is God manifest
in the flesh because (a) God, being infinite "All," cannot be cir-
cumscribed in a finite form, and (b) flesh has no reality. They
cannot believe that Jesus is the Christ because the corporeal man
Jesus cannot be the spiritual "Christ, Truth"—in other words,
matter cannot be spiritual. They cannot believe that Jesus died
on the cross because there was no death and Jesus was alive in
the tomb. They cannot believe that God raised Jesus from the
dead because (a) Jesus never died, and (b) God has no consciousness of the concept of death and thus could not be
involved in the process. They cannot believe that Jesus' sacrificial death on the cross paid the penalty for their sins because
(a) there is in reality no sin, and (b) the penalty for the "belief"
of sin (the false acknowledging of the reality of matter, sin, sickness, death, and evil) cannot be paid by anyone other than the
person doing the sinning (the "believing"), and (c) no single
sacrifice can pay the penalty for sin.

So, you can see how thoroughly Christian Scientists have
been inoculated against the true salvation of God's Word.

In addition to this, God's true salvation is tragically hidden to Christian Scientists even while they read the Scriptures, because Mrs. Eddy has changed the definition of most key Scripture words, thereby fatally altering the true message of God's Word. Such words as God, Christ, Holy Spirit, salvation, atonement, resurrection, sin, heaven, and hell—just to mention a few—mean something entirely different in Christian Science than they do in the Bible. Christian Scientists are essentially speaking a different language from the Bible, and this is another reason it is difficult to witness to them. Clarifying the meaning of key Bible terms at the outset, if possible, could aid the Christian in sharing the gospel with Christian Scientists.

In the final analysis, there is only one way to penetrate the solid faith that Christian Scientists have in Mrs. Eddy and her teachings, and that is PRAYER—persistent prayer. Only the Holy Spirit can open minds and hearts that have been closed by Satan's lies.

Irene Guthrie

Here is my advice to a Christian who is trying to influence a New Age advocate to accepting Christ:

1. *Examine your own motives.* Are you trying to win the person to the Lord for personal glory, or are you under bondage to a church group or affiliation to "win souls"? The best way to witness to a New Ager is to let the Lord lead you to souls that are fertile ground. God knows which of those have a hard heart and which are open to the gospel—you may not know for sure.

2. *Speak the truth in love.* Don't come across as haughty and prideful. Keep a humble spirit and avoid Pharisaism. Remember, "such were some of you"! Don't try to play the role of the Holy Spirit, but let him prick the heart. Keep in mind that one plants the seed, another waters, and the Lord gives the increase.

3. *Show Christ in your actions.* Be kind, courteous and considerate. Try to minister to the other's needs. If a person is sick, offer to do some shopping or fix a meal; if in need, bring groceries, clothing, or a job reference. Remember that the New Age movement is big on sharing!

Give God a chance to prove himself and the infallibility of his Word. For example, offer prayer for healing (and salvation) if the person is sick.

4. *Be properly equipped with the Word of God.* Have a knowledge of the principles of New Age teaching so you can understand their terminology, keeping in mind that they use Christian terms and often confuse us into thinking they are Christian, too. Be ready to compare New Age teachings with sound Bible doctrine.

5. *Don't be discouraged.* You may not see immediate results, and the opposition may seem strong. And, as 2 Timothy 2:23–26 (KJV) tells us, "But foolish and unlearned questions avoid, knowing that they do gender strifes. And the servant of the Lord must not strive; but be gentle unto all men, apt to teach, patient, in meekness instructing those that oppose themselves; if God [notice the "if"] peradventure will give them repentance to the acknowledging of the truth; and that they may recover themselves out of the snare of the devil, who are taken captive by him at his will."

6. *Never compromise your own faith by shaming Christ in your life-style.* For instance, if the New Age advocate invites you to his or her home for an occult meeting of some sort so as to prove to you that it is "harmless," don't put yourself into that position. Or if they want you to meet them at a bar after work to discuss Christianity, decline graciously and suggest another time and place.

Be on guard because "your adversary the devil goes about seeking whom he may devour." Keep your relationship at a safe distance, and use wisdom and discretion.

Will Baron

I'll tell you straight—it is very, very difficult to rescue someone from the New Age. I have even debated with New Agers since I've been out, but even that is difficult.

I believe firmly that any rescue of a New Ager can *only* be done through the Holy Spirit. Of course, if someone is only casually interested in the New Age, the job is easier. But most of them are under such deception from Satan and his demons that only the Holy Spirit's power can get them out. One of the ways he works is through persistent, fervent prayer—my parents prayed for me for fifteen years.

The Holy Spirit can show a Christian how to reach different individuals. For one, a study of how the Bible differs from New Age teachings about Jesus might be useful. For another, a book about someone like myself who left the New Age could be effective.

On a practical level, our biggest asset is our Christian lifestyle and character. We need to live out the character of Jesus Christ in our lives—being compassionate, loving, and charitable. This is what will make an impression. One thing that caught my attention right away was the difference between Muriel and the godly Christian pastors I met. She was dedicated, of course (she had to be—she was practically forced into action by demons), but she wasn't "godly" in the way I expected her to be: patient, kind, humble, and at peace.

16

Teaching Techniques

Are there any teaching techniques that you feel are particularly effective in leading a cult member to Christ?

Which do you think is more important in this process: using the Bible or showing inconsistencies in the cult's doctrine?

David Reed

I think you have to take things step-by-step. Jehovah's Witnesses have been brainwashed as to the meanings of specific verses in the Bible. Many verses have been taught to them out of context, with an organizational meaning attached to each verse. Therefore, if you show them a passage, they may see only the meaning the Watchtower taught them.

A good illustration of this occurred once when some Witnesses came to my door. They didn't know me, so I asked them about their belief that a great crowd of believers will live on the earth and not go to heaven. One of the women showed me Revelation 7, where a great crowd is mentioned. When I pointed out to her that this crowd is before the throne of God, she answered that the whole earth stands before God's throne.

Then I had her turn to Revelation 19:1 and asked her to read it to me from her own *New World Translation*. When she got to the words, "great crowd in heaven," I stopped her and asked her where the great crowd was, and she answered me, "on earth." Even when I pressed her to look again, she insisted that even though it read, "in heaven," the great crowd was really on earth, and that men at her headquarters in Brooklyn could explain it. This incident really demonstrates two things: the "blinders" that the Watchtower Society puts on people, and the fact that their doctrine is often based not on what the Bible says, but on what their leaders *say it says*.

Because of this, I advise Christians to use *The Watchtower*, not the Bible, as a starting point, to show how it has flip-flopped back and forth on doctrine and not gone forward with higher, brighter doctrines, as they have been taught.

Just quoting discrepancies in *The Watchtower* won't do the job, because a Witness will simply assume you don't know what you're talking about. They usually don't know their own history, so you must show them photocopies of pertinent documents. I have assembled about fifty good ones in my book, *How to Rescue Your Loved One from the Watchtower* (Baker Book House, 1989).

However, it's important not to let them know you got these photocopies from a book by an apostate. I advise people to go to a public library and make photocopies from original sources of at least of a few of the documents. That way you can tell Witnesses that you have seen some of the statements with your own eyes, and that they can go to the library and personally look them up.

It is important to approach the Witness as a questioner, not as an attacker. Instead of saying, "Here's proof that *The Watchtower* made a false prophecy," ask a specific question. For instance, "What about this information I looked up in the book, *Millions Now Living Will Never Die* (published by the Watchtower Society in 1920), which states that in 1925 Abraham, Isaac, and Jacob were going to be resurrected here on the earth? Can you show me some documentation of where and when that resurrection took place?"

With that type of approach, you are not attacking the organization, you are just challenging the individual to think. I know that Christians who have the truth often find it very difficult to sit and just humbly ask questions. But this was a teaching technique that Jesus himself used to open the minds of the Jews.

If you can just show a Witness some evidence, and bite your tongue and refrain from wagging your finger under his nose, he will come to the right conclusions himself, because the wagging finger he will not be able to ignore will be in his own conscience.

You may not see results right away. Sometimes you can only share a few thoughts with the Witness at your door. But if, down the road, another Christian does the same thing, it will be like the process Paul talked about, where one plants, another waters, and eventually there is a harvest. I know that because I remember the few times that Christians shared truth with me, and though I didn't respond to it right then, I filed it away in the back of my mind. When God began to lead me out of the Watchtower, these things came to mind and bore fruit years later.

Joan Cetnar

Jehovah's Witnesses are taught that the Watchtower Society is the only channel of truth on the earth today (*Watchtower*, 5/15/55); that it is the "faithful and discreet slave" appointed by Jehovah to give spiritual food at the proper time; that the Watchtower Society—the Jehovah's Witnesses—is God's prophet (*Watchtower*, 4/1/72; *Awake*, 6/8/86) and the only right religion.

Witnesses were told in the February 15, 1983, issue of *The Watchtower* that the four requirements for gaining eternal life were: taking in knowledge, obeying God's law, being associated with God's channel (his organization), and loyally advocating his Kingdom rule to others (preaching door-to-door). There is not one mention of trusting in Jesus for eternal life. Once one accepts the above requirements for gaining eternal life and pleasing God, that person has allowed the organization to take control of his or her mind.

In order to free this mind, the lofty claims of the organization must be carefully examined with the help of the Bible and the Witnesses' own literature. Because the organization teaches that the Bible cannot be understood without the aid of the Watchtower publications, the only real source of authority is the writings of the organization. Therefore, Christians must go directly to those publications and use photocopies to show Witnesses what they have claimed and what actually happened.

I believe there are four areas in which Christians can effectively question the authority of the Watchtower organization:

1. *The Watchtower Society claims to be a true prophet of God.* According to Deuteronomy 18:21–22 and Matthew 7:15–20, anyone who makes this claim must consistently produce true prophecies, for he would ostensibly be speaking not from his own mind but rather with information directly from God. However, eight times—in 1874, 1914, 1918, 1925, 1941, and 1975, to name some dates—the Watchtower organization predicted the second coming of Jesus Christ. They are also false prophets in that they have had to change their "truth" frequently. Truth that originates with God, however, never has to be changed.

2. *The Watchtower Society has deliberately changed the Word of God to agree with their doctrine.* They have produced their own translation of the Scriptures called *The New World Translation.* In it, they have added words, taken words out, and paraphrased words and passages to make them agree with their own doctrine. This is in violation of strict commands by God not to add to or take away from this book, his Word.

3. *The Society has deliberately misquoted what others have written and lied about what the books these people have written say.* In their publication *Insights Into The Scriptures*, they have defined "lying" as speaking an untruth to someone who deserves to know the truth. Therefore, if they feel you do not *deserve* to hear the truth, you will not hear it from them.

4. *They have violated the commands of God in his Word not to consult spirits or spirit mediums.* In the February 15, 1956, issue of

The Watchtower, Jehovah's Witnesses were warned not to have anything to do with Johannes Greber and his translation of the New Testament, which was done with the help of demon spirits. Six years later, however, the Watchtower Society began both to quote from and advocate this translation because its rendering of John 1:1 agrees with their *New World* wording: "the Word was a god."

Honest-hearted, truth-seeking Jehovah's Witnesses will soon realize that they have put their trust into a false prophet. When this occurs, a Witness will want to know, "If this is *not* the truth, where is it?" That will be the opportunity we Christians have been seeking to show that faith and trust must be placed in the person of Jesus Christ, not in any organization. Then, too, that Witness will be willing to discuss Bible doctrine with you with a desire to learn what the Bible *really* teaches—not just what the Watchtower says it means. He or she will want to know the truth, not just to argue with you, so you can show how anyone can have assurance of salvation, which is not just for 144,000 people.

The fact that we Christians can *know* we are saved is a wonderful blessing. In fact, one effective way you can convey that to a Witness is to ask this question: "If I were to study with you and become a Jehovah's Witness, what would you have to offer me that I don't already have—since I have Jesus, and John 5:24 says that hearing the word and believing means I have eternal life? As a Christian, I have assurance that I will live with him in eternity. Would I trade that for living forever on 'paradise earth,' never being able to see Jesus?"

But again, I would caution Christians to *lovingly* turn the focus on the false nature of the *organization* before letting any Witness get you into a discussion of the Trinity, resurrection, the deity of Christ, or other areas where Watchtower teaching has dulled his or her ability to see Bible truth.

Carolyn Poole

I believe there is great power in the Word, and that it can convict in ways that people cannot. The Bible should be emphasized first, and then as a person opens up to its truth, he or she will be able to see how it contrasts with Christian Science doctrine.

Sometimes this is a slow process. Many times in the women's Bible study I attended, I would read a Bible passage that I had never before read while I was a Christian Scientist. More often, though, the verses that showed Christian Science doctrine to be in opposition to the Bible were ones that Mary Baker Eddy had twisted to make them seem like they were saying something completely different, and I had accepted her explanation over the plain truth of what the passage actually *said*. You see, even though she stated in *Science and Health* that "as adherents of Truth we take the inspired Word of the Bible to be our sufficient guide to eternal life," she also made it clear that she believed there were human errors and misinterpretations in it. And of course, as my practitioner told me, we needed Mrs. Eddy to spiritually interpret the Bible for us, so that we could avoid the errors in it.

But, again, the Word itself is so powerful that it can show some of the errors in Christian Science. For instance, when I started reading in the Bible that Jesus called himself "the Way," it was easy for a Christian to point out to me that this was very different from Mary Baker Eddy's teachings that he was merely "the Way Show-er."

I am very grateful to the women of those first Bible studies that I attended, for the way in which they presented the Bible and the way in which they treated me with respect and love.

Elaine Dallas

The only people whom I personally have been able to help bring out of Christian Science were people who were not totally indoctrinated and were able to do some independent thinking.

Getting past the Christian Science refusal to even look at conflicting views is very difficult. With some people, I would say that from a human point of view it is even impossible; but thank goodness, "with God all things are possible." In hearing the testimonies of other people who have left Christian Science, it seems that for each person there was a different idea or concept that caused each to begin independent thinking.

I don't think you can just use the Bible or just point out inconsistencies in Christian Science doctrine to try to convince someone to leave it. They are both important.

One approach I might suggest is to appeal to the Christian Scientist's name. Real scientists in search of truth will not look at just the evidence that supports their own particular ideas. They will try to look at all facets of a case, taking into consideration all the facts available, before coming to a conclusion. The reliability of any hypothesis is only determined by testing it against all the information at hand.

Christian Scientists who consider only those portions of Holy Scripture and other writings that substantiate the teachings of Mary Baker Eddy are bound to come to faulty conclusions. I have noticed that when they are defending these conclusions, they will claim to have the "higher spiritual understanding," while others are looking at things from only a "material" standpoint. That shifts the blame from the inconsistencies in Christian Science to the person who sees those inconsistencies. When I first started seeing that Christian Science was not true to the Bible, this alone was not enough to take me out of it. I simply thought that with a deeper understanding I would find that these inconsistencies would disappear.

What finally had an effect on me was seeing from my study of certain words in the original Hebrew and Greek Scriptures how blatantly Mrs. Eddy had changed their meanings. I also was helped by verifying in the Scriptures the gospel message I kept hearing on the radio. But again, each person is different.

Irene Guthrie

First of all, I am particularly uncomfortable with the word *technique*, only because as a former New Age advocate the technique of mind control was used on me. I certainly would not want to use the same techniques as a Christian. Unfortunately, since becoming a Christian I have seen many examples of abuse and manipulation of the minds of those who were seeing God. Therefore, for me, "technique" is equated with manipulation.

Most probably, however, the Bible is more effective in teaching New Age believers than showing their own inconsistencies, though there is a place for both. They will challenge your view of their inconsistencies, because their own pantheistic worldview will have justification for those inconsistencies.

A lot depends on the individual. Since New Age is very broad in its philosophies, personal beliefs vary widely. In any event, you must draw on the wisdom and knowledge of the Holy Spirit to lead you and guide you in whichever godly "technique" he chooses. Perhaps a Christian book about the New Age, or a visit to your church, may be a good teaching tool.

Will Baron

I don't think there are any particular "techniques" that work. I believe the best thing is to witness to a cult member about yourself. If you have never been in the New Age, you cannot talk about that, but you can talk about Jesus and what kind of differences he has made in your life.

If you can't do this—that is, identify blessings that Jesus has brought into your life—you are not going to be an effective witness. There is something wrong in your own relationship with God, and that must be tended to before you try to lead someone else to him.

After telling about your own experiences, I think it is good to go straight to the Gospels, to the very words of Jesus. Point out that he did claim to be the Son of God and that he said that belief in him would erase the penalty of sin. And show the cultist that believing in Jesus can help people change their characters so that they can actually become like him.

Another important area to discuss with a New Age believer is what Jesus said about his own second coming. Using Scripture, point out that this world is not promised another two thousand years in "the Age of Aquarius," as the New Age teaches, but that Jesus will come back in a very specific way, in the clouds of the sky and with power and great glory!

One thing you have going for you is that most New Agers do believe that the Bible is inspired. Of course, their interpretations will usually differ from yours. But allow the Holy Spirit to act through the Word to open their eyes and ears and bring them into a relationship with Jesus Christ.

17

Helpful Resources for Decision Making

What books, literature, speakers, or other resources were most effective and helpful to you personally during your time of decision and transition from the cult?

Which would you recommend for Christians? Which for cult members?

David Reed

It was the Bible alone that brought my wife and me out of the Watchtower and led us to Christ. I recommend that Jehovah's Witnesses read the New Testament—by itself.

In general, the other books most helpful to me at that time were written by ex-Witnesses. A really good book in this category is *Crisis of Conscience* by Raymond Franz (Commentary Press: 1983). The author was at one time on the Watchtower headquarters staff. Of course, I try to give my insights in my books: *Jehovah's Witnesses Answered Verse by Verse* (Baker Book House, 1986); *How to Rescue Your Loved One from The Watchtower* (Baker Book House, 1989); *Index of Watchtower Errors* (Baker Book

House, 1990); and *Behind the Watchtower Curtain* (Crowne Publications, 1989).

Books written by Christian cult experts who had not been involved in the Witness organization were more helpful to me *after* I had fully left the Watchtower. In my opinion, books written by non–ex-Witnesses are not usually the best to give to a Witness.

Joan Cetnar

When we left the Watchtower organization in the 1960s, there was very little literature available for people who were coming out of the Jehovah's Witnesses. In fact, we felt for a long time that we must be the only ones who had left simply because we disagreed with the organization's teachings.

Through contact with some former Jehovah's Witnesses who had left the organization in 1914 and 1925, we were able to acquire some important documentation proving the false prophecies of the Watchtower Society. But since these folks were still holding on to many of the doctrines of the first president of the Society, Charles Taze Russell, they could not help us learn the truth about who Jesus is and how to have a personal relationship with our Savior.

Later we came in contact with the works of Edmond Gruss. We found excellent documentation in his book *Apostles of Denial* (Presbyterian and Reformed Publishing Company, 1970) and his later book on prophetic speculation, dealing with the dates of 1914 and 1975, *Jehovah's Witnesses and Prophetic Speculation* (Presbyterian and Reformed Publishing Company, 1972).

There is a wealth of good material available today. *Crisis of Conscience* (Commentary Press, 1983) by Raymond Franz gives a firsthand account of what goes on inside the Watchtower organization. Although this book does not contain what I would call a "salvation message," it can be very effective in helping a Witness come out of the organization, as long as it is followed up with Christian teaching.

David Reed's *How to Rescue Your Loved One from The Watchtower* (Baker Book House, 1989) helps a Christian to understand the mind and attitudes of a Jehovah's Witness and to avoid pit-falls in dealing with them. Randall Watter's two books on doctrine, *Rehealing Jehovah's Witnesses* and *Defending The Faith* (both published by Bethel Ministries), and his quarterly newsletter from Manhattan Beach, California, are excellent, too.

For thirteen years, Bill and I hosted an annual convention for ex-Witnesses, for people involved in ministry to Jehovah's Witnesses, and for those who have relatives or friends in the Society. Jehovah's Witnesses who want to come are always welcome, too. The convention takes place each October in Pennsylvania. It fills a great need that we had when we left the organization—to know that you are not alone and that such things as unconditional love do exist outside of the Society. Anyone wanting more information about the convention can write to us or may call (215) 381-3661.

Our conventions have spawned many smaller support groups all over the country. There is also a network of ministries that have answering-machine messages for Witnesses and will provide help if you are having a study with a Jehovah's Witness. (Please call us at the above phone number for information on the support group closest to you.)

I would also recommend a film that has been out for about three years: "Witnesses of Jehovah" (produced by Jeremiah Films and Leonard and Marjorie Chretien). It is available on video from us or at most Christian bookstores and is helpful both for people just coming out of the organization and those who are just beginning to get involved with it. This film gives an overview of what it is like to be a Witness, what the organization teaches, and documentation of false prophecies—and it ends with a good solid gospel message!

Carolyn Poole

When I was making my decision, I read *Born Again* by Charles Colson (Fleming H. Revell, 1976) and cried over every page. One of the most significant things he said in that book was that, in effect, you can't take just part of Jesus. Colson says, "I had to take Him, as he reveals Himself, not as I might wish Him to be."

Colson's eloquent words said what the Holy Spirit had been showing me—that I couldn't continue to just pick and choose the parts of the Bible that I wanted to believe and reject other parts, like the teachings on the reality of hell.

Another book that other people, especially young people leaving Christian Science, have found helpful is Hal Lindsey's *The Late Great Planet Earth* (Zondervan, 1970).

When a Christian Scientist who is beginning to have doubts is referred to our "Christian Way" ministry, we recommend that they read an "unauthorized" biography of Mary Baker Eddy (in other words, an account of her life that is not advocated by the Mother Church). Two such books (which are out of print but can often be found in used bookstores) are *The Life of Mary Baker G. Eddy* by Georgine Milmine (Baker Book House, 1971) and *Mrs. Eddy, The Biography of a Virginal Mind* by Edwin Franden Dakin (Scribner and Sons, 1930). These are heavily documented and show how Christian Science has deified Mrs. Eddy instead of accurately portraying her as a human being who went against her own doctrines. Of particular interest is documentation on how she took morphine for kidney stones while teaching that others should not take medicine.

The Christian Way ministry has pamphlets available. They are: "New Beginnings" by Nancy Kind and "A Former Adherent Exposes Christian Science" and "Christian Science: Cult for the Cultured Mind," which are both written by me, and "I Said 'No' to Christian Science" by Stanley D. Myers. We also have a tape by Elaine Dallas entitled, "Amazing Testimony of Elaine Dallas, Third-Generation Christian Scientist." All are available at P. O. Box 1675, Lancaster, CA 93539; telephone (805) 948-8308.

Elaine Dallas

The radio was where I really began to learn what the Bible actually said. I listened to J. Vernon McGee's "Through The Bible," Chuck Smith's "Word For Today," and David Hocking's "Sounds of Grace" (now called "Solid Rock Radio").

Another program I listened to was "The Bible Answer Man," which is a ministry of the Christian Research Institute. Periodically, people would call in with questions about Christian Science, and at first his answers would make me so angry. I realized gradually that what he was saying about the unscriptural nature of Christian Science was true. I would have to say that he was very instrumental in opening my eyes, because it was through his teaching that I began to see and deal with the problems and inconsistencies in Christian Science doctrine.

There were two books that were very important in bringing me out of Christian Science. The first was *Strong's Concordance*, with its Greek and Hebrew dictionaries in the back. I began to compare Mrs. Eddy's definitions of words with their true meanings, and a whole world opened up to me. I realized that she had redefined nearly every major concept in the Bible, including God, sin, salvation, atonement, resurrection, and others, in ways that took them far from their original meanings. Just her changing the meaning of one word alone—Christ—changed the entire message of the Scriptures.

Another book that was very helpful to me was Josh McDowell's *Evidence That Demands a Verdict* (Here's Life Publishers, 1979). I spent quite a bit of time looking up things in that book and investigating what the author said. I highly recommend both this book and Strong's for working with Christian Scientists.

There are two other good books that I didn't know about at the time I left Christian Science. The first, *Many Infallible Proofs* by Henry Morris (Master Books, 1974), gives wonderful evidences of the truth and historicity of Christianity. It has answered a lot of questions for me. The second is *Divine Healing Under the Spotlight* by Samuel Fisk (Regular Baptist Press, 1978). This little book examines the healings and miracles of both the Old and New Testaments and could shed new light on healings for Christian Scientists.

Of course, getting a Christian Scientist to look at such books is difficult. Perhaps you could pose a challenge, saying, "If you're a true scientist, look at the evidence that is here."

Irene Guthrie

I would like to preface my response with a comment that my transition from the New Age movement was not an overnight happening, as was my time of decision. I did not become a mature Christian the day I was saved. I have come to realize that the transition has taken several years. New Age ideals and philosophies that have been carried into churches by members have been construed to be Christian teachings, and it took me a long time to see the difference. Only reading God's Word and continually seeking the truth will deliver us from such deception and false teachers. From that perspective, I found the following resources very useful:

1. *The Bible*. It will always be number one for me, because it truly was the source that God used for my deliverance. A major step in my conversion was destroying all my witchcraft and astrology books and icons, as explained to me in the Book of Acts. I also renounced all my occultic practices and the New Age movement, thereby breaking my allegiance to Satan.

2. *Testimonies and ministries on local television*. When I was a newborn in Christ, anyone who named the name of Jesus had my ear. But, like an infant, I found that not everything I tried to eat was edifying—or even edible. However, as I have grown, I have learned through trial and error to discern what is real soul food—Berean soul food—sound Bible-based doctrine.

3. *Christian books on prophecy*. Because New Age doctrine is so mystical in experience, and New Agers consult mediums, seers, and prophetesses for insights into the future, the Christian books and speakers that most captured my attention were those on Bible prophecy. Prophecy was the "bait" that hooked me in the beginning, and the books that were most helpful to me were those authored by Hal Lindsey, such as *The Late Great Planet Earth* (Zondervan, 1970) and *There's a New World Coming* (Harvest House, 1973).

4. *Books on Eastern mysticism/New Age*. One book especially helpful to me was *The Beautiful Side of Evil* by Johanna Michaelson (Harvest House, 1982). I could identify with much that the

author said, and she has been inspiring and helpful in encouraging me to pray for the witches in my area.

5. *Other books on the New Age.* These include *The Hidden Dangers of the Rainbow* (Huntington House, 1983) and *A Planned Deception* (Pointe Publishers, 1985). Because I had put New Age behind me when I got saved, I just ignored the movement for a while. When I heard Constance Cumbey's lectures and read her books, it sparked me to research the movement so that I, too, could help Christians recognize and oppose its ugly plan.

Texe and Wanda Marrs also show the enemy's battle plan against Christianity in *Mystery Mark of the New Age* (Crossway Books, 1988); *Dark Secrets of the New Age* (Crossway Books, 1987); *Ravaged by the New Age* (Living Truth Publishers, 1989); and *New Age Lies to Women* (Living Truth Publishers, 1989).

Hypnosis and the Christian by Martin and Deidre Bobgan (Bethany House, 1984) is a small but powerfully written examination of the question of whether hypnosis is a viable treatment with which a Christian can be involved. I strongly recommend this book!

Another eye-opener for me was Pauline MacPherson's *Can the Elect Be Deceived?* (Bold Truth Press, 1986). I found that even after renouncing New Age, I was deceived by occultic doctrine that was being promoted amongst Christians.

Movies and videos I recommend include "Gods of the New Age" by Caryl Matrisciana (Jeremiah Films, available through most Christian bookstores); and "The New Age Movement," "Seduction and Deception," "Visualization," "Psychology and Inner Healing," "Selfism" (all produced and distributed by The Christian Information Bureau of Bend, Oregon); and a three-hour documentary, "The New Age: A Pathway to Paradise" by Dave Hunt (produced by WSCS-TV, Chicago, and available through "The Berean Call," P. O. Box 7019, Bend, OR 97708).

For Christians, I would recommend: the Bible, books by Constance Cumbey, Texe and Wanda Marrs, the Bobgans, Johanna Michaelson, Pauline MacPherson, and any videos or books by Dave Hunt.

For New Age believers, I recommend books by Hal Lindsey; *Death of a Guru* (published by Harvest House, 1986) by ex-guru Rabi Maharaj; *Hypnosis and the Christian* by the Bobgans; and *Gods of the New Age* by Caryl Matrisciana (Harvest House, 1985).

Will Baron

At one point I was planning to start a New Age meditation group at Hope Chapel in Hermosa Beach—with the blessings of a pastor there. As part of my preparation, I tried to learn all I could about Christian doctrines. I went to local Christian bookstores and would browse through books, even those that attempted to discredit the New Age movement. I found them entertaining, and wished I could talk to some of the authors to show them there was no conflict between Christianity and New Age. I believed I possessed the "full gospel," a fusion between the two.

My eyes were not opened, in fact, until I read *Ellen G. White, Prophet of Destiny* by Rene Noorbergen (Keats Publishing, 1972). It was Ellen White's vivid description of Satan that let me see I had in reality been serving the devil.

I spent six months studying the Bible before I really made a commitment to baptism in Christ. I have a New International Version, and the Gospels were especially important to me. Because I wanted to be grounded in the words of Jesus, they were the first thing I read in the mornings and the last thing I read each night. I also made a special study of the Book of Revelation.

I tried to immerse myself in Christian teachings and fellowship. One book that really helped me was C. S. Lewis's *Mere Christianity* (Macmillan, 1943). I also listened a lot to media preachers. One who helped me tremendously was Lloyd Oglivie, whose program "Let God Love You" was one I would listen to each day as I drove to work. I would also listen with great enthusiasm to Chuck Smith of Calvary Chapel, and I went to hear Billy Graham when he came to Anaheim.

The primary book that all of us—New Agers and Christians alike—need to study is the Bible. But, specifically for New Agers

I recommend my book, *Deceived by the New Age* (Pacific Press, 1990). Maybe I'm biased, but I think it would be a good book to give to a New Ager. I would like to write a book sometime in the future that would be just for them, something that would be marketed in secular bookstores.

18

Helpful Resources for Spiritual Growth

Since you have become a Christian, which books, literature, speakers, or other resources have been most helpful and edifying in your spiritual life?

David Reed

My focus continues to be on the Bible, on God's Word. Even though I'm the author of Christian books, I believe Christians ought to be spending most of their reading time in the Bible, not in books *about* the Bible. Just because an author with a Ph.D. says something doesn't mean he or she has a relationship with the Lord that is more meaningful than we do; our hearts can be just as open to the Lord.

Although Christian books have their place, and reading them can be like spending evenings with mature Christians, a kind of fellowship with other believers, they can't take the place of prayer and listening to the Lord. As one elderly lady once told me, the best learning about God is not in a school of theology, but in a school of "knee-ology."

There are two speakers who have greatly influenced me. One is Pastor Robert Hinkley of the First Baptist Church I attended for nine years. His down-to-earth approach to Scripture has helped me understand that Christianity is a personal walk that is achievable by anyone.

I have been helped quite a bit, too, by Wayne Monbleau, who hosts a radio program carried across the eastern United States called "Let's Talk About Jesus." I really admire the way he always turns the spotlight on Jesus and helps callers to focus on him. He also has tapes and books that I have really enjoyed, which are available through his radio ministry.

Joan Cetnar

I'd have to say that the single most influential book has been my Bible. It has been wonderful to read it with my eyes now opened and with the help of the Holy Spirit to understand it.

Matthew Henry's *Bible Commentary* has helped me with difficult passages, and I've used Dr. Robert Morey's books that deal with subjects that Jehovah's Witnesses need particular help with (*Death and The Afterlife*, published by Bethany House, for instance). Another good resource is Josh McDowell's *Jesus, A Biblical Defense of His Deity* (Here's Life Publishers, 1983), which deals with this subject not in depth, but with very helpful information. I also like Chuck Colson's *Loving God* (Zondervan, 1983).

My favorite speakers have been Charles Stanley, David Hocking, Dr. Tony Evans, and Chuck Smith, whose church we attended in southern California before we moved back to Pennsylvania.

I enjoy listening to Christian radio and recommend it to Witnesses because the music and teaching are generally so uplifting. But I always counsel them to be careful, because these speakers are only men, not infallible authorities.

Carolyn Poole

Christian radio and television have been very helpful to me since I have become a Christian. I used to watch Pat Robertson every morning, and I first prayed "the sinner's prayer" with a television preacher.

In 1976 I met Dr. Walter Martin at a "charismatic clinic." He was a great encouragement to me and helped me establish contact with other ex-Christian Scientists. It was with his help that our Christian Way ministry got its start, and we have ministered to hundreds of ex-Christian Scientists and the Christians who are witnessing to them over the past twelve years of this organization.

Other speakers who have been a great influence in my life include Dr. Billy Graham and Dr. James D. Kennedy, as well as numerous pastors of small congregations.

Here are the study guide books that have been most helpful to me: *Halley's Bible Handbook* (Zondervan, 1927 and many subsequent updates); *The Open Bible New American Standard Version* (Thomas Nelson, 1977), whose "Christian Life Study Outlines" are especially good; and *Logos International Bible Commentary* (Logos International Publishers, 1981).

Elaine Dallas

I continue to use and benefit from *Strong's Concordance* and reading my Bible. Also, since leaving Christian Science, I have found a number of books that have further substantiated for me the fact that this religion is indeed a non-Christian cult. I think these particular books could help any ex-Christian Scientist who might still feel some pull of loyalty to Mrs. Eddy and her doctrines. They could also possibly be given to practicing Christian Scientists, for they reveal facts that could crack the solid faith they have in Mrs. Eddy's doctrines, allowing the light of God's truth to begin to penetrate their minds.

One of these is *The Kingdom of the Cults* by Dr. Walter Martin (Bethany Fellowship, 1965). This book deals with many non-Christian cults, including Christian Science, comparing their teachings with the Bible. Another is *Twisting the Truth* by Bruce Tucker (Bethany House, 1987), which shows the way that cult groups subtly distort basic Christian doctrine. Tucker's chapter on salvation is excellent.

A third resource is *The Cult Explosion* by Dave Hunt (Harvest House, 1980). It deals with many different cults and shows the disturbing similarity of Christian Science to Eastern religions. A fourth is *Know the Marks of Cults* by Dave Breese (Victor Books, 1975). This book helps a Christian recognize the distinguishing marks of cults.

Just as Christian radio played a very important part in my conversion, it continues to be influential in my life. I also enjoy listening to tapes purchased through various radio ministries, particularly those of Dr. David Hocking's in his "Solid Rock Radio" ministry. For many years previously, he had been the speaker on the "Biola Hour" radio ministry.

There are many good new radio programs that have come out since I left Christian Science. I appreciate the fact that the programs we have on our local Christian radio station remain true to the Word.

Irene Guthrie

Speakers who have been most helpful to me are: David Hocking, Chuck Smith, Hal Lindsey, Johanna Michaelson, David Breese, and Charles Stanley.

The following have been excellent sources of literature and information: The Christian Information Bureau (P. O. Box 7349, Bend, OR 97708); "The Gospel Truth"—a publication of Southwest Radio Church (P. O. Box 1144, Oklahoma City, OK 73101); Al Dager, "Media Spotlight" (P. O. Box 290, Redmond, WA 98073-0290); Texe Marrs, "Flashpoint"—Living Truth Ministries (8103 Shiloh Court, Austin, TX 78745); David Wilkerson, World Challenge, Inc. (P. O. Box 260, Lindale, TX 75771); "Eagle Forum Newspaper" (1823 W. 102nd Avenue, Denver, CO 80221).

Finally, a book that made a lasting impression on me and that I strongly recommend as "must reading" for a new convert is *The Calvary Road* by Roy Hession (Christian Literature Crusade, 1950).

Will Baron

Because of my background, I have made a specialty of keeping up with what is going on in the New Age. I subscribe to Texe Marrs' "Flashpoint" and read all the materials from the

Christian Research Institute and the Spiritual Counterfeits Project. I have been called to be on programs like "The 700 Club"
and other shows on CBN and TBN. My ministry also involves
doing a lot of counseling and answering letters. So I need to
keep abreast of Christian/New Age issues.

For people who have come out of the New Age movement
or who have been harassed by demons, I recommend *Over-
coming the Adversary* by Mark I. Bubeck (Moody Press, 1984).
This is a book about warfare praying against demonic activity,
and it is tremendous. I also recommend many of Dave Hunt's
books, especially *The Seduction of Christianity* (Harvest House,
1985).

The book I personally have enjoyed the most is one I keep
handy any time I study the Bible: *Halley's Bible Handbook* (Zondervan, 1965). It helps me understand time periods and the historical and cultural background of the Old and New Testaments.
I think there would be a lot more personal Bible study if everyone had a copy of this book.

19

Advice to Parents About Cults

What would you tell parents that could help them protect their children from cultist indoctrination?

David Reed

I think it is important for parents to level with their children, especially with teenagers, about problems in churches and in communities of Christians. If you bring up your children to believe that everything is just hunky-dory in your church—that God approves of everything Christian churches do, that all ordained people are "God's men," and that whenever we fight a war, God is on our side—your children may be in for a rude awakening later. They will also be very vulnerable to a Jehovah's Witness who may show them a picture of a religious leader shaking hands with Hitler, or may smear some other dirt on Christianity. Let your child know that there are true Christians as well as false and that things go on in churches that we should be ashamed of instead of proud of.

This means that the focus has to be on the Lord, not on people. God lets us see in the Bible both the good side and the bad side of believers like King David. We should do the same with our children, while always showing Jesus to be the only perfect example.

Parents must also put their children into direct contact with the Bible. You can't do that by just telling your kids to go to Sunday school; you have to go with them. And seeing husband and wife reading the Bible together will make much more impact on them than giving them even the nicest children's Bible.

Emphasize to your children how important it is to have a personal relationship with Jesus and feed on the Word as an individual. If you are worshiping in a church where the children are not being nurtured—or where there is hypocrisy or agendas that are obstacles—leave! Don't let the inspiring music or your position there keep your family in a place that is detrimental to your children's personal walk with Jesus.

Joan Cetnar

It is most important that children be grounded early in true doctrine by seeing what the Bible teaches. One way to do this is to make sure they attend Sunday school and church services, but you personally must help them come to Jesus at an early age and learn to appreciate that Jesus is their Savior.

Once they have a solid foundation, young people can recognize error when they hear it. In fact, you have to teach them to look for error—Jesus warned of false prophets and false christs. He said they would come "in sheep's clothing." Parents must explain to their children what this means and what a false prophet today would look like.

Carolyn Poole

It should be a number-one priority with parents to help their children understand who Jesus is. Children need basic teachings that will protect them from error. For instance, they need to understand that all have sinned and come short of the glory of God, as the Bible teaches, and thus we need a Savior.

If they understand these two things, they will not be fooled by the Christian Science teachings that man is perfect because he is made in the image of God. Nor will they have doubts about the fact that Jesus is God. You can emphasize the reality of hell, too, but teach them that God does not send us to hell—we make that choice by rejecting his free gift of salvation through his Son.

Elaine Dallas

The most important thing I feel parents should do is teach their children the Bible so that they know what it says. It has been said that the best way to recognize counterfeit money is to be familiar with what real money looks like. The only way a person can recognize false teaching is to know what the true teachings are in the Scriptures.

It is important for parents to start giving their children sound Bible teaching very early in their lives. And, as they grow older, they should be encouraged to read carefully any books given to them, verifying whether what is said is in agreement with the Bible.

My advice for children, and for anyone, is to not just believe what someone says *about* the Bible, but know and believe the Bible itself.

Irene Guthrie

1. The best and most important protection for your children is to introduce them to Jesus early in life. Involve the whole family in a Bible-believing church where sound doctrine is taught. At home, encourage Bible study and prayer time on a consistent basis, allowing each one to participate. In other words, "Train up a child in the way he should go: and when he is old, he will not depart from it" (Prov. 22:6 KJV).

2. Live the gospel in front of your children, never compromising it for fear of rejections from either peers or family. Reverence God and gain the trust of your family by exhibiting Christ-like attitudes. Set biblical standards for your family's lifestyle: ". . . but as for me and my house, we will serve the Lord" (Josh. 24:15 KJV).

3. Foster open communication at all costs by having frequent family meetings to discuss (not argue about) problems, questions, doubts, fears, and so on. Offer spiritual help and bibli-

cal guidance for reaching solutions. Know your children intimately and keep aware of what is going on in their lives. Make
time with them a priority over your job and even, sometimes,
ministry.

4. Know what the New Age movement is all about, understanding its principles and philosophies well enough to recognize it in movies, games (especially computer games), toys,
books, and music. Pray that the Holy Spirit will help you discern things you cannot alone detect as New Age. A helpful
guide to this is Phil Philips, who wrote *Turmoil in the Toy Box*
(Starburst Publishers, 1986).

Replace New Age-influenced forms of entertainment with
healthy activities. Your local Christian bookstore has wholesome toys, videos, and games that will edify your children and
glorify God.

5. If at all possible, home-school your children or enroll them
in a reputable Christian school. Spare them the daily battle with
secular humanism and the pagan religion they may be taught
in the public schools, where Christian children are often
ridiculed because of their faith. On the other hand, it is an honor
to be persecuted for his name's sake.

If it is not possible to home-school your children or send them
to a Christian school, you must take an active part in their education. Watch for occult training in the books they read and protect them from exposure to occultic practices in the classroom,
such as meditation/relaxation and out-of-body experiences. A
good book for parents on this subject is Johanna Michaelson's
Lambs to The Slaughter (Harvest House, 1989). Another good
source of information is John Whitehead, who has written "The
Rights of Religious Persons in Public Education" (Crossway
Books, 1991). He offers a toll-free number: (800) 441-FIRE.

6. Encourage Christian social activities with other children,
such as vacation Bible school, church youth/family camps, picnics, parties—any healthy alternative to the worldly activities
that lure our children. Invite non-Christian children, but cen-
sor your children's involvement with non-Christian friends.

Remember, you know your children better than anyone and can judge whether or not a certain friend will be good for your child.

7. Teach your children how to recognize the New Age in general. Spare them (especially younger children) the more fearful aspects of New Age, but show them through Scripture and prophecy that we live in an exciting time and that God has a perfect plan for the end of this age. It will help them influence others for Christ if they see your compassion for lost souls.

8. Love your children. The security you offer as godly parents through the Holy Spirit's guidance will instill confidence in them. If they know who they are in Christ, they will have "God-esteem" instead of a slanted, psychological view of self-esteem. When they see that you as parents know that God has a wonderful plan for their lives, and that you are committed to seeing them through that plan, they will not be so apt to search for attention from people who seek after and serve foreign gods.

A book that is generally helpful for parents is *Your Child and the New Age* by Berit Kjos (Scripture Press/Victor Books, 1990).

Will Baron

I believe this is the most profound and important question a Christian could ask.

New Age thinking has already permeated our society in many ways. Ronald Reagan used an astrologer to govern his schedules. I was shocked the first time I heard President Bush talking about "a new world order." No politicians have used that phrase in the past—only New Age leaders had done that up until then. But there have been occultic forces in our nation for years. The motto "Novus Ordo Seclorum," which is on our dollar bills, actually means "new world order." And it appears underneath an occultic symbol, the all-seeing eye of Horus atop a pyramid.

Mysticism is all around us. Movies like *Star Wars* and *E.T.* are full of it. George Lucas has openly acknowledged that his inspiration for the mystical concepts in *Star Wars* came from Carlos Castaneda's books—and those were books that heavily influenced my entry into New Age.

Much of television, especially children's shows, focuses on magicians and sorcerers and magical powers. As a result, there is a generation of people who are growing up thinking that the occult is *normal*. I am single, have no children, and don't own a television set, but I can certainly see how it would be tempting for parents to let their children just watch these things. However, I think it would be important to talk to them about what they are watching or reading and show them which elements are New Age and which are not.

Try to find out what might attract a child to the occult. Because fantasy is so prevalent now, parents should encourage their children to face their own problems, not look for some sort of mystical solution or escape. Of course, this would require that parents themselves be able to recognize New Age influences.

I believe our society is changing so much and so fast that New Age thinking will soon become the norm. In Western Europe, Christianity was once the norm, but today over there the norm is now atheism and secular humanism. Maybe the answer to this is to educate one's children in Christian schools, where they can learn to distinguish truth and then be well prepared to deal with New Age error.

20

Effective Nurturing

Is there anything you would say to the Christian body as a whole that would be helpful in teaching a cult member or nurturing a new Christian who has left a cult?

David Reed

When a Christian is talking to a Jehovah's Witness, he or she must be aware that the Witness has been trained to set certain "traps." Typically, Witnesses will try to pit their organization against a specific church, or against Christendom as a whole.

Don't fall into that trap! The churches that Peter, and Paul, and James wrote to in the Bible all had problems, and churches will always have problems. Since the issue is not the Watchtower versus Christianity, but the Watchtower versus Jesus, the question must be: "Will I follow an organization or follow him?" If a Witness tries to turn the focus back on churches and their problems, I agree that following an organization will always get you into trouble, but then I point out that Jesus himself is the only solid rock.

New Christians who are ex-Witnesses must, I believe, be allowed some freedom and some time to reevaluate their thinking on such things as the Trinity, the future state of the dead, and other doctrines. Show them respect and confidence in their ability to follow Jesus, read the Bible, and be led by the Spirit.

Don't tell them, "Look, your doctrines are all wrong, and you're going to have to change and believe everything I say." Focus on what is basic in Scripture, what is essential for a follower of Christ, and don't try to make an ex-Witness walk in lockstep with you on every little detail. A Witness who has broken free from obedience to men won't want to fall into obedience to another group of men. Give them freedom and time, and don't expect them to stand at attention and salute like little soldiers on everything.

Joan Cetnar

I believe that most Jehovah's Witnesses are sincere people, just as sincere as I was when I was a Witness. They are well trained, and this makes many Christians afraid of them. There are three ways, I think, to counter this fear.

First of all, remember that though Witnesses are sincere, they are seriously mistaken and deceived and need your help. Second, don't forget that "greater is He who is in you than he who is in the world" (1 John 4:4 NASB). And, third, you don't have to be afraid to show them love. Even if your only contact is the Witness at your door, you can show that person a loving attitude, share your own testimony, and tell him or her that you have assurance of salvation from the Bible.

As to nurturing ex-cultists who are new Christians, I think the key is patience. For example, it takes time for many ex-Witnesses to overcome what they have been through in the Watchtower Society. A great deal depends on how long they were involved, what traumas they sustained, and how much of their families they had to leave behind. Christians must be very sensitive and allow the Lord to love them, through us.

We also have a responsibility to help them learn true doctrine. Ex-Witnesses are always anxious to replace false doctrine with the truth, but they need guidance. One way to do this is to have Bible studies with them.

Again, love them! Help them get into the mainstream of Christianity.

Carolyn Poole

I had an experience that was devastating to me when I was a new Christian. I was filled with enthusiasm and shared openly with people at church about my salvation. A woman I hadn't met before was talking with me, and I told her, "I was a Christian Scientist."

She reacted to me with a shocked look. If I had been in the Mafia or had participated in terrorist raids, I don't think she could have regarded me with more open horror. It hurt me deeply.

Christian Scientists need to be invited into the Christian world. They are so isolated. A lot of them send their children to the Christian Science Principia School, read only "authorized" literature, associate only with other members, and even retire in the church-owned nursing home. They are not going to seek out the Christian—the first step must be taken by the Christian, perhaps by inviting them to a concert, Bible study, or other Christian activity.

What will "work" with one Christian Scientist may have no effect on another. It has been my experience that many—if not most—Christian Scientists will cut a Christian off completely. The only thing that will help bring out those who ultimately come out is a combination of time, patience, prayer, and kindness. Let the Holy Spirit do his work—and don't give up!

Elaine Dallas

Christian Scientists are possibly some of the most sincere and dedicated religious people one could ever find. Their religion is not just a Sunday-only thing. Every day they are conscientiously attempting to keep their thoughts "pure"—which means striving to keep uppermost in their minds the "truth" that "God is All" and that therefore the material world, sickness, disease, death, and evil have no reality and can have no effect on them.

With this "knowing the truth" comes the assurance that none of the aforementioned "errors" needs to be feared. From my fifty-plus years in Christian Science, I know the sense of assurance and peace this gives, but I know now that this is simply a "pretend" security, a false peace. Neither God's Word nor life itself supports any of Mrs. Eddy's claims—they refute them. Christian Scientists have been terribly deceived.

It is ironic that Christian Science attracts "intellectual" people and that they see Christian Science as a very logical religion. It *is* based on logic, but unfortunately its premise, "God is All," is totally unscriptural. Consequently, all conclusions based on this premise are equally unscriptural.

Even Mrs. Eddy's reasoning itself is not always correct. For instance, she made the statement in *Science and Health* that only one of the following can be true: (1) everything is matter or (2) everything is Mind. She then asks, "Which one is it?" The question carries with it the assumption that one of these statements is indeed true, and a Christian Scientist, having been preconditioned to deny the first and choose the latter, will have no problem with this assumption. The possibility that neither one is true is not even considered—but in this case, *neither* is true.

This is somewhat like the old question, "Have you stopped beating your wife yet?" Here the question again carries with it the assumption that you have indeed been beating your wife, whereas the truth probably is that you have never done so.

Christian Scientists who are new Christians need very quickly to get into a sound church where they can begin growing spiritually and receiving the support they will so desperately need during the "no-man's-land" feeling they will be experiencing. Without this growth and support, they can be easily drawn back into Christian Science, falling back into their old accustomed and comfortable feeling of "security," mistaken though it is.

I thank God for opening my eyes and enabling me to see the false nature of Christian Science and the truth of the Scriptures. I praise God for the assurance of *true* eternal security, which is founded upon his holy Word, not on what Mrs. Eddy said.

At the same time, my heart is heavy for all the others who are still deceived and trapped in Christian Science. May they be like the noble Bereans of Acts 17 who "searched the Scriptures daily" to see if the things Paul and Silas told them were true. And may Christian Scientists likewise search the Scriptures daily to see if the things Mrs. Eddy said are true.

Irene Guthrie

Keep in mind that the New Age is not new. It is an old lie, started by the serpent in the Garden of Eden when he deceived Eve into eating from the tree of the knowledge of good and evil. A verse that has been especially meaningful to me is Jeremiah 6:16, from the Amplified Bible: "Thus says the Lord, Stand by the roads and look, and ask for the eternal paths, where is the good, old way; then walk in it, and you will find rest for your souls. But they said, We will not walk in it!" (Matt. 11:29).

The answer to the world's problems is not a "new world order," but God's *old* order by his Word. I am not advocating falling back to legalism, but a return to God's own "eternal paths." We can testify to the New Ager that the "old way" doesn't mean the ancient, mystical, religions, but the way of the true God, who is the Ancient of Days and is from before the foundation of the world.

Our world is in serious spiritual trouble and has only two kinds of people: the saved and the unsaved. New Agers have been blinded to the truth by Satan; they are walking on a broad, pantheistic path that is leading them to destruction. When dealing with a person lost in the New Age movement, you are wrestling not with flesh, but with powers and principalities. Expect struggle—you are born-again in the Spirit, a human being dealing with an unregenerate New Ager who has not come to a knowledge of the truth.

The New Ager who is willing and open to listen to the teaching of the Bible will have a heart hungry for the things of God. For this type of person, "preach the word; be ready in season and out of season; reprove, rebuke, exhort, with great patience and instruction" (2 Tim. 4:2 NASB). Commit the willing heart to

God in prayer and fasting. Be patient and seek the Lord's guidance in how best to fill that person's needs with books, tapes, videos, or other helpful literature.

Sometimes a zealous New Ager will profess Jesus Christ as Lord and Savior but lack submission to God, refusing to come to him on *his* terms. In such a situation, I would reevaluate the issue of salvation with the person. Restate the basic Bible doctrines from the Gospel of John, and if you still have a problem getting past the truth of salvation-by-faith-and-not-works, perhaps the teaching should not be pursued. In this case, avoid arguing. Instead, discreetly turn the individual over to someone who may be able to get through to him or her. As a last resort, shake the dust off your feet—and go on.

Nurturing a former New Ager who is now a Christian is often a long and slow process that demands affectionate care and personal attention. Although it requires great patience, remember that God is long-suffering toward us.

Because of former brainwashing, you must allow time for the newborn to show signs of maturity. The transition may take years, as it did for me. Be available to answer questions and be honest with your answers. If you don't know the answers, don't be too proud to get help from pastors, elders, or other ex-cultists who may have more experience than you.

Finally, here is a promise for believers who are in ministry to ex-cultists. It is from Daniel 12:1–3 (NASB):

> "Now at that time [of the end] Michael, the great prince who stands guard over the sons of your people, will arise. And there will be a time of distress such as never occurred since there was a nation until that time; and at that time your people, everyone who is found written in the book, will be rescued.

> "And many of those who sleep in the dust of the ground will awake, these to everlasting life, but the others to disgrace and everlasting contempt [cf. John 5:29].

> "And those who have insight will shine brightly like the brightness of the expanse of heaven, and those who lead the many to righteousness, like the stars forever and ever" [cf. Matt. 13:43].

Let *your* light shine!

Will Baron

From my experience as a New Ager, I know there are many sincere people involved in that way of thinking. A lot of them would make excellent Christians, so it's up to us to bring them the truth of Scripture and the truth about Jesus Christ. All heaven rejoices when someone comes out of the New Age, just as it did when the prodigal son came home.

I believe that most New Age believers are above average in intelligence. Of course, the movement covers a wide spectrum of people, but all of them need love and caring from us—just like Christ cared for the adulteress who was about to be stoned.

Above all, Christians should remember that New Agers are not directly satanists! Satanism is a different religion, where people acknowledge Satan as a powerful being who can give them wealth and power. New Agers are looking for God. They are searching for happiness and some sort of harmony with God, but they are deceived by the arch-deceiver, Satan, and his demons. They need the gospel message, and they will hear it as much from our example to them as anything else.

People who come out of the New Age have special problems. Often, they are harassed by demons, as I was. They need special counseling and especially need the ministry of prayer. There is not a lot known about the specifics of how to nurture new believers who have come out of the New Age, but I would like eventually to be able to help in this area, too.

Epilogue

The more I listened to what these six people had to say, the more convinced I became that the image of the cults as an archipelago was an appropriate one. Little by little, the water around the apparently separate islands became clearer, and I could see interconnecting links.

Reincarnation—once strictly an Eastern religious concept—showed itself as a primary tenet of both Christian Science and New Age thinking. Masonic symbols connect both Mormonism and the New Age. Pyramidology, spiritualism, and phrenology, which I thought were peculiar to the New Age, are deeply embedded in the past history of the Jehovah's Witness movement. Christian Scientists share an affinity with Jehovah's Witnesses, who deny any real eternal punishment for the wicked. Christian Scientists, Mormons, and New Age believers teach that we can be as godlike as Jesus, while Jehovah's Witnesses say that Jesus was a little closer in stature to us than to Jehovah God.

I saw the effect that cultic thinking has had in the lives of these six people. I should not have been surprised to find, for example, that the two ex-Christian Scientists still use some of the formalized speech patterns of their expressive former mentor, Mary Baker Eddy. (No criticism is implied here. After all, I still—after eighteen years out of Mormonism—unconsciously grab my elbows instead of folding my hands when someone says, "Let us pray." We all have holdovers from our cultic pasts.)

But there were some other kinds of surprises, too. For instance, when I read the ebullient testimony of former New Ager Irene Guthrie, I thought I would have to have a long tether to pull her back down to earth to get her to answer the questions I posed. To my delight, I found that she was as organized and complete in answering questions as she was enthusiastic in telling her own story. I found that the way the different people approached the task reflected aspects of both their personalities and their backgrounds. Some were highly narrative, others quite concerned with documenting and backing up anything they considered disputable.

I have learned to respect the amount of work that some of these people have invested in their full-time ministries to cults. David Reed, who has written what I consider to be the most authoritative and readable books on Jehovah's Witnesses, is also the editor of a publication for Witnesses, ex-Witnesses, and concerned Christians called "Comments from the Friends." Joan Cetnar and her beloved husband, William (who passed away just before this book went to press), have not only spent many years in ministering to Witnesses but have also hosted an annual convention for ex-Witnesses. Carolyn Poole has used her years of experience in the Christian Science movement to counsel with people through her "Christian Way" ministry, an organization that also features as part of its literature ministry a testimony tape by Elaine Dallas, whose meticulous answers to questions in this book have been such an asset. Irene Guthrie is actively involved in multimedia presentations on the New Age, which she has presented to groups. She is beginning to be contacted by Christian television producers to tell her story of her years as a white witch. And, finally, Will Baron ministers through *Deceived by The New Age*, a book that Pat Robertson called "an unbelievable, extraordinary story" about his oppression by the demonic beings to which the New Age made him vulnerable.

In that sense, then, this book is just a continuation of the ministry in which these people have long been involved. I know from listening to tearful voices on tape as they told their testimonies that this delving into the past was at times a painful process for some of them. Many expressed a real desire to share even their pain, acknowledging that while they know they cannot relive the past, perhaps the telling of it will keep others from repeating their mistakes.

I found that they had in common with the ex-Mormons I interviewed for my previous book a characteristic lack of what I called "territorial instincts" when it comes to current church affiliation. Some, in fact, actually expressed an aversion to the concept of denominations, echoing what is apparently a widespread contemporary sentiment expressed in the headline of a recent article from the Fort Lauderdale *Sun-Sentinel*: "Denomination a 'Bad Word' Among New Churches."

I saw a tie-in between this feeling and one of the questions that I asked the participants, which had to do with the way their perceptions about church leadership have changed. I believe that one of the areas in which most Christians seriously underestimate the effect of cults on their adherents is in the view of church leadership. Consider, for instance, the plight of someone coming out of the old Worldwide Church of God, whose leader, Herbert W. Armstrong, claimed he was answerable only to God. Or the ex-Mormon whose former cult's founder, Joseph Smith, said, "No man ever did a work like me—even Jesus was deserted by his disciples"—and whose more modern "General Authorities" have proclaimed, "When the leaders speak, the thinking has been done." Or consider the person newly out of Christian Science who was repeatedly told that the Bible needed to be corrected and that Mary Baker Eddy was the only one authorized by God to do the job (a privilege claimed also by David Berg, founder of the Children of God cult).

Many times, a new Christian just out of a cult doesn't know *how* to look at church leaders. Followers of Jim Jones had watched in awe as he held aloft his hands, supposedly dripping with the blood of the stigmata. Other leaders of cults have claimed outright to be gods or at least to be in the process of becoming gods: Mary Baker Eddy, Charles Manson, Adolf Hitler, Sun Myung Moon, and all Mormon prophets and leaders.

I asked the question of my participants about their view of church leadership not so that they could express their dismay at the recent televangelist scandals (which we all feel), but rather so that other Christians could see what they did indeed so articulately express: the need to plainly teach ex-cultists the difference between blind obedience to leadership, by which they were earlier oppressed, and the biblical injunctions to honor and respect those who labor among us in ministry and service.

Two things impressed me about the participants' changed views of the Bible. The first was their joy at both the freedom to study God's Word in different translations and the encouragement by others to come to their own conclusions about what the Scriptures said. Of the three cults represented in this book, only one—Jehovah's Witnesses—made any claim to guiding members to look at the original Greek and Hebrew words. However, the Witnesses share an undesirable characteristic with most other cults in that they only allow reading from an "approved" version and/or commentary. In the case of the Jehovah's Witnesses, this translation was expressly tailored to fit the cult's doctrine.

The second thing that the question about the change in the view of the Bible brought out was that most of the warnings in the Bible against cultic activity simply had no meaning for them while they were involved in the cult. It was not that the group or its leadership forbade them to read these warnings; members simply ignored or redefined the warnings so as to be of no threat to the cultic mind. For example, the few times that I was encouraged as a Mormon to read the Bible, no one ever directed me to the passages in Isaiah 43, 44, and 45 that state clearly that there is only one God and that there will be no others. Nor did I read Paul's warning in Galatians against "another gospel," even if it be brought by an angel, and ever dream of a connection with the angel Moroni, whose likeness stands on top of the Salt Lake Mormon temple. When Will Baron was involved in "Christian New Age," he was apparently nonplused by Revelation 9:20–21, which tells of worshiping demons and practicing magic arts. Nor did he ever identify with those characterized by Paul in 1 Timothy 4:1 as following deceiving spirits and doctrines taught by demons. I'm sure that David Reed and Joan Cetnar read in their *New World Translation* of false prophets in Matthew 24:24 without ever suspecting that they were following such prophets. When Elaine Dallas and Carolyn Poole read Mrs. Eddy's notes on 2 Thessalonians 2:11–12, they never thought *they* were the ones who had swallowed a powerful delusion and believed a lie. Only Irene Guthrie—whose main contact with the Scriptures in her days of training at a New Age school was seeing a large Bible on a table behind her teacher—could use the excuse that she didn't know what the Bible said. The others studied it, but because their eyes were blinded by cultic teachings, they simply could not see that what it plainly said about false teaching applied to *them*.

After these six people shared their changed attitudes about the Bible, I felt that I and most other Christians are ungrateful for (and unaware of) the two great blessings we have in reading the Bible: an uncensored freedom to read from multiple translations and an unclouded vision that gives us the ability to understand what we read, because we have not had our minds programmed to *mis*-understand it.

This problem of "vision" shows up in another area, too. One trait of a cult not included in the list of cultic characteristics in my introductory material on "The Archipelago of the Cults" is the absolute inability of people deceived by cults to see that they *are* in a cult. For example, you could give that list of thirty characteristics to a Jehovah's Witness and he or she could tell you just how many of them apply to a Mormon friend (and vice versa). A cult, I have concluded, is only obvious to those outside its bounds. Those inside a cult see all their frantic behavior to earn salvation simply as "devotion to God." Their aberrant doctrines are "normal" to them, and everyone else who differs is the one who is strange. (Elaine Dallas grew up incredulous of other people who couldn't see the "logic" of Christian Science, for instance.)

One question that I think is very significant is the one about the "personal cost" involved in leaving a cult. Most committed

Christians who are ex-cult members don't really make a "big deal" out of this and must be asked about it to say anything at all. (I personally feel a little foolish talking about giving up friends and other benefits of Mormonism when there are Christians around the world who are daily in jeopardy of their very lives for the cause of Christ.) But, on the other hand, before a Christian asks a cult member to leave the security blanket of the group that has ensnared him or her, the Christian must be aware of what the cult has already extracted from that cultist, and what the break with the cult is likely to cost in the future. Jesus urged disciples to count the cost, pointing out that there would indeed be a price involved.

Regarding the price already extracted from the cult member, because most cult members believe their salvation is dependent upon their working to serve the cult, they may already be physically spent in that process. (For instance, there is an inordinately high suicide rate among Mormon women, who are expected to be perfect wives, mothers of many children, and ideal homemakers as well as great spiritual examples at all times.) Of course, cult members pay high soul-prices, too—they are robbed of the most precious elements of Christianity.

A Christian's faith is bound up in and defined not by an organization, but by a person: Jesus Christ. But, to many cult members, Jesus is just one of many god-men, not *the* God-Man. He is drained of personality by those who concentrate on "Christ consciousness" instead of on how he related on earth to human beings. For some, his precious name is no more than part of a chant—"Christ in me is health, Christ in me is wealth" (Unity)—to manipulate cosmic powers into what they want.

The cults also rob their members of the significance of the most powerful symbols of Christianity. When I was a Mormon, I disdained the cross because I believed that Jesus' atonement did not take place there but in the garden. And why, I wondered, would I want to wear an instrument of torture as a charm around my neck? Thus, the cross was truly emptied of its power for me and for all Mormons—and also for all Jehovah's Witnesses, who believe that Jesus was impaled on a pole. The cross is equally meaningless for any New Age believer, because it signifies denial of self. New Agers maintain that self is supreme and must be preserved at all costs, never "sacrificed," for self to them *is* God.

Jehovah's Witnesses also have corrupted one of the most poignant symbols of Christ's sacrificial love for us by making blood a distasteful thing, something that must be avoided. And the incarnation—the taking on of flesh by God—is absolutely denied by Christian Scientists, who thus squander the significance of this ultimate "demonstration" of God. Again and again there are examples of how the cults have taken the most precious elements of the message of Christ and made them something to be despised in their eyes. Cult members who escape come to Christianity needy; they are poverty-stricken of the riches of both grace and truth.

Here's the bottom line in dealing with cult members: Christians must realize that even after escaping, ex-cultists are not immediately "like us." They cannot be discipled or nurtured like garden-variety unbelievers who come to Christ. There are certain elements that must be considered.

First of all, David Reed once observed that when you show a cult member—especially a relatively new one—that the group with which he or she is allied is not based on truth, often the first reaction will be that the cult member will feel that he or she is "bad" for making a wrong choice of religion. Some cults sow the seeds for this kind of thinking. Remember how Elaine Dallas always assumed that if she didn't understand a concept in Christian Science, it was *she*, not it, that was lacking, and she just needed to work harder at understanding. We Christians who can see "the big picture" might feel anger at Satan and see the cult member as someone who was sold into slavery. But the once-duped cult members' anger may well be directed at themselves for buying into it in the first place.

Even after a final decision to leave a cult, there is still a long uphill road ahead. Cults are unique in their treatment of apostates. Although 1 Corinthians teaches that those who will not repent of sin must be deprived of Christian fellowship, in the

hopes that they will want to come back, the heavy-handed tactics used by Jehovah's Witnesses, for example, go far beyond
that. Joan and Bill Cetnar, and David Reed and his wife, Penni,
were all led to believe that not only were they to be isolated from
former Witness friends, but that each couple was unique—they
would never fit in among other people either. This was a deliberate attempt to isolate them from any source of fellowship
based on commonality. I had similar feelings when I left the
Mormon church and was warned by my branch president,
"Don't you know you'll never be happy again?" And, indeed,
my feelings of aloneness, of singularity, were not abated until
five long years later, when I met for the first time another ex-
Mormon Christian.

The issue of submission is going to be an emotionally charged
one for the ex-cultist. If my own experience is any gauge, a new
Christian will approach the subject with an ambivalence so violent that it may border on spiritual schizophrenia. Why is that?
Well, we tell a new Christian that he or she must humble self
before God, must submit even thinking processes to him and
learn to have "the mind of Christ."

All that is necessary, of course, and biblical. But consider how
it might sound to someone like Will Baron, who knew full well
that the last time he surrendered himself to a governing power,
the cost was almost unbearable. In fact, I would venture to say
that the more compelling and mystical the cultist's former experiences, the harder it will be for him or her to "open up" spiritually to God.

Here's how that played out in my own case. I was willing for
God to be my Savior. He could even be my Lord, and I would
obey everything I read in Scripture to do. But I was going to
keep my emotional distance from him, because the last time I
had fallen in love with a god, he had broken my heart. It was
years after becoming a Christian that I began to feel a desperate need for God—began to pant for him as a deer pants for
water, as David said. Maybe it was because I never before then
knew how lost I had been.

Christian brothers and sisters, if you have never been involved in a cult, listen to what the people in this book have to say. Many Christians feel that they themselves are "too smart" ever to get involved in a cult, not realizing that pride and feelings are the two wedges that cults use to get under the skin of a believer. Ironically, feeling "superior" to someone with a cultic past is a trap that can make us become vulnerable to cultic lies, because we are then lowering our guard.

Likewise, a Christian who immediately rejects "junk about visions and mystical experiences" places himself in great jeopardy—for Christians who rely only on what they themselves see and touch are among the most arid of souls. Perhaps we have forgotten that the life-style taught by Jesus is anything but practical and wise by the world's standards. Faith itself demands that we base our entire salvation on that which we do not see.

The definition of what is "real" has to be clearly outlined for an ex-cultist Christian. New Age believers who become Christians, for instance, must learn to put aside all they think they know and let the Bible define what is real and what is valuable. Even feelings have to be trained by the Word.

Christians, therefore, do not have to worry about treating ex-cult members who are new Christians differently—they themselves already *know* they are different. But there are other things that they probably are unable to recognize. For instance, many people come out of a cult and make the transition to a Christian church without ever feeling that they are "newborn in Christ." Often, the pride and self-sufficiency (or, at the very least, feelings of superiority) so inbred in them by the cult will fool them into thinking they are making a simple transition from one realm of adulthood to another. They must be taught openly that true conversion to Christ involves being *born again* and truly becoming like a little child, something for which they are not likely to feel any need until shown.

When I wrote about this phenomenon as it related to ex-Mormons, I stated that ex-Mormons who are new Christians are not just newborn babes, they are newborns who are born addicted. They must be cared for differently than other new-borns, for they have very real needs that other babies do not have. They cannot be blamed for their addiction but must be lovingly weaned from it.

Furthermore, people who escape cults and come to Christ are not just babies born addicted. They are born *abused*. Child abuse occurs when an authority figure, someone bigger and stronger, uses a position of trust to hurt a child. Therefore, I don't think any of us who have lived as faithful members of cults have escaped unscathed from the experience. Cults, after all, exist as the result of a conscious plan in the mind of Satan to define a subculture and control the people within it. You can't live under that kind of deliberately destructive leadership for long with-out dire consequences.

I can say what I am about to say because I, too, was ravaged by the aftereffects of a cult. I don't believe anyone who escapes from one gets out whole. We are all skewed by that experience in one way or another and in varying degrees. Denying that fact doesn't help us heal.

Neither addiction nor abuse is healed until it is first recog-nized and then dealt with. You can't tell a victim of cultism just to pray and be more spiritual and everything will work out. There are no quick fixes and instant cures. Someone has to teach God's way of truth, and love, and forgiveness. This will take time and patience. It will be very hard.

But here's the truth that Jesus died for: Children—*all* his chil-dren—are worth it.

Glossary

The following is a listing and informal definition of terms that may be unfamiliar to some readers. They are associated with Jehovah's Witnesses (JW), Christian Science (CS), or New Age (NA).

Acupressure (NA)—the application of pressure through fingertips to activate certain sites on the body without needles (see **Acupuncture**).

Acupuncture (NA)—5,000-year-old Chinese practice based on philosophy and astrology. Intended to harmonize the physical and mental aspects of an individual by puncturing sites on the body with needles to reduce pain or cure disease.

Age of Aquarius (NA)—2,000-year-long period that New Agers believe we are entering as a result of our planet's movement into the influence of the astrological constellation Aquarius. As a result of this, the consciousness of mankind will be raised to produce a level of spirituality known as "the New Age."

Anointed class (JW)—small minority of Jehovah's Witnesses who expect to go to heaven.

Armageddon (JW)—a future event that Jehovah's Witnesses believe will be the intervention of God to destroy the entire non–Jehovah's-Witness population of this planet.

Astrology chart (NA)—a circular diagram that is the result of charting on paper one's life, activities, and characteristics by the divination process of astrology, as determined by the date, time, and place of birth of the individual.

Automatic writing (NA)—also known as "journaling," it is the writing of a message from a spirit entity, using the hand of a medium.

Bethel (JW)—Brooklyn, N.Y., headquarters of the Watchtower Society.

Bible-study servant (JW)—an assistant-overseer position in a local congregation of Jehovah's Witnesses.

Biofeedback (NA)—the use of monitoring machines to teach people to control involuntary functions, such as heart rate and tension.

Black witchcraft (NA)—male principle of occultic forces used for evil purposes: black art, demonism, satanism, magic circles.

Branch church (CS)—a local church organized under the Mother Church but having its own democratic government. A member must adhere to the Tenets but not necessarily be a member of the Mother Church.

Channel (NA)—a verb that refers to the process by which a spirit entity, usually identified as an individual who has passed on (such as Lazarus, Moses, Cleopatra, etc.), speaks forth messages through a medium.

Channeling (NA)—as defined by John Ankerberg and John Weldon, a New Age term for spirit possession where a willing human "channel" or medium relinquishes his or her mind and body to an invading spirit, who then possesses and controls that person for its own purposes, usually as a mouthpiece to give the spirit's own teachings. Also referred to in the past as mediumship.

Christ, Truth (CS)—a term that Mary Baker Eddy used interchangeably with "Christ"; eg., "Christ, Truth, was demonstrated through Jesus to prove the power of Spirit over the flesh . . ." (*Science and Health* 316:8–9).

Christhood (NA)—a supposed immortal state achieved by a New Age disciple as a result of undergoing the mystical "Christhood" initiation following several lifetimes of strenuous spiritual endeavor. After this initiation, the disciple is said to become an Ascended Master.

Circuit overseer (JW)—a traveling Jehovah's Witness elder assigned to visit and supervise 16 to 20 congregations, spending a week at a time with each.

Class instruction (CS)—a once-in-a-lifetime class comprised of thirty students and a teacher who meet together daily for two weeks. From this a lifelong student-teacher bond is formed which is renewed at annual "Association Meetings."

Congregational servant (JW)—the presiding overseer of a group of Jehovah's Witnesses.

Cosmic mind (CS)—unknown force in the universe by which living creatures have their subsistence, according to both New Age and Eastern religions.

Demonstration (CS)—the result of "knowing the truth" and experiencing healing or the solving of a specific problem.

Devil (CS)—as defined by Mary Baker Eddy, "Evil; a lie; error . . . a belief in sin, sickness, and death."

Disfellowshiped (JW)—status of a Jehovah's Witness who has been sentenced by a judicial committee to be shunned by all other Witnesses, including family and friends.

District assembly (JW)—a semi-annual gathering of Jehovah's Witnesses in a designated area.

District overseer (JW)—the next rung up in the Jehovah's Witness hierarchy from a circuit overseer; a traveling elder assigned to supervise several circuit overseers.

Divination (NA)—foretelling of the future or obtaining secret knowledge; the opposite of biblical prophecy.

Divine Mind (CS)—term that Mary Baker Eddy used for God: "God is incorporeal, divine, supreme, infinite Mind, Spirit, Soul, Principle, Life, Truth, Love" (*Science and Health* 465:8–10).

Djwhal Khul (NA)—one of forty-nine Ascended Masters who functioned as messenger to Alice Bailey for her New Age writings and to others; probably the alias for dozens of demons.

Executive board (CS)—the group of members in charge of membership meetings and conducting the business of the church.

Externalization (NA)—a process through which the Ascended Masters will soon begin to reveal themselves visibly to individuals and groups of people in preparation for the future public appearance in the world of "the Christ," or New Age messiah.

Extrasensory perception (NA)—the ability of a person to perceive information by some human faculty other than the normal sense mechanisms of sight, touch, smell, hearing, and taste.

Good witch (NA)—an individual, usually a Wiccan, whose religion is based on the worship of nature, who uses magic in his or her ceremonies through familiar spirits for supposed benevolent purposes; anyone consciously channeling energy for a positive purpose.

Guided imagery (NA)—visualization exercises directed by a leader wherein some in the audience merely relax, while others enter into altered states of consciousness, which include trance, a sense of astral projection, and connection with a spirit guide.

Hearings (JW)—official proceedings of Jehovah's Witness judicial committees; kangaroo courts at which the same three elders serve as prosecutor, judge, jury, and executioner.

Higher self (NA)—identified in *Your Child and the New Age* as equated with "the God-self," "the I-AM," "my inner self." It contains all cosmic knowledge, wisdom, and power, just as each unit of a hologram contains all the characteristics of the whole. Normally it is only accessible through New Age consciousness-raising techniques, such as Eastern meditation.

Hypnotic regression (NA)—the use of an altered state of consciousness, achieved either through meditation or hypnosis, to search the mind to reminisce on supposed past lives.

Icon (NA)—pictorial representations or religious images or articles, which are venerated or worshiped.

Incantations (NA)—spells; verbal charms spoken or sung as a part of magic rituals; a written or recited formula of words designed to produce a particular effect.

Intuitive healing (NA)—a psychic reading whereby the spirit guide reveals the nature of a problem in the subject, whether it be physical or emotional. Usually followed by the laying on of hands for a healing or by a comforting positive message about the future from the psychic.

Invocation (NA)—verbalized prayer statements used boldly to command into action certain supernatural energies and forces for the attainment of a desired result.

Journaling (NA)—see **Automatic writing**.

Judicial committee (JW)—a group of at least three men in authority in a local Jehovah's Witness congregation.

Kingdom Hall (JW)—local Jehovah's Witness meeting-place. (Jehovah's Witnesses become very upset if it is referred to as a "church.")

Lesson-Sermon (CS)—material printed in the "Christian Science Quarterly" composed of selected passages from *Science and Health with Key to the Scriptures*, which serve to corroborate and explain Bible passages. Weekly Lessons are to be read daily by Christian Scientists and then read by the Readers at the following Sunday service.

Lord Maitreya (NA)—the Ascended Master who holds the executive office and title of "the Christ" and presides over the "White Brotherhood of Masters." Traditional New Age teaches that Lord Maitreya's "soul" actually "possessed" Jesus of Nazareth and that Maitreya will soon appear in public as "the second coming of Jesus."

Mantra (NA)—a practice of Hindu origin; the repetitious chanting of a word, a God-name, or a formula, used to place oneself into an altered state of consciousness.

Masters (NA)—one of a group of forty-nine immortal human beings who have achieved Christhood and now live in seclusion in various remote parts of the earth, telepathically inspiring humanity to carry out "the will of God"; in actuality, demonic spirits or evil angels under the control of Satan.

Material (CS)—that which consists of matter, defined by Mary Baker Eddy as "Mythology; mortality . . . illusion . . . mind originating in matter . . . the opposite of God; that of which immortal Mind takes no cognizance: (*Science and Health* 591:8–14).

Medium (NA)—a human contact between the natural and the supernatural; between inquisitive people and evil spirits.

Metaphysical (NA)—adjective relating to occultic philosophical knowledge concerned with the supernatural realm and the ultimate realities of the nature of man, God, and the universe.

Membership board (CS)—a small group of members who interview prospective members and pass approval on those who qualify and submit their names at the general membership meetings.

Mind Sciences (CS)—collective name for such religions as Unity, Christian Science, Religious Science, and Divine Science, all of which basically believe in the power of the mind for healing. They are actually based on the Gnostic doctrines refuted by John in his first epistle in the New Testament.

Ministerial servant (JW)—a man appointed in a congregation to care for literature supplies, financial accounting, sound system, and so on, under the direction of the elders.

Mother Church (CS)—The First Church of Christ, Scientist, in Boston, Massachusetts; the publishing, central administrative, and religious headquarters of Christian Science. Organized by Mary Baker Eddy and now governed by a five-member board of directors, which oversees all church activities worldwide. Any Christian Scientist who adheres to church Tenets may become a member of the Mother Church while simultaneously belonging to one of its local branch churches.

Mysticism (NA)—"the experience of mystical union or direct communion with ultimate reality reported by mystics" (*Webster's New Collegiate Dictionary*, 1973).

Necromancy (NA)—the occult practice of consulting the dead.

New Age movement (NA)—a worldwide satanic conspiracy to overthrow the kingdom of God through political, spiritual, and educational means.

***New World Translation* (JW)**—version of the Bible produced by the Watchtower Society; contains about three hundred changes in verses to make them support Jehovah's Witness doctrines.

New truth (JW)—doctrine proclaimed by the Watchtower Society that is different from the previous understanding on the subject.

New world society (JW)—esoteric term used by Jehovah's Witnesses to refer to themselves.

Numerology (NA)—an occult form of divination that assigns significance, qualities, and characteristics to numbers.

Occult (NA)—the practices of witchcraft, satanism, spiritualism, and divination through supernatural means.

Ouija board (NA)—a "game" board used as a point of contact through which spirits give messages to the user.

Palmistry (NA)—the practice of determining one's character or future from the markings on one's hands.

Pantheism (NA)—the belief that God is in everything (rocks, trees, people, etc.) and that everything is God.

Paranormal (NA)—adjective describing phenomena that cannot be explained by natural or scientific laws.

Parapsychology (NA)—field of study seeking evidence for telepathy, clairvoyance, and psychokinesis.

Past-life regression (NA)—see **Hypnotic regression**.

Pioneer (JW)—a Jehovah's Witness who has committed to putting in a large number of monthly hours going door-to-door. "Auxiliary pioneers" serve 60 hours a month; "regular pioneers" serve 90 hours a month; and "special pioneers" serve 120 hours a month.

Practitioner (CS)—a person who devotes his or her time to the work of Christian Science healing and has no other occupation. Practitioners give mental treatments for people who call on them in time of need; they are paid for these treatments.

Principle (CS)—one of Mary Baker Eddy's terms for God (see **Divine Mind**).

Prophet or prophetess (NA)—one who is able to foretell future events; a spiritual seer.

Psychic (NA)—one who is sensitive to, and perceptive of, supernatural forces; a medium who possesses abilities not normal to the natural world.

Psychic healing (NA)—the direction of "healing energy" to individuals by psychics who lay on hands for the purpose of healing.

Psychic reading (NA)—a consultation between a psychic and a client in which the psychic uses extrasensory perception to "read" and reveal hidden issues and solutions pertaining to a problem faced by the client.

Psychic surgery (NA)—associated mainly with Brazil and the Philippines, this is the supposed ability of the hands of a spiritualist "healer" to magically enter a patient's body, remove diseased tissue, and have the incision heal instantly as the psychic surgeon's hands are withdrawn.

Psychokinesis (NA)—the ability to move physical objects by using only the power of the mind.

Psychosynthesis (NA)—a New Age personal-development program developed by Roberto Assagioli, M.D., which is a form of psychotherapy focusing on spiritual evolution as a means of achieving healing and wholeness of being.

Pyramidology (NA)—the philosophical idea that precise geometric measurements and alignments of pyramids, especially that of Cheops, can be used to produce an inexplicable electromagnetic field, force, or energy.

Readers (CS)—three-year term of office for those who conduct Sunday services and present readings from the Bible and from the writings of Mrs. Eddy. One man and one woman are selected by the board of directors to be Readers at the Mother Church; two Readers (who are also members of the Mother Church) serve at the local level.

Reflexology (NA)—manipulation or massage of areas of the feet to affect the rest of the body.

Reincarnation (NA)—the belief that when an individual dies, he or she may return to life on earth in a new body, either animal or human.

Science and Health with Key to the Scriptures **(CS)**—book by Mary Baker Eddy: textbook that, along with her other writings, is studied by Christian Scientists as the final word on what they believe. First published in 1875 but revised many times.

Self-hypnosis (NA)—the act of putting oneself into an altered state of consciousness by means of a deep trance or sleeplike state.

Service overseer (JW)—local Jehovah's Witness elder assigned to supervise door-to-door work in the congregation.

Society (JW)—shortened term typically used by Jehovah's Witnesses to refer to their Brooklyn headquarters organization, the Watchtower Bible and Tract Society of New York, Inc., and related corporations.

Spell (NA)—an uttered word or form of words said to have magic power (see **incantations**).

Spirit guide (NA)—a "familiar" spirit who resides in a medium and provides the medium with information to be sought through divination (revealing of past and future events).

Spiritism (NA)—phenomena shown through such things as extrasensory perception, apparitions, and spiritist cults.

Sunday school (CS)—instruction for Christian Scientists under the age of twenty only; held every Sunday concurrently with the church service.

Tarot cards (NA)—cards containing occult symbols, used in divination.

Telepathy (NA)—communication that is supernaturally conveyed from one mind to another.

Therapeutic touch (NA)—an occultic healing method derived from the ancient Hindu principle of *prana* (vital energy force of life), believed to realign energy for healing and health.

Treatment (CS)—the mental process of "knowing the truth" that only God and his reflection (man) exist and that, since God is good and is spiritual, man and all else is good and spiritual. In a "treatment," sickness, sin, disease, and death are declared unreal.

Trinity (JW)—doctrine denied by Jehovah's Witnesses, but which summarizes the Bible's revelation that the Father is God, the Son is God, and the Holy Spirit is God—and yet God is one.

Truth (JW)—whatever the Watchtower Society teaches.

Visualization (NA)—(see **Guided imagery**) the process by which one can through an altered state of consciousness create reality. Based on a Hindu concept that *maya*, or illusion, is universal—what we see (reality) is a figment of the imagination, and what we cannot see (spirituality) is the true reality.

White magic (NA)—voodoo, shamanism, New Age "glamour"; the female principle of occultic forces used for supposed benevolent purposes; in reality, a form of sorcery used to cast spells and bring about changes in the natural world.

Witness (JW)—a person recognized as a fellow-Witness only if he or she has been baptized by the Watchtower organization and is active in its works program.

Watchtower, The **(JW)**—magazine first published in 1879 by Pastor Charles Taze Russell; see also **Society**, his publishing organization and Jehovah's Witness headquarters.

Wizard (NA)—a spiritistic medium with supernatural wisdom derived from the spirit that inhabits his or her body.

White Brotherhood of Masters (NA)—see **Masters**.

Yin/Yang (NA)—an astrologically based belief system in which *yin* (lunar) and *yang* (solar) cause the energy or life-force (*Ch'i*) to flow through one's body.

Zodiac (NA)—the use for astrological purposes of the twelve imaginary horoscope "signs" or constellations (see **Astrology chart**).

Table of Contents

Introduction

The greatest adventure we face as human beings is to explore the meaning of life. Questions like "Where does the universe come from?" and "Is there a God?" and "What happens to us when we die?" challenge us to think, love, and live. It is the conviction of Catholic Christians that the answers to these questions are found most surely in Jesus Christ. This book has been written to explain how Catholics try to follow Jesus in thinking about the meaning of our existence, in loving God and neighbor, and in experiencing life as a beautiful gift from God.

I have tried to be faithful to authentic Catholic teaching as it is rooted in Scripture and sacred tradition. Bible passages are quoted frequently; and the documents of the Second Vatican Council, while not quoted directly, provide the foundation for the development of each chapter.

This book is intended for those who are interested in joining the Catholic Church and for Catholics who wish to increase their understanding of their faith. It can be useful for adult religious education classes, RCIA programs, Catholic high school and CCD religious classes, college classes, discussion groups, and private study. I have tried to make it long enough to provide a survey of the important aspects of Catholicism but brief enough to allow busy people to read it in a reasonable amount of time.

Our study of Catholicism should help us to know about Christ and to know Christ. Religious education is a matter not only of the head but also of the heart. It is important to learn as much about Jesus and his Church as possible, but our study should also help us to know Jesus as our Savior, our Friend, our Lord and our God, to commit our lives to him, and to be active members of his Church.

This book has been developed out of my experiences of more than twenty years as a priest and teacher of adult religious education classes. I am indebted to the Daughters of Charity, who taught me in grade school; to the seminary professors who prepared me for ordination to the priesthood and to the authors who have helped form my understanding of Jesus Christ and his Church, especially those listed in the bibliography. Down through the years I have used material from many sources in my teaching and preaching, material that finds expression in this book. If any source has not been properly acknowledged, I apologize.

I want to express my gratitude to Father Patrick Kaler, C.SS.R., Father David Polek, C.SS.R., Jean Larkin, Cecelia Portlock, and to the editorial staff at Liguori Publications for their assistance and support. I am grateful to Jim and Toni Walters, who first encouraged me to write for Liguori; to Paul and Carol Berens, who proofread most of the original manuscript; to my Vincentian confreres and to priests of the diocese of Springfield-Cape Girardeau who helped with advice and suggestions; to the parishioners at St. Denis Church in Benton, Missouri, especially those who attended the "pilot project" class for this book; to the members of Most Precious Blood Church in Denver, Colorado, and St. Vincent de Paul Church in Cape Girardeau, Missouri; to the Cape Girardeau "discussion group"; and to my family. May God bless you all!

I pray that this book may help people come to a deeper understanding of the teachings of the Catholic Church; to put their faith in God the Father, Son, and Holy Spirit; and to commit their lives to Jesus Christ. "And this is my prayer: that your love may increase ever more and more in knowledge and every kind of perception, to discern what is of value, so that you may be pure and blameless for the day of Christ" (Philippians 1:9-10).

Father Oscar Lukefahr, C.M.

CHAPTER ONE

Our World and Our God

How did our universe come to be? When did life begin? Is there a God? Could everything have come from nothing? Is there a meaning or purpose to life? How can we find true happiness? What happens to us when we die? These are the most basic questions that face us as human beings, and people have wondered about them for ages.

Ancient cave drawings and burial sites indicate that early humans believed in deities and in an afterlife. Today, polls show that most human beings believe in God and in eternal life. But some people believe there is no God, no purpose to life, and no life after death. We believe in God or in "nothing" as the ultimate reality. In spite of scientific advances, we still must "believe."

The Need to Believe

Why must we believe? Some knowledge can be obtained through our senses or by scientific investigation. We don't have to believe that apples are red. We can see that. We don't have to believe that water is made up of two parts of hydrogen and one part of oxygen. We can establish that by scientific investigation.

But the knowledge essential in life and the answers to questions about ultimate reality can be acquired only by faith. For example, psychologists say that to be happy we must love and be loved. We cannot prove scientifically that others love us. We must either believe it or go through life without love. We'll never be able to put love under a microscope, but we can see that believing in love is worthwhile because love enriches our lives. The emptiness of a loveless life and the joy of a love-filled life demonstrate that love is real.

So it is with faith in God. We can't put God under a microscope. (If we could, God would be just a part of our limited material world.) We can't have scientific proof that God exists and is the origin of the universe. On the other hand, we can't have scientific proof that nothing is behind the universe because we can't put nothing under a microscope either! Ultimately, we must believe in God or in nothing.

Reasons for Belief in God

If we choose to believe in God rather than nothing, what are the reasons? Many have been given, and we will focus on three of them.

The first is that the universe must come either from a God who put it into being or it must come from nothing. There are no other alternatives. To most human beings it is more reasonable to believe that the universe comes from Someone than to believe that it comes from nothing. If there is no Creator, why does anything exist? A philosophical argument puts it this way: "Why is there something rather than nothing? The universe as we know it exists without a sufficient reason for existing. Its only sufficient reason must be in Another, a Being beyond the world, supernatural, namely God."

The second reason is built around the laws of chance. Chance means that something occurs without intention or cause. For example, if I take ten coins dated 1971 to 1980 and try to draw 1971 without searching for it, I depend on chance. If so, the "odds" are ten to one. If I try to draw 1971 and 1972 in order, the odds jump to one hundred to one (assuming that I return each coin after it is drawn). The odds against pulling out 1971 to 1980 in order are ten billion to one! What would the odds be that the whole universe could have been formed by accident, by chance? Truly incredible! If there were no God, everything would have to be an accident. Few people would bet that anyone could drop a bomb on a junkyard and produce a *Boeing 747* or throw a stick of dynamite into a print shop and create Webster's dictionary! But the odds for this happening are better than the odds of producing an entire universe by accident. That is why some thinkers feel that it is reasonable to believe in God from the laws of chance alone.

The third reason has to do with us. Nothing in this world can bring us complete happiness. Life doesn't make sense unless we are moving toward a God who will give us what we long for. As Saint Augustine said: "You have made us for yourself, O Lord, and our hearts are restless until they rest in you." We have a hunger deep inside that this world cannot fill because it is meant to be filled by God. Further, belief in God makes sense because it brings out the best in us. When we see how belief in God is the foundation of the beautiful lives of people like Mother Teresa of Calcutta, we realize that it makes us better than we would be otherwise. We can be fully human only when we believe in God.

So just as we make a choice to accept love, so we make a decision to accept belief in God. As a life without love is shriveled and weak, so a life without belief in God is hollow and empty. As love enriches life, so faith in God enriches life. It is reasonable to believe in God. And when we say, "We believe in God," we are making a positive statement about life and about ourselves. Life has meaning because it comes from God. We are not accidents but God's children. Faith in God is a positive stance which can only enrich our lives as human beings.

Belief in God
for the Twentieth Century

While the reasons for belief in God can be quite convincing, many believers are troubled by doubt or by the skepticism of non-believers. Doubt can arise when we reflect on the evil in the world. The horrors of modern warfare, the sufferings of victims of cancer and other illnesses, the catastrophe of an earthquake can make us wonder why, if there is a good God, such things can happen. Skeptics can mock believers with the notion that a "truly enlightened intellectual" couldn't believe in such a "medieval" notion as God.

Evil and suffering do raise difficult questions about the existence of God. In our time these questions are perhaps more evident than ever because of modern communications; war, sickness, and natural disasters are brought into our living rooms via television. On the other hand, our ability to answer these questions is enhanced by modern Scripture scholarship and by a better understanding of human freedom and the laws of nature. In later chapters we will explore these issues. Here we simply acknowledge that evil and suffering are a part of human life. They raise the most difficult objections to belief that we encounter. In fact, if there were no evil, no suffering, there would perhaps be no unbelief! But we must recall also that great believers have faced up to the worst possible evils and have experienced the presence and strength of God. Maximilian Kolbe in a Nazi concentration camp during World War II suffered torture, degradation, and death; through it all he believed in a good God, and he brought that belief to others who were suffering with him.

Suffering may raise difficult questions, but it need not destroy belief in God. Kolbe and all the martyrs testify that God becomes more present as suffering intensifies. And if believers have to answer the question, "If God exists, why is there evil in the universe?" then nonbelievers must answer a far more difficult question, "If there is no God, why is there good in the universe?"

As to the objection that truly intelligent people couldn't believe, the fact is that many intellectuals and scientists do believe in God. Some of the most brilliant individuals of modern times, like author C.S. Lewis and philosopher Mortimer Adler, have professed belief in God and have written books explaining their belief. There is no statement less enlightened than the one which says that intelligent people do not believe in God!

What is more, the arguments for believing in the existence of God have, if anything, been strengthened by the discoveries of recent years. Prior to the twentieth century most people thought that the universe was limited to the few thousand stars visible in the nighttime sky. Even astronomers had only vague ideas about the nature of our Milky Way galaxy and were uncertain if other galaxies might exist. That such a small and relatively uncomplicated universe could come about by accident might seem at least remotely possible.

But what was thought to be the universe proved to be only a tiny speck of it. Using tools like radio telescopes, scientists have discovered that the universe is incredibly vast. Astronomers use light-years as a measure of the universe. A light-second is the distance light travels in one second: 186,282 miles. A light-year is the distance light travels in one year: about six trillion miles! We can gain some insight into the distances involved when we reflect that our moon is less than two light-seconds away, 240,000 miles, and that the universe is perhaps forty billion light-years across! The star closest to our own sun, Alpha Centauri, is "only" 4.3 light-years away. Yet if astronauts traveled in today's fastest spaceship to Alpha Centauri, it would take one hundred thousand years to arrive! Once there, they would have taken only the first step in our galaxy, which contains about two hundred billion stars! They would still have the rest of the galaxies in our universe to explore — one hundred billion or so of them! They would encounter brilliant quasars and black holes with gravitational fields so strong that light is pulled into them and space and time are distorted. They would discover galaxies organized into huge structures awesome in their order, gigantic building blocks for our amazing universe.

If our age has uncovered the vastness of the universe, it has also discovered the almost infinite "smallness" of the atom. Scientists have found that everything in the universe is built of incredibly small particles which are as highly organized as the universe. Using electron microscopes, they have found, for example, that the dot of an "i" on this page contains perhaps a million ink molecules. These, in turn, are formed of atoms, each made up of a nucleus surrounded by electrons which whirl around it. The nucleus is made up of protons and neutrons, combinations of yet smaller particles called quarks, and electrons are only one class of subatomic particles called leptons. There is a galaxy in the dot of an "i"!

Every breath we take contains trillions of atoms. We live on a planet surrounded by trillions of stars. We could spend an eternity trying to grasp the smallness of the atomic building blocks of the universe or the vastness of the whole picture. And we would still be left in awe.

If there is no God, all of this must come from nothing! All of its organization must be an accident! If we sometimes find it hard to believe in God, then we should try to believe in nothing. Believers in God are sometimes mocked with the notion that they are putting faith in a fairy tale. On the contrary, there is no fairy tale more incredible than that the universe — infinite in its smallness and in its vastness, astonishing in its structure and organization — could come from nothing! The more we know of the magnificence of the universe, the more we are drawn to believe that it must have a Master Architect to design it and a Creator to build it.

As we take a good look at ourselves, small creatures on a small planet in a small solar system in a small galaxy in our vast universe, we discover that we have within us a desire to come to know the One who made us. Doctors and psychologists have learned that our bodies react in a positive or negative way to certain emotions. Fear, self-pity, and despair release chemicals into our systems that can poison us. Faith, hope, love, and peace can make us healthier.

Two people are standing at the grave of a loved one. The first says, "There is no God. I will never see my friend again. Soon I will die and that will be the end of everything." The second says, "God has received my friend into his care. When I die, we will be together again. God loves us, and death brings us to eternal life." The first individual is experiencing feelings likely to cause the release of chemicals harmful to the human body; the second is experiencing feelings that promote health. It is almost as if even our bodies are telling us that we are made for belief in God!

From Now to Yesterday

So it is reasonable to believe in God, now more than ever! And while our faith is suitable for today, it is not new. We who believe have a family history. Our tradition stretches across the centuries to a man called Abraham, to a people called the Israelites. Their efforts to come to know God and to believe in him are recorded in the "family album" we call the Bible. It is to the Bible we now turn in order to explore our roots, to gain a better understanding of our beliefs, and so to strengthen our faith.

Questions for Discussion or Reflection

When have you felt closest to God? When have you experienced the most serious doubts about God's existence? Which of the reasons for belief in God seem most convincing to you? Are there other reasons for belief that are important to you?

Activity

Read chapter 43 of the Old Testament Book of Sirach. Spend a few minutes reflecting on this chapter; then read it again as a prayer of praise to God. Close your eyes and think about the universe as astronomers now describe it to us. Picture yourself from some vantage point in space: You are a tiny human being on a tiny planet in the vastness of the universe. Thank and praise God for creation. Ask God to help you know that his greatness includes the ability to pay attention to you and to love you!

CHAPTER TWO

Our Religious Tradition

W hen we reflect on the magnificence of the universe, we can only wonder at how great its Maker must be. As we are dazzled by the marvel of created things, we realize the wisest of us can have only the faintest notion of their Creator. So it is not surprising that human beings have had many diverse opinions about God and have developed many different religious traditions.

Some of these have placed limits on God and have stated that God has weaknesses and cannot satisfy our hopes for perfect happiness. But the Creator of our universe is infinite. Nothing about God is "too good to be true."

The Judeo-Christian Religious Tradition

One religious tradition has placed no limits on the greatness of God or on God's ability to fulfill our dreams, the Judeo-Christian tradition.

It begins with Abram, a native of Ur, an ancient city north of the Persian Gulf. In about 1900 B.C., Abram's family migrated to Haran, a city near the present-day Turkish-Syrian border. (All dates in this chapter are B.C. unless otherwise noted.) In Haran, Abram received a call from God to move to Canaan, present-day Palestine. God made a "covenant" (an agreement) with Abram, changing his name to Abraham and promising that he and his wife, Sarah, would have a son, the first in a long line of descendants. They did have a son, Isaac, who in turn became the father of Jacob. Jacob had twelve sons and with them migrated sometime after 1750 to Egypt, where their descendants, the Hebrews, became slaves.

About 1250 a Hebrew named Moses heard God commanding him to lead his people to freedom in the land of Canaan, the Promised Land. After escaping, the Hebrews (who became known as Israelites and later as Jews) wandered about in the desert for forty years. Moses died on the border of the Promised Land, and his lieutenant, Joshua, led the people into Canaan. There followed a period of conquest, with the twelve tribes (divisions of the Hebrew people named after the sons of Jacob) settling in various parts of Canaan. They fought with the inhabitants (Philistines and others) through a long "frontier period" called the time of the Judges.

About 1020 Saul, a member of the tribe of Benjamin, began to bring the tribes together and was named king. He eventually went insane and was killed in a battle with the Philistines. Into the breach stepped a young military leader, David. Beginning about 1000, David united the tribes, set up Jerusalem as the center of his government, defeated the enemies of the Israelites, and made Israel a force to be reckoned with in the Middle East. His son, Solomon, succeeded him as king and built a magnificent temple in Jerusalem. But in his later years Solomon became involved in the worship of false gods and alienated the people with heavy taxes and forced labor. Solomon's son, Rehoboam, continued these policies, and in 927 a civil war split the people into two kingdoms — Israel in the north with its capital in Samaria, and Judah in the south with its capital in Jerusalem.

Both kingdoms were plagued by poor leadership and by the people's unfaithfulness to God. In 721 the northern kingdom was attacked by Assyria; its leading citizens were slaughtered or dragged into exile. Other captives from foreign lands were brought into Israel by the Assyrians; they intermarried with the few Israelites who had been left behind, forming the people known as the Samaritans. In 587 the southern kingdom was conquered by the Babylonians. Jerusalem was sacked, its walls destroyed, and its temple demolished. The survivors were taken into exile in Babylon.

A few decades later Cyrus, the king of Persia, conquered Babylon. He allowed the Israelites to return to their homeland in 539. Those who returned to Judah found their land devastated, their homes destroyed, and Jerusalem a heap of ruins. Harassed on every side by enemies, they managed to build a temple about 515 and to rebuild the city walls, completing the task in 445. Their hopes of regaining the glory of King David were doomed to disappointment.

Alexander the Great conquered Palestine in 332. After his death, Egypt and Syria vied for control of the Jewish nation, and in 200 the Syrians launched a terrible persecution of the Jews. In 167 a family of warriors, the Maccabees, led a revolt against the Syrians and succeeded in gaining a measure of independence in 135. This lasted until 63 when the Romans, under Pompey, conquered Jerusalem and made Palestine a vassal state. In 39 Herod the Great was set up by the Romans as king. A man who committed many horrible atrocities, he was also a tireless builder, constructing fortresses, palaces, and a magnificent temple which outshone that of Solomon. It was under his rule that Jesus Christ was born.

Not a very impressive history! Except for a brief period under King David, the Israelite nation had little political or military influence. But somehow they kept their belief in the God of Abraham. Somehow they kept alive a hope that God would intervene in history by sending a Savior. When God did send that Savior, there were Israelites ready to welcome him.

The Bible — Origin, Nature, and Interpretation

Throughout the history of the Israelite people, there were those who were inspired to record their experience of God. History and stories, poetry and preaching, laws and legends, proverbs and prophecy, were passed on from generation to generation. These inspired writings were recognized by spiritual leaders as revelations from God and cherished as God's own Word.

They have come down to us as the books of the Old Testament. Catholics recognize forty-six Old Testament books as divinely inspired, that is, as having God as their Author. This does not mean that God dictated the books, but that he guided the human authors to write in such a way that the books teach religious truth. The human authors played an important part, and we can understand the message of the inspired books only when we have some awareness of who wrote them, when and why they were written, and what the authors intended to convey.

This approach to the Bible is called the "contextual" approach. It means that we must have the context of any given passage if we are to understand it. Another approach to the Bible is the "fundamentalist," which states that the words of the Bible must be taken only at face value: If the words say that Jonah was swallowed by a fish and lived in its belly for three days, then such an event occurred. The contextual approach would lead us to study when, where, why, and by whom the book was written and so arrive at the conclusion that Jonah is a parable designed to teach that God loves all nations.

Some people are frightened by the contextual approach and feel that it leads us to treat the whole Bible as a fable. This is not the case. There is history in the Bible, as well as parables, laws, poetry, songs, and many other forms of writing, each of which can teach religious truth in its own way.

We shouldn't be surprised at this because we use the contextual approach every day. For example, any newspaper has the front-page news, editorials, sports, comics, classifieds, and advertisements, and we understand each differently. On the front page we might read the words, "An armed guard gunned down robbers as he tried to steal the company payroll." On the sports page we might read, "The Cincinnati catcher gunned down the St. Louis left fielder as he tried to steal second base." The same words are used, but they have a very different meaning! We don't have any difficulty understanding them (at least if we know something about baseball) because we are aware of the context of each sentence. On the other hand, if we took the second sentence in a fundamentalist fashion, we might be misled to suppose that baseball is a very violent sport!

Learning to read the Bible intelligently is something like reading the newspaper. But because the Bible was written so long ago, in a different culture, we must become acquainted with the "context" of its books. Most Catholic Bibles have introductions that present the information needed, and there are many fine books available to make Bible reading easy, enjoyable, and beneficial.

Reading the Bible

Another important thing to remember in reading the Bible is that its various books are not organized according to subject matter or chronology. Therefore, it's not best to start on page one and try to read straight through. Many people who do this find themselves bogged down in difficult passages and become discouraged. Readers should first become familiar with the "whole picture," then they can read the Bible with understanding.

Someone who is investigating the Judeo-Christian tradition for the first time and is handed a Bible might be compared to a refugee from a war-torn country who is being adopted into a family. Such a person might be told, "We want you to feel at home, so we are giving you copies of all the documents that relate to our family. Look through them and you'll discover what we are like." The documents might include genealogies, blueprints for the family home, stories told by grandparents, letters written by family members to one another, songs used at family gatherings, and so on. The individual might browse through these documents and find some to be very helpful and others of limited usefulness. Family letters might be essential in giving insight about the love and care of family members for one another. Blueprints, on the other hand, might not be all that interesting, unless the individual being adopted happened to be an architect!

Some parts of the Bible are very important to any believer. The Psalms are frequently used in private prayer and public worship. Some parts of the Book of Numbers, with long lists of names and places, might be of interest only to specialists. Once we become familiar with the general structure of the Bible and do some "sampling," we can find those passages which will be most helpful.

A Global View of the Old Testament

Geographers today bemoan the fact that many people have little knowledge of our world. Some Americans are not familiar with the geography of North America, much less that of other continents. Yet knowledge of the earth and of the interrelationship of its parts is crucial to our survival: the burning of the rain forests in Brazil could bring about the melting of polar icecaps and the flooding of New York. We should gain at least a general awareness of the globe, then become more acquainted with our own country.

Similarly, many Christians have little knowledge of the "geography" of the Bible, which is as essential to our spiritual survival as knowledge of the globe is to our physical survival. We need some understanding of the Bible as a whole — a global view. This global view can come through an awareness of the main categories of books in the Bible, of their content, and of when they were written.

Such a "view" is presented in the following pages. The categories follow those given in *The New American Bible*. The books of the Bible are listed in the order in which they are found in the Scriptures.

The Pentateuch

The Pentateuch (from the Greek words for "five" and "books") is the collection of the first five books of the Bible. It includes Genesis, Exodus, Leviticus, Numbers, and Deuteronomy. The Pentateuch is meant to answer the basic questions in life and to explain the origins of the Jewish people. Like many other parts of the Bible, the Pentateuch was not written at one time by one author. Rather, it includes traditions, stories, and historical data passed on by word of mouth from generation to generation, put into written collections from about 1000 to 550, and then edited into its present form between 500 and 400.

Genesis reflects the Jewish belief that God created the world and that the world is good. Evil is a result of human sinfulness. When people sin, God calls them back through covenants, inviting them to obedient and loving service. Genesis introduces Abraham, the "Father" of all who believe in the true God. *Exodus* recounts the story of the birth of the Jewish nation as the Hebrews are called out of slavery under the leadership of Moses. *Leviticus* stresses the holy nature of God's people. *Numbers* describes the organization of the Jewish nation. *Deuteronomy*, largely in the form of a sermon attributed to Moses, shows the spirit of love and obedience which should characterize the people of the covenant.

The Historical Books

These books cover the period from the entry of the Israelites into the Promised Land in about 1225 to the end of the Maccabean wars in about 135. They are not to be equated with modern history, for ancient historians did not have printing, videorecorders, and telephones. They did not achieve the accuracy we expect from modern historians and often were not concerned about it. Their primary purpose was to teach the story of the encounter of God and humankind, and their works are called "salvation history" to distinguish them from modern history. Nevertheless, the Bible contains much accurate historical data, and many of the names, places, and events have been verified from other sources.

The *Book of Joshua* continues the story of the Israelite people after the death of Moses. Led into the Promised Land by Joshua, they warred against the inhabitants and established footholds throughout Palestine. *Judges* describes the time after Joshua's death a two-hundred-year-long "frontier" period of war and settlement under leaders called "judges." *Ruth* is a beautiful story about love and loyalty in the life of one of King David's ancestors who lived in that frontier period.

The *First* and *Second Books of Samuel* tell about the last judges, Eli and Samuel, and relate how the Israelites were united in 1025 under Saul, their first king. They then describe the troubled relationship of Saul and David, and the long reign of King David. *First* and *Second Kings* take up the story of David's old age, describe how he was succeeded by Solomon, and explain the long decline of the Jewish people that began after David's death. Significant events of this period were the split of Israel into north and south — the fall of the north to Assyria and that of the south to Babylonia. The *First* and *Second Book of Chronicles* are mostly a theologically oriented repetition of material in the Books of Kings.

The *Books of Ezra* and *Nehemiah* cover the return of the Israelites from exile in Babylon and the rebuilding of the Jerusalem temple and walls. *Tobit, Judith,* and *Esther* are the sort of literature we might call "historical novels." They are stories set during the exile and restoration that teach trust, courage, care for others, and the importance of remaining faithful to God.

The *First Book of Maccabees* contains the account of Israel's heroic resistance to the persecution of Antiochus IV, a Syrian king who attempted to abolish Jewish religious practices between 171 and 164, and of the struggle for independence waged by the Jews down to 135. The *Second Book of Maccabees* relates in more detail events already narrated in First Maccabees.

The Wisdom Books

These books are an inspired search into the meaning of life. Using poetry and proverbs, sayings and songs, they face the problems of our origin and destiny, human suffering, good and evil, right and wrong. They deal with homely everyday situations and with the most critical issues of life and death.

The *Book of Job* is a great poem written around 500. It attacks the theory that all suffering is sent by God as punishment for sin and concludes that we cannot give easy answers to the riddle of suffering. Suffering does not separate us from God, and his presence can help us accept and overcome it.

The *Book of Psalms* is a collection of one hundred and fifty prayers in the form of Hebrew poetry. Most were written in the years between King David and the restoration after the Babylonian exile. They address every human emotion and situation, and vary greatly in style, length, and approach. As Hebrew poetry, they depend on the balance of thoughts rather than on rhyme. A good way to use the psalms is to read through them, keeping a list of those that are meaningful for private prayer and reflection.

The *Book of Proverbs* is a collection of wise sayings. The oldest ones date back to the time of Solomon (970) and the newest to about 400. They cover every subject imaginable, from down-to-earth worldly wisdom to lofty theological reflection. *Ecclesiastes* is a book that points out the limitations of human life and the difficulty of knowing its meaning. The author, unaware of the reality of eternal life, advised his readers to live a moral, balanced life, without expecting too much happiness. Written about 300, it demonstrates our need for the wisdom only Christ can give. The *Song of Songs* is a dramatic poem praising the beauty of human love. Created about 300, it is seen by many commentators as symbolic of the love God has for people. *Wisdom* may be the last book of the Old Testament to have been written. Composed around 75, it presents a philosophical reflection on the meaning of Hebrew history and expresses belief in eternal life. *Sirach* (called in some Bibles Ecclesiasticus), written around 180, is a book similar to Proverbs. It organizes sayings according to subject matter on topics from table etiquette to religious worship.

The Prophets

Many people think of prophets as those who foretell the future. Prophets in the Bible, however, are those who "speak for God," and the prophets were primarily concerned with their own contemporary situations.

The official leaders of the northern and southern kingdoms often failed to give the people proper guidance; as a result, both leaders and common folk turned away from God. The prophets condemned the leaders and warned the people of terrible judgment if they did not return to God. When both kingdoms were destroyed, the prophets encouraged the exiles to turn back to God and hope for a better future, a future which promised a "Messiah," a savior from God.

The *Book of Isaiah* was composed by several authors. The first thirty-nine chapters come from the prophet Isaiah (740-687); mindful of God's holiness, he tried to bring Judah back to the Lord. Chapters 40-55 were written by an unknown poet during the Babylonian captivity (586-539) and are noted for the Suffering Servant passages foretelling a Messiah who would suffer for his people. Chapters 56-66 contain poems by unknown prophets who wrote in the spirit of Isaiah. *Jeremiah* (626-585) presents the sermons of a great man who prophesied in Judah during its collapse. It gives much autobiographical data remarkable for its honesty and depth of feeling. *Lamentations* is a collection of poems on the misery caused by the destruction of Jerusalem and the exile (587). *Baruch* is a meditation on the exile and a prayer for forgiveness and restoration; it was written long after the exile, as late as 200. *Ezekiel* (597-550) used dramatic visions, symbolic actions, and picturesque language to encourage the people to be faithful to God during the Babylonian exile. *Daniel* takes its name from its hero rather than its author, who is unknown. It was written around 165 as an "apocalypse," a common literary form from 200 B.C. to A.D. 200, characterized by figurative language, visions, symbols, and stories designed to teach that God cares for his people, even in persecution. *Hosea* (750) comes from a prophet in the northern kingdom; his marriage to an unfaithful wife and his willingness to take her back represent God's relationship to the unfaithful Israelites. *Joel* is an apocalyptic work composed about 400, using a terrible plague of locusts as a symbol of impending judgment. *Amos* (750) gives the life, times, and prophecies of a shepherd from Judah who prophesied in Israel during a time of prosperity. He warns that Israel will be punished for its injustice toward the poor and oppressed. *Obadiah* (475) is a short, harsh condemnation of the people of Edom who harassed the Jews after they returned from exile in Babylon. *Jonah* (450) is a parable rather than a prophecy. It is meant to show God's love and mercy toward all people, even pagans. The author of *Micah* (725-697) was a prophet who condemned the corrupt leaders of Samaria and Jerusalem and promised that a ruler would be born in Bethlehem who would bring restoration and peace. *Nahum* (612) is a song of joy at the destruction of Nineveh, the capital of Assyria, the savage nation which had destroyed Israel and ravaged Judah. *Habakkuk* (600) foretold that Babylon would conquer Judah but that God would use the occasion to purify his people and restore the covenant. *Zephaniah* (620-600) prophesied judgment against Jerusalem at a time when many Jews had gone over to pagan worship. The book looks forward to better days when God's people would respond to his love and mercy. *Haggai* (520) encouraged the Jews who had returned from exile in Babylon to rebuild the temple and to trust in God. *Zechariah* (520), through a series of visions, also urged the returning exiles to rebuild the temple. The second part of the book was written by unknown authors and foretells the coming of the Prince of Peace. *Malachi* (450) is the last book in the Old Testament (though not the last to be written). It shows the need for constant reform and looks forward to the coming of the Messiah.

From Good to Bad to Hope for Better

The Old Testament begins in Genesis with a clear statement that all God creates is good. It teaches that human beings bring evil into the world through sin. The Old Testament ends with the hope that evil can be overcome by good: God will send a prophet before the final day to bring about conversion (Malachi 3:23-24).

The Old Testament is as honest a presentation of the human condition as can be found. Life as we experience it is neither all good nor all bad. And in the worst of times, most people are able to find hope for the future — usually with an awareness that "doom" is possible if we repeat the mistakes of the past.

The people of the Old Testament are just like us. We see the foolish mistakes and the sins of their political and religious leaders repeated in the follies of some of the political and religious leaders of our day. Samson and Delilah, Saul, David and Bathsheba, Solomon — all have parallels in our time, and in every age. We see the faith of Abraham and the courage of Moses in people of today who put their trust in God and serve him. We see ourselves in page after page of the Old Testament as we seek out the good in life and turn away from the bad. We find reason to hope in the future because the hopes of the Jewish people for a Messiah have been fulfilled — in Jesus Christ.

Questions for Discussion or Reflection

Have you read the Old Testament? If not, what have been the obstacles? When you read the Bible or hear it, do you consciously think of it as God speaking to you? A retreat master asked: "When you stand before God at your judgment, what will be your response when God asks you, 'How did you like my Book?' " What will be *your* response if God asks you this question?

Activity

Open your Bible and page through the Old Testament. Note the main categories of books and their length. Read a few introductions. Read some passages you are familiar with. Choose a book; read it from start to finish. Ask God to give you a great love for his Word and a real sense of belonging to the Judeo-Christian family, with its rich heritage, history, and traditions.

Reflect: You have just been adopted into God's family. Jesus stands before you, gives you the Bible, and says, "I want you to feel at home, so I am giving you all the documents that relate to our family. Look through them and you'll learn what we are like." Take the Bible from his hands, then sit quietly and observe your feelings. Talk to Jesus about them.

CHAPTER THREE

Jesus Enters
Our Tradition

The Jews who lived in Palestine during the last years of the reign of King Herod the Great (37-4 B.C.) hoped for better things. Senior citizens could remember how the Roman general Pompey had conquered Jerusalem in 63 B.C. The glory days of David were almost a thousand years in the past. People wondered, as they worshiped in the beautiful temple built by Herod, if there would ever be another David, as the prophets had foretold.

While the Jews were proud of their new temple, most of them resented Herod. He was a puppet of Rome, a master of intrigue, ruthless in putting down opposition. The situation in Palestine was tense, and there seemed to be little chance of getting rid of Herod or the Romans.

Some Jews in positions of wealth and power had adjusted to the presence of the Romans and cooperated with them. They were the *Sadducees*. Most of them were in the priestly class; they followed only the Torah, the written law. They did not believe in life after death, and their hopes were that peace and prosperity might prevail in this life. Other Jews, relatively few in number, hoped that God would send a Messiah to lead the Israelites to "a military" victory over the Romans. These were the *Zealots*. Still others neither collaborated with the Romans nor fought against them. They centered their lives on observing the written law and thousands of other detailed prescriptions handed down as oral tradition. They believed in eternal life and hoped for a heavenly reward. These were the *Pharisees*. There were those who looked for peace in the desert, forming communities that practiced elaborate rituals. They hoped that their devotion would call down a Messiah who would lead them to heavenly glory. These were the *Essenes*.

The common people must have been influenced to some degree by all these groups. They met in their synagogues to hear the Scriptures and must have wondered how prophecies of a conquering Messiah could be reconciled with those of a Suffering Servant. How could Psalm 72:8 talk about a victorious Messiah and Isaiah 53:5 speak of this same person as being "pierced for our offenses"?

They pondered what Jeremiah could have meant when he said, "The days are coming, says the LORD, when I will make a new covenant with the house of Israel and the house of Judah" (Jeremiah 31:31). No one could have imagined the answer which lay hidden in the mind of God and that was now about to unfold.

The New Covenant

God had plans that far surpassed all human hopes. God knew what no one could imagine, that the new covenant would change the course of human history because God would become a member of the human family.

And so, toward the end of King Herod's reign, God sent the angel Gabriel to Mary, a young woman of Nazareth in Galilee in the northern part of Palestine. Gabriel announced that Mary, engaged to a carpenter named Joseph, would have a child, the Son of God, by the power of the Holy Spirit. When Mary consented, "the Word became flesh and made his dwelling among us" (John 1:14). Mary soon left to visit her cousins Elizabeth and Zechariah who were expecting a child, though Elizabeth seemed past her childbearing years. Three months later Mary returned to Nazareth. When Joseph discovered that she was pregnant, he decided to end the engagement quietly. But an angel explained that Mary had conceived her Child by the Holy Spirit, and Joseph took Mary as his wife.

Shortly thereafter they had to go to Bethlehem to register for a census mandated by the Roman emperor. While they were there, Mary gave birth to her Son, named Jesus at his circumcision. When Jesus was presented at the Temple in Jerusalem, he was recognized as the Messiah by two elderly Jews, Simeon and Anna. He was honored with gifts by the magi from the East who had followed a star to his birthplace. Herod learned of Jesus' birth through the magi and tried to get information on his whereabouts. But they, warned in a dream that Herod actually wanted to kill the Child, returned home secretly. Herod, in a rage, ordered the execution of all male boys two years old and under in the vicinity of Bethlehem. Mary and Joseph escaped the massacre by fleeing to Egypt, where they remained until Herod died. They then settled in Nazareth, where their life was so ordinary that the only thing reported was a pilgrimage to Jerusalem when Jesus was twelve years old. Left behind by Mary and Joseph when they departed from Jerusalem, he was found in the Temple, his "Father's house."

The infancy narratives of the Gospels of Matthew and Luke are meant to convey what is beyond history, that God became human in Jesus Christ. They hint that in the person of Jesus the Old Covenant was being transformed into the New. They cover the next eighteen years of his life by stating only that he "advanced [in] wisdom and age and favor before God and man" (Luke 2:52).

The Kingdom of God Is at Hand

When Jesus was thirty years old, his cousin John, son of Elizabeth and Zechariah, began to preach at the Jordan River. Huge crowds flocked to hear his call to "prepare the way of the Lord" (Mark 1:3) and to be baptized as a sign of repentance. It was now time for Jesus to begin his mission. He went to John for baptism. John objected that he himself should be baptized by Jesus, then complied at Jesus' insistence. As Jesus came out of the water, the Spirit descended on him in the form of a dove, and a voice from heaven called out, "You are my beloved Son; with you I am well pleased" (Mark 1:11).

Jesus then withdrew into the Judean wilderness for forty days of fasting and prayer. As a human, Jesus needed to seek out his Father's way of bringing about his kingdom. The gospels tell us that he was tempted by Satan to choose other ways, perhaps those of the Sadducees, Pharisees, and Zealots. The Sadducees were content with earthly comfort; Jesus was tempted to use his miraculous power to turn stones into bread for his own comfort. The Pharisees wanted to win favor by showy displays of holiness; Jesus was tempted to "win the crowds" by a spectacular leap from the Temple. The Zealots wanted a war-won kingdom; Jesus was tempted to accept all the kingdoms of the earth from Satan. Jesus resisted these temptations, went to Galilee, and began to teach.

Some time afterward, John the Baptizer was imprisoned by Herod Antipas, son of Herod the Great and ruler of Galilee, because John had rebuked him for marrying his brother's wife. John had pointed out Jesus as the "Lamb of God" to his disciples, and some began to follow Jesus. From these and others Jesus formed a special group of twelve apostles (John 1:35-51; Matthew 4:18-22; 10:1-4).

The Message of Jesus: His Parables

Jesus began his preaching with the words: "This is the time of fulfillment. The kingdom of God is at hand. Repent, and believe in the gospel" (Mark 1:15). He painted colorful pictures in his parables, stories which illustrated important truths about God's kingdom and described it to his listeners.

1. The kingdom of God is present in Jesus. It is like a hidden treasure or a pearl of great price, of more value than anything (Matthew 13:44-46). To accept the kingdom is to build our lives on solid rock (Matthew 7:24-27). We accept it not by praising ourselves like the proud Pharisee but by seeking God's mercy like the humble tax collector (Luke 18:9-14). The seed of God's kingdom is his word; we must be like fertile soil, well prepared to receive it (Matthew 13:1-23).

2. The gospel, the Good News, is that God wants to give his mercy and forgiveness to all. God loves us with a gentle tenderness beyond our wildest dreams. God is like a shepherd who seeks the lost sheep, a woman who searches for a lost coin, a loving father who welcomes back his wayward son (Luke 15).

3. We cannot receive God's mercy unless we share it with others. We must not imitate the servant who sought mercy from his master, then denied it to a fellow servant (Matthew 18:23-35), or the rich man who let a beggar starve at his gate (Luke 16:19-31). Our model is the Good Samaritan, who cared for an unfortunate stranger (Luke 10:25-37). Our eternal destiny will depend on how we treat Christ who comes to us in the hungry, thirsty, and neglected (Matthew 25:31-46).

4. God is almighty, and the kingdom he establishes through Jesus cannot be destroyed. No matter how much the kingdom is opposed, it will triumph. Just as a farmer is sure of the harvest even after an enemy has planted weeds in his wheat (Matthew 13:24-43), so God's kingdom cannot be snuffed out. As a mustard seed grows into a large shrub, so the seed of the Church planted by Christ will surely flourish (Matthew 13:31-32). As leaven placed in dough will make the whole loaf rise, so Christ's kingdom will have its effect on the world (Matthew 13:33).

5. All this calls for a response. With Jesus a decisive turning point in history has arrived. We must change our lives and put God's kingdom first. If we miss this opportunity, we are like a farmer who built huge barns to store his crops, only to die before he could enjoy their benefits (Luke 12:16-21); we are like foolish young women who are invited to a wedding but don't have oil for their lamps (Matthew 25:1-13). We are invited to the banquet of heaven, and Jesus urges us to accept the invitation (Matthew 22:1-14).

Thus the parables teach us that God offers us the kingdom — life and joy through Jesus. Now is the time to accept it, rejoice in it, and share it.

The Message of Jesus: The Sermon on the Mount

A good summary of the content and style of Jesus' teaching may be found in the Sermon on the Mount in chapters 5-7 of Matthew. The sermon begins with the beatitudes, in which Jesus turns the values of the secular world upside down: happy are they who place their trust in God and put God's kingdom first.

Jesus is not afraid to make serious moral demands: fidelity to God's law, victory over anger and lust, commitment in marriage, forgiveness, love of enemies, generosity. God has been generous to us. We must imitate him.

Jesus teaches us to pray to God as "our Father." In the Lord's Prayer we acknowledge the preeminence of God. We ask for the grace to do God's will and so help bring about his kingdom. We place the present, past, and future in God's hands: We pray about our present needs (our "daily bread"), seek forgiveness for past misdeeds, and ask to be delivered from future trials.

Jesus teaches us to put God first — a god second to money or to anything else is not God. He assures us that God holds us close to his heart and that we are of great value because we matter to the Maker of the universe.

Here in the Sermon on the Mount is a pattern for living that is psychologically and spiritually sound: healthy self-esteem, generous love for others, belief in God as origin and goal of life.

The Message of Jesus: The Last Supper Discourse

In the Last Supper discourse of Jesus (John 14-17), Jesus reveals the inner life of God as Father, Son, and Holy Spirit. He invites his followers to share God's love. He offers us the closest possible intimacy with God. He encourages us to love one another with the love he has for us. He promises a peace that cannot be taken away. He assures us that nothing, not even death itself, can separate us from the life, love, joy, and peace he came to bring.

The Miracles of Jesus

Jesus' words alone would have been enough to gather huge audiences. But he also worked miracles, astounding signs that had no natural explanation and which attracted multitudes. Jesus healed. He gave sight to the blind and hearing to the deaf. He helped the lame to walk and the paralyzed to move. Jesus exercised power over nature. He changed water into wine to keep a wedding party going, and he multiplied bread and fish to feed a hungry crowd. He calmed the raging sea. Most remarkably, Jesus conquered death. He brought back to life the daughter of a Jewish official (Mark 5:21-43), a widow's son, (Luke 7:11-17), and his friend Lazarus (John 11:1-44).

Jesus worked these miracles because he wanted to bring God's love to people and to demonstrate the power of God (Mark 2:1-12). At times Jesus worked miracles in response to the faith of individuals (Matthew 8:5-13; Luke 8:43-48). At times there is no mention of faith in those he cured (Luke 7:11-17). He healed many, but surely there were many others he did not heal. There is no formula to explain miracles as they occurred during Jesus' ministry or as they occur today. Miracles are free actions of God, and we do not know why God works miracles in some cases and not in others. We accept them as signs of God's love and leave the mystery in God's hands.

Jesus' Power Over Satan

When Satan tried to tempt Jesus at the very beginning of his mission, Jesus resisted, and he continued to exercise authority over the devil. The gospels tell how Jesus drove evil spirits from people (Mark 1:23-28; Matthew 8:28-34) and state that he did this on many other occasions (Mark 1:34, 39).

The Bible takes the existence of good and evil spirits for granted. God has created spiritual beings called angels; some of them (devils, demons) have rebelled against God and try to get human beings to join in their rebellion. Jesus' power over these demons is another sign that the kingdom of God is present in him (Matthew 12:28). God does not annihilate his creatures when they misuse their freedom, and so demons continue to exist. But Jesus brings victory over Satan, and he gives others the power to conquer Satan (Luke 10:17-20).

The Response to Jesus

Jesus preached the Good News that God wants to fulfill our fondest hopes for life, joy, and peace. He worked miracles that revealed God's presence, mercy, and power. He demonstrated mastery over evil. We might expect, then, that all would have accepted him as Savior — but such was not the case.

It is true that large crowds flocked to Jesus, but they were looking for a Savior who would establish an earthly kingdom, and Jesus had to resist their attempts to proclaim him king (John 6:15). At times he commanded people not to say anything about his miracles (Mark 1:40-45; Mark 5:40-43). He had to correct even his own apostles for seeking a worldly kingdom (Matthew 20:20-28).

Jesus' popularity alarmed the Sadducees, who were afraid that the large crowds might start a civil war which would end in the destruction of Israel (John 11:45-54). The Zealots certainly noticed the large crowds, and no doubt they had hopes of recruiting Jesus and his followers, more so because one of the Twelve Apostles seems to have been a member of the Zealot party (Luke 6:15).

While the Sadducees feared that Jesus might cause a civil disturbance, the Pharisees were enraged by the content of his teaching. Jesus refused to sanction their practice of keeping thousands of detailed regulations. The Pharisees and Scribes (specialists in Jewish law) accused Jesus of breaking the law and criticized him for speaking with sinners. They accused him of driving out demons by the power of Satan. In time they allied themselves with Sadducees and Herodians (supporters of King Herod Antipas) and began to plot against Jesus (Mark 3:6).

So Jesus was faced with huge crowds of people who misunderstood his message, with the wealthy and powerful who feared him, with subversives who hoped to use him to their advantage, and with the religiously influential who opposed his teaching. The wonder is that Jesus continued to preach! He realized that his enemies were growing stronger in their resolve to destroy him, but he had come to bring God's mercy to all, even his enemies. He refused to use his miraculous power to crush his foes, relying only on love to call them to repentance. They refused to respond, and Jesus began to tell his apostles that he would be delivered into the hands of his foes.

Finally, Jesus decided to go to Jerusalem to face his enemies in their own stronghold. He went at Passover time when the population of Jerusalem, normally about one hundred thousand, was increased tenfold by pilgrims. Accompanied by throngs of followers, Jesus rode into the city on a donkey, not a war-horse, as if to show that he was not interested in an earthly kingdom. There he confronted his enemies directly. He drove from the Temple those who were changing money and marketing animals for sacrifices, extorting huge profits from the poor (Luke 20:28-48); he thereby angered the priests and Sadducees who benefited from those profits. He denounced the Pharisees, apparently in a last attempt to shock them into recognizing their hardness of heart (Matthew 23). But they, along with the Sadducees and Herodians, only intensified their efforts to have Jesus killed.

The Crucifixion and Death of Jesus

Because of Jesus' popularity with the multitudes of pilgrims, the Sadducees, Herodians, and Pharisees could not risk arresting Jesus publicly. Then Judas Iscariot, one of Jesus' apostles, went to the chief priests and offered to betray Jesus for thirty pieces of silver. On Thursday evening after Jesus had shared the Last Supper with his apostles, he went with them to pray in a garden on the Mount of Olives outside the city walls. Soldiers led by Judas arrested Jesus, who was abandoned by his apostles, and took him to the chief priests. He was questioned, subjected to an unfair trial, and sentenced to death.

But because the Jewish leaders did not want to be blamed for Jesus' death, and because they wanted him to undergo the humiliation of a Roman crucifixion, they led him to the Roman governor, Pontius Pilate, and accused him of treason. Pilate questioned Jesus and decided that he was innocent. After sending him to Herod Antipas, in Jerusalem for the Passover, he had Jesus scourged to placate the Jewish leaders. He then tried to release Jesus, but the chief priests gathered a mob to shout for Jesus' execution. Finally, Pilate gave in and condemned Jesus to death.

Jesus was led to a place outside the city walls called Golgotha. There he was crucified between two criminals. He suffered the horrors of crucifixion for at least three hours. In his agony, he showed concern for his Mother, who was there at the Cross with his apostle John and a few faithful women. He promised heaven to one of the criminals who turned to him as Lord. He forgave those who had crucified him. He commended his spirit to his heavenly Father and died. A Roman soldier thrust a spear into his side to guarantee the fact of his death.

Joseph of Arimathea, an admirer of Jesus, asked Pilate for his body. Aided by Nicodemus, he placed the body of Jesus in a tomb and covered its entrance with a huge stone. The chief priests and Pharisees, having heard of Jesus' statement that he would rise from the dead, went to Pilate and asked for soldiers to guard the tomb to keep his apostles from taking the body. This was done, and a seal was placed on the stone blocking the entrance. Jesus' enemies felt that they were rid of him once and for all.

Why the Crucifixion?

Why did Christ die on the cross? One reason may be that God's love is a threat to evil, and evil will always lash out against it. When God made himself "vulnerable" by becoming human, evil nailed Jesus to the cross.

That would be true in any age. If Jesus came to earth today and went to a troubled spot, asking enemies to love one another, he would be quickly eliminated. Once Jesus had become one of us, it was only a matter of time until he would be murdered. He knew and accepted this. He came armed only with love, completely vulnerable to his enemies, "like a lamb led to the slaughter" (Isaiah 53:7), and it was this love that saved us: "No one has greater love than this, to lay down one's life for one's friends" (John 15:13).

The Resurrection

Jesus had been crucified on a Friday. The burial arranged by his friends was hastily done before the Sabbath rest. On the third day after his death, some women went to the tomb to anoint his body with spices. They were astonished to find the stone rolled back and the tomb empty; they ran to tell his apostles, who were in hiding. No one knew what to make of the empty tomb until Jesus appeared to his followers risen and glorious, no longer limited by time or space.

For a period of forty days Jesus appeared often to his apostles and to others. The gospel narratives of the Resurrection (Matthew 28; Mark 16; Luke 24; John 20-21) show that Jesus' followers were certain that he had risen. The faith of the early Church is expressed by the reluctant believer, Thomas, who fell on his knees before Jesus and said, "My Lord and my God!" (John 20:28).

At first the Resurrection of Jesus had seemed to the apostles too good to be true. Then they realized that it was true and too good to hide. The very apostles who had abandoned Jesus at his arrest now began fearlessly to proclaim him as the Savior foretold in Old Testament prophecies. In the face of determined opposition and persecution they preached that Jesus had come to bring salvation to all. The risen Jesus "worked with them and confirmed the word through accompanying signs" (Mark 16:20).

Questions for Discussion or Reflection

Is Jesus real to you? Do you talk to him as you talk to other friends? Do you feel comfortable talking about Jesus with others? Do you realize that Jesus is truly closer to you and more present to you now than he would have been if you had lived in Palestine two thousand years ago?

Activities

Write down in your own words answers to these questions: "Who is Jesus Christ?" "What are the most important elements of Jesus' message?"

Read John 1:35-42. Hear Jesus inviting you to spend some time with him. Remember that Jesus is with you as you pray and enjoy being with him.

Read John 20:24-29. Kneel and speak the words of Thomas to Jesus, "My Lord and my God!" Hear Jesus saying to you, "Blessed are those who have not seen and have believed." Ask Jesus to strengthen your faith in him.

CHAPTER FOUR

Jesus in His Followers and in His Word

" **A**ll power in heaven and on earth has been given to me. Go, therefore, and make disciples of all nations, baptizing them in the name of the Father, and of the Son, and of the holy Spirit, teaching them to observe all that I have commanded you. And behold, I am with you always, until the end of the age" (Matthew 28:18-20). With these words the risen Jesus commissioned his disciples and assured them of his continuing presence. Jesus then ascended to heaven on a cloud (Acts 1:9) to God's right hand (Mark 16:19).

Jesus promised to be with his followers, then departed. How could this be? The cloud, the ascension, and the expression "at God's right hand" are meant to show that Jesus is truly "Lord and God," no longer limited by space or time. Jesus was not taken away; he is where God is — everywhere.

The Coming of the Holy Spirit

After the Ascension, the apostles gathered in an upper room with Mary, the Mother of Jesus, and with other believers. They prayed. They chose Matthias to replace Judas Iscariot, who had committed suicide after betraying Jesus (Acts 1:13-26). They must have discussed over and over again the incredible things that had happened since they had first met Jesus. They must have wondered how they, such a tiny group of uneducated people, could possibly "make disciples of all nations."

Their waiting ended and any misgivings vanished in a mysterious outpouring of courage and wisdom, which Luke describes as a strong driving wind and tongues of fire. "They were all filled with the holy Spirit" (Acts 2:4). Led by Peter, the apostles left their upper room and began to preach to the crowds assembled in Jerusalem for the feast of Pentecost.

Peter announced that Jesus was the fulfillment of Old Testament prophecies and had been raised from the dead as Lord and Messiah. He invited his listeners to repent and be baptized in the name of Jesus for the forgiveness of their sins and promised that they too would receive the Holy Spirit. Three thousand were baptized on that day, and as the apostles continued to preach, more and more people put their faith in Jesus (Acts 2:14-47).

When Peter and John healed a crippled beggar, the Jewish authorities arrested them and threatened punishment if they continued to preach in Jesus' name. Peter and John responded, "Whether it is right in the sight of God for us to obey you rather than God, you be the judges. It is impossible for us not to speak about what we have seen and heard" (Acts 4:19-20).

As the apostles continued to proclaim Jesus as Messiah and Lord, the number of believers grew, and so did the opposition to them. A deacon named Stephen was executed. Saul, the overseer of this murder, "was trying to destroy the church; entering house after house and dragging out men and women, he handed them over for imprisonment" (Acts 8:3). It was about A.D. 37, five or six years after Christ's Resurrection. (All dates are A.D. unless otherwise noted.)

Then came a dramatic and unexpected development. Saul, on his way from Jerusalem to Damascus to arrest followers of Jesus, had a vision of the risen Christ. He became a believer and began to proclaim Jesus as the Messiah. Soon the persecutor became the persecuted and when some Jews tried to kill him, he escaped and spent the next few years in Tarsus and Arabia (Acts 9).

The Spread of the Gospel

Meantime, the believers began to preach the gospel to Jews and Gentiles alike. They made converts in towns south of Jerusalem, like Gaza, and moved west and north along the Mediterranean coast to Lydda, Joppa, Caesarea, Tarsus (Saul's hometown), and Antioch, where they were first called "Christians" (Acts 10-11).

Another persecution broke out in 44, this one started by Herod Agrippa, grandson of Herod the Great and ruler of Judea from 41-44. He killed James, the son of Zebedee, and arrested other Christians, including Peter, who miraculously escaped from prison (Acts 12). In spite of such troubles Christians continued to preach, grow in number, and care for one another. Christians at Antioch, for example, sent relief aid to famine-stricken believers in Judea (Acts 12). Such instances of concern united Christians. At the same time they were gradually moving away from their Jewish ties because of the persecutions against them and because so many Jews refused to accept Jesus as the Savior.

After Herod's death in 44, Saul (now known as Paul) and Barnabas (another early missionary) were sent by the Church at Antioch to preach the gospel in Cyprus and Asia Minor. They first spoke in Jewish synagogues but met with much hostility and persecution. They then turned to the Gentiles (non-Jews) and brought many people to Christ (Acts 13-14).

Some Christians of Jewish background, however, objected to what Paul and Barnabas had done; these Christians stated that all believers must keep the Law of Moses. This view was rejected by Church leaders at a council in Jerusalem in 49. The crucial argument was given by Peter: "We believe that we are saved through the grace of the Lord Jesus" (Acts 15:11).

The Jerusalem council illustrated a profound truth. Jesus Christ is the Word of God and the revelation of God; any other word or revelation must be judged in the light of Jesus' life and teaching. Salvation can be found only in Christ. Christians now clearly recognized this as the foundation of their tradition, and henceforth the Old Testament would be judged in the light of the New. Christianity was no longer seen as a Jewish sect, but as a religion for all people — a "catholic" religion.

Christianity soon spread throughout the civilized world. The Acts of the Apostles focuses on Saint Paul, telling how he brought the gospel to many parts of Asia Minor and Europe, including the very heart of the Roman Empire, Rome itself. Other missionaries took the gospel to Africa, India, and Asia, their task made easier by Roman roads and by the Roman peace.

But Rome soon became a foe. The Emperor Nero instigated a persecution against the Christians in the mid sixties and, according to tradition, both Peter and Paul were martyred in Rome at this time.

By every logic the mighty Roman Empire should have crushed Christianity, but the "blood of martyrs is the seed of Christians," and the Church continued to grow.

Rome played a major part in another development. After the death of Herod Agrippa in 44, the Zealots pressed for a "holy war" against the Romans. In 66 the unrest exploded into a full-blown revolt. In 70 the Romans besieged Jerusalem, slaughtered its inhabitants, and reduced the city to ruins. The Temple was no more, and Christianity was separated even further from its Jewish roots.

Formation of the New Testament and Christian Bible

For twenty years after the Resurrection of Christ, missionaries spread the Good News of Jesus by preaching. Eventually, Christians began to feel a need to preserve their heritage in writing. Collections of the sayings of Jesus, liturgical prayers, and professions of faith began to appear. In 51 or 52 Paul started to write letters to the towns and cities he had evangelized. These letters were preserved and shared and soon were recognized as having a special authority. By 65 or 70 the Gospel of Mark was written. Other gospels and writings followed. Some were accepted by the Church as inspired, while others were rejected. At the same time books regarded by Jews as inspired were evaluated by Christians, and gradually a list or "canon" of books was compiled.

The process by which the Catholic Church came to accept the Bible as we have it today is a long and complex one. At the time of Christ there were different opinions among Jews about which books should be accepted as divinely inspired. While there were probably no definitive lists until well after the time of Christ, there were two collections which have come to be known as the Palestinian (written in Hebrew) and the Alexandrian (written in Greek). The former contained thirty-nine books and the latter forty-six. The Alexandrian canon gradually prevailed and was accepted by such Church councils as those of Hippo in 393 and Carthage in 397. There was little dissent until the Protestant Reformation, when Protestant leaders rejected the Alexandrian canon in favor of the Palestinian. In 1546 the Council of Trent defined the Alexandrian as the official canon of Old Testament books for Catholics. As a result, the Catholic Old Testament canon contains seven more books than the Protestant: Tobit, Judith, First and Second Maccabees, Wisdom, Sirach, and Baruch (and additions to Esther and Daniel). These books are placed in some Protestant Bibles as the "Apocrypha."

By 125 all twenty-seven books of the New Testament were written and by 200 were recognized as inspired. The complete canon was listed by the Councils of Hippo and Carthage and was not challenged until Martin Luther dropped Hebrews, James, Jude, and Revelation. However, other Protestants maintained the traditional New Testament canon, and today all Protestant churches accept the same twenty-seven books as does the Catholic Church. We move now to a "global view" of these books.

The Gospels

No books have touched the hearts and lives of people so dramatically as have the four gospels. Through the gospels we are put in touch with Jesus himself, we hear the preaching of the early apostles, and we read the words of the Evangelists who gave us the gospels in their present form.

The gospels were not written immediately after the Resurrection of Jesus. First came oral preaching, then collections of the sayings and miracles of Jesus, hymns, and professions of faith. The work of the gospel writers, the Evangelists, consisted in collecting materials about Jesus and adapting them to meet the needs of specific audiences.

Matthew, the first Gospel in our present New Testament arrangement of books, was written after Mark, and most likely used Mark as a source. The book is named after the apostle Matthew, but its actual author is unknown. He wrote around the year 80 and probably intended his Gospel for Jewish Christians. In many ways the Gospel shows that Jesus is the fulfillment of Old Testament prophecy, and the main body of the Gospel is divided into five sections, which would remind Jews of the Pentateuch.

Mark was written in 65 or 70, probably for non-Jewish Christians. It is the shortest of the gospels, and presents Jesus as the suffering Messiah who was misunderstood and rejected until his Resurrection. Many think that the author is John Mark, a missionary who traveled with Paul and had some contact with Peter.

Luke appeared about the same time as Matthew and probably used Mark as a source also. Luke was a skilled Greek author who addressed his Gospel and its companion volume, the Acts of the Apostles, to Greek-speaking Christians. The author is usually identified as a missionary who traveled with Paul. He emphasizes the mercy and forgiveness of Jesus, as well as the joy his salvation brings. For Luke, Christ's life was a "journey to Jerusalem," to suffering and death and glory.

John was written twenty or more years after Luke and differs from the other three gospels in language and style. The author has been identified as the apostle John, or one of his disciples, but this is uncertain. The Gospel may have been written for Christians around Ephesus in Asia Minor. Rich in symbolism, it reflects upon the life and teachings of Jesus as he lives in the Church and the sacraments.

Acts, Letters, and Revelation

The *Acts of the Apostles* takes up where the Gospel of Luke leaves off. Written by the same author and at the same time as the Gospel of Luke, Acts describes the beginnings of the Church in Jerusalem (chapters 1-5), the first missions outside Jerusalem and the conversion of Paul (6-12), the missionary journeys of Paul (13-21), and Paul's arrest and trip to Rome (21-28). Acts gives us a unique view of the early Church and of its preaching.

The next twenty-one books of the New Testament are called the "letters." Some can properly be called letters in our modern sense, but others are actually sermons or theological treatises. They include the earliest and latest writings of the New Testament. Thirteen are attributed to Saint Paul. However, Paul dictated many of his letters to secretaries, and others may have been composed by fellow workers who depended on outlines or basic themes drawn up by Paul. Some of the letters attributed to Paul or other New Testament leaders may have been composed after their deaths by writers who used ideas originating with Paul and the other leaders.

None of the letters is a complete theological explanation of Christian doctrine. They were written to meet specific needs of the early Christians to solve problems as they arose. They represent increasing insight into the meaning of Christ's life and message as gained by the apostles and early Christians under the guidance of the Holy Spirit. Since many of the problems they encountered are the same as those we face today, the letters speak to us, giving insights into the life of the early Church and addressing God's Word to us.

Romans, written by Paul in about 58, is a strongly reasoned argument that we are saved by faith in Jesus Christ, not by observance of Old Testament law. Paul devotes the last four chapters to an explanation of the moral duties of Christians and to the meaning of life in Christ.

First and *Second Corinthians* were written between 54 and 58. Corinth was a Greek city known for its loose morals, and the Christians of Corinth needed a great deal of encouragement and correction from Paul after their conversion from paganism. In these letters Paul addresses issues like cliques in the community, sexual morality, virginity and marriage, Eucharistic assemblies, charismatic gifts, love, and the Resurrection.

Galatians was written by Paul in about 54 to believers in Galatia (modern Turkey). Paul refutes those who demanded that Christians be circumcised, and he reminds believers that we are saved by faith in Christ.

Ephesians may have been written by someone in the Pauline tradition about 90, well after Paul's death. It is addressed to the Christian community in Ephesus (a seaport in Turkey). It proclaims the uniqueness of Christ as Son of God and the oneness of the Church with Christ, and it lays the foundation for our understanding of the Church as "one, holy, catholic, and apostolic."

Philippians is a beautiful document that may contain parts of three letters sent by Paul to converts at Philippi, a city in northern Greece. Paul thanks the Philippians for their generous assistance, assures them of his love for them, and exhorts them to remain one in Jesus the Lord.

Colossians proclaims Jesus as Son of God and Head of his Body, the Church, echoing many of the ideas of Ephesians. It encourages Christians to die to sinful ways and to live in union with the risen Savior. Addressed to the community of Colossae, a small town in southwestern Turkey, it may well be a sermon written after Paul's death, using Paul as a "heavenly spokesman."

First Thessalonians is the oldest book in the New Testament. Written by Paul in about 51 to the Church at Thessalonica, a seaport in northern Greece, it reminds the Christians of Paul's loving mission to them and encourages them to be faithful as they await the coming of Christ, which they apparently expected in their lifetime.

Second Thessalonians was written later to answer more questions about the coming of Christ.

First and *Second Timothy* and *Titus* are called the "pastoral letters" because they are addressed to early Church leaders as guides for the pastoral care of their communities. They probably are letters by inspired writers who wanted to give Pauline advice and guidance to Christians around the year 100. The letters reflect the growth of the Church and emphasize the importance of faithfulness to the gospel and to the teaching of the apostles.

Philemon is a personal letter written by Paul in 58 asking Philemon, an influential friend, to take back a runaway slave whom Paul had converted.

Hebrews is a carefully composed sermon whose author is unknown. It was probably written late in the first century to Christians in general and presents Christ as the Word of God, as Priest who saves us by his death, and as Leader who opens heaven to us.

James is the title of the next letter, but Scripture scholars debate about who James really is. The book is a sermon of the late first century, teaching that a living faith must show itself in good works and a holy life.

First and *Second Peter* are probably sermons written in Peter's name to encourage Christians of the late first century. The first letter uses baptismal liturgies, hymns, and other sources, including perhaps Peter's sermons, to comfort and encourage persecuted Christians. The second exhorts believers to remain faithful to Christ and always to be ready for his coming.

First, Second, and *Third John* are commonly believed to have come from the same Christian community that produced the Gospel of John. They were written late in the first century. First John proclaims Jesus as Son of God but also truly human; God is love, and therefore we are to love one another. Second John urges believers to remain faithful to Jesus. Third John is a short note requesting aid and hospitality for missionaries.

Jude is a short sermon written about 100, warning Christians to avoid false teachers and remain faithful to the teaching of the apostles. Much of Jude's message is found in chapter two of Second Peter.

Revelation belongs to that category of literature called "apocalypse," popular two hundred years before and after Christ. This literature uses figurative language, symbols and numbers, visions, heavenly messengers, and picturesque descriptions of the struggle between good and evil. The author of Revelation calls himself John (1:1, 4, 9), but we do not know just who this John is. The book may have been written in Ephesus to give encouragement to Christians of Asia Minor during times of persecution by the Roman Emperor Domitian (81-96). Many people have tried to use Revelation as a "heavenly timetable" to determine the end of the world, but Revelation was not intended for this. Indeed, our best way of understanding it may be to see it as a biblical *Star Wars,* that is, as an epic presentation of the battle between good and evil. As in the *Star Wars* movies, good is threatened as all kinds of monsters are unleashed by the forces of evil, but these are vanquished. Seen in this way, Revelation is a powerful statement that God will prevail over Satan. It says at the end of the Bible what Genesis states at the beginning: God is good, and God created the world as good. Evil has entered the world because of sin, but God will overcome it. All people are called to be faithful to God in order to share in Christ's great triumph and heavenly joy.

The Bible:
God Speaks to Us

The Bible has been a "bestseller" for two thousand years. It addresses every human situation, reflects every emotion, paints vivid pictures of all kinds of people — good and bad. But the most important reason why the Bible is a bestseller is that it is inspired: God speaks to human beings through its pages. "All scripture is inspired by God" (2 Timothy 3:16; see Hebrews 4:12 and 2 Peter 1:19-21).

This does not mean that the writers "took dictation" from God. Rather, in various ways, they were touched by God to record his presence and activity in their lives. They may have experienced God through extraordinary visions, dreams, or angelic messengers; through ordinary kinds of prayer; or by recognizing God in his saving actions. New Testament writers experienced God through the words and actions of Jesus. In these ways, and in many others, God spoke to his people, and they expressed what they heard in the Bible.

When we pick up the Bible, because God is not limited by space or time, he speaks to us through the same words as those addressed to Moses, to David, to the prophets. When we pick up the Bible, Jesus speaks to us here and now just as he spoke to the apostles.

People of faith realize this unique aspect of the Bible, and all Christians should understand that when we open the Bible, we "dial God's number." We can take any other book from a library shelf, read it, and learn valuable information. All the while, the book's author is not aware of what we are doing. But when we pick up the Bible, God says, "Hello."

God's words are right there for us with answers to today's problems. "Indeed, the word of God is living and effective...and able to discern reflections and thoughts of the heart" (Hebrews 4:12). When we are discouraged, Jesus says to us, "Come to me, all you who labor and are burdened, and I will give you rest" (Matthew 11:28). When we are frightened, Jesus tells us, "Peace be with you" (John 20:19). When we are lonely, Jesus reminds us, "I am with you always" (Matthew 28:20).

When God speaks to us through the Bible, he invites us to respond. We respond through prayer: we read God's words, then talk to God as we would to any friend. We respond also through our life choices: we read until we come to a phrase that challenges us to make a change in our lives; then we make some practical decision based on what we have read. There is no other book that allows this kind of communication with God. Down through the centuries Christians who have understood this have revered the Bible as a sacred book, as a beloved companion, and as a treasured friend.

The Bible, Tradition, and Revelation

By the end of the first century most of the books of the Bible had been written. By the end of the second century most Christians accepted the forty-six books of the Old Testament and twenty-seven books of the New Testament. By the end of the fourth century official lists of these seventy-three books were approved by Church councils.

By proclaiming these books to be inspired by God and by rejecting others as not inspired, the Church, guided by the Holy Spirit, was saying, "This is what we believe about God, about Jesus, about life and death, about what we are as a Church. And this is what we reject." The books of the Bible, in turn, helped shape the beliefs of each new generation of Christians.

All of this was a dynamic process involving some conflict. In the first four centuries after Christ there were those who wanted to put limits on the saving action of Jesus by claiming that all Christians should follow the Law of Moses. There were those who said that Jesus was God, but not human; others said that Jesus was human, but not God. Some said that Jesus revealed God as Father, Son, and Holy Spirit; others denied this. The early Church expressed its beliefs about these and other matters in the biblical books it accepted as inspired, in the decisions of councils, in formulas of belief called creeds, and in its worship. As this happened, believers became the kind of Church which we recognize as "Catholic."

The process by which the Bible was formed can help us to understand what the Catholic Church means by sacred tradition. "Tradition" means "handing on," and sacred tradition includes the way the Church has handed on and interpreted the Bible, as well as creeds, worship, decisions of councils, and the consistent teaching of the Church down through the centuries. These may not contradict the Bible but are based on the Bible and expand upon it.

The Bible and sacred tradition comprise what the Church understands as divine revelation. Catholics do not think that our belief can be limited to the Bible alone because early in the life of the Church there was no New Testament! Further, tradition is necessary if the Church is to apply the teaching of the Bible to changing circumstances. We believe that the Church does this under the guidance of the Holy Spirit. Jesus said, "I have much more to tell you, but you cannot bear it now. But when he comes, the Spirit of truth, he will guide you to all truth" (John 16:12-13).

We have studied the books of the Bible. Now we turn to a study of what the Church proclaims as its belief about God, Jesus, and itself.

Questions for Discussion or Reflection

Do you think that the Catholic Church could have come into being and that the New Testament could have been written if the Resurrection of Jesus were not a reality? What reasons could Peter and the apostles have possibly had to preach Jesus as Lord if he had not actually risen from the dead? If Jesus had not risen, can you imagine yourself as Peter trying to convince the apostles that they should pretend that Jesus was alive, even though the only things they stood to "gain" were persecution, suffering, and death? Does this strengthen your faith in the risen Christ?

"Jesus is more present to me today than he was to the apostles before he rose from the dead." "Jesus speaks to me today just as surely as he spoke to the apostles before his Resurrection." Are these statements true or false? Why?

Activities

Open your Bible and page through the New Testament. Try to note the main categories of books and the length of the various books. Read a few of the introductions to the books. Look for passages you may be acquainted with and read some of them.

Pick up your Bible and ask the Holy Spirit to help you realize that you are "dialing God's number." Open your Bible to the Gospel of John and read chapter 17. Place yourself at the Last Supper with Jesus and his apostles. Listen to Jesus' prayer to his Father. When you get to verses 24-26, picture Jesus looking directly at you, speaking your name instead of "they" or "them."

CHAPTER FIVE

The Church — Jesus Unites Us to the Trinity

The first disciples of Christ believed that he had called them to proclaim his life, death, and Resurrection (chapter three). They spread the gospel and began to identify certain writings as valid expressions of his life and teaching (chapter four). They had received a new vision of God from Jesus and began to recognize their unity with Christ in his Church. Their vision and their recognition can help us realize what it means to be "Church."

The Trinity

As Jews, the apostles believed in one God. But Jesus spoke to them of Father, Son, and Holy Spirit (John 14-17). Jesus was their "Lord and God" (John 20:28). Mysteriously, God was One, God was Three, and God was Jesus.

The disciples expressed their vision of God as Father, Son, and Holy Spirit in the New Testament. The life of Jesus began when Mary was overshadowed by the Holy Spirit and conceived the "Son of God" (Luke 1:35). As Jesus was baptized in the Jordan, the Father's voice was heard and the Spirit descended as a dove (Mark 1:10). The risen Jesus told his followers to baptize "in the name of the Father, and of the Son, and of the holy Spirit" (Matthew 28:19).

In time Church leaders began to speak of Father, Son, and Holy Spirit as the "Trinity." They chose formulas which expressed the Church's beliefs about the Trinity: there are "three Persons in one divine nature," the Son is "begotten" by the Father; the Holy Spirit "proceeds" from the Father and the Son. We use these formulas today when we recite the Nicene Creed at Mass.

The phrase "three Persons in one divine nature" expresses a mystery we cannot fully understand. But we can gain some insight into it. The word "person" refers to "who" we are. The word "nature" refers to "what" we are. If someone asks us, "Who are you?" we respond with our name…person. If someone asks us, "What are you?" we respond that we are human…our nature. With humans there is only one person in each human nature. But God is three divine Persons in one divine Nature (*divine* means "of God").

The word "begotten" is used in the Creed because it means that the Father and Son are of the same nature. When parents "beget" a child, they beget someone of the same nature as themselves. When people "make" something, they make something different. When we say that the Son is "begotten" by the Father, we profess our belief that the Son is equal to the Father, "true God from true God." When we say that the Holy Spirit "proceeds from the Father and the Son," we also express the equality of the Spirit with Father and Son.

Theologians have tried to offer insights into the Trinity by saying that the Father knows himself from all eternity, and this Knowledge is the Son. The Father and Son love each other with infinite love, and this Love is the Holy Spirit. I can know myself, and this idea, or mental picture, is real. I can love myself, and this love is real. But God's Knowledge is so limitless that it is a Person, the Son. The love of Father and Son is so limitless that it too is a Person, the Holy Spirit.

Such insights may be helpful, but we can no more understand the inner life of God than a daisy can understand higher mathematics. We can realize, however, that Jesus revealed God as a Community of love because God wants to draw us into that Community. We are destined to spend eternity with the Trinity, and this "heaven" begins here on earth when we know God as Father, Son, and Holy Spirit.

The Father

God is Father. This does not mean that God is like human fathers but that all good qualities in human parents come from God. The Bible tells us about these qualities. God cares and is close to us: "I will never forget you. See, upon the palms of my hands I have written your name" (Isaiah 49:15-16). God wants us to be free: as

God freed the Israelites from slavery, so he frees us from sin (Deuteronomy 26:5-9). God forgives us our sins and wants us to experience his forgiveness even more than we want to be forgiven (Luke 15). God loves us beyond imagining: "With age-old love I have loved you" (Jeremiah 31:3). God promises that good will win out over evil and that life will conquer death: "For I am convinced that neither death, nor life…will be able to separate us from the love of God" (Romans 8:38-39). To these qualities Jesus adds a special note of tenderness and affection when he addresses God as "Abba," equivalent to "Daddy" or "Dear Father" (Mark 14:36; Romans 8:15; Galatians 4:6).

God is Father-Creator. Some Christians say that Genesis teaches exactly *how* God created the world and that the Bible cannot be reconciled with the theory of evolution. But Catholics believe that the Bible teaches the *why* of creation, while science studies its *how*.

Why are we here? Because God exists and created us, and so life has meaning and we have hope for the future. *Why* is there right and wrong? Because God created us free and invites us to choose the right. *Why* is there such a thing as married love? Because God created us male and female to form marriage covenants modeled on God's faithfulness and love.

How did creation occur? According to the most common scientific theory, creation began fifteen to twenty billion years ago in an incredible explosion of power (the "Big Bang") which threw out all that now forms the universe. From that life developed. For Catholics there is no necessary contradiction between such scientific theory and biblical teaching, as long as it does not deny God's existence.

The Son

God is Son. From all eternity, there is a relationship in God's being which we can best understand as "Father-Son." Then the New Testament teaches that the Son, the second Person of the Trinity, became human. "In the beginning was the Word, and the Word was with God, and the Word was God.…And the Word became flesh and made his dwelling among us" (John 1:1-14).

That God the Son became human is a miracle we call the Incarnation. It is a mystery completely beyond our comprehension, but some have tried to bring the mystery down to a level we could understand. Some have denied that Jesus was truly human (2 John 7-9). Others have denied that he was truly God. The Catholic Church has always taught that Jesus is truly divine and truly human.

The Church explains that Jesus has a divine nature and a human nature, united in one divine Person, the "Word." We cannot understand how Jesus can be both God and a human being, but we believe it on the testimony of Scripture and of the Church. We believe it because Jesus worked miracles and because miracles still occur in his name. We believe it because Jesus rose from the dead, and in his victory over death, we see the presence of God. With Thomas the apostle, every Catholic can say to Jesus, "My Lord and my God" (John 20:28).

It was, of course, through his human nature that his contemporaries made contact with Jesus, and it is still through his human nature that we encounter Jesus. Christ's human nature gives us our truest insights into the nature of God. Therefore, we should learn all we can about the human, Jesus.

What kind of a man was Jesus in his mortal life on earth? The Bible shows us that he was a real down-to-earth human being. Raised in a small town, he was so normal that when he came back as a teacher and miracle worker, people refused to believe he was special (Mark 6:1-6). He was enough of a boy to go off on his own and get lost at the age of twelve (Luke 2:41-52). He observed life and loved nature: the sun and rain, wild flowers and vines and trees, moths and birds and foxes, people building houses, farmers planting crops, women baking bread, and fishermen casting their nets (Matthew 5-7; 13). He celebrated life (John 2:1-11). He was courageous yet knew fear (Mark 14:32-42). He was born like us and experienced death as we will (Luke 2:1-7; Luke 23).

Jesus liked people and people liked him. He was always getting invited to meals (Luke 4:39; 7:36; 10:38; 14:1). He enjoyed being with people (John 1:35-51). He cared about little children (Mark 10:13-16) and noticed people others missed (Mark 10:46-52). To him elderly widows and despised sinners were important (Mark 12:41-44; Mark 14:3-9).

Jesus was merciful and compassionate. He defended a woman accused of adultery (John 8:1-11). He shed tears at the death of Lazarus (John 11). He wept over the fate of Jerusalem (Luke 19:41-44).

Jesus was, and is, a friend. "No one has greater love than this, to lay down one's life for one's friends. You are my friends" (John 15:13-15).

This is the reality of the Incarnation: The kindness and mercy of Jesus, his concern for "little people," his love even to dying on the cross for us, his forgiveness of sinners, are the kindness, mercy, concern, love, and forgiveness of God. Jesus is Emmanuel, "God is with us" (Matthew 1:23)

The Holy Spirit

God is Holy Spirit. We Catholics believe that the Holy Spirit is the love eternally proceeding from the Father and Son. The Holy Spirit, then, is the cause of all that is good and loving in the universe. If we want to know where the Holy Spirit is, we need only look for whatever is good and loving: the beauty of nature, the warmth of family life, the care people show one another.

The Holy Spirit is Love, and love is power, our source of strength as we follow Christ. Just as the Spirit descended as a dove upon Jesus at the beginning of his ministry (Matthew 3:16-17), so the Spirit descends upon us to guide us. The Holy Spirit is like the wind and fire which strengthened the apostles to witness for Christ (Acts 2:1-4). Wind is capable of moving huge ships across the water, but the ship must open its sails if it is to go anywhere. Fire can generate warmth and light, but it takes effort to utilize its energy.

Just so, we must "open our sails to the Spirit" to experience the power of God. We must open our hearts and lives to the warmth and light of the Spirit's fire. We do this by study of the Scriptures and by prayer and by humbly admitting our weakness to God. For the Holy Spirit works through our weakness and humanity, giving us strength to do what we could not otherwise accomplish. Hebrews 4:14-16 says that God sympathizes with our weakness and that we can confidently go to him for help in time of need. The apostles, ordinary people like us, touched by sin and failure, were able through the power of the Spirit to spread the faith throughout the world. The Spirit helped them; "the Spirit too comes to the aid of our weakness" (Romans 8:26), bringing us power, warmth, and light. So Jesus calls the Holy Spirit our "Advocate," our Helper, who guides us to the truth (John 14:15-18; 16:7-14).

In God We Live and Move and Have Our Being

We human beings are made in such a way that we need to know and be known, love and to be loved. Why is this? Because we exist in a "Trinitarian universe," designed by God's infinite Knowledge, created by God's infinite Love. We are made in the image and likeness of God (Genesis 1:27). Therefore, the Trinity is the most basic of our beliefs and the most practical. Our lives are "Trinitarian" because God is the Trinity.

We can make this realization a part of our lives each time we pray. In prayer we address God as the One from whom we come — the Father. We are aware of God at our side, teaching us to say "Our Father," standing with us as we pray — the Son. We are conscious of God within us, inspiring us to lift up our hearts, giving depth and feeling to our prayer — the Holy Spirit (Romans 8:14-17). In prayer we can picture God as our Father who gives all creatures life, Jesus as our Brother who walks alongside us, the Holy Spirit as the Guest of our souls. Through prayer we know Father, Son, and Spirit as our God, in whom "we live and move and have our being" (Acts 17:28).

The Church, the Body of Christ

We do not come before the Trinity as solitary human beings. Along with our inborn need to know and love God, we have a need to know and love other people and to be known and loved by them. Because we are made in the image and likeness of God, who is "Community," we need community.

Jesus came to draw us into the "Community love" of the Trinity. He lived, died, and rose to bring all people into one family (John 10:16-18). At the Last Supper, Jesus asked us to love one another as he loves us (John 15:12). He prayed that we would be one, as he and the Father are one (John 17:20-21).

He formed the community of believers into the sign of his continuing presence on earth. He said, "Where two or three are gathered together in my name, there am I in the midst of them" (Matthew 18:20). When Paul was persecuting Christians, Christ asked him, "Why are you persecuting me?" This helped Paul to understand the unity between Christ and believers. He later wrote to them, "You are Christ's body" (1 Corinthians 12:27), and explained that Christ, "is the head of the body, the church" (Colossians 1:18).

Paul uses the terms "Body of Christ" and "church" interchangeably. The word "church" is a translation of the Greek word *Ekklesia,* an assembly of people called forth, "the People of God." Christ calls forth believers to bring him to the world, especially by their love and community: "This is how all will know that you are my disciples, if you have love for one another" (John 13:35). It is the task of the Church, then, to perpetuate the love of Christ on earth and to mirror the love of the Trinity.

The Imperfect Church: Christ's Beloved Church

Since the Church is made up of human beings who are not perfect, it is to be expected that the Church will be less than perfect. Some people are scandalized by failures in the Church and say that Christ never intended a Church with its leaders, rituals, laws, and potential for scandal and sin.

But the first generation of Christians believed that Christ intended to establish a Church (Matthew 16:18) with leaders who would make decisions ratified by God: "Whatever you bind on earth shall be bound in heaven, and whatever you loose on earth shall be loosed in heaven" (Matthew 18:18). They believed that Christ gave them ritual observances by which to remember him: "This is my body, which will be given for you; do this in memory of me" (Luke 22:19). They accepted from Jesus strict rules of conduct (Matthew 6:21-22) and guidelines for marriage (Mark 10:11). They believed that Jesus expected his followers to have standards for membership in the Church, and that those who violated them were to be excluded: "If he refuses to listen even to the church, then treat him as you would a Gentile or a tax collector" (Matthew 18:17).

Jesus knew that those who would represent him were subject to failure. Peter denied him three times, but Jesus, after his Resurrection, gave Peter a threefold commission to care for his sheep (John 21:15-18). The apostles ran away when Jesus was arrested, and yet he appeared to them after his Resurrection and sent them to preach the gospel to all nations (Matthew 28:16-20). Jesus patiently helped the unbelieving Thomas to put faith in him (John 20:24-29).

The early Church had all the problems found in churches today. There were liars and hypocrites (Acts 5:1-11). There were complaints of unfairness (Acts 6:1). There were those who used religion for personal gain (Acts 8:9-24). There were disagreements about doctrine (Acts 15). There were conflicts among Church leaders (Acts 15:36-41). There were sermons that failed to make an impact upon the preacher's audience (Acts 17:22-34) and sermons so long that they put people to sleep (Acts 20:7-12). There were questions about pastors' salaries, disorder at worship ceremonies, lust and scandal, and neglect of the poor (1 Corinthians 5-11). There were all the problems which arise when people try to follow Jesus and fall short of the mark because of human weakness and sin.

Because the Church is the Body of Christ, it has never lacked goodness and grace. If there were villains in the early Church, there were also heroes (Acts 7). If there was sin, there was holiness (Acts 2:42-47). If there was selfishness, there was generosity (Acts 4:32-37). If there were laws and leaders, it was because no society can exist without them (Acts 6:1-7). If there were ritual ceremonies, it was because these were faithful responses to Christ's will (1 Corinthians 11:23-26). If there were times when the followers of Jesus failed him, there were also times when they were heroic in professing his gospel (Acts 4:1-22).

In the Church there have always been good and bad people, good and bad times. The history of the Church has been the history of Christ living in us, inviting us to follow him faithfully, and calling us back when we fail.

Christ in the History of His Church

If there had been such a thing as the "evening news" in the first century, the activities of the first Christian preachers would probably have not been reported. A tiny religious movement proclaiming that an executed man was alive would hardly have been thought important by the worldly wise. But as we read in the Acts of the Apostles, those first preachers converted thousands to Christ, and communities of believers were established in many major cities of the Roman Empire. In a few years they came to the attention of the Emperor Nero, a madman who launched a bloody persecution of the Church in 64, killing Peter, Paul, and many innocent men, women, and children. Other persecutions followed, but Christianity continued to spread. There were about half a million believers by the year 100 and several million by 300. During this time patterns for Church structure were established, as local churches were led by bishops and assisted by priests and deacons. Disputes about the real nature of God and Christ led bishops to clarify the Church's beliefs in conciliar decrees and creeds.

In 313 the Church entered a new era. The Roman Emperor Constantine issued the decree of Milan, granting religious tolerance to Christians. Soon he began to support Christianity in various ways. This ended the persecutions, but it also opened a door to church-state entanglements that would create new problems for the Church. When the African priest Arius taught falsely that Jesus was not truly God, interference by emperors complicated the bishops' efforts to state the true belief of the Church. Eventually the teaching of the Councils of Nicea in 325 and Constantinople in 381 prevailed, and the Creed formulated by these Councils is still prayed by Catholics at Mass.

In the fifth century the Roman Empire began to collapse as barbarian tribes invaded her once secure boundaries. The Church became a civilizing force among these tribes as they were slowly converted to Christ. Monastic communities, which had been in existence for several hundred years, began to expand in the sixth century under Saint Benedict and were instrumental in the spread of the gospel. In the seventh century the Church in the East came under the attack of Islamic armies. The eighth century saw the continuing conversion of European peoples. In 800 Charlemagne was crowned as Holy Roman Emperor. He promoted Christianity, but he also renewed church-state ties, laying the groundwork for corruption and decay in the Church during the period known as the Dark Ages.

The tenth, eleventh, and twelfth centuries saw such diverse movements as the Crusades to free the Holy Land, monastic reform, establishment of the great universities, and Gothic architecture. A serious setback occurred in 1054 when divisions between the East and West led to the schism or separation of the Eastern Church from Rome. The thirteenth century was marked by the presence of great saints like Saint Francis, Saint Dominic, and Saint Thomas Aquinas. Unfortunately, the fourteenth century brought confusion to the Church when the popes moved from Rome to Avignon in France from 1305 to 1376 and when two or three men claimed to be pope from 1378 to 1417. In the fifteenth century corruption among many Church leaders and increasing interference by the secular authorities in ecclesiastical matters made reform imperative. There were many saintly Catholics, both clergy and laity, who called for renewal, but their messages were not heeded.

In 1517 Martin Luther, a Catholic monk, posted his "Ninety-five Theses" on a chapel door in Wittenburg, Germany, calling for an end to the abuses in the Church. He wanted reform, not a new church; but poor communications, stubbornness on the part of Luther and his Catholic counterparts, and interference by secular authorities led him to a "protestant" position, accepting the Bible as the only true authority and teaching salvation by faith alone. He was followed in his break from the Church by Jean Calvin (Switzerland), John Knox (Scotland), Henry VIII (England), and many others. Division followed division, and Christianity has since been split into many hundreds of churches.

The Protestant break from the Catholic Church finally shocked Catholic leadership into serious efforts for reform. The Council of Trent (1545-1563) clarified Catholic belief, corrected abuses, and set up the seminary system for the education of clergy. New religious orders like the Jesuits arose to aid in renewal. Many great saints promoted spiritual growth in Europe and led missionary activities in the New World and elsewhere, bringing hundreds of thousands of new members into the Church. The Church suffered more persecutions, during the French Revolution, for example, but survived them.

Since the Council of Trent there has been a steady movement in the leadership of the Catholic Church away from secular entanglements toward a more spiritual focus. New understandings of church-state separation arose from the Constitution of the United States. Scientific knowledge advanced from the seventeenth to the twentieth centuries, and the Church has had to reexamine the relationship of faith and science. The coming of so many Catholic immigrants to North and South America and the success of missionary activities all over the world have helped to make the Church more universal.

At the end of the twentieth century there are about nine hundred million Catholics, almost one sixth of the world's population. The last one hundred years have seen a succession of remarkable popes who have led the Church through rapidly changing times to a point where the papacy is perhaps more respected and more influential than it has ever been. But these popes have also pointed out the ongoing need for reform if the Church is to be faithful to Christ. The Second Vatican Council, a gathering in Rome of all the Catholic bishops of the world in the 1960s, restated Catholic beliefs for the modern world and instituted many changes in worship and structure, encouraging Catholics to renew their efforts to follow Christ. There are many challenges facing the Church today: materialism, atheism, Communism, the unstable condition of the international political scene, a shortage of vocations to the priesthood and religious life, just to name a few. And all its members are human, as fallible as were Peter and the apostles. Yet the Church is still the Body of Christ, and we can trust that he will continue to guide and strengthen the Church as he has from the beginning.

One, Holy, Catholic, and Apostolic Church

From New Testament times to the present, through all the ups and downs of history, the Church has described itself as "one holy catholic and apostolic." These words were used by the Councils of Nicea and Constantinople in the fourth century, and they are used by Catholics today when we pray the Nicene Creed at Mass. What do they mean?

The Church is *one*. We believe that the Catholic Church is built on the rock of Peter's faith (Matthew 16:18) and that it is united under Peter's successor, the pope. We do not say that other churches have no relationship to Christ. But we believe that Christ wants all his followers to be united in him. He prayed "that they may all be one" (John 17:21). Vatican II taught that while divisions exist, we should see the good in other churches, and work and pray for unity.

The Church is *holy*. "You are...a holy nation" (1 Peter 2:9). Christ died to make us holy. This does not mean that we are sinless (as is obvious from our history), but that we are given a share in the holiness of God through Baptism and are called to reject sin and live in union with Christ (Philippians 1:4-11).

The Church is *catholic*. This word means "universal" and refers to Christ's Church throughout the world. When divisions arose among believers, "catholic" also became a proper word, like a first name. Thus, Saint Augustine spoke of himself as a "Catholic Christian." We are proud to be Catholic, and we believe in our union with other followers of Christ over all the earth. Together, we are "Christ's body" (1 Corinthians 12:27).

The Church is *apostolic*. This means that the Church traces its authority back to Jesus through the apostles: Jesus commissioned them, and they ordained others who did the same through the centuries up to the pope and bishops today. The Church is apostolic because it faithfully proclaims the teaching of the apostles. The church is apostolic in the sense that it is missionary: an apostle is "one who is sent," and the whole Church is sent to preach the gospel to the world. Our Church, then, is "built upon the foundation of the apostles" (Ephesians 2:20).

The Church: The Sacrament of Christ

Jesus made God visible on earth, and theologians say that Christ is the "sacrament" of God, meaning that Christ was a visible sign to his contemporaries of the invisible God. The Church makes Christ visible today, and so is the "sacrament" of Christ, a visible sign of his presence in our world.

Christ put a great deal of trust in his apostles and in us! He depends upon us to continue his work, and the success of this mission depends to a great extent on how well we fulfill our role of being Christ to the world. Before Jesus was crucified, he had his own mortal body through which he could speak, listen, touch, forgive, heal, comfort, share, pray, love, unite, and bless. Now we are his Body.

We give Christ our lips to speak his words of love and comfort. We give him our hearing to listen to the troubled. We give him our eyes to look with love upon others. We give him our hands to touch the lonely. When we forgive, Christ forgives and brings peace to those seeking pardon. When we heal, Christ heals; when we comfort the sorrowful, Christ consoles. Christ needs our generosity so that he may help the poor. He needs our prayers so that his prayer can be lifted up to the Father from every age and place. Through our love, Christ's love takes human form. When we work for unity, we answer Christ's prayer for unity, "that they may all be one" (John 17:21). When we bless, Christ blesses.

We are members of the Body of Christ. Saint Paul writes, "So we, though many, are one body in Christ and individually parts of one another. Since we have gifts that differ according to the grace given to us, let us exercise them" (Romans 12:5-6). Parents raising their children, students attending class and participating in school activities, adults at their jobs and professions, priests and religious in their ministries, the elderly in nursing homes…all are the Body of Christ. "Now you are Christ's body, and individually parts of it" (1 Corinthians 12:27).

As we look at the weaknesses in ourselves and in other members of the Church, we may feel that it is presumptuous to see ourselves as the "body of Christ." Yet "Christ loved the church and handed himself over for her to sanctify her, cleansing her by the bath of water with the word, that he might present to himself the church in splendor, without spot or wrinkle or any such thing, that she might be holy and without blemish" (Ephesians 5:25-27). The "church in splendor" will exist only in the fullness of eternity, but the Church on earth, which needed cleansing in New Testament times and needs cleansing today, is nourished and cherished by Christ "because we are members of his body" (Ephesians 5:30).

Questions for Discussion or Reflection

In what ways can the Trinity be a doctrine that has practical implications for your daily life? What human characteristic of Jesus do you like most? Is it possible to really love Christ without loving the human beings who make up the Church? Do you think that Christ needs you? In what sense are you Christ in your home? At work? In your social life? At church?

Activities

Read Romans 8:14-17 and Galatians 4:4-7. Think of God as the Goal of your life and as the One from whom you come — the Father. Think of Jesus at your side, teaching you to call God "Father," standing with us as you pray — the Son. Think of God within you, inspiring you to lift up your heart to the Father, giving depth and feeling to your prayer — the Holy Spirit.

CHAPTER SIX

Christ in His Sacraments — Baptism and Confirmation

H uman life is enriched by celebration and ritual. Balloons and flowers send congratulations at the birth of a child. Birthday cakes and graduations mark milestones along the road to maturity. Meals bring families and friends together. Words of forgiveness and a handshake or a hug melt the coldness of a quarrel with the warmth of reconciliation. Ceremony and music and dancing tell the world that a man and woman have joined in marriage. Those who lead, teachers or police or government officials, are commissioned for their tasks. Funny cards and visits encourage a friend in the hospital, and floral wreaths or words of sympathy comfort bereaved family members at the loss of a loved one.

Jesus Christ was no stranger to celebration and ritual. Angels sang at his birth, and he was circumcised according to Jewish law. At the age when Jewish boys become bar mitzvah (a son of the law), he went to the Jerusalem Temple with Mary and Joseph. Jesus shared meals with friends. He forgave sinners with words of comfort and peace. He changed water into wine to keep the party going at the wedding feast of Cana. He commissioned his apostles to teach all nations. He healed the sick, and he wept at the grave of Lazarus.

The first Christians saw Jesus' presence in all that celebrates the goodness of human life. They knew that Christ had come to sanctify everything we do, that he had entered life as sunlight enters crystal, filling it with light and beauty.

The Sacraments

How did Christ enter the lives of his followers? The apostles believed that it was through signs of celebration and ritual given them by the Lord. On the first Pentecost, Peter told the crowds, "Repent and be baptized" (Acts 2:38). Paul reminded the Corinthians at the Last Supper that they proclaimed Christ's death and shared his body and blood by doing what he did at the Supper (1 Corinthians 11:23-27). Christ gave new life through the sign of Baptism; he was present through the sign of the Eucharist.

At first there was no organized theology of such signs, but one was gradually developed under the guidance of the Holy Spirit. By the thirteenth century the Church recognized seven signs, or sacraments, given to us by Christ, and the Council of Trent declared as dogma that these are Baptism, Confirmation, Eucharist, Penance, Matrimony, Holy Orders, and Anointing of the Sick.

These sacraments are "meetings with Christ," where he does today what he did in Palestine two thousand years ago. He gives eternal life through Baptism as he offered it to his contemporaries (John 17:2). He pours out the Holy Spirit in Confirmation as he sent the Spirit upon the apostles (Acts 2). He gives us himself in the Eucharist as he gave the apostles his body and blood at the Last Supper (Matthew 26:26-28). He forgives us through Penance as he forgave the sinful woman who wept at his feet (Luke 7:36-50). Through Matrimony he brings God's grace to husband and wife as he did at the wedding feast of Cana (John 2:1-11). He sends others to teach, lead, and sanctify in Holy Orders as he sent the apostles (Matthew 28:18-20). Through the Anointing he heals as he cured the sick who came to him, or he leads the dying to eternal life as he promised heaven to the thief on the cross (Mark 1:32-34; Luke 23:43).

A sacrament may be defined as a sign from Christ by which he comes to us and gives us his life and love. The sign may be clearly expressed in the Scripture, like the water of Baptism and the bread and wine of the Eucharist. Or it may be the result of the Church's experience and reflection, such as the exchange of vows in Matrimony. Each sacrament includes the use of Scripture. In every sacrament Christ acts through the signs and speaks through Scripture.

Because Christ is truly present through the sacraments, they can always have an effect in our lives. However, we must approach the sacraments with faith and devotion. We need the eyes of faith to look beyond the signs to the reality they contain and devoted hearts to focus on Christ's presence. Like the two disciples on the way to Emmaus who recognized the risen Jesus as he broke bread with them and opened the Scriptures to them (Luke 24:13- 35), we must recognize in the sacraments the risen Jesus giving us the "righteousness of God" (2 Corinthians 5:21).

Baptism — the First Sacrament

"It was like a miracle," parents often say of the birth of their child. "God seemed to be there in the hospital room with us!" There are few events more moving than the birth of a child. As the parents hold new life in their arms, they may be filled with faith in God, with hope for their child, and with love for each other as their eyes fill with tears of joy and awe.

But birth can also make us realize how fragile life is and how quickly it passes. Grandparents whisper to new parents, "It seems only yesterday that we were holding you." Life goes swiftly by, and faith can be lost, hopes dashed, and love weakened. If only there were a birth that did not have to end in death! If only we could be "reborn" to a life where faith, hope, and love could not be destroyed!

Jesus came to give us such a birth. By God's grace any human being can be reborn to a new life that will never end. That birth is Baptism, the sacrament which unites us to the life of Christ himself and opens for us the pathway to the other sacraments and to eternal life.

The Origins of Baptism

The first mention of Baptism in the New Testament is made in reference to John the Baptizer, who invited people to be "baptized" in the Jordan River as a sign of repentance (Matthew 3:1-17). John's Baptism symbolized a desire to be freed of sin and to live more worthily. Jesus was baptized by John, not because he needed to repent but because he wanted to show his oneness with humanity.

John's Baptism was not the Baptism given by Jesus. John said he was baptizing with water for repentance but Jesus would baptize with the Holy Spirit (Matthew 3:11). The Baptism of Jesus is not merely a symbol of repentance but a powerful action of Jesus that brings God's life to us. As Jesus explained, "No one can enter the kingdom of God without being born of water and Spirit. What is born of flesh is flesh and what is born of spirit is spirit" (John 3:5-6).

After his Resurrection, Jesus told the apostles to "make disciples of all nations, baptizing them in the name of the Father, and of the Son, and of the holy Spirit" (Matthew 28:19). So Peter told his hearers on the first Pentecost, "Repent and be baptized, every one of you, in the name of Jesus Christ for the forgiveness of your sins; and you will receive the gift of the holy Spirit....Those who accepted his message were baptized" (Acts 2:38-41).

The Effects of Baptism

Saint Paul explains the effects of Baptism. "We were indeed buried with him [Christ] through baptism into death, so that, just as Christ was raised from the dead by the glory of the Father, we too might live in newness of life" (Romans 6:4). A Christian is a "temple of God," in whom "the Spirit of God dwells" (1 Corinthians 3:16). Baptism makes us one in Christ: "For in one Spirit we were all baptized into one body" (1 Corinthians 12:13).

Baptism brings "death" to sin, *forgiveness of sins.* In traditional Catholic theology, this includes deliverance from original sin and from any personal sins one has committed. Original sin refers to the condition of alienation from God in which we are born, as well as the tendency which makes it easier for us to give in to temptation than to resist. We still face temptation after Baptism, of course, but we have through Baptism a "claim" to God's assistance (traditionally called "actual grace"). Baptism gives us the *life of Christ* (traditionally called "sanctifying grace"). Baptism offers *union with God:* Jesus promised to send the Holy Spirit to be with us always (John 14:15) and promised also, "Whoever loves me will keep my word, and my Father will love him, and we will come to him and make our dwelling with him" (John 14:23). The Church teaches that in Baptism we are given the virtues of faith, hope, and love, by which our union with God is established and strengthened.

Finally, Baptism confers *membership in the Church,* the Body of Christ.

And so there is a life which does not have to end in death. There is "rebirth" to a life where faith, hope, and love cannot be destroyed, because they are given to us by God.

Baptism
and the Church

In New Testament times people who heard the Good News of Christ were baptized soon after professing faith in Jesus (see Acts 2; 8; 10; 16). But when persecutions started, the Church began to require a period of instruction lasting one or more years. The weeks before Easter were a special time of preparation and prayer, leading up to the Easter Vigil celebration when new converts were baptized, confirmed with the Holy Spirit, and given the Eucharist.

At first, Baptism was conferred by immersing the candidate. Paul implies this when he says that we are buried with Christ in Baptism and rise to new life. In time Baptism was also administered by the pouring of water over a candidate's head, perhaps because immersion proved to be inconvenient in colder climates.

Preparation for Baptism was shortened when mass conversions began and entire tribes were received into the Church with their leaders. As Christianity spread, the practice of infant baptism became common. It may be that children had been baptized even in New Testament times because families were baptized together, and this presumably included children (Acts 10; 11:14-15; 16:15, 33). Baptism of infants would not have seemed strange to Jewish Christians, for Jews practiced circumcision of boys eight days old (Luke 2:21). After infant baptism became the norm, adults who wished to join the Church were usually instructed by a priest and baptized privately.

In the Catholic Church today Baptism may be done by immersion or by pouring water over the head of the candidate. A bishop, priest, or deacon is the usual minister of Baptism. In an emergency anyone can baptize by intending to do Christ's will and by pouring water over the person's head while saying, "I baptize you in the name of the Father, and of the Son, and of the Holy Spirit."

The water and prayer are the signs essential for a valid Baptism, but in the full ceremony of Baptism other signs are used. Blessed oil and chrism (oil mixed with balsam) signify the comfort and strength given by the Holy Spirit. A baptismal candle is a reminder that Christ is the Light of the World (John 8:12). A white baptismal garment recalls Paul's words: "For all of you who were baptized into Christ have clothed yourselves with Christ" (Galatians 3:27). Sponsors represent the Christian community and help welcome the candidate into the Church.

Infant Baptism Today

Infant Baptism has a long tradition in the Catholic Church going back to its antecedents in Judaism and at least hinted at in the New Testament. It is based on our belief that Christ wants to "take into his arms" the little children of today, just as he embraced the children of his time (Mark 10:13-16). It also shows that we don't have to do anything to earn God's love, which is freely bestowed even upon infants whom God cherishes simply because they are his children.

However, parents who have their children baptized should have a serious intention of bringing the children up in the Catholic faith. In the Baptism ceremony parents make solemn promises to do just that. Parents should pray for and with their children, be the first teachers of the faith to their children by word and example, and lead them to the other sacraments of the Church. If parents have their children baptized and then do not raise them as Catholics, they are denying the children the very life begun by Baptism. This is like giving a child physical life and then denying that child food, clothing, and shelter. Parents who do follow Baptism with prayer, instruction, and good example give their children the assurance that they are loved and cared for by Jesus.

Some Catholics have been taught that unbaptized infants go to "limbo," a place of eternal natural happiness, without the intimate closeness to God enjoyed by those in heaven. Limbo, however, is not Catholic doctrine; it is a theological opinion not commonly accepted today. The Church does not have an official teaching concerning the eternal destiny of unbaptized infants, but many Catholics believe that Christ, who said, "It is not the will of your heavenly Father that one of these little ones be lost" (Matthew 18:14), waits for each "little one" with the same warm embrace he gave the children of his time.

Adult Baptism Today

The Second Vatican Council recommended that the Church renew its way of receiving adult candidates. A revised rite called the Rite of Christian Initiation of Adults (RCIA) was approved by Pope Paul VI in 1972 and has become the norm for the Church. The RCIA stresses formation in doctrine, liturgy, Church life, and service and involves the larger Church community in welcoming, instructing, helping, and praying for the candidates.

The RCIA has four stages. The first is the *Period of Inquiry* or *Pre-catechumenate,* which may last from several weeks to many months. During this stage candidates are invited to ask questions about the Church, share their own faith stories, and decide whether or not they wish to continue. Those who do continue celebrate the Rite of Becoming a Catechumen and enter the second stage, the *Catechumenate.* This is a more intense period of instruction and introduction to liturgy, faith-life, and service and may last about a year. The Rite of Election, which usually takes place on the First Sunday of Lent, marks the transition between the Catechumenate and the third stage, *Enlightenment and Purification.* This stage covers the season of Lent and includes special liturgical ceremonies at the Lenten Masses, as well as more intense preparation through prayer and study. It climaxes at the Easter Vigil with the Sacraments of Initiation, Baptism, Confirmation, and the Holy Eucharist. The final stage of the RCIA is the *Post-baptismal Catechesis (Mystagogia).* This stage, lasting from Easter to Pentecost, focuses on the mysteries ("mystagogia") of Christ's death and Resurrection and helps the newly baptized to develop a deeper understanding of their faith. They now share fully in the Eucharist and are asked to live the gospel in their daily lives and to perform works of service for others.

The RCIA is the process by which nonbaptized candidates are received into the Catholic Church. Baptized members of other Christian denominations who wish to join the Catholic Church are not baptized again but are received into the Church through Penance, Profession of Faith, Confirmation, and the holy Eucharist. The stages of the RCIA may be adapted to meet their needs.

The RCIA can also serve as the focus for ongoing conversion for all the members of the Catholic Church. As the members of a

66

parish see new candidates learning Church doctrine, they may be encouraged to study their faith. As "cradle Catholics" participate in the liturgical ceremonies welcoming new members into the Church, they may wish to renew their own commitment to Christ. As they see newly baptized Catholics begin ministries of service, they may be encouraged to serve more generously. And Catholics who act as sponsors, teachers, and "prayer-partners" for the candidates have abundant opportunities for growth in their own lives.

Baptism and Salvation

It is the belief of Catholics that Baptism frees us from sin, unites us to the saving power of Christ's death and Resurrection, incorporates us into the Church, and sets us on the path to salvation. Obviously, this is all God's gift and cannot be earned, but Baptism is a gift that invites a response. It is birth to a new life of following Jesus. It is not yet salvation fully completed in heaven.

There are some who believe that an individual is saved once and for all by being baptized or by "accepting Jesus as Lord." Such people may ask others, "Have you been saved?" The question assumes "once-saved-always-saved," which is not biblical. Saint Paul urged the Philippians (people who had already been baptized): "Work out your salvation with fear and trembling" (2:12). Paul also wrote, "How much more then, since we are now justified by his blood, will we be saved through him from the wrath" (Romans 5:9).

We might compare salvation to traveling by ship through the waters of this life to the safe haven of eternal life. The ship has been built. Christ has done everything necessary by his life, death, and Resurrection to bring us to heaven. In this sense salvation has been accomplished (John 3:16). But we must book passage on the ship and be an active part of the crew. We must "work out" our salvation. Jesus warned: "Not everyone who says to me, 'Lord, Lord,' will enter the kingdom of heaven, but only the one who does the will of my Father in heaven" (Matthew 7:21). Saint James asks: "What good is it...if someone says he has faith but does not have works? Can that faith save him?" (2:14; see Matthew 25; 1 Corinthians 15:58; 2 Corinthians 3:18). The Bible makes it clear that we can "jump ship" and choose another destination (1 Corinthians 9:27;

1 Timothy 4:1; 6:10; 6:20-21; 2 Timothy 2:11-13; Hebrews 4:1-11; 6:4-12; 2 Peter 2:20-22).

But we trust that Jesus will see us to our final goal: "I continue my pursuit toward the goal, the prize of God's upward calling, in Christ Jesus" (Philippians 3:14). We trust that Christ, to whom we are united by Baptism, will give us salvation and that we will continue to accept it until we arrive in heaven.

Salvation of the Unbaptized

Is Baptism necessary for salvation? Jesus said, "No one can enter the kingdom of God without being born of water and Spirit" (John 3:5). Some Christians think this passage means that anyone not actually baptized in water is condemned to hell. But Catholics believe that John 3:5 must be interpreted in the light of Jesus' words at his Ascension: "Whoever believes and is baptized will be saved; whoever does not believe will be condemned" (Mark 16:16). This passage implies that the condemned are those who hear the gospel and refuse to accept it. So the Catholic Church teaches that those who learn of Christ's gospel and culpably reject it are rejecting eternal life. But there are many who are unbaptized through no fault of their own, and the Church believes that they can be saved.

This understanding came very early because some catechumens were martyred before they could be baptized. The Church believes that those who shed their blood for Christ are joined to him by "baptism of blood." Others desire Baptism but die before they can receive it; these people have a explicit "baptism of desire." Still others sincerely try to do what is right but have no opportunity to learn about Christ. These are said to have an implicit "baptism of desire," and the Church teaches that they can be saved.

This teaching has a basis in Scripture. The parable of the Last Judgment in Matthew 25 implies that some will be saved because they ministered to Christ in the poor and hungry, even though they were unaware of his presence in them. It is also common sense: we do not expect people to follow rules they could not have known. Similarly, God would not expect people to obey the command to be baptized if they had no opportunity to learn about it. People who love and do what is right can be saved. They may not know Christ by name, but they know God, who is love: "Everyone who loves is begotten by God and knows God" (1 John 4:7).

The Sacrament of Confirmation

In New Testament times the sending of the Holy Spirit was usually associated with Baptism. Peter told his hearers at Pentecost, "Repent and be baptized...and you will receive the gift of the holy Spirit" (Acts 2:38). But there are some instances in the New Testament of a special "sending" of the Holy Spirit after Baptism. Chapter 8 of Acts tells how the people of Samaria were evangelized and baptized by Philip. When the news reached Jerusalem, the apostles "sent them Peter and John, who went down and prayed for them, that they might receive the holy Spirit, for it had not yet fallen upon any of them; they had only been baptized in the name of the Lord Jesus. Then they laid hands on them and they received the holy Spirit" (Acts 8:14-17; see Acts 19). Such passages provided a basis for the celebration of Confirmation, a sacramental bestowal of the Holy Spirit apart from Baptism, and once infant baptism became common, Confirmation was celebrated later in life.

By the Middle Ages a theology had been developed wherein Confirmation was seen as the sacrament which gives the Holy Spirit to us for strength, service, and evangelization. The bishop was the ordinary minister of Confirmation, and the custom arose of having the bishop visit individual churches to minister the sacrament.

Down through the centuries the age at which individuals might receive Confirmation has varied greatly. In the United States today, those baptized as infants are most often confirmed sometime during the teen years, ordinarily by the bishop. Before Vatican II those baptized as adults were confirmed later by the bishop at his parish visit. But with the RCIA, adults who are baptized or become Catholic through Profession of Faith are confirmed by the priest who receives them into the Church.

The sign used for the bestowal of the Holy Spirit in Confirmation is the laying on of hands (Acts 8:14-17) and anointing with sacred chrism. The use of oil goes back to the anointing of priests, prophets, and kings in the Old Testament. As the minister anoints the confirmand, he says, "(Name), be sealed with the Gift of the Holy Spirit." The term "sealed" indicates the Church's belief that Confirmation bestows a character, a permanent change, as does Baptism, so that these sacraments are not repeated. Each candidate has a sponsor who should help by prayer, example, and support.

The candidate may choose a "Confirmation name" taken from a favorite saint, who is both model and heavenly intercessor.

Pentecost and the Gifts and Fruits of the Holy Spirit

At Pentecost the Holy Spirit came upon the apostles in power, symbolized by fire and a mighty wind (Acts 2), offering friendship and grace to the apostles, allowing them to accomplish what they could not on their own. Confirmation is our Pentecost, when the Spirit offers us grace and friendship.

The effects of the Holy Spirit upon our lives have been expressed traditionally as the *gifts* of the Holy Spirit: wisdom, understanding, counsel, knowledge, courage, reverence, and piety (Isaiah 11:2). The results of the Holy Spirit's friendship are called the *fruits* of the Spirit: love, joy, peace, patience, kindness, generosity, faith, mildness, and chastity (Galatians 5:22-23). These are qualities that can help us lead happy, loving, worthwhile lives, and Confirmation makes them available to us. We are no longer alone when we try to be kind, for example: Jesus models kindness for us, and the Spirit helps us to imitate Jesus. What we could not achieve by our own efforts, we can achieve with God's help as kindness becomes a "fruit" of our relationship with the Holy Spirit.

Confirmation and Friendship With God

Good friends are a source of happiness. Jesus tells us that we can be friends with God (John 15:15). Father, Son, and Spirit love us personally (John 17:23) and want us to be filled with divine life and love. Confirmation is a sacrament that should "confirm" our friendship with God. And while the celebration of Confirmation may take only a short time, it can and should have an effect on our lives.

Two friends might take a vacation together. The event may last only a week but can strengthen friendship for a lifetime. Confirmation is something like that. It is an event that can deepen our friendship with God and change our whole life for the better. But just as the results of a vacation might depend on how well the friends keep in touch afterward, so the results of Confirmation will depend largely on how well we keep in touch with God.

Friends can write, call on the phone, or visit. God won't send us a letter through the postal service, but he has written the Bible for us. He won't call us on the phone, but we can talk to him anytime in prayer. God won't ring our doorbell, but he will visit with us anytime. Bible, prayer, worship: These are crucial to a life of friendship and intimacy with God. Confirmation offers us God's friendship now and forever!

Confirmation and Service

The coming of the Holy Spirit upon the apostles deepened their friendship with God, but it also moved them to do Christ's work. Pentecost got the gospel out from behind locked doors and into the world. Confirmation should help us continue the work of Christ and minister to others. The Holy Spirit offers us gifts like healing and leadership (1 Corinthians 12) for this very reason and helps us understand what we *can* and *should* do.

"Charity begins at home." We begin with our families and acquaintances. When we see someone lonely, hurt, or misunderstood; hungry for food or friendship; imprisoned by fear, worry, or heartache; needing a loving touch or kind word; our response should be what Christ would do if he were in our place.

Next, our parish. We should be a loving community of people who care for one another. Christ asks us to be kind to parishioners by friendliness in the parking lot, words of congratulation after a Baptism, presence at a funeral. Most parishes offer many opportunities for service such as committee work, liturgy, and social-concern organizations.

Then, our world. The Catholic Church provides disaster relief and aid to the needy everywhere in the world. Our gifts to special collections, joined to the gifts of millions of others, can save lives and ease suffering. The Catholic Church joins with other churches to defend the most helpless of human beings, the unborn, and other groups deprived of justice. It is not possible to be actively involved in all social causes, but we can choose at least one organization where we can make a difference through participation, prayer, and monetary gifts.

At home, in our parish, in our world, "if we live in the Spirit, let us also follow the Spirit" (Galatians 5:25).

Signs of the Spirit's Presence

One of the most interesting religious phenomena of this century has been the charismatic movement. It has reached many traditional denominations, including the Catholic Church, and many parishes have charismatic prayer groups.

The charismatic movement emphasizes the importance of the Holy Spirit, of the Bible as God's Word, and of group prayer. Charismatics believe that the Holy Spirit still manifests his presence through gifts like healing, prophecy, and speaking in tongues. These gifts might become evident through the laying on of hands and the "baptism of the Holy Spirit." Charismatic prayer groups often express emotions freely in prayer and worship, and they can have an enthusiasm for their faith which reflects that of the early Church.

Many bishops are actively involved in the charismatic movement, and popes have given their blessing to it. Paul's Letters to the Corinthians show that the Church at Corinth was actively charismatic. But the Church does not teach that all its members should speak in tongues or exercise all the Spirit's gifts. Other churches addressed by Paul in his letters were not as "charismatic" as that of Corinth, and even there not all spoke in tongues (1 Corinthians 12-14). There is room in the Church for a great variety of gifts and ways of worship.

Still, a Catholic might hear about dramatic manifestations of the Holy Spirit in the charismatic movement and wonder, "Have I received the Holy Spirit?" In 1 Corinthians 12:3 Saint Paul states, "No one can say, 'Jesus is Lord,' except by the holy Spirit." In 1 Corinthians 12:31—13:13 he describes love as the greatest gift of the Spirit. Therefore, if we can say with faith that Jesus is Lord, and if we truly love others, we have received the Holy Spirit. Yet we should strive for other spiritual gifts and always try to be more open to the Holy Spirit.

Catholics have the beautiful custom of making the Sign of the Cross with holy water as a reminder of Baptism and Confirmation. This practice should call to mind the great gifts and responsibilities bestowed by these sacraments: "So then you are no longer strangers and sojourners, but you are fellow citizens with the holy ones and members of the household of God, built upon the foundation of the apostles and prophets, with Christ Jesus himself as the capstone. Through him the whole structure is held together and grows into a temple sacred in the Lord; in him you also are being built together into a dwelling place of God in the Spirit" (Ephesians 2:19-22).

Sacraments and Sacramentals

The "Sign of the Cross" and "holy water" are examples of what Catholics call "sacramentals." Sacramentals are sacred signs which resemble the seven sacraments but are not instituted by Christ and do not convey Christ's grace as the sacraments do. Instead, they are instituted by the Church and symbolize spiritual effects. They open us to God's grace if we use them with faith, just as prayer can open our hearts to God. Sacramentals dispose us to receive the grace of the sacraments and sanctify various occasions in human life.

Some sacramentals are related to the sacraments. Holy water, for example, is blessed water that recalls our baptism. All sacramentals remind us of the goodness of the things God has created. Important sacramentals are blessed ashes, bells, candles, crosses, crucifixes, statues, sacred images, medals, oils, palms, rosaries, and prayers of blessing.

Questions for Discussion or Reflection

What are the happiest memories you have of family rituals? What religious rituals and ceremonies have meant the most to you? Have Baptism and Confirmation made a difference in your life?

Activities

Place yourself in God's presence and think of your Baptism, picturing Jesus as the one baptizing you. Feel the water on your forehead as a sign from Christ that he is filling you with his life. See yourself as the dwelling place of Father, Son, and Holy Spirit. Ask the Holy Spirit to make you more aware of these realities. Think about the fruits of the Holy Spirit listed in this chapter. Which of these qualities do you need most? Pick out one, think of how Jesus had that quality, and ask the Holy Spirit to help you be more like Jesus.

CHAPTER SEVEN

The Eucharist — Christ's Meal and Sacrifice

S oon after children are born they let the world know they are hungry. A baby's cry for food is a dramatic expression of our human need for nourishment. But meals do more than sustain the body. When a mother holds her child to her breast, she satisfies not only the need for food but also the need for closeness and love. Meals bring people together when families gather around the dinner table or teenagers have a pizza or friends enjoy a meal at a restaurant. At meals we remember...an anniversary dinner. We celebrate ...a birthday party. We anticipate...a rehearsal meal.

Through Baptism, Christ gives us a share in God's life. This life requires spiritual food and drink, which Christ provides at the Eucharist, a meal that nourishes, unites, remembers, celebrates, and anticipates.

Origins of the Eucharist

On the night the Israelites fled from slavery in Egypt, they were told to slaughter a lamb and smear its blood on the doorpost of their homes. This sign would cause the destroying angel to "pass over" their homes when he struck down the firstborn of the Egyptians. They then ate the lamb with unleavened bread and bitter herbs. They were to repeat this meal each year to commemorate their deliverance from slavery (Exodus 12:1-28; Deuteronomy 16:1-8).

The Passover meal became an occasion which fed the Israelites, body and soul. It nourished them and joined them to God and one another. It recalled God's saving deeds and celebrated their freedom. It anticipated the full redemption God would one day bring them through his Messiah.

It was at a Passover celebration that Jesus gathered his apostles for the Last Supper before his Crucifixion. At this meal Jesus "took bread, said the blessing, broke it, and giving it to his disciples said, 'Take and eat; this is my body.' Then he took a cup, gave thanks, and gave it to them, saying, 'Drink from it, all of you, for this is my blood of the covenant, which will be shed on behalf of many for the forgiveness of sins' " (Matthew 26:26-28). The apostles could not have fully understood these words that night. But after Christ's death and Resurrection, they realized that in some mysterious way the bread and wine had become Jesus Christ. Christ was their spiritual food and drink!

"This Is My Body. This Is My Blood."

Catholics believe that when Jesus said the words, "This is my body....This is my blood," he meant exactly what he said. For Jews, "body" meant the person, and "blood" was the source of life identifiable with the person. So Jesus was saying over the bread and cup, "This is myself," and we believe that the bread and wine truly become the very person of Jesus.

The traditional theological term for this miracle is "transubstantiation." It means that the "substance" of the bread and wine becomes the "substance" of Christ's body and blood, while the appearances of bread and wine remain. When a priest says the words of Jesus — the words of consecration — over the bread and wine, they still retain the appearance and taste of bread and wine, but they become Christ himself, who is then as truly present to us as he was to the apostles.

The New Testament bears witness to the reality of Christ's presence in the Eucharist. The Gospel of John devotes the entire sixth chapter to Jesus as the "Bread of Life." First, Jesus multiplies loaves and fish, a miracle which foreshadows his ability to "multiply his presence" in the Eucharist. Then he walks on water, showing his divine power over nature, a power capable of changing bread into his body. Finally, he urges the crowd to work not "for food that perishes but for the food that endures for eternal life" (John 6:27). This food is Jesus: "I am the living bread that came down from heaven; whoever eats this bread will live forever; and the bread that I will give is my flesh for the life of the world" (6:51).

When his listeners objected, Jesus declared: "Unless you eat the flesh of the Son of Man and drink his blood, you do not have life within you. Whoever eats my flesh and drinks my blood has eternal life, and I will raise him on the last day. For my flesh is true food and my blood is true drink. Whoever eats my flesh and drinks my blood remains in me and I in him. Just as the living Father sent me and I have life because of the Father, so also the one who feeds on me will have life because of me. This is the bread that came down from heaven. Unlike your ancestors who ate and still died, whoever eats this bread will live forever" (6:53-58).

These words stunned his disciples. "This saying is hard," they said "Who can accept it?" (6:60) Many "returned to their former way of life and no longer accompanied him" (6:66). But Jesus did not call out, "Wait, you misunderstood. I didn't mean that the bread is my body, but that it only *represents* my body." Instead, he asked his apostles, "Do you also want to leave?" Peter answered, "Master, to whom shall we go? You have the words of eternal life. We have come to believe and are convinced that you are the Holy One of God" (6:67-69).

Jesus did not "water down" his statements in the least. They were hard to accept, and Peter did not claim to understand them. He simply accepted them on the authority of Jesus, who had "the words of eternal life."

Saint Paul also believed in the words, "This is my body." After criticizing the Corinthians for their irreverence in receiving the Eucharist, he stated bluntly, "Whoever eats the bread or drinks the cup of the Lord unworthily will have to answer for the body and blood of the Lord" (1 Corinthians 11:27).

Catholics do not claim to understand how bread and wine become Christ's body and blood. We accept, as Peter did, the "words of eternal life." We believe, as Paul did, that the bread and wine are the "body and blood of the Lord."

The Eucharist as a Meal:
Jesus Gives Nourishment and Life

The Eucharist is a meal, for Christ gave us the Eucharist at a Passover meal, and he chose food and drink as the elements to be changed into his presence. The early Christians saw the celebration of the Eucharist as a meal: Saint Paul called it the "Lord's supper" (1 Corinthians 11:20).

Jesus spoke of the Eucharist as food and drink: "My flesh is true food, and my blood is true drink" (John 6:55). Jesus wants us to draw a parallel between what food and drink do for us and what the Eucharist does for us. Food and drink nourish our body and become our body. The Eucharist nourishes us, but in this case we become what we receive. We are transformed into Christ!

Using the imagery of vine and branches, Jesus explains that we receive life from him: "Remain in me, as I remain in you. Just as a branch cannot bear fruit on its own unless it remains on the vine, so neither can you unless you remain in me. I am the vine, you are the branches" (John 15:4-5). The Eucharist is the means by which we remain in Christ and receive his life. "Just as the living Father sent me and I have life because of the Father, so also the one who feeds on me will have life because of me" (John 6:57). As a healthy branch receives life from the vine, so we can thrive when we are sustained by the life of Christ.

The Eucharist as a Meal: Jesus Unites Us to Himself

Meals join people to one another. When we receive Jesus in the Eucharist, we are joined to him. Jesus loves us so much that he died for us. He spoke of us as God's gift to him and prayed that we might be one with him (John 17:24). Jesus gave us the Eucharist to unite us to him. "Whoever eats my flesh and drinks my blood remains in me and I in him" (John 6:56).

To really grasp the meaning of this we need to think about special moments of human closeness: parents holding a child, a husband and wife together, time spent with a best friend. The Eucharist is all this — and more. The Eucharist is union with Jesus, with the Father, and with the Holy Spirit, and traditionally Catholics have referred to the reception of Jesus in the Eucharist as "Holy Communion."

The Eucharist as a Meal: Jesus Unites Us to One Another

The Eucharistic meal joins us not only to Christ but also to one another. Those who receive Jesus are one because they receive the one Christ. "The cup of blessing that we bless, is it not a participation in the blood of Christ? The bread that we break, is it not a participation in the body of Christ? Because the loaf of bread is one, we, though many, are one body, for we all partake of the one loaf" (1 Corinthians 10:16-17). We long for unity and peace. So does Jesus: "I pray...for those who will believe in me...that they may all be one, as you, Father, are in me and I in you, that they also may be in us, that the world may believe that you sent me" (John 17:20-21). He even died "to gather into one the dispersed children of God" (John 11:52), and at every Mass, Jesus brings us together: husband, wife, parents, children, brothers, sisters, friends, strangers.

The Eucharist as Sacrifice

The Passover meal was also a sacrifice, an offering to the Lord. After the escape from Egypt, Moses sacrificed young bulls at Mount Sinai, splashed some of their blood on God's altar, and sprinkled some on the people. This was a covenant sacrifice expressing the union between God and his people. At the time of Jesus, lambs for the Passover were slaughtered at the Temple; their blood was shed and their flesh was eaten with unleavened bread. The Israelites thereby recalled the Exodus and renewed their covenant with God.

With this as background Jesus celebrated the Last Supper. He told his disciples, "No one has greater love than this, to lay down one's life for one's friends" (John 15:13). He made it clear that the Supper was intimately linked to his coming death. He took bread, "broke it" as a sign that his body would be "broken" on the cross, and said, "This is my body, which will be given for you" (Luke 22:19). He took wine and said, "This is my blood of the covenant, which will be shed on behalf of many for the forgiveness of sins" (Matthew 26:28).

This is why Catholics speak of the Eucharist as a sacrifice. Jesus gave his life; he shed his blood for us. In doing so he established a New Covenant between God and us (Hebrews 9:11-15). As the Last Supper anticipated Christ's death on the cross, so each celebration of the Eucharist remembers that death. Saint Paul wrote: "As often as you eat this bread and drink the cup, you proclaim the death of the Lord until he comes" (1 Corinthians 11:26). Catholics believe that the Eucharist makes present the death of Jesus. This does not mean that Christ dies again (Hebrews 7:27). But the Eucharist is a miracle that rolls away the centuries and allows us to stand at the cross of Christ. "The cup of blessing that we bless, is it not a participation in the blood of Christ? The bread that we break, is it not a participation in the body of Christ?" (1 Corinthians 10:16-17).

The "separate consecration" of the bread and wine serves as a reminder that once in history Christ's blood was separated from his body when he died on the cross. When the Eucharist is celebrated today, however, Christ's blood is not separated from his body. The Christ who becomes present at the words of consecration is the risen, glorified Christ. Catholics believe that Christ is fully present in both the bread and wine and that we receive Christ when we communicate under the form of either bread or wine. At the same time we remember that Christ once gave his life for us in the sacrifice of Calvary.

The Eucharist and Everlasting Life

The Jesus who sacrificed his life for us rose from the grave on Easter Sunday, and we receive him in the Eucharist (Philippians 2:5-11). The Eucharist nourishes the life given to us in Baptism and Confirmation, and that life is eternal (Romans 6:3-11). For these reasons the Eucharist is a special sign of hope that we will live forever.

Jesus wanted this to be so. He said, "Whoever eats my flesh and drinks my blood has eternal life, and I will raise him up on the last day....Whoever eats this bread will live forever" (John 6:54, 58). For Saint Paul the Eucharist was not a memorial to someone dead and gone, but to Christ who is alive and will come again (1 Corinthians 11:26). At every Eucharist we look with confidence to that day when Christ will come to lead us through death to everlasting life.

The Eucharist Through the Centuries

The first Christians in Jerusalem "devoted themselves to the teaching of the apostles and to the communal life, to the breaking of the bread and to the prayers" (Acts 2:42). This passage may well refer to the prayers, readings, and celebration of the Lord's Supper. Christians certainly developed patterns for the Eucharist very early, for Saint Paul had to correct the Corinthians about abuses at meals they shared in connection with the Lord's Supper (1 Corinthians 11:20-34).

Around A.D. 150 Saint Justin described a celebration of the Eucharist that closely resembled today's Catholic Mass. ("Mass" comes from the Latin word for dismissal from the assembly.) The people gathered together on Sunday, the "Lord's day," participated in prayers and hymns, and listened to readings from the Old Testament and from the writings of the apostles. Then bread, wine, and water were offered, and the words of Jesus at the Last Supper were prayed by the one presiding. The people received the body and blood of Christ, and Communion was brought to the sick. A collection was taken for the poor and needy.

There were many variations around this basic pattern. With the passage of time came a tendency to emphasize the mystery of the Mass as a ceremony performed by the priest and watched by the people. In 1570 after the Council of Trent, Pope Pius V decreed that all Masses in the Roman Catholic Church should be celebrated according to definite rules set up in the *Roman Missal*. For almost four centuries Mass was prayed in Latin from this missal.

By the middle of the twentieth century a movement for liturgical renewal encouraged more participation on the part of the congregation, along patterns observed in the early days of the Church. Since Vatican II, Mass has been celebrated in the language of the people, and participation by the congregation and by ministers such as lectors and Eucharistic ministers has become common.

Liturgy of the Word
and Liturgy of the Eucharist

"Liturgy" means "work," and the liturgy is certainly one of the most important works of the Church. Liturgy embraces all official worship of the Church, but it is often used to refer specifically to the Mass. Within the Mass itself there are two main divisions — the Liturgy of the Word and the Liturgy of the Eucharist.

The Liturgy of the Word begins with the Sign of the Cross and greetings exchanged by priest and people. There is a brief pause to call to mind our sins and an act of sorrow. On Sundays (and other special days) we may pray the Glory, a hymn of praise. After the priest offers a prayer, the Scriptures are read. The usual pattern for Sundays and special feasts is a first reading from the Old Testament, a responsorial psalm, a second reading from a New Testament book, an acclamation verse, and a reading from a gospel. On weekdays, before the gospel there is only one reading from either the Old or New Testament, followed by the responsorial psalm. Then a "homily" is given, applying the readings to everyday life. On Sundays and major feasts the congregation professes its faith by praying the Nicene Creed. The Liturgy of the Word closes with the Prayer of the Faithful, in which we place our needs before God.

The Liturgy of the Eucharist begins when the offerings of the community and the bread and wine are brought to the altar. These are presented to God by the priest, who then washes his hands as a sign of our need for purification. After a prayer over the gifts, and one said by priest and congregation asking God to accept the sacrifice, we move to the Eucharistic Prayer. Its introduction is called the Preface, chosen from many options to suit the occasion. There are nine different Eucharistic Prayers, including three for children's Masses and two for reconciliation. All include the words used by Jesus at the Last Supper, by which the bread and wine become Christ (the "Consecration"). The Eucharistic Prayer concludes with the Great Amen, proclaimed by the congregation as its "yes" to all that has gone before. We then recite the Our Father, which is followed by a prayer for deliverance from evil and a prayer for peace. Remembering that we must be at peace with one another before we can approach God's altar (Matthew 5:23), we offer a sign of peace. Those taking holy Communion receive Christ under the sign of bread or both bread and wine. After Communion there is time for quiet reflection and thanksgiving. The Mass draws to a close as the priest says a prayer, then blesses and dismisses the congregation.

Within this general structure of the Mass there are many options possible. People just starting to attend Mass can become familiar with it by requesting one of the missalettes available at many churches. Some may feel self-conscious and fearful of making a blunder at Mass; a good rule is to observe what others are doing, whether standing, sitting, or kneeling, then imitate them.

Hymns may be sung at Mass, and many parts of the Mass may be sung by priest and congregation. "Singing is praying twice," according to Saint Augustine, with words and melody. Singing praises God and brings people together.

Guidelines for Receiving Communion

From the earliest days of the Church, receiving the Lord in holy Communion was seen as a sign of unity with the Church. Those preparing to join the Church did not receive Communion until they were baptized and confirmed at the Easter Vigil. Today Communion signifies unity with the Church in sacramental life, belief, and morals. This is expressed in guidelines for the reception of holy Communion issued by the National Conference of Catholic Bishops on November 8, 1986:

For Catholics:
Catholics fully participate in the celebration of the Eucharist when they receive Holy Communion in fulfillment of Christ's command to eat His Body and drink His Blood. In order to be properly disposed to receive Communion, communicants should not be conscious of grave sin, have fasted for an hour, and seek to live in charity and love with their neighbors. Persons conscious of grave sin must first be reconciled with God and the Church through the sacrament of Penance....

For Other Christians:
We welcome to this celebration of the Eucharist those Christians who are not fully united with us. It is a consequence of the sad divisions in Christianity that we cannot extend to them a general invitation to receive Communion. Catholics believe that the Eucharist is an action of the celebrating community signifying a oneness in faith, life and worship of the community. Reception of the Eucharist by Christians not fully united with us would imply a oneness which does not yet exist and for which we must all pray.

(*Origins,* January 15, 1987, Vol. 16, No. 31, pg. 554)

The Eucharist and the Liturgical Year

We celebrate great events each year. We have holidays to recall events like the birth of our nation. We anticipate special days with decorations, parties, and family traditions. We may relive certain events by re-creating battles and sponsoring pageants. Between holidays life returns to its ordinary routine.

The "liturgical year" is the Church's way of celebrating and reliving the great events of our salvation. Each year follows a pattern, and the readings and prayers for Mass have been organized to fit into it. The liturgical year begins with Advent, four weeks of preparation for Christmas. On December 25 we observe the birthday of Christ and reflect on the Incarnation. After Christmas other feasts prolong the celebration: Holy Family Sunday, the Solemnity of Mary, Mother of God (New Year's Day), Epiphany, and the Baptism of the Lord.

There follows a period of Ordinary Time, the length of which depends on the date of Easter. The Lenten preparation for Easter begins on Ash Wednesday, when we are marked with ashes on our foreheads as a sign of willingness to do penance and reform our lives. As catechumens make final preparations for Baptism, all Catholics are challenged during Lent to die to sin and rise to new life. Lent ends at the sacred triduum, three days which relive the events of the first Holy Thursday, Good Friday, and Holy Saturday. We celebrate the Resurrection with the Easter Vigil and the Masses of Easter, the greatest feast of the Church year. Easter season continues through Ascension Thursday (forty days after Easter) and ends on Pentecost Sunday (ten days after Ascension).

Ordinary Time resumes the day after Pentecost, but the next two Sundays commemorate the Trinity and the Body and Blood of Christ. Ordinary Time continues through the last Sunday of the liturgical year, the Solemnity of Christ the King, after which the First Sunday of Advent starts the cycle again.

Christ is free of the limits of space and time and relives with us the events of his life through the liturgical year. Through Scripture readings and prayers appropriate to the events being celebrated, God speaks to us. We respond by participating in the liturgy, and so are joined to the birth, life, dying, and rising of Christ, as once again Jesus walks the pathways of our world.

All through the liturgical year, special place is given to Sunday, observed as the Lord's day because Christ rose on the first day of the week. Most major liturgical observances occur on Sunday, but there are also special feasts in the liturgical year called holy days of obligation. In the United States we observe six: Christmas on December 25; Solemnity of Mary, Mother of God on January 1; Ascension Thursday, Mary's Assumption on August 15; All Saints'

Day on November 1; and the Immaculate Conception on December 8.

There is a cycle of Scripture readings at Mass found in the book called the *Lectionary* following a three-year pattern for Sundays and a two-year pattern for weekdays. Prayers, found in the altar book, the *Sacramentary,* are repeated annually.

Throughout the liturgical year the Catholic Church observes feast days in honor of the saints. As we remember their lives in special prayers at Mass and ask them to pray for us, we heed the biblical command: "Remember your leaders who spoke the word of God to you. Consider the outcome of their way of life and imitate their faith" (Hebrews 13:7).

The Sunday Obligation

Sundays are special. Christians in New Testament times met for the breaking of the bread on the first day of the week (Acts 20:7). They thus obeyed the third commandment: "Keep holy the Lord's day." Jesus had said, "Do this in remembrance of me," and they hastened to do what the Lord had asked of them.

As time passed, some Christians fell away. The author of the Letter to the Hebrews urged his readers to be faithful: "We should not stay away from our assembly, as is the custom of some, but encourage one another, and this all the more as you see the day drawing near" (Hebrews 10:25). Worthy participation in the Eucharist is essential to life in Christ, as Saint Paul noted (1 Corinthians 11:29-30). In times of persecution Christians risked their lives to share the Eucharist. For them it was a great privilege to be invited to the Lord's Supper.

Today, almost two thousand years later, the Catholic Church maintains its belief in the importance of the Eucharist. Surely we ought not say, "No, thank you," to the Lord's own invitation to "do this in remembrance" of him, and so the Church points out the necessity of the Eucharist by requiring that we attend holy Mass on Sundays and holy days. Except when we are prevented from sharing in the Mass by illness or responsibilities such as caring for the sick, we should attend Mass as gladly as we would respond to any personal invitation from Jesus himself.

All at Mass have a unique part to play in offering their lives to the Father in union with Christ's offering of his life on the cross.

All can bring to Mass the events of the past week and their hopes for the week ahead. Our offering is incomplete when some believers are absent. Further, we go to Mass in order to be with others. Attending Mass is not like attending a movie, where many happen to be together to see the same show. It is rather like a family reunion, which we attend precisely to meet others and to express and strengthen our unity. When any Catholic is missing, our family reunion in Christ is less than it should be.

Sight, Scent, Sound, Touch, and Taste

Jesus loved the world he entered through the Incarnation. His parables are full of sight, scent, sound, touch, and taste. He obviously believed that truth, beauty, and grace can be conveyed through created things. In Catholic liturgy material things are used to "incarnate" spiritual realities, and Catholic churches are typically full of sights, scents, sounds, and things to touch and taste.

Colors are used in vestments and altar adornments to express various meanings. Purple and violet signify anticipation, purification, or penance, and are used in Advent and Lent. Red is the color of blood and symbolizes the supreme sacrifice of life given for others; it is used for Passion Sunday, Good Friday, and the feasts of martyrs. Red is also the color of fire and is used on Pentecost Sunday. White expresses joy, purity, and eternal life; it is used for most feasts of our Lord, for the seasons of Christmas and Easter, for funerals, for feasts of saints, and for angels. Green, the color of growing things, is symbolic of life and the vitality of faith, hope, and love. It is used for Ordinary Time.

Anyone attending Mass will see the crucifix, vessels containing bread and wine, candles, statues, stained-glass windows, familiar faces, flowers, and many other sights which delight the senses, teach the mind, and warm the heart.

Scent enhances worship. Incense is used to signify our adoration of God and our hope that prayer will rise up as does the smoke and odor of incense (Psalm 141:1-2; Revelation 5:8). Flowers add the beauty of scent, as well as of sight.

Sound is a part of worship. Bells are rung to summon the congregation, announce a death, or proclaim our joy. Musical instruments express every human emotion and nuance of worship. Prayers are said and hymns are sung.

As many Catholics enter a church, they touch their fingers to holy water and sign themselves with the cross. Touch becomes a way for us to reach out to others at the sign of peace and other times. Kneeling and standing and sitting are postures for worship, prayer, listening, and reflection.

"Taste and see how good the LORD is," exhorted the psalmist (Psalm 34:9). We experience the truth of this when we receive the Lord in Holy Communion. The taste of bread, the staff of life, tells us of the eternal life Christ gives in the Eucharist. The taste of wine, that gladdens our hearts (Psalm 104:15), opens our minds and hearts to the joy and peace that only Christ can give.

God loves the world he made. We Catholics believe this, and following Jesus we find in sight, scent, sound, touch, and taste ways to worship our God and to receive blessings from his hands. We thus open our lives to the central reality of the Eucharist, Jesus Christ, the Word made flesh.

All I Want Is to Know Christ

Some people say they get nothing out of Mass, that the sermons are boring, and that churchgoers are no better than anyone else. They should recall that Jesus' own townspeople rejected him because they didn't like his sermons and because he seemed so ordinary (Luke 4:16-30). Without denying the importance of good sermons and the need to strive for holiness, we must remember that Christ does not need perfect preachers to touch our hearts and that he came to save sinners.

The Mass does not depend on any one thing for its value or meaning. There are prayers and Scripture readings which never lose their power as God's Word. There are the avenues of sight, scent, sound, touch, and taste by which we can draw closer to heaven. There is always the Lord. The church may be humble, the singing off-key, the preacher ordinary. But at Christ's words, "This is my body," all limitations are stripped away and we stand in the very presence of God. It is, above all, at the Eucharist that we make Saint Paul's wish our own: "All I want is to know Christ and to experience the power of his resurrection, to share in his sufferings and become like him in his death, in the hope that I myself will be raised from death to life" (Philippians 3:10-11, *Good News Bible*).

Questions for Discussion or Reflection

Why do you think people have risked their lives to smuggle bread and wine into concentrations camps to celebrate the Eucharist? Some Protestant denominations have an "altar call," inviting people to come to the altar and accept Jesus as Savior. How is Holy Communion like an altar call? And much more besides? When you attend Mass, you are standing at Calvary near the cross of Jesus. Compare your attitude with the attitudes of those who witnessed Christ's death on Calvary. Is your attitude like that of Mary, of the soldiers, of the Jewish leaders, or of indifferent passers-by?

Activities

If you find Mass boring, it may be that you are coming because you "have to" or only to "get something" out of Mass. Try coming because you want to give something. Come to give God your thanks and worship. Come to give Jesus your love and friendship. Come to give prayers for others, a smile to others, a helping hand to the elderly. Come to give a part of your income to the work of the Church. Come to give God all the events of your past week and your hopes and plans for the next week. If you come to church to give, Mass will never be boring!

CHAPTER EIGHT

Reconciliation — Jesus Forgives

"**N**othing is new under the sun" (Ecclesiastes 1:9). We constantly rediscover old truths. One truth redis-covered in our time is that "confession is good for the soul." Psychiatry and psychology are relatively new sciences, but they frequently depend on the old art of listening to problems, which often include guilt. Guilt can eat away at people, causing physical and emotional ills, but when it is brought to the surface, healing begins. Confession is good for the soul.

Jesus knew this well. He came to call sinners (Mark 2:17), wel-comed them, and ate with them (Luke 15:2). He listened to people unburden themselves of guilt and spoke words of healing, "Your sins are forgiven" (Mark 2:5).

The Reality of Sin

Karl Menninger, a psychiatrist, wrote a book entitled *Whatever Became of Sin?* In it he said that people worry about crime, violence, terrorism, war, cheating, unethical conduct, and a host of other problems, but still avoid talk of sin. Yet sin exists and should be spelled "s-I-n," for it means that I set myself and my choices against those of God and others. Sin is pride and self-centeredness.

"Nothing is new under the sun." The Bible tells us how God created human beings and invited them to choose what was right. Instead, Adam and Eve ate from the "tree of knowledge of good and bad." In effect, they said to God, "We will tell you what is right and wrong." They set their choices against God's, and sin entered the world, alienating people from God, from one another, and from creation: Adam and Eve hid from God, blamed each other, and felt pain and suffering. And over everything fell the dark shadow of death (Genesis 2-3).

Adam and Eve are all those who make sinful choices and live in a world which is less than paradise because it is limited by the sins of countless generations. "All have sinned and are deprived of the glory of God" (Romans 3:23).

Repeatedly, the world has been overwhelmed by sin, nations destroyed by war, and societies undermined by lust. Sin immerses people in a flood of self-inflicted evil, as the story of Noah illustrates (Genesis 6-9).

What is true for society is true for us as individuals. When we oppose the will of God and choose our way over his, we inevitably suffer. Through sin we lose peace of mind and find instead the anguish of guilt and self-reproach.

The Mercy and Forgiveness of God

Sin is a flood of evil from which we can be rescued only by the ark of God's forgiveness. The good news of the Bible is that forgiveness is available, for God is "gracious and merciful, slow to anger and of great kindness" (Psalm 145:8). The Israelites experienced that forgiveness, even for crimes as great as those of David, who murdered a loyal soldier and stole his wife (2 Samuel 11-12). Again and again they turned from God. Again and again overwhelmed by the consequences of sin, they returned to God for mercy and forgiveness.

But the human race as a whole was unresponsive to God's law and call for repentance. We were held captive by sin (Romans 1-3), but God did not abandon us. Instead, he revealed his great mercy: "When the fullness of time had come, God sent his Son, born of a woman, born under the law, to ransom those under the law, so that we might receive adoption" (Galatians 4:4-5).

Jesus, Messenger of God's Mercy and Forgiveness

The message of Jesus presumed the existence of sin and the opportunity for forgiveness: "This is the time of fulfillment. The kingdom of God is at hand. Repent, and believe in the gospel" (Mark 1:15). Whereas many of Israel's religious leaders shunned sinners, Jesus associated with them and extended God's mercy to them with remarkable sympathy, sensitivity, and understanding.

There was the sinful woman who knelt before Jesus while he was dining at the house of Simon the Pharisee. She bathed Jesus' feet with her tears, wiped them with her hair, and anointed them with ointment. This act of contrition drew scorn from the Pharisees, but Jesus praised her great love. He spoke the words she wanted so much to hear: "Your sins are forgiven....Go in peace" (Luke 7:48, 50).

There was the tax collector, Zacchaeus (Luke 19:1-10), who heard that the famous teacher, Jesus, was coming to Jericho. Unhappy in his wealthy isolation, he must have longed for the mercy and understanding of Jesus. Small of stature, he could not see Jesus because of the crowds, so he climbed a tree. Jesus looked into his heart and saw a need for forgiveness, a desire to change, and promptly invited himself to Zacchaeus' house. Some grumbled, saying, "He has gone to stay at the house of a sinner." But Zacchaeus knew that Jesus was offering him a new life. He stood his ground and said, "Behold, half of my possessions, Lord, I shall give to the poor, and if I have extorted anything from anyone I shall repay it four times over." Jesus responded, "Today salvation has come to this house...for the Son of Man has come to seek and to save what was lost." And so a man imprisoned by greed was set free by the love, understanding, and mercy of Jesus (Luke 19:1-10).

The full extent of Christ's capacity for forgiveness was shown as he died on the cross. He prayed even for those who had crucified him: "Father, forgive them, they know not what they do" (Luke 23:34). Then one of the criminals nailed beside him asked for mercy, "Jesus, remember me when you come into your kingdom." Jesus assured him of pardon, "Amen, I say to you, today you will be with me in Paradise" (Luke 23:42-43).

These people, and so many others, experienced interaction with the Divinity which had previously been impossible. They looked into God's eyes and saw sympathy and understanding, stood in God's presence and shared their sorrow and shame. They heard God say, "Your sins are forgiven. Go in peace."

Parables of Pardon and Peace

Jesus showed by word and action that God is more merciful than we ever imagined. Lest we still underestimate God's readiness to forgive, Jesus described it in parables. The most beautiful of these are found in Luke's Gospel.

There is the parable of the Lost Sheep. The shepherd searches until he finds the sheep, "sets it on his shoulders with great joy and, upon his arrival home, he calls together his friends and neighbors and says to them, 'Rejoice with me because I have found my lost sheep' " (Luke 15:5-6).

There follows the parable of the Lost Coin. A woman loses a coin. She searches until she finds it, then calls friends in to celebrate (Luke 15:8-10).

Finally, Jesus tells the parable of the Prodigal Son. A young man insolently asks his father for his inheritance, leaves, and squanders everything. Reduced to destitution, he decides to return home, asking only to be allowed back as a servant. His father sees him coming, rushes out to embrace him, and welcomes him back with a magnificent party (Luke 15:11-32).

These three parables convey the same message: the unbelievable love and mercy of God. In each parable there is a party even though, by human standards, there is really no reason for it. Sheep are always wandering off. A shepherd throwing a party because he found one sheep would be thought strange. The same could be said for a woman who calls friends to celebrate because she found a misplaced coin. And any Jewish father who killed a fatted calf because an ungrateful son came crawling back in desperate need would be judged insane. That is precisely the point! God is so merciful that by human standards he is "off the scale." We might suppose that one sinner out of billions of people on the globe couldn't possibly matter to God. On the contrary, there is "rejoicing among the angels of God over one sinner who repents" (Luke 15:10).

Christ Shares With His Church
the Power to Forgive

Christ offered forgiveness and taught us about God's mercy. Then he made the supreme sacrifice of love, giving his life for us. "For Christ, while we were still helpless, yet died at the appointed time for the ungodly. Indeed, only with difficulty does one die for a just person....But God proves his love for us in that while we were still sinners Christ died for us" (Romans 5:6-8).

In light of all this it would have been surprising if Jesus had not given his Church a sacrament for the forgiveness of sins. The Catholic Church believes that Jesus did so in the Sacrament of Penance, known also as Reconciliation or Confession.

The Sacrament of Penance

The gift of forgiveness was the very first gift made by Jesus to his apostles after the Resurrection. "On the evening of that first day of the week, when the doors were locked, where the disciples were, for fear of the Jews, Jesus came and stood in their midst and said to them, 'Peace be with you.' When he had said this, he showed them his hands and his side. The disciples rejoiced when they saw the Lord. [Jesus] said to them again, 'Peace be with you. As the Father has sent me, so I send you.' And when he had said this, he breathed on them and said to them, 'Receive the holy Spirit. Whose sins you forgive are forgiven them, and whose sins you retain are retained' " (John 20:19-23).

Scripture scholars debate about whether these words refer to Baptism, to Penance, or to both. But they certainly convey the belief of the first Christians that Jesus had entrusted to them his mission to forgive sins, and they shared his forgiveness in many ways: Baptism, Eucharist, Anointing, prayer, and the Sacrament of Penance.

The Sacrament of Penance has undergone many developments. The earliest evidence indicates that those who sinned after Baptism were reconciled to the Church through the bishop. Some heretical groups denied that serious sins could be forgiven, but this opinion was condemned by the Council of Nicea in 325, and at this time this Sacrament of Penance was applied to sins such as adultery, apostasy, and murder. Sinners went through a long period of public penance and were reconciled to the Church at Easter. In the sixth century, through the influence of Irish monks, Penance became available for less serious sins, and private confession of sins replaced the rigorous discipline of earlier times.

In the twelfth century the theology of Penance took on dimensions that shaped usage of the sacrament to our own day. Theologians explained that Penance included contrition (sorrow and conversion), confession of sins to a priest, satisfaction (doing penance for one's sins), and absolution (declaration of forgiveness) by a priest. These four elements were affirmed by the Council of Trent in 1551 after the sacraments were questioned by Protestants. By the twentieth century it was common for Catholics to go to confession quite frequently, usually following a set pattern for the sacrament.

Vatican II called for a revision of Penance in order to express more clearly its nature and effects. A new Rite of Reconciliation was established in 1974. It expanded the use of Scripture, emphasized the role of the priest as a healer in Christ's name, pointed out the importance of the Church in reconciling us with God, and offered options for the reception of the sacrament.

The first option is individual reception of the Sacrament of Penance, either behind a screen or face to face. The second is a communal service, where many people gather to pray and prepare for the sacrament, and then have the opportunity for individual confession of sins. The third option, general confession and absolution, is used in emergency situations where enough priests are not available for individual confessions.

Preparing for the Sacrament of Penance

The Sacrament of Penance is a meeting with Christ. We should begin preparation for it by praying for the faith to be fully aware of Christ's presence. We should pray also for the grace to see our lives as Christ does, recognize our sins, understand how they offend God, and then confess them honestly.

Next we examine our conscience. There are pamphlets and books available for this, or the following guide may be used. All unconfessed serious (mortal) sins should be told. "Mortal sins" are those that involve serious matter and are committed with full knowledge and full consent of the will. Less serious sins are called venial sins. (More will be said about this in chapter thirteen). We should look for our most significant venial sins, pick out two or three, and confess them. We should not make a "grocery list" of sins but look into the reasons why we fail and into the attitudes behind our sins.

An Examination of Conscience Based on the Ten Commandments

(See Exodus 20:1-20 and Deuteronomy 5:1-21.)

1. I am the Lord your God. You shall not have other gods besides me. Do I think about God and put God first in my life? Do I set aside time each day for prayer and Bible reading? Am I superstitious? Am I too materialistic? Am I proud or self-centered?

2. You shall not take the name of the Lord your God in vain. Do I use God's name reverently? Do I often think of God the Father as my Creator, Jesus as my Savior, the Holy Spirit as my Helper? Do I sin by cursing, swearing, or careless use of God's name?

3. Remember to keep holy the Lord's day. Do I worship God faithfully at Sunday Mass, holy days, and other times? Do I do anything special — like prayer, Bible reading, and family time — to make Sunday the "Lord's day"? Have I done my share for my parish through volunteer service?

4. Honor your father and your mother. Do I respect and care for my parents and other members of my family? Do I find ways to show my love for them and tell them I love them? Do I show gratitude to them? Do I fulfill my responsibilities and do my share of work at home? Do I pray with members of my family? If a parent, do I offer spiritual leadership? Have I disobeyed those who have authority over me?

5. You shall not kill. Have I reached out to the sick, elderly, and lonely? Do I pray and work for peace and justice? Have I been courteous? Have I ever injured anyone? Have I taken part in an abortion? Have I injured myself through alcohol, drugs, smoking, overeating, or excessive dieting? Have I hated or refused to forgive? Am I prejudiced? Do I belittle or discourage others?

6. You shall not commit adultery. Have I been pure in words and actions? Does my clothing reflect the standards of Christ? Have I sinned by adultery, fornication, or other impure actions? Have I indulged in bad movies, television, reading, or other entertainments that offend against decency?

7. You shall not steal. Have I given an honest day's work for my wages? Have I been fair to employees? Have I been generous in my gifts to the poor and to the Church? Do I let Christ's teachings guide me in business matters? Have I stolen anything, been dishonest, or cheated?

8. You shall not bear false witness against your neighbor. Have I consciously tried to speak well of others? Have I been truthful? Have I gossiped? Have I judged others? Have I betrayed secrets?

9. You shall not covet your neighbor's wife. Have I been holy in my thoughts, a "temple of the Holy Spirit"? Have I indulged in impure thoughts and desires? Have I led others into sexual sin?

10. You shall not covet your neighbor's goods. Have I made heaven my true goal in life and focused my hopes on God? Do I appreciate God's free gifts, such as the beauties of nature? Have I been generous with my time, talents, and treasure? Have I been envious or jealous of others? Do I make myself and others unhappy by my complaints, my self-pity, or my selfishness?

Celebrating the Sacrament of Penance

In most Catholic churches there are reconciliation rooms furnished with a kneeler, screen, and chairs. The penitent has a choice of kneeling behind the screen and confessing anonymously or sitting in a chair and confessing face to face. Reconciliation is celebrated as follows:

1. Reception of the penitent. After the penitent exchanges greetings with the priest, the two make the Sign of the Cross. The priest says a short prayer to which the penitent responds, "Amen."

2. Reading of God's Word. The priest may read or recite a brief passage of Scripture, or the penitent may do so.

3. Confession of sins. The penitent tells how long it has been since the last confession (an approximation is sufficient) and confesses sins for which forgiveness is needed. The priest may offer words of advice or encouragement, then gives an act of penance or prayer.

4. Prayer of penitent and absolution. The penitent expresses sorrow through any act of contrition (for example, "Jesus, I am sorry for all my sins. Have mercy on me"). The priest says the prayer of absolution, and the penitent responds, "Amen."

5. Proclamation of praise of God and dismissal. The priest says, "Give thanks to the Lord, for he is good." The penitent answers, "His mercy endures forever." The priest closes with a short blessing or prayer.

After confession, we should thank God for the grace of the sacrament and carry out the penance given us by the priest.

In communal services, people gather at church at a scheduled time. The ceremony may begin with a song. There are prayers and Scripture readings, examination of conscience, an act of sorrow, then individual confessions and absolution. People may remain after confession for a closing prayer, blessing, and hymn. Such celebrations remind us that sin has a communal dimension; any sin, even the most private, harms the Church, just as a wound to any part of the body injures the whole person. Communal services of penance also let people pray with and for one another, allowing Christ to touch hearts in remarkable ways.

The Value
of Confession

It is one thing to know how to go to confession. It is another thing to go! Most people find it hard to admit guilt, and they ask, "Why must I confess my sins to another human being? Why can't I confess them directly to God?"

We can and should confess directly to God as soon as we are aware that we have committed any sin, large or small. The Sacrament of Penance is regarded as absolutely necessary by the Church only when a Catholic has committed a serious sin and wishes to receive the Eucharist. Since Catholics are required, as a minimum, to receive Communion at least once during the Easter season (Ash Wednesday to Trinity Sunday), Penance is necessary then for those in serious sin. Those free of serious sin are not required to go to confession.

Hopefully, however, we who are followers of Jesus will look beyond what we "must" do to what we "should" do. Jesus has given the Sacrament of Penance to us. Our response ought not be, "Must I accept your gift?" It should rather be, "Thank you, Lord. How can I best make use of your gift?"

We will make the best use of Penance when we realize its tremendous value. First, there is value in the very act of admitting our guilt to another human being. When guilt is brought to the surface, it begins to lose its power to hurt. The old phrase "skeleton in the closet" is indicative of the harm which hidden guilt can do. Some of the most successful self-help groups, like Alcoholics Anonymous, believe that we must tell our failings to another. The Fourth and Fifth of the Twelve Steps in A.A. are: "We made a searching and fearless moral inventory of ourselves" and "We admitted to God, to ourselves, and to another human being the exact nature of our wrongs." (The Fourth and Fifth Steps from the Twelve Steps are reprinted for adaptation with permission of Alcoholics Anonymous World Services, Inc.) Common sense teaches the same thing. A friend may come to us and say, "Something is bothering me. I feel so guilty and just don't know what to do about it." Our first response will probably be, "Would you like to talk about it?" In Penance we can honestly and openly admit our sins to the priest, and we will be better for it. "Therefore, confess your sins to one another and pray for one another, that you may be healed" (James 5:16).

Second, there is value in hearing that we are forgiven. When we apologize to someone, we need to hear our apology accepted. "I am sorry." "I forgive you." If the person to whom we apologize says nothing, we can't be sure that we have been forgiven. When we apologize to God for our sins, no voice booms from the sky to say that we are forgiven. How does God accept our apology and tell us, "I forgive you?" Through the Sacrament of Penance! Jesus told the apostles: "Whose sins you forgive are forgiven them" (John 20:23).

Third, confession helps us when we have sinned seriously. People can do shameful things, then think, "If others knew me as I really am, they could not accept me." Those who fear that no one could accept them put themselves at the bottom of the human race. But when a sinner confesses, then is accepted and assured of God's pardon, that sinner begins to realize: "Yes, I have done evil things, but I am not evil. If the confessor and God accept me, then I can accept myself as a good person who has done evil but now wishes to turn away from sin."

Fourth, confession helps us when we have not sinned seriously. We can drift along in life, spiritually lazy, failing to see "little" sins like selfishness, gossip, and impatience. People who use Penance faithfully are encouraged thereby to examine their consciences, take stock of their failings, and look to God for the forgiveness and help he alone can give. (People who feel they have no need of confession might say to members of their family: "I'd go to confession, but I can't remember any faults. Can you think of any I might have?")

Fifth, Penance helps us realize that while sin may be classified as "serious" and "less serious," it is never trivial. Sin is always an offense against God. Sin crucified our Savior. Penance reminds us that sin must not be taken lightly.

Sixth, confession brings out the fact that sin is not just a personal matter between me and God. The Church is the Body of Christ, so every sin against Christ offends the Church, and reconciliation with Christ requires reconciliation with the Church. Confession allows this because the priest is a representative of the Church. Further, all churches believe that we must be baptized by another; we do not baptize ourselves. The Catholic Church believes that we must be reconciled by another; we do not absolve ourselves!

Confession as a Meeting With the Forgiving Christ

When the Church forgives, Christ forgives. The priest is a sign of Christ's Real Presence in Penance. We confess our sins to Christ, and Christ forgives us.

This means that the priest has a serious responsibility to show the same compassion and understanding Christ showed to sinners. Most priests realize this and act accordingly. However, priests are human; they can fail to show Christ's mercy to penitents, just as parents can fail to show Christ's love to their children. Penitents who encounter a priest seriously lacking in compassion or understanding should pray for that priest, but they should also seek out another confessor.

All priests are bound to observe the "confessional seal." They may not disclose what is told in confession and may not use it against a penitent in any way.

Some penitents are afraid that the priest might look down on them because of their sins. Such penitents should remember that any priest who did this would be committing a terrible sin of pride, worse than anything the penitent might have confessed to him. Further, confessors hear every sin imaginable, and nothing they are told will shock them. Most priests would agree with this statement of an experienced confessor: "When people confess sins they think especially shameful, I don't look down on them but respect them for their courage and honesty." Finally, penitents should remember that priests go to confession too!

Overcoming Problems

We can learn many things by observing others, but we cannot learn about Penance in this way. As a result, people who join the Church are sometimes uneasy about Penance, even after it has been explained. Catholics who have been away from confession for many years may be uncertain about what to do or may fear that they will panic and forget everything. Such individuals need only mention to the priest that they are unsure or fearful and ask for his help.

At times we may confess our sins and afterward realize that we forgot something we had intended to tell. If this happens, we can simply mention it the next time we go to confession. A person may deliberately fail to confess a serious sin out of fear or shame, then carry a burden of worry and doubt, perhaps for many years. Such an individual can tell the priest, "Father, I was afraid to confess something a few years ago, and I need your help."

At times people are terribly damaged by their own sins or the sins of others. People who are weighed down by burdens of infidelity, abortion, child abuse, or other sins sometimes tell the priest: "I feel so guilty. I just don't see how Christ can forgive me." Such a person should meditate on the following: "Suppose someone came to you with exactly the same sins and feelings of guilt you now have. Would you treat that person harshly? If you can be understanding and forgiving (because you know how that person feels!), will not Christ be at least as understanding and forgiving as you are?"

Another problem is described by this complaint: "I use Penance regularly, but I keep confessing the old sins. It doesn't seem to do me any good." People who feel this way may not realize that if they were not using Penance they would be slipping back! Actually, they may be making progress but feel otherwise because they are becoming more sensitive to the sin in their lives.

When we become discouraged with our weaknesses and the frequency with which failings seem to rise up, we should realize that the soul is like a flower garden. The better the soil is, the more beautiful the flowers. But good soil means that weeds can grow too. We pull them out, and they grow back again! Pulling out weeds is a necessary part of gardening. So it is with our lives. The soul may be beautiful with the flowers of virtue, but the weeds of sin keep coming up. We "pull them out" in the Sacrament of Penance…over and over again. And we never forget: "A saint is a sinner who keeps trying!"

Questions for Discussion or Reflection

When a penitent confesses serious sin, does Christ change his attitude toward that person? Does God love us less before confession? If God does not change when we confess, what does?

Some people criticize Catholics because "they go to confession and then commit the same sins again." Is there some truth in this accusation? Can our sins be forgiven if we fear we may commit the same sins again? If we intend to commit the same sins?

How often should Catholics go to confession? Once a year? Once a month? Why?

Activities

Spend a few minutes thanking Jesus for Penance. Ask the Holy Spirit to give you God's attitude toward this sacrament. Meditate on the Lord's Prayer: "Forgive us our trespasses as we forgive those who trespass against us." Reflect: When I am asked for forgiveness by others, do I show the kind of compassion and mercy I want from Jesus? (Matthew 18:21-35).

CHAPTER NINE

Marriage — Christ Shares God's Love With Us

She lay quietly on her bed, staring out the window. Occasionally a moan escaped her lips, twisted downward at the corners by the same stroke which had immobilized her years before. Her husband entered the room, smiled, kissed her gently on the cheek, and repeated the words he'd spoken to her for sixty years, "Honey, you look beautiful. I love you." Ever so slowly, the expression on her face softened into a look of contentment and peace.

"Husbands, love your wives, even as Christ loved the church.... So [also] husbands should love their wives as their own bodies. He who loves his wife loves himself. For no one hates his own flesh but rather nourishes and cherishes it, even as Christ does the church, because we are members of his body. 'For this reason a man shall leave [his] father and [his] mother and be joined to his wife, and the two shall become one flesh.' This is a great mystery, but I speak in reference to Christ and the church" (Ephesians 5:25-32).

In this passage Saint Paul sees marriage as a sign, a sacrament, showing how Christ loves the Church. For almost two thousand years Christian married couples have shown the world that "God is love" (1 John 4:16), that Christ loved the Church, and that the greatest gift of the Holy Spirit is love (1 Corinthians 13).

When we witness an old man kissing his wife with gentleness and love, we stand in the presence of the sacred. We are touched by the realization that such love elevates human life to its most solemn beauty. We picture the couple sixty years ago, young newlyweds with hopes and dreams for the future. We see them

101

raising their children, sharing hard work and hard times. We walk with them through middle age to where they are today. We visualize friendships and partings, fun and failure, health and sickness, prayer and pain, days and weeks and months and years of all the building blocks of life.

Then we understand why Jesus chose marriage as the sacrament to reflect his love for his Church. We realize that many marriages fail, that building a marriage and a family is difficult. But this underscores the greatness of marriage, and if we appreciate this greatness, we will want to stand up and be counted with those who believe in marriage and work to build up the family.

Marriage and the Bible

The greatness of marriage flows from the very nature of God. God is Father, Son, and Holy Spirit, a "family" of three Persons. Human beings are made in the image and likeness of God (Genesis 1:27), and because God is "family," men and women are called to be family. The three Persons of the Trinity love one another eternally, and people must love. God is creative, and people must share in God's creative action if human life is to continue.

Marriage, then, brings us close to the unity, love, and creativity of God. Old Testament writers expressed this fact in vivid imagery which married God to his people: "For he who has become your husband is your Maker" (Isaiah 54:5). "On that day, says the LORD, she shall call me 'My husband' " (Hosea 2:18).

In the New Testament Christ is wed to his Church. Saint Paul writes, "I betrothed you to one husband to present you as a chaste virgin to Christ" (2 Corinthians 11:2). When human history ends, the "Church triumphant" will be betrothed to Christ: "For the wedding day of the Lamb has come, his bride has made herself ready" (Revelation 19:7). Marriage, of all human institutions, seems best suited to express the unity between God and us.

Marriage as God's Design

Marriage is not merely a human institution; it comes from God: "God created man in his image; in the divine image he created him; male and female he created them. God blessed them, saying: 'Be fertile and multiply' " (Genesis 1:27-28).

Jesus clarified God's design for marriage in many ways. He was born into a human family, thereby showing the holiness of ordinary family life (Luke 2). He worked his first miracle at the wedding feast of Cana (John 2:1-11), putting the seal of God's approval on marriage: The love of husband and wife is worth celebrating! He taught that married love must be faithful: "You have heard that it was said, 'You shall not commit adultery.' But I say to you, everyone who looks at a woman with lust has already committed adultery with her in his heart" (Matthew 5:27-28). He proclaimed that married love should last forever: "From the beginning of creation, 'God made them male and female. For this reason a man shall leave his father and mother [and be joined to his wife], and the two shall become one flesh.' So they are no longer two but one flesh. Therefore what God has joined together, no human being must separate....Whoever divorces his wife and marries another commits adultery against her; and if she divorces her husband and marries another, she commits adultery" (Mark 10:6-12).

Marriage in the Church

With such a background in Scripture, marriage should have been appreciated as a sacred and a sanctifying vocation by all followers of Christ. But some, influenced by philosophies regarding the soul as good and the body as bad, have taught that marriage is evil or, at best, only tolerable for the continuance of human life. Such attitudes had to be faced even in the New Testament era (1 Timothy 4:1-5), and they have resurfaced at various times through history. Vatican II stated the official position of the Church when it praised the goodness of family life and taught that married love is a sharing in God's love.

Marriage is a sacrament given to the Church by Christ. Christ did not create marriage, of course, but raised it to a new level. By participating in family life, by his presence at the wedding feast of Cana, and by his solemn declarations concerning the fidelity and permanence of marriage, Christ touched marriage with the grace of God in such a way that Paul could describe it as a great mystery "in reference to Christ and the church" (Ephesians 5:32).

So marriage is not just an arrangement between husband and wife. Every marriage affects others for good or ill. Each marriage is important to the children. A stable, loving marriage gives children an environment where they can mature into happy, loving adults; a marriage that is unhappy or shattered by divorce will be traumatic to them. Each marriage is important to the extended families of the couple. A happy marriage is a great blessing to parents and relatives. A marriage that fails, however, separates people from one another, creates pressures, sets up barriers between grandparents and grandchildren, and weakens the structures so necessary for happiness and peace.

Every marriage is important to God and the Church. "God is love" (1 John 4:16), but God depends on people to share his love with others. Marriage and family life, as Ephesians 5:32 indicates, should show the world how Jesus loves his people. It is no exaggeration to say that Jesus Christ depends largely on married couples for credibility in the world today. When a man and a woman stand before God on their wedding day and pledge their lives to each other, and then are faithful to their promises year after year, people take notice. They see Christ as the couple's source of strength and love. Christ's words at the Last Supper are verified: "This is how all will know that you are my disciples, if you have love for one another" (John 13:35). Christ's prayer at the Last Supper is answered: "I pray…that they may all be one, as you, Father, are in me and I in you, that they also may be in us, that the world may believe that you sent me" (John 17:20-21).

Because marriage has such important implications for the Church and for society as a whole, the Catholic Church has developed laws to safeguard the sacredness of marriage. Husband and wife must intend to be faithful, to make their marriage permanent, and to be open to the possibility of children. The "ministers" of the Sacrament of Matrimony are the bride and groom. A priest and two witnesses must be present, and it is through the vows and the presence of the community that Christ joins the husband and wife in love.

Interfaith marriages are common today, and engaged couples who are planning one should discuss areas such as worship, religious upbringing of children, and prayer. Catholics have a serious responsibility to share their faith with their children, and this may conflict with the partner's belief. Openness, prayer, and consultation are necessary in such cases. Interfaith marriages involving Catholics may be witnessed in a Catholic church. For a sufficient reason and with a dispensation from the bishop, they may be witnessed elsewhere.

Most dioceses have required programs designed to help couples prepare for marriage. The couple also meets with a parish priest to do necessary paperwork, plan the ceremony, and reflect upon the meaning of the sacrament. These preparations help couples make better decisions about marriage and can lead to stronger, healthier families.

After husband and wife make their vows, they continue to minister the grace of Christ to each other by every loving word and action. Their sacrament continues in all they do: work, play, communication, prayer, sexual intercourse, raising children, forgiveness, healing, all the ingredients of life. Married life, therefore, is a means by which Christ enters the home and fills it with his grace and love. Every Christian family should be a "little Church," a point of contact between God and his people, so that family life can be the path of grace walked by most people to eternal life.

Living the Ideal
in the Real World

This is a very high ideal, and because we are human, we will not live it perfectly. But if couples appreciate the beauty and holiness of marriage, they are likely to do the practical things that make a marriage work. There are many fine books and resources available to help couples develop the skills necessary for marriage and family life. Couples must work at these skills, such as communication and child raising. A good marriage does not just "happen." It is built by love, attention, and constant effort.

Family counselors have observed that most marriages go through certain stages. First, there is the "honeymoon," the rosy months when husband and wife see each other as perfect and are buoyed up by romantic feelings. Eventually, however, comes the second stage, "disillusionment," as they begin to see the faults in each other, the same faults that exasperated their families before they married! This stage is followed by a third, "unhappiness," as husband and wife wonder if it was a mistake to marry, quarrel, and try to change each other into the "ideal" person they thought they had married in the first place. Many marriages break up at this point, often because unhappy couples do not realize that all people struggle with such problems. Couples who are realistic come to terms with the fact that no one is perfect, and each spouse learns to love the person he or she married, not the imaginary ideal of the romantic stage. This is the fourth stage of "acceptance." Now husband and wife realize that their love is genuine, that they can depend on each other, that they are accepted and loved just as they are. This makes possible the fifth stage, the "happiness" each hoped for on their wedding day. Such stages may be repeated, as after the birth of a child or when the last child has left home. Couples who expect such patterns will not be surprised at disillusionment or pain and can work through these stages to real happiness.

Another fact basic to a successful marriage is that real love goes beyond emotions. Many people suppose that love is comprised of feelings of warmth and affection. Such emotions, often equated with "falling in love," make people feel good. However, they inevitably pass, and when they do, many people quickly "fall out of love." Real love is a decision that endures even when romantic feelings are absent, the decision to put the good of the other on a par with one's own, to love the other as one's self. It includes many other decisions to be patient and kind, to put away selfishness, rudeness, and pride, to forgive and to endure (1 Corinthians 13).

For a successful marriage there must be good communication and mutual respect between husband and wife. The Bible says: "Be subordinate to one another out of reverence for Christ. Wives should be subordinate to their husbands as to the Lord. For the husband is head of his wife just as Christ is head of the church.... Husbands, love your wives, even as Christ loved the church and handed himself over for her" (Ephesians 5:21-25). This passage is sometimes construed to mean that the husband has the right of dominance over his wife. Not so. If "wives are to be subordinate to their husbands," then husbands are to love their wives "as Christ loved the church." Both wives and husbands are encouraged in Ephesians to give of themselves, generously and lovingly, in imitation of Christ.

When husband and wife are blessed with children, they have the first responsibility to teach them the gospel by word and example. Parents must spend time with their children, pray with them, talk to them about Jesus, instruct them about right and wrong, and live according to their beliefs. Parents must set priorities for important activities like family meals, working and playing together, and family discussions. In these and other ways, parents bring Christ into the home.

Some couples want children but cannot have them, and for this reason they bear the burden of disappointment and loss. Hopefully, such couples can find strength in the realization that their marital love is a great blessing to the whole Church. Their love can be fruitful, as they reach out and share that love with relatives, friends, and others.

Resources for Growth in Married Love

Many professions and businesses offer programs to help people upgrade their skills. Marriage and family life require skills that are basic to happiness, and couples should put as much energy into upgrading family-life skills as they put into upgrading their abilities for work and business.

Every couple can benefit from the resources available through the Catholic Church and through other agencies. Marriage Encounter has been strengthening marriages all over the world. It teaches the beauty of sacramental marriage, as well as the communication skills that can make a good marriage better. Many dioceses and parishes offer Marriage Enrichment programs, counseling, and family-life seminars. Retreats for married couples and for families are available in most parts of the country. In recent years a new program has been developed to help save marriages of couples on the brink of separation or divorce. This program, *Retrouvaille* (the French word for rediscovery), has helped many couples find happiness and fulfillment in marriages once thought hopeless.

The most important resource for growth in married love is prayer. Research has shown that couples who worship together, read the Bible together, and pray together have an extremely high success rate in their marriages. There are many reasons for this. First, couples who seek from God the joy and peace that only he can give will not expect a spouse to be god! Human beings have longings in their hearts that can be filled by God alone. Those who expect them to be filled by a spouse will be disappointed. Second, marriage is built on love, and God is the source of all love. Married couples who fail to pray together on their pathway through life are like desert wanderers who die of thirst as they walk past springs of water. Third, couples who pray together express feelings that strengthen marriage and family life: gratitude, sorrow, forgiveness, praise, hope, and love. When a husband and wife, praying with each other, speak to God about such feelings, intimacy between the couple and God is strengthened.

Marriage and Sexuality

The Book of Genesis teaches that God created man and woman, commanding them to "be fertile and multiply." The sexual nature of human beings, like all of God's creation, is "very good" (Genesis 1:28). The beauty of marital love is expressed in such books of the Bible as Ruth, Tobit, and the Song of Songs. As long as people have been on the earth, the sexual drive and the pleasure associated with it have brought men and women together to build homes and create families.

But if sexuality has great power for good when properly directed, it has great potential for creating tragedy and pain when misdirected. Sexuality then loses its connection with love and begets lust, which has wreaked havoc on human lives in every age. Lust can motivate the foulest treacheries, as when David murdered Uriah to steal his wife, Bathsheba (2 Samuel 11-12). Sexual activity, therefore, must be guided by God's laws, clearly expressed in the Bible.

"You shall not commit adultery." "You shall not covet your neighbor's wife." The sixth and ninth commandments (Exodus 20:14, 17) forbid genital activity outside marriage. Jesus gave his followers even higher standards. He forbade divorce, teaching that husbands and wives must be faithful to each other forever (Mark 10:1-11). He said that "everyone who looks at a woman with lust has already committed adultery with her in his heart" (Matthew 5:28), prohibiting even lustful desires. Saint Paul wrote: "Do not be deceived; neither fornicators nor idolaters nor boy prostitutes nor practicing homosexuals...will inherit the kingdom of God" (1 Corinthians 6:9-10). He further warned, "Be sure of this, that no immoral or impure or greedy person, that is, an idolater, has any inheritance in the kingdom of Christ and of God" (Ephesians 5:5; 1 Corinthians 6:15-20; Hebrews 13:4). These passages are very blunt in saying that genital sexual activity outside marriage excludes one from the kingdom of God.

The Bible forbids sexual activity outside marriage, not because sexuality is bad but because it is so good that it can have its fullest meaning only in marriage. Sexual activity is a means of communication, and God wants it to say: "I love you totally, faithfully, forever, and with openness to new life. You are the only person I love in this way." But intercourse can say many other things, like "I hate you" in rape, "Let's do business" in prostitution, "I like you but let's not get serious" in casual sex, or "I think I love you but let's try it for a while" in a living-together arrangement. Sexual activity can communicate the very opposite of love, or less than it should, and so lose its power to express what God wants it to say. This perhaps explains why many married couples find sex boring or meaningless after a few years and why couples who live together before marriage have a higher divorce rate than those who do not. Sexual activity outside marriage is seriously sinful because it trivializes one of God's greatest gifts.

Many people of the twentieth century may think that such an approach to sexual morality is quaint and outmoded. On the contrary, sexual immorality is quaint and outmoded. The Greeks of Old Testament times and the pagans of New Testament times wallowed in immorality. Historians have observed that they, and all other societies that followed their example, were weakened and destroyed by the erosion of morality. Sexual immorality weakens individuals; many are the leaders who have fallen as a result of sexual indiscretions. Sexual immorality weakens families, and when the building blocks of society fail, society crumbles. Sexually transmitted diseases threaten civilization, today more than ever. History reveals that those who have been hurt by sexual immorality are countless. We will search in vain for any helped by it. Countless are those who have benefited from following the standards of Christ. We will find no one hurt by them.

But tragically the modern media is largely controlled by individuals who deride the standards of Christ and promote sexual promiscuity. We who are Christian must have the courage to reject the "tired old sins" of the past and to walk in the light of the life-giving and love-giving principles of Jesus Christ.

Catholic Family Planning

There are many movements today to avoid the artificial and seek out the natural. Many food additives are harmful. Many chemicals pollute the environment. Many artificial substances will be hazardous to living things long after they are disposed of. Human life can be endangered by pollutants in the atmosphere. Aware of such problems, people are trying to live "in harmony with nature."

The official teaching of the Catholic Church on family planning would seem to fit very well with modern efforts to follow the patterns of nature. As presented by recent popes, Church teaching states that sexual intercourse has been given us by God to express love and to bring new human life into existence. To place an artificial barrier between the act and its natural result is to thwart God's purposes and is therefore wrong. The Church teaches that couples should plan their families, but they should use only natural means to do this.

In a world where "natural is beautiful," we might expect that the Church's teaching would find much support, but this has not been the case. After Vatican II many Catholics expected the Church to permit the use of artificial contraceptives. Pope Paul VI, however, in the encyclical letter *Of Human Life* affirmed traditional Catholic teaching that has been strongly upheld by Pope John Paul II. The popular press has often presented papal teaching in negative fashion, influencing public opinion against an honest investigation into the values of natural family planning. Many Catholics are unaware of new natural methods, supposing the old "rhythm" approach to be the only one available, and so have not considered natural family planning as a viable option.

Yet Catholics who do follow the Church's teaching find that it has been a great blessing for marriage and family. The Couple to Couple League, a nonprofit organization founded in 1971, helps couples learn and practice the Sympto-Thermal Method of family planning. Couples using this method report that natural family planning has a positive effect on their marriages: It helps them become aware of their bodies and their natural fertility patterns, is very effective, keeps their sexual relationship alive, improves communication, and helps them understand the different needs of man and woman. Similar results are reported by couples using the Billings/Ovulation Method.

On the other hand, artificial methods of birth control have had some very negative results. There are serious health risks. IUDs (Intrauterine device) have caused death and sterility. Medical reports show a higher incidence of cancer among women who use contraceptive pills, especially those who begin as teens or use the pill for a long time. If chemicals in vegetables, fruits, and animals can be dangerous to human beings, if people are concerned about side effects of medications, we may well wonder about the side effects of powerful drugs and chemicals whose whole purpose is to reverse the human reproductive process or render it ineffective. We may well wonder why more research has not been done to help couples determine when they are fertile, so that artificial means would be unnecessary.

Another negative effect of artificial methods of birth control is that they have placed emphasis more on the frequency of sexual acts than on their meaning. For many married couples sexual intercourse is not seen in its fullest meaning as an expression of love, and the emotional needs of spouses are neglected. A nationally syndicated columnist asked her women readers: "Would you be content to be held close and treated tenderly and forget about the act?" More than ninety thousand women responded; seventy-two percent said "yes." Obviously, for these women intercourse did not convey the love and affection they were looking for.

More sexual activity does not necessarily mean more happiness or better marriages. Since the advent of the pill, the divorce rate has increased, and there is evidence that infidelity among spouses is more common than it was fifty years ago. This does not mean that artificial birth control is the cause of divorce or infidelity, but it does indicate that couples who want successful marriages must look beyond mere sexual activity to other important issues.

Natural family planning includes discussion of other important issues. Couples who use natural family planning talk about the meaning of sexual intercourse. They weigh spiritual, emotional, and physical values. As a result, intercourse takes on new meaning, and their marriages are strengthened.

Catholic couples owe it to themselves to seriously examine the teaching of the Church on natural family planning and to study the natural methods available to them. Natural family planning is not always easy, but when people fit their lives into the patterns God has designed for life, they can expect God's blessings.

Ceremony Without Marriage

Married life can bring happiness and meaning to life. Unfortunately, it can also end in betrayal, failure, broken homes, and broken hearts.

The Catholic Church believes that "what God has joined, no one may divide." But a man and woman can exchange vows and rings at a wedding without being joined by God. For a real marriage husband and wife must intend what God intends: that marriage be permanent, faithful, and open to children. They must be emotionally capable of such a marriage, and they must be free to marry.

Some people have intentions incompatible with Christian marriage. "I'll stay married if my spouse makes me happy; if not, we'll divorce." "No one person can keep another happy; therefore, we retain the right to have sex with other partners." "We will not have children because they interfere with the lifestyle we enjoy." The Catholic Church teaches that attitudes such as these "invalidate" a marriage, that is, they make a real marriage impossible.

A marriage ceremony is invalid if a spouse is incapable of entering into a loving union because of immaturity, psychological problems, or similar reasons, or if forced to marry. A ceremony is also invalid if one of the spouses is not free to marry because of a previous marriage or because marriage is forbidden by Church law or by a just civil law.

In these cases the wedding ceremony, even if Catholic, does not result in a valid marriage. Often such apparent marriages end in civil divorce, and one or both of the spouses may wish to marry in the Catholic Church. The official statement by the Church that no valid marriage existed between the two parties is called a declaration of nullity, or an annulment. An annulment is given by a diocesan tribunal, an office of the bishop, after a thorough investigation. It does not have civil effects and does not affect the legitimate status of children.

The Church may, on the authority of Saint Paul (1 Corinthians 7:12-15), dissolve a marriage of unbaptized persons when one wishes to be baptized and the other refuses to live with the baptized person. This is called a "Pauline Privilege." The marriage of a baptized and an unbaptized person can also be dissolved under similar circumstances by the "Petrine Privilege," or "Privilege of the Faith."

The Catholic Church recognizes as valid the marriages of non-Catholics. In the eyes of the Church, civil divorce does not dissolve the marriages of Catholics or non-Catholics, although either may be declared invalid if the conditions for an annulment are present. Further, civil divorce does not exclude a Catholic from the practice of the faith. At times civil divorce may even be necessary to protect a spouse or children from abuse or mistreatment.

A person who wishes to inquire into the possibility of a declaration of nullity should contact a parish priest. Each diocese has its own procedures; the priest can explain these and help get the process started.

Many dioceses and parishes offer retreats and group experiences to help divorced individuals cope with their problems and live their faith. In these and in many other ways, the Catholic Church tries to show the compassion of Christ to those who have suffered from the trauma of divorce.

Marriage and Eternal Life

The elderly gentleman who shared love and marriage with his wife for sixty years experienced the pain of parting as she died several years before he did. After her death he expressed confidence that he would join her again in heaven.

People often ask if husbands and wives will have a special relationship to each other after death. Some deny this, quoting Jesus' words: "When they rise from the dead, they neither marry nor are given in marriage, but they are like the angels in heaven" (Mark 12:25). But in this passage Jesus was simply meeting an objection to the resurrection placed by the Sadducees. His main point was that we do live after death. We will have spiritual bodies, "like the angels," and there will be no more death or birth. But the knowledge and love of this life will be intensified in the next, and surely God's love will keep us close to our loved ones.

Couples who walk down the aisle and through the pathways of this world together can look forward to walking hand in hand through the "new heaven and new earth," where God "will wipe every tear from their eyes, and there shall be no more death...or pain" (Revelation 21:1, 4).

Questions for Discussion or Reflection

Do you think that priests and religious should be "holier" than married people? Why or why not? Do you think that most married couples and families pray together often? What would be your reaction if you asked your priest when he prayed and his response was "Sundays and mealtimes?" What if you asked a married couple the same question and received the same answer? Is it possible to be a good priest or a good married couple without prayer?

Activities

Couples should set aside time for prayer and should learn various ways of praying together. One fine method of praying is as follows:

1. Let God speak to you. Read aloud a passage from the Bible (one of the passages quoted above would be a good place to start). Talk about it together and reflect on the passage until you come to a decision that makes a change for the better in your lives, like spending more time with each other.

2. Pray out loud in your own words, talking to God about what is important to you and about anything suggested by the Scripture reading. This can include thanking God, praising him, telling him that you love him and each other, asking for help, asking pardon for failings. Focus on three areas of prayer: (a) yourselves, family and friends; (b) Church; and (c) world.

3. Close with the prayer Jesus taught us, the Lord's Prayer. (Holding hands is a good way to express your unity in Christ.)

This prayer might take five minutes or an hour. There are many options for the second step, such as the "Lord, hear our prayer," a format used in the Prayer of the Faithful at Mass. And remember, God doesn't need elegant phrases. He just wants to talk with you as a couple!

CHAPTER TEN

The Priesthood — Jesus Ministers

A prisoner had escaped from Auschwitz. In retaliation, the Nazi commandant summoned the other prisoners and chose ten to be starved to death. One of them sobbed, "My wife, my children!" A forty-seven-year-old Catholic priest, Father Maximilian Kolbe, stepped forward. "I want to die in place of this prisoner," he said. The commandant hesitated, then snapped, "Request granted."

Bishop Fulton Sheen looked into the camera and into the eyes of the largest television audience of his day. He ended his explanation of Catholic doctrine with a smile and the words, "God love you."

Tens of thousands of people stood in Yankee Stadium. Pope John Paul II began Mass, "In the name of the Father, and of the Son, and of the Holy Spirit."

These are twentieth-century images of the priesthood.

A businessman paused at his desk. He was struggling with a decision that would affect all his employees. He picked up his Bible, read from it, and prayed.

The young family hurried into a pew. They knelt for a few moments, then rose with the congregation to sing the opening hymn — but only after the mother separated the two smallest children who had been busily elbowing each other.

A schoolteacher, tired after a long day with twenty squirming first graders, stood on "bus duty." She chatted with the children, tossed a ball back and forth with a shy little girl, and answered questions about a homework assignment.

These too are twentieth-century images of the priesthood.

The Ordained Priesthood
and the Priesthood of the Faithful

Most Catholics could easily identify Father Kolbe, Bishop Sheen, and Pope John Paul II as priests. They might not recognize the businessman, family, and teacher as priests. But they are, according to God's Word in the Bible.

The word "priest" comes from the Greek *presbyteros,* meaning "elder," and refers to someone authorized to perform the sacred rites of a religion, someone who is a mediator or link between God and people. In the Old Testament priests came from families tracing their lineage to Aaron or Levi. As consecrated ministers they held a special place of leadership in worship. But there was also a "priesthood of the people." God said to the Jews, "You shall be to me a kingdom of priests, a holy nation" (Exodus 19:6). All the people were dedicated to God and participated in the sacrifices offered by the consecrated priests.

The New Testament Church laid the foundation of an ordained priesthood. But it also recognized a priesthood of the faithful: "You are 'a chosen race, a royal priesthood, a holy nation, a people of his own, so that you may announce the praises' of him who called you out of darkness into his wonderful light" (1 Peter 2:9).

The Second Vatican Council in its document the *Dogmatic Constitution on the Church* taught that the baptized are consecrated as the "common priesthood of the faithful." This differs from the ordained priesthood but is a real participation in Christ's priesthood. According to the Council, the faithful exercise their priesthood by joining in the offering of Mass and sacraments, by prayer, and by the witness of a holy life.

This has important implications for all Catholics. It means that they come to Mass not as mere spectators but as people who offer their lives with Christ to God. All Catholics have a priestly offering, their own particular circumstances of life, which no one else can present (Romans 12:1). Catholics can also be active participants in the celebration of other sacraments in union with Christ.

The priesthood of the faithful means also that our prayers are part of the priestly prayer of Christ. Whether we pray individually or with others, we make our prayer with Jesus. This reality encourages us to pray with faith and confidence. Jesus Christ, our High Priest, is always at our side. "Therefore, since we have a great high priest who has passed through the heavens, Jesus, the Son of God, let us hold fast to our confession....Let us confidently approach the throne of grace to receive mercy and to find grace for timely help" (Hebrews 4:14-16).

The priesthood of the faithful means that Christ depends upon us to carry on his priestly mission by the witness of our lives. Christ offered himself as his priestly sacrifice (Hebrews 7:27). All our thoughts, words, and actions can become a part of the offering of Christ and give witness to the loving action of God in our world. The traditional Catholic practice of the morning offering, by which we offer to God our day, is a beautiful expression of this fact. "Through him [Christ] then let us continually offer God a sacrifice of praise, that is, the fruit of lips that confess his name. Do not neglect to do good and to share what you have; God is pleased by sacrifices of that kind" (Hebrews 13:15-16).

The Single Vocation

The context of the priesthood of the faithful is an appropriate place to point out the importance of the single vocation. Many individuals are called to follow Christ as single Catholics, and this vocation offers abundant opportunities to do great things for God.

By Baptism and Confirmation single Catholics are united to Christ and commissioned to continue his mission. They are to be Christ in the workplace and other arenas of daily life. By participating in the Mass and sacraments, by prayer, and by the witness of their lives, single Catholics bring Christ to the world.

Being single gives many Catholics the opportunity to pursue specialized fields of service. Doctors, nurses, teachers, and others can choose to be single in order to help others. Their vocations allow them to bring Christ into situations that might not be reached as effectively by priests, religious, or married couples.

Singles should realize that their first ministry is their daily lives. They serve Christ by going to work, participating in government and civic affairs, interacting with family and friends, and enjoying recreational and social activities. Many singles are also active in church ministries: They teach religion, sing in choirs, read Scripture at Mass, help as Eucharistic ministers, and serve on parish councils and other parish organizations.

The single vocation is a call to be part of the priesthood of the faithful, to continue the work of Christ, who served his Father as a single person in the world.

The Ordained Priesthood

Old Testament traditions place the origins of the priesthood with the tribe of Levi (Deuteronomy 33:8-11) and with the family of Aaron (Exodus 28-29). Priests led the people in worship, interpreted God's will, and taught the law of God. After the exiles returned from Babylon, the office of high priest developed into the most important position in Israel. The high priest was the head of Israelite worship, president of the Sanhedrin (the main Jewish tribunal), and chief representative of the people to the various foreign powers that ruled Israel.

The followers of Jesus at first worshiped in the Temple after his Resurrection and met in their own homes for the "breaking of the bread." When Jewish leaders began persecuting the Church, Christians developed their own structure and positions of leadership. The New Testament mentions the Twelve Apostles as having special prominence. There were also other apostles (like Paul), prophets, teachers, miracle workers, healers, helpers, administrators, interpreters (1 Corinthians 12:38), evangelists, pastors (Ephesians 4:11), deacons (Acts 6:1-6), presbyters (1 Timothy 5:17-22), and bishops (1 Timothy 3:1-7; Titus 1:5-9). In the New Testament there is no clear explanation of the interrelationship among these offices, and their functions probably varied in different locations.

But there is evidence from other sources that the offices of bishop, priest, and deacon began very early to take on the characteristics we see in them today. Ignatius of Antioch, who died in A.D. 108, wrote letters to local churches presided over by a bishop; he provides evidence that bishops and priests celebrated the Eucharist. Hippolytus of Rome, who died in A.D. 236, describes how the bishop ordained other bishops, priests, and deacons by the imposition of hands. This pattern of ordination is essential to the Catholic Church, which traces a line of succession from the apostles to the bishops of the present day.

As the Church grew, bishops became leaders of geographical areas called dioceses; they were assisted by priests and deacons. There have been times when Church leaders exercised considerable power over temporal governments and times when political rulers controlled ecclesiastical leaders. Generally, when the roles of church and state became intertwined, the Church suffered, either because it was oppressed or because it became too involved in temporal matters. In the past one hundred years the Church has moved away from political entanglements. As the result, its influence in spiritual matters has been strengthened, and Church leaders have grown in credibility and influence.

Deacons

In the Acts of the Apostles we read that deacons were first ordained by the apostles to care for the poor (Acts 6:1-7). (The Greek word *diakonia* means helper.) They soon began to carry out other ministries. Stephen preached the gospel and was martyred for witnessing to Jesus (Acts 6-7). Philip preached in Samaria and elsewhere, instructing people and baptizing (Acts 8).

Eventually, the role of deacon disappeared except as a final step to the priesthood. It was revived as a ministry after Vatican II. Deacons, both married and single, assist the priest at the altar during Mass, read the gospel, preach, baptize, witness marriages, conduct funerals, and perform many other functions important to the life of the Church.

Priests

"You are a priest forever, according to the order of Melchizedek" (Psalm 110:4). These words from the Old Testament were understood by early Christians as prophetic of the priesthood of Jesus Christ. The lineage of Jesus did not go back to Levi or Aaron, and the author of the Letter to the Hebrews saw in Psalm 110 an indication of God's intent to replace the Israelite priesthood with a new one. Melchizedek was a king and "priest of God most high." He offered bread and wine to the Lord in the presence of Abraham, who gave him tithes, thus acknowledging his superiority. Therefore, the priesthood of Christ is superior to that of Levi and Aaron, descendants of Abraham (Hebrews 5-7; Genesis 14:18-20).

The Catholic Church, guided by the Holy Spirit, saw the Eucharist as an offering of bread and wine, which became the body and blood of the great King and Priest, Jesus Christ. It has been the function of priests to continue this sacrificial mission of Jesus and to continue as well his prophetic mission of teaching and his kingly mission of leading.

Priests continue the priestly ministry of Christ. They celebrate the sacraments and lead others in worship. Their greatest privilege is to pray over the bread and wine the words of Christ, "This is my body. This is the cup of my blood." Priests baptize, confirm (when welcoming adults into the Church), hear confessions, witness marriages, anoint the sick, and bury the dead. They pray the Liturgy of the Hours, the daily prayer of the Church.

Priests continue the prophetic ministry of Christ by preaching, by teaching religion classes in elementary schools, high schools, universities, and by explaining the faith to converts. They counsel individuals and families.

Priests continue the kingly ministry of Christ by serving as administrators. They work with parish councils and other organizations to keep parish life functioning effectively. They may be involved in works of charity, social justice, and ecumenism. They cooperate with other priests at neighboring parishes and with diocesan leaders to coordinate the work of the Church in their diocese.

Priests must witness to Christ by the manner of their lives. A well-known aspect of priestly witness is celibacy, the voluntary state of not marrying and of abstaining from sexual intercourse. The roots of celibacy are found in the New Testament. Christ himself was celibate. He spoke of those who "have renounced marriage for the sake of the kingdom of heaven" (Matthew 19:12). Saint Paul praised celibacy as a means of focusing on "the things of the Lord" (1 Corinthians 7:32-34). Some priests in the early Church freely embraced celibacy, and eventually laws required celibacy of priests in various places. In A.D. 1139 the Second Lateran Council made celibacy mandatory for priests of the Latin Rite of the Roman Catholic Church. Married men may be ordained priests in Eastern Rite Catholic Churches, and today married ministers of other faiths who join the Roman Catholic Church and are ordained to the priesthood may remain married.

Recent popes have praised celibacy as a great gift of God to the Catholic Church, and it is surely that. Celibacy offers a unique opportunity to imitate the celibate Jesus. Celibacy frees priests from many concerns, as Saint Paul suggests, to devote themselves to "the things of the Lord." Celibacy is a positive surrender of self to Christ, not just a negative renunciation, just as marriage is the positive choosing of one spouse, not just the renunciation of all others. Celibacy is a constant reminder to the priest that Jesus Christ is his first love and his source of strength. Celibacy creates a need that can be filled only by Jesus: It "demands" a strong prayer life between the priest and Jesus, just as marriage "demands" communication between husband and wife. Celibacy also frees a priest to relate to many families, and it is one of the ways Jesus fulfills his promise: "Amen, I say to you, there is no one who has given up house or brothers or sisters or mother or father or children or lands for my sake and for the sake of the gospel who will not receive a hundred times more now in this present age: houses and brothers and sisters and mothers and children and lands, with persecutions, and eternal life in the age to come" (Mark 10:29-30).

Priests are usually addressed as "Father." This title suggests the family relationship a priest should have with members of the Church, as well as the attitudes of sacrifice and generosity with which a priest should serve his people. Thus, Saint Paul said to the Corinthians: "I became your father in Christ Jesus through the gospel" (1 Corinthians 4:15). Some people criticize Catholics for calling priests "Father," stating that Jesus forbade this when he said, "Call no one on earth your father" (Matthew 23:9). But from the context it is clear that Jesus was speaking against false attitudes of pride and superiority. If this passage should be taken in a slavishly literal sense, then "father" could not be used in reference to parents!

Another term sometimes used of priests is "monsignor." This is an honorary title conferred by bishops on priests because of important positions they may hold or because of special service to the Church.

An issue much debated in recent years is the question of whether women should be ordained priests. The official teaching of the Church is that only men may be ordained because this is Christ's own design for the priesthood. Those who disagree state that the reason Christ did not call women to the priesthood was founded on cultural conditions of his time. However, Christ did not hesitate to challenge other cultural limitations, including those that oppressed women. In any event the issue is a painful one, and we should pray that it will be handled with charity and openness to the Holy Spirit.

In all that priests must be and do, they follow in the footsteps of Christ, the Good Shepherd. They have the responsibility and privilege of bringing the compassion, kindness, and generosity of Christ to the world. Being human, priests can fail, just as married couples can fail to show the love of Christ to their families and to the world. Some years ago priests were often "placed on a pedestal," as if their vocation alone raised them to a special level of sanctity. It wasn't so then and isn't so now. Priests have the same weaknesses as other human beings and struggle with the same temptations. They depend upon the grace of Christ just as all others do. They need the support, love, and prayers of friends to keep them going.

Bishops

Bishops are leaders of church communities called dioceses, which vary in size and in number of parishes (local churches) and members. The word bishop comes from the Greek *episkopos,* meaning "overseer." Bishops are the successors of the apostles, and have the "fullness" of the priesthood. By A.D. 100, bishops were overseeing local churches. When problems arose, bishops met in councils to teach and guide church members over wider areas. Today all the bishops of the world in union with the pope are called the College of Bishops and as such are responsible not only for their own dioceses but also for the worldwide Church.

Originally, local bishops were elected by the people. Now the pope selects bishops, usually in consultation with the bishops and perhaps the priests of a given area. Bishops are usually ordained by other bishops, and in certain cases they may be ordained by the pope himself. In either event they are spiritual leaders in their dioceses, not just representatives of the pope.

Bishops carry out many of the same duties as priests but on a diocesan scale. Bishops ordain priests by the laying on of hands and invocation of the Holy Spirit. The bishop is a leader for the priests in his diocese, their "shepherd," and priests are in turn responsible to their bishop. Bishops have direct pastoral contact with laypersons when they travel to parishes for Confirmation ceremonies and special events like church dedications. The church of the bishop is called a cathedral, and his office the chancery. The chancery is staffed by priests, nuns, and laypersons who are responsible for the administration of such diocesanwide ministries as education, media, marriage preparation, annulments, finances, social justice, youth, Catholic organizations, and worship.

Bishops also fulfill responsibilities to the Catholic Church at large by cooperating with other bishops at regional and national levels. On the regional level dioceses are grouped together around an archdiocese, which is presided over by an archbishop. Regional groupings of bishops might meet to set common guidelines for marriage preparation, discuss problems in the area, or cooperate in charitable endeavors. The archbishop might preside over such meetings, but he does not have authority over the bishops in their own dioceses. On the national level in the United States, bishops belong to the National Council of Catholic Bishops and meet regularly to discuss national issues and determine policies. Documents issued by the NCCB, such as the recent statement on atomic weapons, can have considerable influence.

Some bishops and archbishops are named cardinals by the pope. Usually these are leaders who are in charge of important dioceses or who have high administrative positions in the Church. There are about one hundred cardinals from all over the world. They meet in Rome after the death of a pope to elect a new one.

The Pope — Our Holy Father

The United States has a president. College football teams choose captains. Civic groups elect chairpersons. Societies and organizations of every kind have leaders who are a sign of unity and purpose for each group. So it should not be surprising that the Catholic Church has a leader who is a sign of unity and purpose for its members. We call our leader the pope, a word which can be traced back to the Latin *papa* and the Greek *pappas,* both of which mean "father."

The Catholic Church believes that the papacy finds its origin in the mind of Christ and in the New Testament Church. One day Jesus asked the apostles, "Who do people say that the Son of Man is?" When they responded with John the Baptizer, Elijah, Jeremiah, or one of the prophets, Jesus asked, "But who do you say that I am?" Simon Peter replied, "You are the Messiah, the Son of the living God." Jesus was pleased with this answer, acknowledging that it had been inspired by God and that it indicated a special role for Peter: "Blessed are you, Simon son of Jonah. For flesh and blood has not revealed this to you, but my heavenly Father. And so I say to you, you are Peter, and upon this rock I will build my church, and the gates of the netherworld shall not prevail against it. I will give you the keys to the kingdom of heaven. Whatever you bind on earth shall be bound in heaven; and whatever you loose on earth shall be loosed in heaven" (Matthew 16:13-19).

The Catholic Church understands this passage as mandating a special place of leadership and authority for Peter. Many other New Testament passages reinforce this view. Peter is named first in the lists of the apostles (Mark 3:16-19); he is the central figure in gospel events such as the Transfiguration (Matthew 17:1-8). Even after denying Jesus, he is singled out by the Lord to shepherd the flock (John 21:15-19). In the Acts of the Apostles, Peter is the first to proclaim the gospel publicly and is the chief spokesman for the apostles (Acts 2:14-40).

Saint Peter went to Rome where he was martyred. His successors as bishop of Rome were recognized as leaders among the bishops, just as Peter was recognized as leader among the apostles. Popes have been visible signs of Jesus' presence and action in the world and signs of unity for the Catholic Church, calling all to be one flock under one Shepherd.

There have been about two hundred sixty-five popes. Most have been good men and effective leaders. Many have been saints. Some have been sinners and have failed miserably in their roles as spiritual leaders. Such failures should not surprise us. Jesus chose twelve apostles, and Judas turned out to be a traitor. Peter denied him.

Even though popes can fail, Catholics believe that Christ will not allow the Church to be misled in essential matters of faith and morals. Thus the basis for our doctrine of papal "infallibility," which applies only when certain conditions are met: (1) the pope is speaking *ex cathedra* — that is, as leader of the whole Church; (2) he is dealing with faith or morals; (3) he is expressly defining the doctrine as a matter of faith. This has happened only once in the last one hundred years, when Pope Pius XII defined the doctrine of the Assumption in 1950.

Catholics believe that truths can be infallibly expressed when they are believed by the universal Church or taught by the College of Bishops in union with the pope. When the doctrine of the Assumption was defined, it had been the object of belief by Catholics from time immemorial, and most of the world's bishops recommended that it be defined as Catholic doctrine.

Solemnly defined doctrines of the Catholic Church are called dogmas. These are beliefs that must be accepted by all who wish to be members of the Church. They include such truths as the Holy Trinity, the Incarnation, Christ's divinity, the Real Presence of Jesus in the Eucharist, Mary's Immaculate Conception, her Assumption, and the beliefs we profess in the Nicene Creed and Apostles' Creed.

The Catholic Church, then, has a basic core of beliefs that are essential, but there are many areas of belief which allow for varied opinions. For example, the Catholic Church holds as dogma that the Bible is inspired by God, but the Church has defined very few specific interpretations of biblical passages. Most of what the pope presents in sermons and writings is not infallible teaching. However, Catholics should attend to the pope's noninfallible teaching, since it is an important way Christ guides his Church through the Holy Spirit.

The doctrine of infallibility can be seen as a great blessing for the Church. It gives us assurance that God will not allow the powers of the "netherworld" to lead his Church astray. It helps believers to distinguish what is essential from what is not. A clear understanding of infallibility and its limits may also be seen as a safeguard against the misuse of authority. Where there is no doctrine of infallibility, those in authority can easily claim the aura of infallibility. Some who criticize the Catholic Church because of its doctrine of infallibility will insist that their interpretation of the Bible is the only correct one and that only their church members can be saved. Where there is no doctrine of infallibility, there is the temptation for leaders to claim infallibility in everything!

The popes of the twentieth century have become spiritual leaders to the world. Through modern means of communication and transportation, they have preached the gospel of Christ to "all nations" (Matthew 28:19). The papacy is not just an institution but Christ's gift to his Church. The successor of Peter is not just the pope but our Holy Father: priest, teacher, leader, and sign of unity.

Religious Communities

For much of the Catholic Church's history, religious communities have played an important role in keeping the spirit of Jesus Christ alive in the world. Religious communities are organizations of men and women who take vows of poverty, chastity, and obedience in order to follow Christ more faithfully. They include laypersons, deacons, priests, and bishops in their numbers. There are hundreds of religious communities in the Church, some numbering thousands of members worldwide and some embracing only a few members in a particular location.

By their vow of poverty, religious give up some control over material possessions. By chastity they pledge not to marry and so free themselves for the service of Christ. By obedience they agree to serve the larger needs of their community and of the Church. Some communities may take other vows too, such as service to the poor. Religious communities of men may be made up of priests and Brothers, who take vows but are not ordained. Some communities of men or of women may dedicate themselves to prayer and remain inside monastery or convent walls. Others devote themselves to various kinds of ministries, living where they work. Whereas "diocesan" or "secular" priests are ordained for a certain diocese and usually remain there all their lives, religious may go where they are needed and may serve many different dioceses. Laypersons may be affiliated with religious communities as members of a Third Order, and there are also lay institutes that promote prayer and good works.

Generally, religious communities developed in response to the needs of the Church and to the leadership of a "founder." Thus, the Jesuits, the largest community of men in the Church, were founded by Saint Ignatius of Loyola in 1534 to face the challenges of the post-Reformation era. They are well known today for pastoral, educational, and missionary work. The Daughters of Charity, the largest community of women, were founded by Saint Vincent de Paul and Saint Louise de Marillac in 1633 to serve the poor in schools, hospitals, and orphanages. Some religious communities, like the Benedictines, have been in existence as long as fifteen hundred years. Others, like the Missionaries of Charity, founded by Mother Teresa of Calcutta in 1950, have had a great impact on the Church in a relatively short time.

"A Holy Nation, A People of His Own"

"You are 'a chosen race, a royal priesthood, a holy nation, a people of his own, so that you may announce the praises' of him who called you out of darkness into his wonderful light" (1 Peter

2:9). This passage can help us to see "priesthood" as a vocation of all believers. Hopefully, it will lead us to see ourselves — single, married, vowed, or ordained — as a family, a "people of God's own" who announce the praises of Christ and spread the Good News.

Hopefully, too, this vision of the priesthood of the faithful might help all Catholics to see ordained ministers and vowed religious as brothers and sisters and pray for religious and priestly vocations. That would surely be in accordance with the heart of Jesus who said, "The harvest is abundant but the laborers are few; so ask the master of the harvest to send out laborers for his harvest" (Luke 10:2).

Questions for Discussion or Reflection

Have you thought of yourself as sharing in the priesthood of Christ? What do you have to offer at Mass that no one else can? Do you pray for priests and religious, your bishop, the Holy Father? If a member of your immediate family expressed a desire to become a priest, Brother, or Sister, how would you react? Do you regularly ask God to "send laborers for his harvest"?

Activities

Next time you attend Mass, pray for the priest. If he preaches well, thank God for this. If not, ask God to inspire the priest and to help you get at least one special blessing from each homily.

CHAPTER ELEVEN

The Anointing of the Sick — Jesus Heals

W e look at the beauty of the earth and see the handiwork of God. We discover in our vast universe a plan that bears the seal of a divine architect. We feel secure and loved, and we easily believe that our hearts are made for God.

But when a tornado sweeps across the landscape leaving a trail of splintered buildings and shattered bodies, we may ask whose handiwork we now survey. When we step into the lobby of a children's hospital, we may wonder how this place fits into the divine plan. When we sit in doctors' offices dreading the word "malignant," we may feel fear pushing faith from our hearts.

Tragedy, suffering, sickness, and death pose formidable obstacles to belief. There is so much pain. If there is a good God, why must this be? How can we trust that Jesus will heal when we cannot understand why God allows the pain?

Why?

The temptation is to find an easy answer to the "why" of suffering. In Old Testament times, for example, people did not make distinctions between "causing" and "allowing." Since God is allpowerful, they believed that he had to be the cause of everything. If someone made a wicked choice, it was God who caused it. Thus, "the Lord made Pharaoh obstinate, and he would not let the Israelites leave his land" (Exodus 11:10). The Israelites did not understand natural laws, like the law of gravity: If someone leaped from a building and was killed, they felt that God caused the person's death. They believed also that if God caused something bad, he must have a good reason. Usually that reason was punishment for sin; so if people suffered, it was because they had sinned. The Book of Job was written to challenge these assumptions, as well as other "easy answers" of the time. Job concludes that human beings cannot understand the designs of God.

The contemporaries of Jesus were still confused about the causes of suffering, as is clear from the attitude of Jesus' followers when they saw a blind man. "His disciples asked him, 'Rabbi, who sinned, this man or his parents, that he was born blind?' " (John 9:2). Jesus answered that neither the blind man nor his parents had sinned but that his blindness was permitted "so that the works of God might be made visible through him" (John 9:3). In other words God did not cause the blindness. Rather, God was on the side of the blind man, ready to help, as he did through the healing hand of Jesus. God does not cause our suffering. God may *allow* it for reasons we do not understand, but he is on our side.

God gives us freedom so that we can freely love. God does not take freedom away when we choose the wrong thing or when we choose evil. He won't catch us if we fall from a ten-story window. He won't reach out to stop a bullet from a murderer's gun. He won't destroy a criminal to prevent evil. If God would do these things, all would be forced to make only good choices. We would be mere puppets, incapable of freedom and love.

We live in a world where for hundreds of thousands of years people have been making free choices, many of them bad. As a result the human race is far from what it should be. Instead of using our talents for the past half-million years to learn how to live in harmony with one another and with creation, we have created weapons for destruction and upset the balance of nature. We pass on problems and diseases in ways we may never understand. Long ago, for example, someone might have misused alcohol, introducing genetic mutations that endure for generations and cause cancer in a descendant. God is not punishing an individual today by sending cancer: It is a consequence of human freedom and natural laws just as inevitable as hitting the ground after a fall. It just takes longer. God does not interfere with the natural process. He lets it happen because freedom is so essential to our being truly human, loving, and responsible. Yes, there have been some occasions in human history when God intervened to change the consequences of natural laws, but such interventions are "miraculous." If they were the normal course of events, they would require an entirely different universe, one with no freedom and no love. In a very real sense God cannot eliminate all tragedies, all accidents, and all illness.

God Is Love

But God does everything he can! "God is love" (1 John 4:16). God is always present to help us make the most of whatever happens. If we open ourselves up to his love, presence, and power, God will do what "love" can do.

Since we live in a world that is the result of God's love, when we freely turn to that love, great things can happen. This is true even in natural circumstances. Consider, for example, the case of two children who undergo major surgery. Afterward one is given medical treatment in isolation, while the other is given the same treatment, plus plenty of love and attention from staff, family and friends. The second child, energized by love, will recover more quickly. So, too, when we are in touch with God, his love can do great things for us, even bringing us better physical and emotional health.

Of course, love won't do everything. It won't stop a bullet or heal every illness or eradicate all the effects of old age. But love will help us make the most of every situation. Love will often make healing possible in circumstances that seem hopeless. Love will strengthen us to cope with disabilities and turn them into victories. Finally, love will do what really matters: It will strengthen us to cope with any illness, any accident, any loss, even death itself.

Miracles do happen, by God's power, and we can always hope and pray for them. But they are miracles precisely because they do not fit into any definite pattern. They are not the automatic result of praying with a certain degree of faith. The presence of a miracle does not mean that God loves one person more than another. The absence of a miracle does not show any lack of love on God's part. After all, Jesus suffered the agony of crucifixion and the horror of death on a cross after praying to his Father for deliverance.

The cross teaches us that there is no easy answer to the problem of pain. Jesus did not eliminate suffering but immersed himself in it. When we are immersed in pain, our union with the suffering

Christ can help us to endure. Even when we feel abandoned, as Jesus did when he cried out, "My God, my God, why have you forsaken me?" (Matthew 27:46), Jesus can bring us to trust and peace: "Father, into your hands I commend my spirit" (Luke 23:46).

The cross can help us see that while suffering is not good in itself, it can lead to good. Few things in life involve more love and courage than the patient acceptance of suffering, especially when beneficial to others. A mother accepts the pains of birth to bring her child into the world. A father endures the fatigue of hard physical labor to support his family. A paraplegic ignores disabilities in order to be of service to others. Pain is not good, but the heroism and courage required to overcome pain are among the greatest values of human existence.

The suffering of Jesus on the cross can also help us realize that while God does not cause pain, God is present to us in our pain. When a child is badly injured by a drunken driver, this is not "God's will." But God is there, helping those involved to endure what must be suffered and to rise above it, to foster whatever healing is possible, to comfort the child's parents. God is present to us in every pain-filled hour as he was present to Jesus on the cross.

And just as the suffering of Jesus was redemptive, so our suffering, by God's grace, can be redemptive. Saint Paul wrote, "Now I rejoice in my sufferings for your sake, and in my flesh I am filling up what is lacking in the afflictions of Christ on behalf of his body, which is the church" (Colossians 1:24). Christ's death was sufficient to redeem all humankind, of course, but Christ needs us now if his love and grace are to be channeled to others. When we offer up our suffering on behalf of others, it becomes a powerful prayer calling down the love and mercy of God. Christ allows us to do more than endure suffering. He makes it possible for us to turn suffering into prayer.

We may not fully understand suffering, but it does not separate us from God's love and it can be overcome: "If God is for us, who can be against us?...What will separate us from the love of Christ? Will anguish, or distress, or persecution, or famine, or nakedness, or peril, or the sword?...No, in all these things we conquer overwhelmingly through him who loved us. For I am convinced that neither death, nor life...nor any other creature will be able to separate us from the love of God in Christ Jesus our Lord" (Romans 8:31, 35-39).

Healing in the Bible

People of the Old Testament believed in the power of prayer and in the efficacy of medicine. Seven hundred years before Christ, King Hezekiah became critically ill. He prayed to God, who responded, "I will heal you." The prophet Isaiah then prescribed a poultice for the boil causing Hezekiah's illness. In three days Hezekiah was well (Isaiah 38). The Book of Sirach bids us: "Hold the physician in honor, for he is essential to you, and God it was who established his profession....When you are ill, delay not, but pray to God, who will heal you....Then give the doctor his place... for you need him too....And he too beseeches God that his diagnosis may be correct and his treatment bring about a cure" (Sirach 38:1, 9, 12, 14).

Jesus worked many miracles of healing, sometimes by a word and sometimes by methods then regarded as medicinal. Mark records that Jesus used spittle to heal the deaf and the blind (Mark 7:31-37; 8:22-26). Spittle was thought to have healing properties by the ancients (even today we place a cut or burned finger into our mouths to ease the pain). Jesus might have been quoting a proverb when he said, "Those who are well do not need a physician, but the sick do" (Matthew 9:12), but its truth was taken for granted by his listeners. One of the early preachers of the gospel was "Luke the beloved physician" (Colossians 4:14).

These passages show that the Bible sees no contradiction between prayer and medicine. The Catholic Church has always believed in the power of prayer and in the efficacy of good medical care and has had a long tradition of building both churches and hospitals.

The Anointing of the Sick

Jesus once sent his Twelve Apostles two by two to teach and heal in his name. "So they went off and preached repentance. They drove out many demons, and they anointed with oil many who were sick and cured them" (Mark 6:12-13). Oil and oil-based medications were used for healing in the ancient world, and this is another example of a physical sign being used to mediate the power of God.

After the Resurrection of Jesus, an anointing with oil brought his healing to the sick. "Is anyone among you sick? He should summon the presbyters of the church, and they should pray over him and anoint [him] with oil in the name of the Lord, and the prayer of faith will save the sick person, and the Lord will raise him up. If he has committed any sins, he will be forgiven" (James 5:14-15).

This passage is seen by the Catholic Church as Christ's design for the Sacrament of Anointing of the Sick. It shows that such an anointing was given by the early Church, that the minister was a Church leader, and that Christ was present through the anointing and prayer to bring physical and spiritual healing.

For eight hundred years healing was the primary purpose of the sacrament. Gradually, however, the anointing was associated with critical illness and death, and by the twelfth century the sacrament was commonly seen as preparation for death and was called by such names as Extreme Unction (Last Anointing) and the Sacrament of the Dying. The Council of Trent countered this trend somewhat by pointing out that the sacrament had numerous spiritual and physical effects, including health of body when this would promote spiritual welfare. But until the Second Vatican Council, the emphasis of Anointing continued to be preparation for death. This Council stated that the sacrament should be called the Anointing of the Sick and taught that it is not reserved for those at the point of death but meant to bring healing and salvation to the seriously ill.

The pastoral practice of the Church today calls for the Anointing of the Sick in case of serious illness — physical, emotional, or mental. Thus, a person might be anointed when sick with pneumonia, when preparing for surgery, when seriously depressed, or when weak from the burdens of old age. Anointing would not usually be ministered for colds or other minor illnesses. The sacrament may be repeated in case of long-term illness, especially when there is a change for the worse. The Anointing of the Sick may be ministered in a continuous rite with Penance and holy Communion. When a person is dying, these three sacraments may properly be called the "Last Rites." When holy Communion is given to a dying person, it is called viaticum — "[Christ] on the way with you."

There is a communal Rite of Anointing, which may be celebrated as a healing service for the seriously ill in nursing homes, hospices, hospitals, and parishes. The Anointing may also be given during the celebration of Mass.

Scripture readings and prayers for healing accompany the anointing. All baptized believers who are present join with the priest in asking for God's grace. The priest, after laying hands on the head of the sick person, anoints the forehead with blessed oil as he prays: "Through this holy anointing may the Lord in his love and mercy help you with the grace of the Holy Spirit." He anoints the hands, saying, "May the Lord who frees you from sin save you and raise you up."

The ritual for the Sacrament of Anointing explains that this sacrament gives God's grace to the sick for the good of the whole person. The sick are encouraged to trust in God and are fortified against temptations and anxiety. They are helped to bear suffering bravely and to conquer it. They are strengthened by God for a return to physical health if this will be beneficial to their salvation, or for their entry into everlasting life. If they are unable to receive the Sacrament of Penance, their sins are forgiven by the Anointing.

How to Pray for the Sick

The Catholic Church acknowledges that prayers for the sick may be answered in many ways by God. Sometimes the Anointing results in cures that seem miraculous. Sometimes the healing process is hastened by the Anointing. Sometimes there appears to be little physical improvement, but the sick person is enabled to bear suffering patiently. Sometimes the person is given peace and hope in the face of approaching death. With so many possible outcomes, how do we know what to pray for when we or others are sick?

First of all we should realize that we do not pray as if God had to be convinced to desire what is best for the sick! God always desires what is best, and we pray in order to place the sick in the healing presence of God. Prayer removes the obstacles between us and God, obstacles like sin, materialism, fear, and depression. Prayer opens us up to God's love and to his gift of healing or of eternal life.

Second, we must pray as Jesus did in the Garden of Gethsemane: "My Father, if it is possible, let this cup pass from me; yet, not as I will, but as you will" (Matthew 26:39). We simply do not know how our suffering fits into God's plan, and while we may always pray for healing, it must be with openness to the will of God. In this we are helped by the Holy Spirit: "The Spirit too comes to the aid of our weakness; for we do not know how to pray as we ought, but the Spirit itself intercedes with inexpressible groanings" (Romans 8:26).

Third, we should become aware of the astounding possibilities for healing, which God has built into our human bodies, minds, and emotions, and into our relationships with others. Modern medical research has uncovered incredible agents for healing in our blood and bodily organs. They are most effective when our minds are thinking positively and our emotions are optimistic. Prayer brings body, mind, and emotions together for the battle against illness. Much study is being given to "right-brain" and "left-brain" activity, and researchers are learning that we have God-given powers that we have only begun to tap. Such powers pour reserves of strength into our bodies in crises, as when a mother lifts a car off the injured body of her child after an accident. Such powers allow people to affect others over great distances, as when one identical twin "senses" that the other is undergoing a traumatic experience. There are some researchers who claim that when people pray for the recovery of an individual, the prayer has effects that are measurable. It may be that prayer opens us up to healing gifts which have lain hidden within us and which God wants us to discover and use.

Fourth, we should be wary of the claim, "If you pray with enough faith, you will always be healed." It just isn't so. Saint Paul reports that he suffered from a "thorn in the flesh" and begged the Lord that it might leave him. God's response was, "My grace is sufficient for you, for power is made perfect in weakness" (2 Corinthians 12:7-9). God did not remove Paul's suffering but gave him strength to bear it. Paul is presented in the New Testament as acknowledging the persistent nature of some illnesses. In 1 Timothy 5:23 Paul writes, "Stop drinking only water, but have a little wine for the sake of your stomach and your frequent illnesses." In 2 Timothy 4:20 Paul relates, "I left Trophimus sick at Miletus." If sickness always yielded to prayers of sufficient faith, Paul's prayer would have healed Timothy and Trophimus.

Fifth, we need to realize that we all must die. Every person miraculously healed by Jesus died eventually from sickness, injury, or old age. Death is the only complete healing. Death frees us from a body vulnerable to disease, injuries, and the ravages of age. In death our physical body is transformed into a spiritual body, and we are brought to the fullness of life and vitality, where there will be "no more death or mourning, wailing or pain" (Revelation 21:4).

How do we pray? We pray with confidence in God's love for us. We pray to the Father, "Thy will be done." We pray in the hope of opening ourselves, the sick, and those caring for the sick to the graciousness and guidance of God and to whatever healing is possible. We pray, free from nagging doubts, that healing might come "if we just had more faith." We pray with the peaceful realization that when sickness seems to close a door in death, Christ opens that door to eternal life.

Words, Images, and Gestures

One way to pray for healing for ourselves or others is simply to talk to God. We speak to God about the pain, tell God we want to pray in union with Jesus, and ask for openness to all the healing God can give. If a friend is in surgery, we ask God to grant healing and to guide the doctors and nurses. We ask God to remove any hindrances to healing. We thank God for his loving care.

Another way to pray is with images. If we are sick, we may picture Christ standing at our bedside, placing his hands on us as he did on the sick in the gospels. We picture our disabilities flowing from us, as the strength and healing of Jesus fill our body, mind, and heart. We can pray like this for others, visualizing Christ standing at the side of doctors and nurses as they care for the sick.

When we visit the sick, we should ask if they would like us to pray with them or for them. They may wish to join us in the Lord's Prayer or in other prayers. They might appreciate our reading short Bible passages pertaining to healing. It might be appropriate to hold the hand of the sick person as we pray. We should be sensitive to the needs of the sick, but we ought not refrain from prayer just because we are shy or fearful.

In families prayer can be a great source of healing. When a parent places a bandage on a child's injury, a little prayer like "May Jesus bless you and make you feel better" brings Christ into the healing process. If a small child is sick, other members of the family can gather around, place hands on the child, and ask God for healing. They should remind the child that Jesus is also present, letting his love and healing power flow into the child.

Today many parishes have "prayer lines." When someone is seriously sick or injured, members of the prayer line inform one another by phone and then pray for the person. Often the sick report that they feel lifted up and strengthened by the prayer of so many.

Only God knows how much healing is available in answer to sincere prayer. If believers could see themselves as members of the Body of Christ, the divine Physician, and pray accordingly, wonderful gifts of healing could result.

Comforting the Sorrowful

One of the most important opportunities we have of transmitting Christ's healing power is in comforting those who grieve. Grief comes to those who suffer a serious loss. It is a natural process, but it can be as debilitating as sickness.

When we reach out to others in their grief, we bring them the healing of Christ. In this, as in all things, Christ is our model. We see Jesus, for example, comforting his friends Martha and Mary at the death of their brother Lazarus, and then — as the "resurrection and the life" — bringing Lazarus back to life (John 11). We can't bring the dead back to life as Christ did. But we can bring sympathy and hope to those weighed down by grief.

Grief touches many people: relatives of someone who has died, a couple experiencing a miscarriage, a friend undergoing surgery, a childless couple, people going through a divorce, a family losing their farm or business, an acquaintance who has had to place a parent in a nursing home.

In order to help such people, we should realize that those who grieve may go through five stages: *denial* — "This can't be happening to me"; *anger* — against God, others, one's self; *bargaining* — "God, if you'll change this, I'll do anything you want"; *depression* — sadness, weariness, wanting to give up; *acceptance* — "This is a part of life, and I must go on from here." These stages may come and go, not necessarily in the order given. People may find themselves in and out of them for years. Anniversaries and holidays are especially hard times when painful feelings recur.

What should we do or say when a friend or relative suffers loss? The first thing is presence, just being available — a visit, a card, a gift. Second, we can express our sympathy in simple and honest ways: "I'm sorry about....I'm praying for you." Third, if people want to discuss their feelings, it is crucial that we listen and accept them. If they express denial, anger, bargaining, or depression, we don't have to try to talk them out of it. If they are allowed to go through the process, they'll reach acceptance sooner. Someone, for example, may be saying over and over, "I can't believe this is happening to me; God is unjust" (denial and anger). Our tendency might be to respond, "Well, it is happening, and you mustn't say things like that about God!" It would be much better just to listen and to say gently, "I'm so sorry you have to go through this pain."

The Church comforts the sorrowful through its funeral rites. Prayer vigils at the funeral home, the funeral liturgy, and the final commendation and committal ceremonies acknowledge the grief of the bereaved and affirm Christ's promise of eternal life. Jesus seems to be present in a special way at these rites to comfort the sorrowful and to help his people to place their loved ones in God's merciful care. Jesus touches the bereaved through the prayers and liturgy of the Church and through the presence and love of its members.

Jesus was sensitive to the grief of Martha and Mary. He wasn't afraid to cry. He was there for them and met their needs. Even before he raised Lazarus, he brought consolation and hope. We can bring comfort to others because we are followers of Jesus. We can bring hope because we believe in eternal life. Above all, we can bring Jesus himself, for the Spirit of God dwells in us, and Christ lives in us (Romans 8:10-11). Through us, Christ comforts those who mourn.

Again, Why?

Tragedy, suffering, sickness, and death are indeed formidable obstacles to belief. But when we see them as consequences of human freedom, when we remember that Jesus himself faced up to them, when we believe that God is near us through the Anointing and the prayer of the Church, when we are supported by other members of the Body of Christ, these obstacles can be overcome. Then we can say with Saint Paul, "I consider that the sufferings of this present time are as nothing compared with the glory to be revealed for us" (Romans 8:18).

Questions for Discussion or Reflection

Have you ever heard the questions, "Can God make a square circle?" "Can God make a rock so big that he can't pick it up?" Do these questions mean that there are things that God cannot do? Can God make a world where people are free and then remove all the unpleasant consequences of freedom?

A woman was standing beside the casket of her daughter who had been killed in an automobile accident. A well-meaning friend came up to her and said, "It was God's will." Was it?

These are comments made to people experiencing grief: "Don't cry; it'll be all right." "You'll get over it." "You don't know how lucky you are." "You should be over it by now." "I know just how you feel." "At least you had each other for years." "You're still young and you have plenty of time to have another child." "Time heals all." "God sends such crosses only to real believers." "It's all for the best." "It's God's will." Evaluate these comments. Do you think they bring comfort to the sorrowing? What can we say to the grieving that will be helpful?

What has Jesus done to prove that God is on your side when you are suffering? What more could Jesus do? What do you think of the statement, "Death is the only complete healing"?

Activities

Tonight, before you fall asleep, form a mental image of Jesus coming to your bedside. Picture him placing his hands on your head to comfort and heal you. Ask him to deliver you from any physical illness or pain that may be troubling you. Ask him to replace any harmful feelings such as fear, depression, resentment, anxiety, and hatred with his grace and love. Ask Jesus to fill your heart and your whole being with the blessings of the Holy Spirit mentioned by Saint Paul in Galatians 5:22: love, joy, peace, patience, kindness, generosity, faith, gentleness, and self-control, qualities which will make you open to the healing presence of God.

You may use the same prayer in reference to others. Picture Jesus standing at their bedsides, giving them his healing and peace.

CHAPTER TWELVE

Communicating With God — Prayer

On August 20, 1977, the spacecraft *Voyager 2* was launched from Earth to explore our solar system and send back information about some of its planets and moons. After visiting Neptune in 1989, *Voyager* flew at thirty-seven thousand miles an hour into the vast reaches of the universe, carrying a message, a twelve-inch gold-plated disk with sounds and images from Earth. It is exciting to think that someday other intelligent beings might "get the message" and send a response to us.

It is far more exciting to realize that we human beings can exchange messages, not just with other creatures, but with the Creator of the universe. Communication with God, prayer, can be one of the most interesting and fulfilling experiences of human existence. But we do not first send a message and wait for a reply, as we have done with *Voyager 2*. Rather, prayer begins with God.

Close Encounters

In the science fiction movie *Close Encounters of the Third Kind* people from many places and walks of life suddenly received a mental image of a certain mountain in the western United States. Without knowing why, they painted pictures and produced clay moldings of the mountain and felt a need to find this place they had never seen. Gradually, some of them began to meet one another and share experiences. They came to the realization that intelligent beings from outer space had communicated with them. They learned to exchange information with those beings through light and music and eventually achieved a "close encounter of the third kind," a face-to-face meeting, and received an invitation to visit their world.

This science fiction story may be seen as a pattern for prayer. God has spoken in many ways to all human beings, imprinting messages in our minds and hearts. When we share our experiences with one another, we come to realize that our Creator is calling us. We learn to listen and to speak to God in many ways (including light and music!). We achieve the "close encounter" of prayer and receive an invitation from God to enter "new heavens and a new earth."

Prayer "happens" when we open our senses, mind, will, and heart to the many ways God speaks to us. We reflect on God's Word, letting it touch our hearts. We then respond to God. As we do, we look to the Bible for guidance.

Prayer in the Old Testament

God placed human beings on this earth and invited them to respond to him. God is not a distant Power but a loving Creator who speaks to those made "in his image" (Genesis 1:27). Unfortunately, sin causes people to distance themselves from God; Adam and Eve "hid themselves from the LORD God" (Genesis 3:8). God never stopped reaching out to his people, however, and when anyone listened, communication with God resumed. Abraham began the Jewish tradition of prayer (Genesis 12-25). Moses encountered God in a burning bush (Exodus 3), in the crossing of the Red Sea (Exodus 14), in the thunder of Mount Sinai (Exodus 20), and in the intimacy of the meeting tent (Exodus 33). David heard God calling him to repentance and responded with prayer, fasting, and penance (2 Samuel 12). Solomon built a Temple to the Lord and led his people in a public prayer of praise and petition (1 Kings 8). The prophets, who spoke for God, also spoke with God. Elijah found God in a "tiny whispering sound" (1 Kings 19:12). Isaiah showed that holiness is required for real prayer (Isaiah 1). Jeremiah expressed his deepest feelings to God in prayer (Jeremiah 20:7-18). The Wisdom Books recommend prayer and give beautiful patterns of prayer (Sirach 17:19-27; 36). The Book of Psalms is a collection of prayers for all occasions.

We can learn much about prayer from the Old Testament and

find prayers to suit every situation. For thousands of years people have found comfort in prayers like Psalm 23:1, "The LORD is my shepherd." But Old Testament prayer has limitations. It sometimes reflects a spirit of vengeance: "O God, smash their teeth in their mouths" (Psalm 58:7), and a spirit of ruthlessness and cruelty: "O daughter of Babylon, you destroyer, happy the man...who shall seize and smash your little ones against the rock!" (Psalm 137:8-9). We may "skip over" such prayers, seeing them as expressions of a limited theology. For the perfection of prayer, we move to the New Testament and the prayer of Jesus.

The Prayer of Jesus

Jesus was both God and man, and it may not be easy for us to understand how he could pray. Did he pray as man and answer his own prayer as God? We can never fully grasp the mystery of Jesus' prayer any more than we can fully understand the mystery of the Incarnation, but we can be sure that the divine consciousness did not negate the human consciousness of Jesus. Jesus "advanced in wisdom and age and favor before God and man" (Luke 2:52), and prayer must have been a part of the process by which he knew God as his Father (Luke 2:49) and himself as the "beloved Son" (Luke 3:22). Jesus prayed for the same reason we do, to communicate with God. But his prayer was perfect, and so, like the apostles, we turn to him and ask, "Lord, teach us to pray" (Luke 11:1).

When we look at the prayer of Jesus, we discover that it was as natural to him as breathing. He began his public life with prayer (Luke 3:22), then went into the desert to spend forty days in communion with God (Matthew 4:1-11). He prayed often and long during his ministry, even at the busiest times (Mark 1:35; 6:45-56). He sought guidance from God before making important decisions, like choosing the Twelve Apostles (Luke 6:12-16). His union with his Father could be so intense that it left his disciples awestruck (Luke 9:28-36). He prayed for himself in time of distress (Hebrews 5:7-8), and he prayed for his apostles (Luke 22:31-34). He participated in official Jewish worship (Luke 22:7-9). He prayed in synagogues (Mark 1:21-22) and the Jerusalem Temple (Luke 2:41-52).

We can pray the words of Jesus as recorded in the New Testament. In the Lord's Prayer, Jesus taught us to call God "our Father"

(Matthew 6:9). In other prayers, Jesus praised God for having revealed his mysteries to the childlike (Matthew 11:25-26), thanked God just before he raised Lazarus from the dead (John 11:41-42), and interceded for the disciples and for us (John 17). When troubled, Jesus prayed to his Father (John 12: 27-28), and in his agony he prayed at Gethsemane (Matthew 26:36-44). In prayers said from the cross, Jesus expressed his feelings of desolation (Matthew 27:46), forgave those who persecuted him (Luke 23:34), and commended his spirit into the hands of his Father (Luke 23:46). We can praise and thank God, ask forgiveness, and make requests in prayers said by Christ. It is comforting to know that even when we find it hardest to pray, when we feel abandoned or overwhelmed or at the very threshold of death, Jesus gives us words to speak to our heavenly Father.

Looking beyond the actual prayers said by Jesus, we find that he taught a great deal about prayer. In the Sermon on the Mount, Jesus tells us that we must pray with sincerity, not to impress others; we must avoid the pagan attitude that God owes us a response in proportion to the length of our prayers. Our Father knows what we need before we ask him; therefore, the purpose of prayer is to express our dependence upon God, as in the Lord's Prayer, where we put present ("Give us this day our daily bread"), past ("forgive us our trespasses"), and future ("deliver us from evil") in God's hands (Matthew 6:5-15). Prerequisites for prayer are humility (Luke 18:9-14) and forgiveness of others (Mark 11: 25-26).

We should pray with faith and confidence, for prayer is always answered: "Therefore, I tell you, all that you ask for in prayer, believe that you will receive it and it shall be yours" (Mark 11:24); "Ask and it will be given to you; seek and you will find; knock and the door will be opened to you" (Matthew 7:7). There is a special power in common prayer: "Amen, [amen,] I say to you, if two of you agree on earth about anything for which they are to pray, it shall be granted to them by my heavenly Father" (Matthew 18:19).

If we read only the passages in the previous paragraph, however, we can get a one-sided view of Jesus' teaching on prayer. We have all had the experience of asking and *not* receiving. Because of this we can get discouraged and give up on prayer, or feel guilty, thinking we lack faith. But these passages must be interpreted in the light of Jesus' other teachings about prayer.

To begin with, Jesus implies that God's answer to prayer may

143

take time, for perseverance in prayer is necessary (Luke 11:5-13; 18:1-8). Jesus also shows us that our prayer must always be made in accordance with God's will. In the Garden of Gethsemane, Jesus prayed, "My Father, if it is possible, let this cup pass from me; yet, not as I will, but as you will" (Matthew 26:39). "Thy will be done" must be the foundation of every prayer we say.

The perfect submission of Jesus to God's will was part of his every prayer. When Jesus tells us, "Whatever you ask in my name, I will do" (John 14:13), we can be sure that praying in his name includes the condition, "If this is God's will." When Jesus says, "If you remain in me and my words remain in you, ask for whatever you want and it will be done for you" (John 15:7), we must remember that Jesus, in whom we "remain," endured the agony of Gethsemane, and his words which "remain" in us include "not as I will, but as you will."

Other New Testament Teachings About Prayer

We learn from the New Testament how to pray in the spirit of the first Christians. Prayer is, above all, Trinitarian. God is to be addressed personally as our dear Father (Romans 8:15). We pray to the Father "through Jesus Christ" (Romans 1:8), who always intercedes for us (Hebrews 7:25). The Holy Spirit lives in us and helps us to pray, for "we do not know how to pray as we ought, but the Spirit himself intercedes with inexpressible groanings" (Romans 8:26).

The New Testament encourages us to pray constantly (Ephesians 6:18), in common with others (Acts 2:42), and in song (Colossians 4:16). Prayer may be praise (Romans 14:11), thanks (Colossians 4:17), sorrow for sin (James 5:16), and petition (Philippians 4:6). Prayer intentions include a safe journey (Romans 1:10), salvation of others (Romans 10:1), deliverance from enemies (Romans 15:31), spiritual needs (Ephesians 3:14-21), and peace (1 Timothy 2:1-4). In time of special need, fasting may accompany prayer (Luke 2:37; Acts 13:2-3; 14:23).

We can pray in the very words placed on the lips of Mary (Luke 1:46-55), Zachary (Luke 1:68-79), and Simeon (Luke 2:29-32). We can make our own the brief prayers found throughout the gospels, like that of the distraught father, "I do believe, help my unbelief"

(Mark 9:24), and of Bartimeus, "Jesus, son of David, have pity on me" (Mark 10:48). Paul gives us many beautiful prayers (Romans 11:33-36; 2 Corinthians 1:3-4) and magnificent hymns of praise (Ephesians 1:3-10; Philippians 2:5-11; Colossians 1:15-20). Many other examples of New Testament prayers may be found (for example, 1 Peter 1:3-5; Revelation 4:11).

Catholic Prayer

The Scriptures open up many pathways to prayer. Instructed by the Old and New Testaments, and guided by the Holy Spirit, Catholics have listened to the voice of God and responded in many ways. Catholics have encountered God in thunder and storm as did Moses and in the gentle breeze like Elijah. They have gone into the desert like Jesus to find God in solitude and silence, and they have prayed together as did the early Christians.

Catholics have meditated upon God's actions in their lives like Mary (Luke 2:52), and they have voiced the Psalms and the Lord's Prayer. They have offered up their work in the morning and asked forgiveness at night. They have looked at the crucifix and joined their sufferings to those of Christ. They have fasted and made pilgrimages, breathed the name of Jesus and recited long litanies, fingered rosary beads and savored the fragrance of incense, walked the Stations of the Cross and knelt in silence. They have prayed in joy at the birth of a child and in tears at the death of a friend. In restaurants and at picnics Catholics have said grace before meals. They have made the Sign of the Cross in churches and on baseball diamonds. In great cathedrals glittering with stained glass and in tiny roadside chapels, they have "raised their minds and hearts to God."

Our Catholic tradition is rich and varied. It offers us limitless possibilities for prayer and encourages us to make prayer a part of life. As an aid to this, we offer some "pathways to prayer" and some attitudes toward prayer.

Pathways to Prayer: God Speaks to Us

Prayer is not something we initiate. God has already started the conversation. But how does God "speak" to us? Perhaps some comparisons with human communication will be helpful.

We use words to communicate, but we convey thoughts and feelings in many other ways. Parents often say their first "words" of love to newborn children with a hug and a kiss. Parents "speak of" care and security to their children by clothing and feeding them. All of us speak with "body language," with facial expressions, with gifts and acts of love, even with silence. We learn to communicate also by evoking the memory of others, by stirring up their emotions, by stimulating their intellect, by touching their imagination, and by encouraging them to act. God communicates with us in all these ways, and more.

God addressed us at the moment of our conception. What God spoke to Jeremiah he could say to every human being, "Before I formed you in the womb I knew you" (Jeremiah 1:5). God gives life to each of us and so invites us to respond to his creative love.

God speaks to us through the universe. Every good and beautiful thing is a word spoken to us by the Creator. "The heavens declare the glory of God" (Psalm 19:2). "For from the greatness and beauty of created things their original author, by analogy, is seen" (Wisdom 13:5; see Romans 1:20).

God speaks to us through the events in our lives, by his providential care. "The LORD is my shepherd....He guides me in right paths" (Psalm 23:1, 3).

God speaks to us through his word in the Bible, which is always "living and effective, sharper than any two-edged sword, penetrating even between soul and spirit, joints and marrow, and able to discern reflections and thoughts of the heart" (Hebrews 4:12).

God speaks to us through people like the prophets (Matthew 1:22; Acts 3:18). Above all, God speaks to us through his Son, Jesus Christ (Hebrews 1:1-2). Jesus is "the Word" of God: "In the beginning was the Word, and the Word was with God, and the Word was God....And the Word became flesh" (John 1:1, 14).

God also can address us by evoking memories, by stirring up emotions, by stimulating thoughts and images, and by encouraging us to act. God can use these doorways to our consciousness, our memory, emotions, intellect, imagination, and will, for he created them! When we are quiet, we can learn to hear his voice in the memories, feelings, thoughts, images, and decisions that arise in us. How do we know that they are of God and not just products of our imaginations? When they are of God, they will be in accord with the teachings of Scripture and the Church and will produce the good fruits of love, service, generosity, and peace. In difficult matters, we may consult with a spiritual adviser.

Beyond the ordinary experiences of prayer, many people have reported visions of Christ, Mary, angels, or saints. The Catholic Church is very cautious about verifying such visions but in some cases has declared some like those at Fatima and Lourdes as worthy of belief. Visions and voices are not essential for prayer, and many of the greatest saints never had such experiences.

Pathways to Prayer: Attentiveness to God

We have said that God speaks with us through the words of the Bible. Are we attentive to his voice when the Bible is proclaimed at Mass? Do we often read the Bible with eagerness to hear what God says to us, especially through Jesus?

We must become attentive to God's many other "words" of love. What does God say to us at every moment by the very fact that he has created us and holds us in being? What do his gifts of sunshine and air, sound and color, scent and taste, warmth and cold, light and darkness, say to us? What does he say by giving us family and friends, food and shelter, mountains and seas, forests and plains? Have we learned to feel the gentle caress of God in a warm breeze? Do we experience God's power in the storm, his magnificence in the starry night? Do we sense the presence of God in the goodness of human beings, especially in the kindnesses they show us? Are we aware of this "body language" of God?

Do we allow God to speak to our mind, emotions, imagination, memory, and will? Do we give him our full attention so that he can call forth ideas into our intellect, fill our hearts with love, touch us with images that console and encourage, help us to remember the great things he has done for us, and challenge us to make decisions?

We will hear God speaking only if we become attentive. Scientists have huge radio antennas that are constantly "listening" for any signal from outer space. We need to tune the "antennas" of our minds and hearts to God. This is not easy. Our lives are always busy and often hectic.

First, we must find time. Some people rise early to pray for an hour, half-hour, or fifteen minutes. Others pray during lunch hour or just before retiring. The important thing is to schedule time for prayer and be faithful to it. If we can't find fifteen minutes, then we should set aside five, or even one. Better to pray one minute a day than to pray not at all because we "can't find the time."

After setting a time for prayer, we need a way of quieting ourselves and coming to an awareness of God's presence. We must "tune out" any interference and "tune in" God. There are many ways to do this.

• Sit quietly in a firm chair. Keep your back straight. Close your eyes and become aware of any tension. Relax the muscles in your face, neck, shoulders, arms, torso, legs, and feet. Reflect on the words of Jesus, "Peace I leave with you; my peace I give to you" (John 14:27).

• Pay attention to your breathing. If it is shallow, deepen it. If it is rapid, slow it down. Breathe deeply and try to feel the air entering your lungs. Think for a moment about the first breath you took as a baby and about the last breath you will take on this earth. Reflect on this verse of Scripture: "The breath of the Almighty keeps me alive" (Job 33:4).

• Be attentive to the sounds of life around you, perhaps a bird singing, a breeze stirring the trees, voices in the distance, a car passing. Think of how all activity and life have their origin in God. Meditate on these words: "Listen to the voice of the LORD your God" (Jeremiah 26:13).

• Be sensitive to the experience of touch. Feel the softness of your clothing, the press of the chair against your body and of the floor against your feet, even the gentle embrace of the air surrounding you. Think about these words of Saint Paul, "In him we live and move and have our being" (Acts 17:28).

• Try to feel your heart beating. Think of how it pumps life-giving oxygen to every cell in your body. Think too of how the human heart is a symbol of love, just as necessary for life as a healthy heart. Ponder these words of Scripture: God has "set his heart on you" (Deuteronomy 7:7); "You shall love the Lord your God with all your heart" (Mark 12:30).

Pathways to Prayer: Speaking to God in Private Prayer

After we have become attentive to God's voice, how should we reply? The most natural way is to talk to God in our own words. There are four basic types of prayer: praise, thanks, sorrow, and petition. Elegant phrases are not required. We need only be open and honest, saying what is really in our hearts. Whether we are happy or sad, angry or at peace, we can share our feelings with God. We may vocalize our prayer, or we may speak in the silence of our hearts.

Another common way to respond to God is to use formulas of prayer. Many such formulas may be found in the Bible, as noted above. Others, like the Hail Mary and Glory Be, have been passed down for centuries and are memorized by most Catholics. There are books of prayers for every occasion and circumstance in life, and many Catholics have a favorite prayer book.

Certain kinds of prayer patterns have been popular with Catholics for generations. The rosary is said using beads to count recital of the Lord's Prayer, ten Hail Marys, and the Glory Be, while we reflect on mysteries from the lives of Jesus and Mary. The Way of the Cross is a devotion at which we meditate on the sufferings of Jesus during his Passion and death, and the Stations may be seen on the walls of many Catholic churches.

Catholics also pray without words, using the many forms of mental prayer developed by saints and spiritual guides. One of the best known is that taught by Saint Ignatius of Loyola. After directing our attention to God, we reflect, for example, on some scene from the gospels. We place ourselves in the scene, imagining the sights and sounds. We talk with Jesus. We make some practical resolution as a result of our reflection. Another method is reflective reading, wherein we read from the Bible or a spiritual book, pausing to think and pray each time some passage inspires us. Another is the Jesus Prayer, where we gently and slowly pray the name of Jesus, focusing on his presence and love. The techniques given under "Pathways to Prayer: Attentiveness to God" may be used to prepare ourselves for other forms of meditation, or they may be employed for a long time as our prayer. Mental prayer can also be simple and contemplative: we place ourselves before God in silence, content just to be with the Lord.

"Imaging prayer" is a kind of contemplative prayer. In this prayer we focus on images rather than words. We praise God by picturing ourselves kneeling before the throne of God in heaven. We thank God by visualizing the blessings we have received as gifts flowing to us from God. We express sorrow for sin by mentally standing at the cross of Jesus. We make petitions by forming images of our needs and place them before God. We pray for others by picturing Jesus standing next to them, placing his hands on them and blessing them. "Imaging prayer" is a beautiful way to end our day. After retiring, we visualize Jesus standing watch over people who need his help and over ourselves as we sleep.

Some people keep prayer journals, a daily record of prayer, and may make their prayer to God in writing. If we can send thoughts and feelings to people through letters, we can surely direct them to God in prayer journals.

Pathways to Prayer:
Speaking to God Through Prayer in Common

Most methods of prayer may be used not only by individuals but also by groups of people, and so become common prayer. There is a special value to prayer with others, as we learn from Jesus, "Where two or three are gathered together in my name, there am I in the midst of them" (Matthew 18:20).

The official communal prayer of the Church, and our most important prayer, is the liturgy. This includes the Mass and the sacraments, Benediction, and the Liturgy of the Hours. Sunday Mass should be the heart of all our prayer, and many Catholics attend daily Mass as a way to unite their lives to Christ. All celebrations of the sacraments are prayer and allow us to pray for ourselves and others at key moments in life. Benediction is worship, through song and prayer, of Christ present in the Blessed Sacrament. The Liturgy of the Hours is the daily prayer of the Church, said by priests, religious, and many laypeople.

In many Catholic parishes there are prayer groups that meet regularly. Some recite the rosary. Others study the Bible, then pray and sing together. There are charismatic prayer groups that pay special attention to the gifts of the Holy Spirit, including praying in tongues (1 Corinthians 12-14).

There are many retreat and renewal movements in the Catholic Church today. Some religious orders sponsor retreats for laypeople. There are Marriage Encounter Weekends for married couples, Teens Encounter Christ retreats for young people, Beginning Again Weekends for the widowed and divorced. Such movements encourage participants to meet for prayer and reflection on a regular basis.

Singing is an important form of common prayer. It is often a part of liturgical prayer, especially the Mass. Through singing, we direct melody and words to God as praise, thanks, contrition, or petition. (We may use music in private prayer also. Some listen to recorded religious music as a way to lift mind and heart to God, and some sing favorite hymns to express their feelings to God.)

In today's world there is a special need for family prayer. "The family that prays together stays together." Modern families must realize that prayer is not a luxury but a necessity. We find time for things that are important, and we simply must find time for prayer. Even the busiest families can take a few minutes after the evening meal to read and discuss the Bible or to pray one decade of the rosary or to pray about the events of the day.

Attitudes Toward Prayer

Our first attitude should be an openness to all that God tells us about prayer in the Scriptures. Focusing on one passage to the exclusion of others can give a distorted view of prayer. For example, Mark 11:24, "All that you ask for in prayer, believe that you will receive it and it shall be yours" must be interpreted in the light of Jesus' other statements, especially those counseling submission to God's will. There is an old saying that God always answers prayers, but sometimes his answer is "yes," sometimes "no," and sometimes "wait."

A second attitude is that we must pray in accord with the ordinary laws of life and common sense. If I pray, "Lord, help our basketball team to win this game," I am asking God to be on our team. God might respond, "Only five players are allowed on a team!" A better prayer might be, "Lord, help us to do our best." Prayers to win a game or a lottery ask God to give us an unfair advantage.

A third attitude has to do with the degree of faith with which we pray. On the one hand, it is a mistake to blame ourselves for lack of faith every time a petition seems to go unanswered. On the other hand, it is probably a mistake to assume that our faith is all it should be. Perhaps our prayers might be more effective if our faith was stronger. Without excessive worrying, we should ask God for the grace of faith, then pray, entrusting the answer to his providence.

A fourth attitude is also faith-related. Often we lack confidence, not because God fails to answer our prayers but because we do not recognize his answers. We are given what we ask, then wonder if it wasn't just a coincidence. (Someone has observed: "Coincidences happen more often when I pray!") Or we forget how often prayers are answered. If we kept a journal of our requests and the answers received, our confidence in God might be enhanced.

A fifth attitude is the awareness that God cannot answer some prayers because we build up walls between ourselves and God. We cannot receive forgiveness from God unless we are willing to forgive those who offend us (Matthew 18:21-35). We sever communications with God by sin, whereas we open ourselves up to God's blessings by holiness of life (1 John 3:21-22).

A sixth attitude: God may not answer our prayer as we'd like because we should take responsibility for answering that prayer. When we pray, "Lord, help the poor," God may suggest that we help the poor by sharing. When we ask God for good health, God may respond by urging us to give up unhealthy habits and get more exercise!

Seventh, we should realize that not all people have the same gifts. Some have a special ability to know what to ask for. Some have a gift of praying for the sick. Some report they can "hear" God speaking to them. There are many spiritual gifts, and no one possesses them all. Rather, many individuals with many kinds of spiritual gifts make up the Body of Christ (1 Corinthians 12:12-31).

An eighth attitude has been expressed in the phrase, "The purpose of prayer is not to bring God around to our way of thinking but to bring us around to God's way of thinking." God's way of thinking may not be ours. We may pray that God will take away an illness or disability and receive instead the patience and strength to endure, as Paul did (2 Corinthians 12:7-9). Often, as believers become more experienced in the ways of prayer, they find themselves asking for fewer things and are content simply to place their lives in God's hands.

A ninth attitude is the awareness that we pray to open ourselves up to the blessings God wants us to have. This is true of prayers of praise, thanksgiving, petition, and sorrow for sin. Our praise and thanks do not benefit God but put us in a proper relationship to our Creator. We make petitions not to persuade God but to turn toward him as the source of all good. We express sorrow not to convince God to forgive us but to open our hearts to the pardon he offers through Jesus.

A tenth attitude is that we can pray with more assurance for spiritual blessings than for material benefits. Jesus says, "If you then, who are wicked, know how to give good gifts to your children, how much more will the Father in heaven give the holy Spirit to those who ask him?" (Luke 11:13). We may pray for prosperity, but such a prayer might merit a positive answer less than a prayer for humility! Further, there are complications in praying for material blessings: the rain we want to make our garden grow might wash out our neighbor's picnic.

An eleventh attitude realizes that God respects the free will of those for whom we pray. If they have hardened their hearts, they can refuse the grace God offers them in answer to our prayers. Still, persevering prayer can have a great effect on sinners, as when Saint Augustine was converted after years of prayer by his mother, Saint Monica. Like a farmer who digs one irrigation channel after another, sending water to moisten arid fields; a believer praying for a wayward friend lays channels through which God's grace can soften the hardest heart.

The twelfth is an attitude which keeps us open to exciting possibilities for prayer. Today much research is being done into the activity of the right side of the human brain and into the communication of feelings and ideas through the right side of the brain. Identical twins often seem to be able to communicate without words and to feel emotions experienced by each other. Perhaps we have such abilities that can be developed through prayer. Just as we have learned to harness electricity to power our machines, so perhaps we can learn to use prayer to strengthen our relationships with one another and to experience the power of God.

Better Than *Voyager 2*

We can make comparisons between modern communications and prayer, but while *Voyager 2* will remain in empty space for the next one hundred thousand years and may never be seen by another creature, our contact with God through prayer is instantaneous and certain!

Prayer can also be difficult. At times God seems close, then very far away. After a retreat we may feel that we have reached the heights of perfect prayer, but God may then withdraw to lead us higher still. Even the saints had periods of fervor and dryness, and God led them through such stages to himself.

When we attune ourselves to the many ways in which God speaks to us, when we become aware of the many opportunities we have to speak with God, we leave the narrow confines of planet Earth and open ourselves up to the infinite love and power of God. Prayer is not just a "close encounter." Prayer "joins heaven to earth, and earth to heaven."

Questions for Discussion or Reflection

Have you ever thought of prayer as an adventure even more exciting than trying to communicate with beings from another planet? Can you think of times when you received answers to prayer in a remarkable way? Mention has been made of prayer of praise, thanksgiving, sorrow, and petition. Which of these kinds of prayer do you say most often? Least often? Of the various "attitudes" toward prayer given in the chapter, which seems most important to you? Are there any attitudes given that you disagree with? Which of the pathways to private prayer have you used? Are there any that you would like to try more often?

Activities

Use the prayer exercises suggested under "Pathways to Prayer: Attentiveness to God" (see page 147).

Memorize the following prayers:

CHAPTER THIRTEEN

Morality — Jesus Guides Us Through Life

"Actions speak louder than words." Study of our faith is meaningful only if it motivates us to act in a manner consistent with the teaching of Jesus. "What good is it, my brothers, if someone says he has faith but does not have works? Can that faith save him? If a brother or sister has nothing to wear and has no food for the day, and one of you says to them, 'Go in peace, keep warm, and eat well,' but you do not give them the necessities of the body, what good is it? So also faith of itself, if it does not have works, is dead" (James 2:14-17).

If we believe in Jesus Christ and accept the teaching of the Bible, we must translate our beliefs into action. In his Sermon on the Mount, Jesus said, "Not everyone who says to me, 'Lord, Lord,' will enter the kingdom of heaven, but only the one who does the will of my Father in heaven" (Matthew 7:21).

These words of Jesus presume that we are free to make choices, that our choices should be in conformity with God's will, and that we are accountable for them. In making choices we are called to follow our consciences.

Conscience

Conscience is sometimes portrayed as a little angel hovering nearby, whispering what we should do and what we should avoid. But conscience is actually our sense of the moral goodness or evil of a thing. My conscience is myself, as I have the ability to discern right or wrong and the responsibility to choose what is right.

But how do we know what is right or wrong? Catholics believe that a true conscience must be in conformity with God's will. Something is right and moral if it is right in the eyes of God, wrong and immoral if it is wrong in the eyes of God. Some of the most basic notions of right and wrong are written by God in our hearts, as Saint Paul says (Romans 2:15), but we must move beyond this "natural law" in our search to know God's will.

Forming Our Conscience: The Bible

We begin by responding to the call of Jesus, "The kingdom of God is at hand. Repent, and believe in the gospel" (Mark 1:15). We consciously accept Jesus Christ as our guide, believing that his words and example teach us the best way to live. We study his teachings and try to apply them to the real decisions of daily life. In a practical way we look to Jesus for guidance in the choices we make in our personal lives, family, social circle, work, and civic duties.

Our source for the study of Christ's teachings is the Bible, and our starting point is the guideline that includes everything — love. "You shall love the Lord, your God, with all your heart, with all your soul, and with all your mind. This is the greatest and the first commandment. The second is like it: You shall love your neighbor as yourself. The whole law and the prophets depend on these two commandments" (Matthew 22:37-40; see Romans 13:8-10).

In making this statement, Jesus was echoing the Old Testament, for the "first commandment" is found in the Book of Deuteronomy (6:4-5) and the "second" in the Book of Leviticus (19:18). And when Jesus was asked by a young man, "What must I do to inherit eternal life?" he responded, "You know the commandments: 'You shall not kill; you shall not commit adultery; you shall not steal; you shall not bear false witness; you shall not defraud; honor your father and your mother' " (Mark 10:17-19). The moral teaching of Jesus, then, includes an affirmation of these commandments of the Old Testament.

The Ten Commandments

The Ten Commandments referred to by Jesus in the tenth chapter of Mark are the heart of Old Testament morality. The Jews accepted them as God's will; they were expressed to Moses on Mount

Sinai (Exodus 20:1-20; Deuteronomy 5:1-21). They have stood the test of time as standards of morality for countless generations.

Why are the commandments so significant? Because they can make us truly free. The Israelites had been slaves in Egypt, and once they had escaped from their bondage, God gave them the commandments to safeguard them from falling into a worse slavery — that of sin. People who keep the commandments can enjoy the full range of human freedom without being limited by the restraints imposed by sin. Those who keep the first commandment will not be trapped by superstition. Those who keep the fourth and sixth commandments will not through their own fault be enmeshed in destructive family relationships.

If we are not truly free today, it is largely because the Ten Commandments are not obeyed. We must lock our possessions because the seventh commandment is not kept. We fear to walk the streets at night because the fifth commandment is not observed. The worth of the commandments can be seen if we ask ourselves the simple question, "What would the world be like tomorrow if everyone would do no more than keep the Ten Commandments?"

The commandments can also help us discern the true meaning of love. "Love" is a word used in many ways, and we can deceive ourselves into supposing that our choices arise from love when they do not. The commandments make it clear that murder, adultery, theft, and the like are never the loving thing to do.

Many books have been written on the Ten Commandments, and it is not possible in this chapter to discuss the full range of meaning for each of them. A listing of the commandments and some areas of morality they embrace may be found in the examination of conscience in chapter eight. Reflection on this examination can help us apply the commandments to our lives.

The Moral Teachings of Jesus

Jesus did more than affirm the Ten Commandments. He urged us to strive toward the higher standard: "You have heard that it was said to your ancestors, 'You shall not kill; and whoever kills will be liable to judgment.' But I say to you, whoever is angry with his brother will be liable to judgment" (Matthew 5:21-22). He said that we must avoid lustful thoughts, not just adultery. Old patterns allowing divorce, revenge, and hatred must be abandoned. What was the higher standard given by Jesus? "Be perfect, just as your heavenly Father is perfect" (Matthew 5:48).

Jesus revised the way people were to look at contemporary moral guidelines. The Pharisees of Jesus' time imposed stringent requirements on people with their legal interpretations. When Jesus' disciples were hungry and began to pick heads of grain and eat them, the Pharisees accused them of harvesting, forbidden on the Sabbath (Exodus 34:21). Jesus defended his followers on the principle that the Sabbath was made for people and not people for the Sabbath (Mark 2:23-28). Jesus repudiated the narrowness of the Pharisees and taught that the good of humans must come before mere legalism.

Jesus condemned some legal interpretations then in vogue. He attacked the Pharisees because they allowed people to "dedicate" funds to the temple, meaning that they could use the funds for themselves but not for others, even needy parents! Jesus made it clear that we must always interpret the commandments according to a genuine spirit of love for God and others (Mark 7:8-13).

Jesus nullified portions of the old law. The Old Testament designated some foods as clean and others as unclean — not to be eaten. Jesus explained that what we eat cannot make us unclean, but that the thoughts, words, and deeds which come from our hearts can. "Thus he declared all foods clean" (Mark 7:19). It took the followers of Jesus a long time to understand what this meant, but eventually the early Church felt free to withdraw from Jewish dietary bans and from such important Jewish practices as circumcision (Acts 15). This had profound implications upon moral judgments made by Christians from that time on.

Whether Jesus was teaching that true justice went beyond Old Testament standards in matters like divorce or that dietary regulations no longer applied, he was urging us to move beyond legalism to what truly fosters love. He said, "Do not think that I have come to abolish the law or the prophets. I have come not to abolish but to fulfill" (Matthew 5:17). Laws are necessary and good, but Christ's followers must constantly strive to view them according to his mind and heart.

The Church

Catholics believe that we have another resource available to us as we form our consciences — the teachings of the Church. Jesus is present in his Church and has given its leaders the authority to speak and act in his name. "Whatever you bind on earth," he said to Peter, "shall be bound in heaven; and whatever you loose on earth shall be loosed in heaven" (Matthew 16:19).

Jesus told his disciples to go to all nations, "teaching them to observe all that I have commanded" (Matthew 28:20). After his Ascension the apostles applied the commands of Jesus to the situations they encountered. Thus, guided by the Holy Spirit, they decreed that Christians in Antioch were not bound by Jewish law but did impose a few limitations for the sake of good order (Acts 15). As circumstances changed, even those limitations were dropped.

New Testament Christians looked to their leaders for guidance in moral questions, as when the Corinthians wrote to Paul for advice (1 Corinthians 7:1). Paul issued directives for them concerning such issues as marriage, foods sacrificed to idols, and behavior in liturgical assemblies. All New Testament letters offered moral guidance, and some, notably the pastoral letters, gave rules of conduct in matters of church organization, relationships, and daily life.

Since then the Catholic Church has provided moral leadership for its members through laws and instruction from pastors, bishops, and popes. Circumstances change with time, and people today face moral problems undreamed of by first-century Christians; Church leaders are responsible for teaching how the gospel applies to modern life and for giving us laws such as those in *The Code of Canon Law* (a collection of laws for the Church) to guide us. Catholics should give serious consideration to such teaching, and while leaders today can make mistakes, just as the apostles could (Galatians 2:11-14), the pope and the bishops speaking as a body possess a special authority that should not be taken lightly.

The Teaching of Theologians and Common Practice of Good Catholics

Throughout Church history there have been great teachers of moral theology like Saint Thomas Aquinas and Saint Alphonsus Liguori and great masters of the spiritual life like Saint Teresa and Saint John of the Cross. Their writings have helped form the consciences of generations of Catholics, and they have established moral principles that have been useful for centuries. Today there are theologians and spiritual writers who are especially qualified to offer moral guidance by reason of their education and experience. When we are faced with difficult moral decisions, moral theologians and spiritual advisers, past and present, can render valuable assistance and guidance. The common practice of good Catholics who are led by the Holy Spirit can also guide us. Much of our appreciation of the goodness of marital sexual relationships, for example, comes from the experience of good Catholics.

A Good Conscience

The teachings of Jesus Christ and of the Bible, the guidance of the Church, the instructions of moral theologians, and experience are the sources available to us as we strive to form a good conscience. They provide us with objective guidelines so that our decisions are not merely subjective and emotional. In some cases we may find the right course of action quickly and easily. For instance, the teaching of Jesus and the Bible, the moral directives of the Church, the teachings of good theologians, and experience are one in telling us that it is evil to murder an innocent person. In other cases the answers are not so clear. Is it permissible to kill someone who is attacking an innocent person? If so, under what circumstances? Here a great deal of study may be required.

Catholics should be aware of proper moral guidelines. They should know which areas of morality allow for flexibility and which areas demand a specific response. In some cases Catholics may freely choose between several alternatives without sin because the issue has not been clearly resolved. Thus, one Catholic might choose to serve as a soldier, while another might feel obliged to serve only in a nonaggressive capacity. In other cases Catholics may not licitly make some moral choices because these violate the clear teaching of the Bible and of the Church. Abortion is such a case, and Catholics who take part in an abortion or promote abortions are transgressing the law of God in a serious matter.

Becoming More Christlike in Our Moral Choices

It is possible in the study of moral theology to make the mistake of assuming that our main goal in life is the avoidance of sin. Our real goal, however, is to become more like Jesus Christ, to act out of love rather than out of a sense of obligation. A mother will go to great extremes for her infant, lavishing care both day and night. She does so gladly out of love and goes to extremes of service she might never approach if she were working for pay. So, too, love is a "law without limits," and if we strive to love as Christ loves, we are likely not only to keep the commandments but to go far beyond them in our service of God and neighbor.

The love of Christ will always challenge us to work for peace and social justice and to have a special concern for the poor. Christ cautioned us that our eternal destiny will be determined by our readiness to help others and reminded us that whatever we do for others is done for him (Matthew 25:31-46).

Christ's love will also challenge us to be consistent in our moral choices. We may be generous and loving to people we visit at a nursing home but thoughtless and unkind toward members of our own family. We may use our tongue to praise God in church, then fall into habits of cursing and gossiping in the workplace (James 3:1-12). "Love never fails" (1 Corinthians 13:8).

Sin and Grace

The Bible teaches that sin goes back to the first human beings on earth. The story of Adam and Eve shows how people have rejected God, choosing their own definitions of right and wrong. Through Adam and Eve, sin entered the world, separating us from the fullness of God's grace, weakening our ability to overcome sin, and subjecting us to the dominion of death. This "fallen state" is called original sin, and the Catholic Church teaches that all human beings, with the exception of Jesus and Mary, have been touched by original sin.

The Church teaches that human nature is not evil but weakened by original sin. Baptism rejoins us to God, who dwells within us as a Friend and bestows "sanctifying grace," God's life and love making us sons and daughters in the Trinitarian family. Baptism does not remove our tendencies to sin but gives us access to the helping grace of God called "actual grace." Sanctifying grace may be compared to the love parents have for their children. Actual grace may be compared to the many acts of love parents perform for their children like feeding, clothing, and teaching them. Baptized, we have sanctifying and actual grace to help us live a morally good life. But we must also struggle against the weaknesses of human nature and against the temptations that attract us to evil.

When we choose evil, acting against our consciences, we commit what is called "actual sin" or "personal sin." Sin begins in our free will, as we choose to act in a way contrary to God's will. Sin may find expression in actions whether external, such as murder or theft, or internal, such as lustful thoughts, envy, or hatred. Sin may find expression also in omissions when we fail to do what we ought, as when we neglect the poor or fail to worship God.

Sin can exist in different degrees. We may be trying to follow Christ and direct our lives in accord with God's commandments so that our "fundamental option" is toward God. But we can do something wrong or fail to do what is right because we are weak or selfish. If our failing is of such a nature that it does not sever our bond of love with God, it is known as "venial sin." Examples of such sins might be carelessness in prayer, unkind words, and bouts of temper. These sins may be venial, but we should try to overcome them, for just as minor failings can damage our relationship with others, so venial sins can weaken our friendship with God and lead to more serious failings.

There are sins which are so serious that they reverse the direction of our lives, turning us away from God, changing our "fundamental option" to sin and death. These are called "mortal sins," sins that are deadly because they cut us off from God's love. Saint Paul gives examples of such sins: "Now the works of the flesh are obvious: immorality, impurity, licentiousness, idolatry, sorcery, hatreds, rivalry, jealousy, outbursts of fury, acts of selfishness, dissensions, factions, occasions of envy, drinking bouts, orgies, and the like. I warn you, as I warned you before, that those who do such things will not inherit the kingdom of God" (Galatians 5:19-21). This is not a complete list, and some of these sins can be less serious at times, as when we are selfish in a light matter. But Paul clearly indicates the existence of sins so "mortal" that they exclude us from the kingdom of God.

It is not possible to establish precise guidelines that would determine in every case whether a given sin is mortal or venial. Some sins are clearly mortal, such as murder and adultery, while others are clearly venial, such as little acts of disobedience by a small child. Others can leave doubt. It would be a venial sin for a child to steal a piece of candy from a store and (objectively, at least) a mortal sin for a thief to steal a poor widow's life savings. But we cannot so easily determine degrees of guilt between these two extremes.

Theologians explain that three conditions must be present for a mortal sin. First, there must be *serious matter,* something that causes serious harm to others or ourselves or is a serious affront to God. Second, there must be *sufficient reflection:* the sinner must be fully aware of the wickedness of the action. Most small children do not have the mental capacity to comprehend the evil of sin and so could not commit a mortal sin. Adults who are mentally deficient or who have had no opportunity to learn about right and wrong might also be incapable of mortal sin. Third, there must be *full consent of the will:* the sinner must freely choose to do what is evil. A man forced to steal money because his child is being held hostage would not have true freedom. Some people can be so damaged emotionally by background or illness that they do not have the freedom or moral maturity necessary to commit mortal sin. But when all three conditions — serious matter, sufficient reflection, and full consent of the will — are present, mortal sin exists.

God's Gift to Us and Our Gift to God

Life and freedom are God's gifts to us; what we become through our use of freedom is our gift to God. God places us on this earth and invites us to love and serve him, opening ourselves up to his love for all eternity. Each day we are given life and freedom. Each day we determine the kind of person we will become. On the one hand, we have the grace of God assisting us to make the right decisions. On the other hand, we are tempted by the devil, by people who sin, and by our own inborn weaknesses. When we make our choices in accord with the dictates of a properly formed conscience, we lead a morally good life. When we go against the moral guidelines given by God, we sin.

The more we choose a certain course or way of acting, whether good or bad, the easier it becomes to perform that action. Thus we form either good habits, called virtues, or bad habits, called vices. The more we speak with kindness and gentleness, the more readily kind words come to our lips. The more we curse or gossip, the more these vices become ingrained in us.

Catholic tradition has assigned special importance to certain virtues. Foremost are faith, hope, and love, called the "theological virtues" because they are gifts of God and direct our relationship to God. By *faith* we acknowledge the reality of God in our lives and are able to believe in the truths that God reveals to us. By *hope* we have confident assurance of achieving our eternal goal with the help of God's grace. By *love* we make the decision to put God first with all our heart, soul, mind and strength, and to love our neighbor as ourselves. While these virtues are gifts of God, we must be willing to accept them from God and to live in such a way that they can grow stronger in us.

There are vices that oppose the theological virtues. We can sin against faith by choosing such false gods as materialism, astrology, or superstition or by failing to pray or study our religion. (Doubts against faith do not necessarily mean the loss of faith, for we will experience temptations against faith just as we do against other virtues.) Sins against hope are presumption, by which we attempt to live without reference to God, and despair, by which we renounce trust in God. (Sometimes despair can originate in depression or emotional illness rather than in a deliberate sinful choice.) Sins against love include hatred of God (as in Satanism), sloth (the neglect of God and of spiritual things), and failure to love our neighbor (1 John 4:20-21).

We grow in the theological virtues by turning to God often in prayer, participating in the Mass and sacraments, making "acts of faith, hope, and love," and asking God to strengthen us in these virtues. Study of the Bible and Catholic teaching will fortify faith, hope, and love, as will exercise of these virtues. When we struggle against doubt, despair, or spiritual dryness and act in faithful, hopeful, loving ways, we allow God to strengthen us in the theological virtues.

Other virtues which have a special place in Catholic tradition are the four "moral" virtues, also called the "cardinal" virtues (from the Latin word for "hinge"), because so many other virtues "hinge" on them. *Prudence* helps us to do the right thing in any circumstance. *Justice* enables us to give others their due. *Fortitude* strengthens us to weather the difficulties and temptations of life. *Temperance* helps us control our desires and use the good things of life in a Christlike way. The gifts and fruits of the Holy Spirit (chapter six) are prominent in Christian spirituality. Many other virtues like humility are taught in the Bible; attentiveness to God's Word will help us become familiar with them.

Catholic tradition recognizes certain vices as especially significant because they are at the heart of most sinful decisions. These are the "seven deadly sins" — pride, greed, lust, anger, gluttony, envy, and sloth. When we find evidence of such sins in our lives, we can uproot them by sincere repentance, by turning to Christ in the Sacrament of Penance, and by practicing the virtues contrary to them.

Saint Paul describes Christian life as a process by which we turn away from sin and put on the virtues of Christ. "Put to death, then, the parts of you that are earthly: immorality, impurity, passion, evil desire, and the greed that is idolatry....You must put them all away: anger, fury, malice, slander, and obscene language out of your mouths. Stop lying to one another, since you have taken off the old self with its practices and have put on the new self, which is being renewed, for knowledge, in the image of its creator....Put on then, as God's chosen ones, holy and beloved, heartfelt compassion, kindness, humility, gentleness, and patience, bearing with one another and forgiving one another, if one has a grievance against another; as the Lord has forgiven you, so must you also do. And over all these put on love, that is, the bond of perfection. And let the peace of Christ control your hearts....And whatever you do, in word or in deed, do everything in the name of the Lord Jesus, giving thanks to God the Father through him" (Colossians 3:5, 8-10, 12-15, 17).

The Imitation of Christ

When we speak of freedom and conscience, of observing the commandments, of living in grace rather than in sin, of choosing virtue over vice, we can sum it all up in Saint Paul's phrase, "Life is Christ" (Philippians 1:21). Life for us should be a constant effort to be one with Jesus, making our everyday decisions according to his mind and heart. We should treat the members of our family with kindness because we believe in Jesus. The way we relate to our friends, coworkers, and people on the street should be a result of our relationship with Christ. The books we read, the television shows and movies we watch, the language we use, the clothes we wear, should be in accord with our life in Christ. Our business decisions, political choices, and social relationships should be, insofar as possible, in harmony with what Christ would do if he were in our place.

Living our life in harmony with the love of Christ may put us at odds with secular society. At times we may make choices that will cause others to ask, "Why are they acting in that way?" with the only satisfactory answer being, "Because they believe in Jesus Christ." Actions do speak louder than words, and we should reflect often on a brief and humorous "examination of conscience" expressed in the question, "If you were arrested for being a Christian, would there be enough evidence to convict you?"

Questions for Discussion or Reflection

Can you name the Ten Commandments? Using the examination of conscience based on the Ten Commandments (chapter eight) as a guide, how many sins can you name that are forbidden by each commandment? How many virtues can you name that are counseled by each commandment?

What would the world be like if everyone would keep the Ten Commandments?

Activities

Place yourself in the presence of God and meditate on the following New Testament passage, "Examine yourselves to see whether you are living in faith. Test yourselves. Do you not realize that Jesus Christ is in you?" (2 Corinthians 13:5).

CHAPTER FOURTEEN

Jesus Gives Us Communion With the Saints

Walk into anyone's home and you are likely to find pictures of family members from generations past — grandparents who moved to the area, parents who built the house, relatives who form the family tree. If you inquire, you may be shown mementos like the books they read, the jewelry they wore, keepsakes they treasured, and diaries they kept. We like to recall our past, search for roots, and delve into our background in a quest for information about our ancestors.

We who are Catholic remember those who have gone before us in our Church family. We hope to learn from the saints and so come to a deeper knowledge of ourselves. We look to them for inspiration, courage, and hope.

Remembering and Honoring the Saints

Some people criticize Catholics for honoring the saints. But it is biblical to remember and honor them. The eleventh chapter of Hebrews is a "verbal memorial" in honor of the holy men and women of the Old Testament. Hebrews 13:7 advises: "Remember your leaders who spoke the word of God to you. Consider the outcome of their way of life and imitate their faith."

It is also natural to honor great people from the past. In our national capital, the Washington Monument, the Lincoln Memorial, and many other shrines and statues honor government and military leaders. Catholics name churches after saints and erect statues to honor spiritual leaders.

The Communion of Saints

We do more than remember. We believe in a union, called the communion of saints, between us and those who have died in Christ. We believe that the saints care about us and watch over us, that they pray for us, and that we can pray with them. We base these beliefs on holy Scripture.

In the Book of Revelation, the saints in heaven are pictured as offering to God the prayers of God's people: "Each of the elders held a harp and gold bowls filled with incense, which are the prayers of the holy ones" (5:8). 2 Maccabees 15:12-15 reports a vision in which the martyred high priest Onias and the prophet Jeremiah pray for the Jewish nation; this demonstrates the Jewish belief that saints are aware of earthly events and pray for us. Moses and Elijah appear with Jesus at the Transfiguration and talk with him about his coming Passion and death (Luke 9:28-36). Jesus speaks of the "joy in heaven over one sinner who repents" (Luke 15:7). The Letter to the Hebrews compares life to a race we run while the great heroes of the past are in the stands cheering us on. "Therefore, since we are surrounded by so great a cloud of witnesses, let us... persevere in running the race that lies before us" (Hebrews 12:1).

These passages imply interaction between those in heaven and those on earth, and we should be aware of the presence and loving care of the saints. Those who are "in heaven" are close to the knowledge and love of God and, therefore, are more aware of our needs and more devoted to us than they ever were on earth. We are never alone, for we live "in communion" with the saints.

Praying to the Saints

Sometimes Catholics are asked, "Why do you pray to the saints? Why don't you just pray directly to God?" We should first note that "pray" is used in two different ways by Catholics. We "pray" to God as the source of all blessings. We "pray" to the saints in the sense that we ask them to pray with us and for us. This is illustrated in two prayers frequently said by Catholics. In the Lord's Prayer, we ask God to "give us this day our daily bread" and to "forgive us our trespasses." In the Hail Mary, we ask Mary to "pray for us sinners."

But why pray to the saints at all? The answer lies in the importance of prayer with others and for others. Jesus places a special importance in common prayer: "For where two or three are gathered together in my name, there am I in the midst of them (Matthew 18:20). Since there is a particular value in praying with others, and since the Bible shows that those in heaven pray for us, it certainly makes sense for us to pray *with* the saints.

It also makes sense for us to ask them to pray *for* us. Paul wrote to the Colossians: "Persevere in prayer, being watchful in it with thanksgiving; at the same time, pray for us, too" (Colossians 4:2-3). Paul prayed directly to God, but he felt it was important to have others intercede for him. If the prayers of those on earth have value, then how much more so the prayers of the saints who stand at the throne of God in heaven!

The prayers of others are needed, not to convince God to bless us but to open us up to the blessings God wants us to receive. Since that is the case, the more intercessors we have on earth and in heaven, the more we can be freed of the hindrances of sin and unbelief which keep us from receiving God's assistance.

We can and should pray directly to God. But our prayers to God take on new life and power when we consciously join them to the prayers of the saints. And each time we pray with the saints, including friends and family members who have died in Christ, we are reminded that we are never alone. Prayer to the saints "keeps us in touch" with them until we join them in heaven.

Canonization of Saints

The New Testament addressed Christians on earth as the "saints," but Catholic tradition very quickly began to apply the term to holy individuals who had entered eternal life, especially to those who had been martyred for Christ. Details of their sufferings, death, and last words were recalled. The apostles, martyrs, and holy people were remembered by the Church and invoked in prayer. The tombs of the martyrs were regarded as holy places. When the Church spread throughout the world, groups of believers began to honor their own saints. As stories were told about the great people of the past, legends began to spring up, and it was not always possible to distinguish fact from fiction in the "lives of the saints."

By the tenth century the Church developed a process called "canonization," in which those who had led holy lives were formally named saints. In the sixteenth century a special commission was set up to study the lives of saintly individuals and to make recommendations to the pope about their canonization. More recently there has been much historical research into the lives of the saints, and the Church has limited its formal recognition to saints whose lives could be studied and verified. The Catholic Church has a liturgical "calendar of the saints," honoring those whose lives have a special importance for the whole Church. Many other saints are remembered only in specific localities or by special groups.

Devotions in Honor of the Saints

The Catholic Church has a holy day of obligation in honor of "All Saints" on November 1. This feast acknowledges that there are innumerable human beings who have been saved by the blood of Christ, "a great multitude, which no one could count, from every nation, race, people, and tongue" (Revelation 7:9). We all have our "own saints" before the throne of God.

Masses are often celebrated on weekdays, and occasionally on Sundays, in honor of the saints. This practice encourages us to remember their lives and to ask them to pray for us. There are prayers and private devotions in honor of various saints, and Catholics are encouraged to pray to the saints in their own words.

It goes without saying that devotion to the saints should help us grow in our commitment to Jesus Christ. The saints direct us to Christ and would not want our enthusiasm for them to distract us from Jesus. Real devotion to the saints sees Christ's face mirrored in his faithful followers and leads us closer to him.

The Saints: Models of Christlike Living

When families get together, they often talk about relatives who have gone before them. They remember a grandfather who donated land for a church cemetery and the aunt who worked day and night to support her family during the Depression. Such recollections give us a sense of oneness with the past and encourage us to persevere in our efforts to lead worthwhile lives. In a similar way our Catholic family remembers our "relatives" in the faith. They form a family tree that is rooted in Jesus Christ. They teach us how to follow Christ in every way of life, and they encourage us to persevere.

Carpenters can look to Saint Joseph to discover that they can be "just" men using hammer and saw. Young people can see in Saint Maria Goretti a model of purity and devotion to Jesus. Mothers can imitate Saint Elizabeth Ann Seton in her dedication to her family. Farmers can learn from Saint Isidore that there is holiness in working the soil, caring for animals, and sharing food with the poor. There are "patron saints" for every vocation and way of life. By studying the lives of the saints, we discover how sanctity may be found in every place and age. And what is just as important, we find that the saints were human beings like us. They had faults and failings, even the greatest of them. When we deny Christ by sin, we can turn to Saint Peter, for he knew what it was like to fail and to receive forgiveness from the Lord. When we fear that we have squandered too many years in petty foolishness, we can ask for the help of Saint Augustine, who prayed, "Too late have I loved Thee, O Beauty ever Ancient, ever New. Too late have I loved Thee." When we sin, and when we succeed, there are saints who walked the path before us and found their way to heaven. They inspire us and lead us on.

The Souls in Purgatory

Catholics believe that some people may experience death when they are neither cut off from God by serious sin nor perfectly free from all venial sin. They need further "purification" from sin to achieve the holiness necessary to stand in God's presence where "nothing unclean will enter" (Revelation 21:27). The Catholic Church teaches that such individuals can be helped by the prayers of others. This belief goes back to Old Testament times.

Some Jewish soldiers fighting in the war for independence under Judas Maccabeus had been slain in battle. They were found to be wearing pagan amulets, a practice forbidden by Jewish law. Their comrades prayed for the dead "that the sinful deed might be fully blotted out." Then Judas "took up a collection among all his soldiers, amounting to two thousand silver drachmas, which he sent to Jerusalem to provide for an expiatory sacrifice." The Bible comments that this was "holy and pious" and affirms that "he made atonement for the dead that they might be freed from this sin" (2 Maccabees 12:43-46).

Inspired by this passage, Catholics have always prayed for their beloved dead. Inscriptions in the Roman catacombs, Christian burial places, show that early believers prayed for the dead. In the fourth century Saint Monica made this deathbed request of her son, Saint Augustine, "One thing only I ask you, that you remember me at the altar of the Lord wherever you may be."

In time, the practice of applying indulgences to the deceased came into being. An indulgence is a declaration by the Church that certain prayers or actions have special value because they bestow a sharing in the grace and merits of Christ. The use of indulgences is a graphic way of showing the worth of prayer made in the Church through Jesus Christ. But indulgences can be misunderstood and abused. Eventually, they were granted by some churchmen as "rewards" for donations, and the selling of indulgences was bitterly opposed by Martin Luther. Unfortunately, in rejecting indulgences, he also rejected the practice of praying for the dead. As a result most Protestant denominations today do not pray for the deceased, and they do not accept 2 Maccabees as part of the Bible.

The Catholic Church has continued to pray for the deceased, and this practice has brought consolation and peace to the bereaved. When we stand at the grave of a loved one, we are not helpless onlookers. By God's grace we can reach across space and time to assist the faithful departed by our prayers. We believe as well that their prayers can help us.

Mary: Our Blessed Mother

Catholics give special honor to Mary, the Mother of Jesus Christ. She was chosen by God to be the Mother of his only Son. Without doubt, this was the greatest privilege and the most significant of all human accomplishments, after those of Jesus. The Bible states that "all ages" will call Mary blessed (Luke 1:48) and, in fulfillment of this passage, generations of Catholics have been proud to call Mary our "Blessed Mother."

Mary has a unique place in Scripture. She is greeted by the angel Gabriel with words that show God's esteem for her: "Hail, favored one! The Lord is with you" (Luke 1:28). She is the faithful "hand-maid of the Lord" (Luke 1:38) who assents to God's will. Elizabeth salutes Mary, "Most blessed are you among women" (Luke 1:42). In the Gospel of John it is Mary who occasions the first miracle worked by Jesus (John 2:1-11), and John's use of the term "woman" in reference to Mary may well be a reference to the "woman" of Genesis: Mary is the "new Eve" and Mother of all the living. Mary is again addressed as "woman" at the Crucifixion. "When Jesus saw his mother and the disciple there whom he loved, he said to his mother, 'Woman, behold, your son.' Then he said to the disciple, 'Behold, your mother' " (John 19:26-27). The beloved disciple may be seen to represent all Christians, and Mary is given to us as our Mother.

The Bible clearly teaches that we are the Body of Christ. Since there is a mystical, but real, identification of Jesus with his followers, the Mother of Jesus is our Mother too. And the very fact that Mary is our Mother should help us realize what Vatican II taught explicitly that Mary is one of us, a member of the Church, and one of those redeemed by Christ.

The Immaculate Conception

The Catholic Church believes that Mary was conceived without sin. Many people confuse this doctrine with that of the virginal conception of Christ, but the two are different. The doctrine of the Immaculate Conception teaches that Mary, by God's grace, was preserved from all stain of original sin and that she herself never sinned. When the doctrine was proclaimed by Pope Pius IX in 1854, he explained that Mary shared in the redemptive act of Christ in that she was saved by the foreseen merits of Christ. The Immaculate Conception is an example of Catholic doctrine that is not clearly taught in Scripture but which, congruent with Scripture, was believed universally by Catholics for centuries before it was formally defined as doctrine by the pope.

Mother of God

Catholics believe that Mary is truly the Mother of God. This does not mean that Mary was the source of the divine nature of Jesus, but that she was the Mother of his human nature and that there was no time when the human Jesus was not God. The second Person of the Trinity existed from all eternity, but when the "Word became flesh," Jesus was both human and divine from the first moment of his conception. Mary was not the Mother of a human being who was adopted as God's Son. She was Mother of Jesus Christ, both God and a human. Therefore, it is proper for us to call Mary the "Mother of God."

The Assumption

The doctrine of the Assumption is the only clearly infallible statement made by a pope in the last one hundred years. It was defined in 1950 by Pope Pius XII, not on his own initiative but in answer to millions of petitions from all over the world. Like the Immaculate Conception, the Assumption of Mary was accepted by Catholics for centuries before it became dogma. This doctrine proclaims that at the end of Mary's life on earth, Christ gave her victory over death, and her body shared fully in his Resurrection as ours will only at the end of time. Because Mary never sinned, she was able to experience complete union with her Son, Jesus. This doctrine is a sign of hope because it points the way to heaven for us, who are, like Mary, members of the Church.

Apparitions of Mary

Mary is our Mother, and Catholics have experienced her intercession in many ways. Generations of believers have praised Mary as one who has led them to the grace of God. Many trustworthy and holy individuals have reported visions of Mary, often accompanied by messages that have been the source of countless blessings. Shrines at the sites of such appearances are visited by millions of people every year, most notably at our Lady of Guadalupe in Mexico, at Lourdes in France, and at Fatima in Portugal.

The Catholic Church does not require that its members believe in such appearances, but there have been official declarations that certain apparitions and the messages associated with them are not contrary to Catholic doctrine and are worthy of belief. We believe on the evidence of Scripture that God sends angels as messengers of his love, and it is reasonable to believe that Jesus can send his Mother as an emissary. Many miracles of healing have occurred at

Marian shrines; hundreds of them have been carefully studied by medical bureaus and have been declared to be beyond any medical explanation. The shrine at Lourdes is especially noted for its miracles and the care with which any reported miracles are examined by doctors, non-Catholic as well as Catholic. Anyone who studies these miracles, as they have been described in numerous books and magazine articles, cannot help but be amazed at the evident presence of God's power and grace working through the intercession of Mary.

Jesus said that we can judge a tree by its fruit, and we can see the good fruit of God's blessings flowing from Guadalupe, Lourdes, and Fatima. They are evidence of God's loving care and of Mary's maternal affection for us.

Devotions in Honor of Mary

Mary has been honored in great works of architecture like Notre Dame in Paris, in beautiful music like Schubert's "Ave Maria," and in priceless masterpieces like the "Pieta." Churches, religious orders, universities, hospitals, streets, and cities have been named for Mary. But the greatest respect the Catholic Church pays to Mary is through the liturgical feasts in her honor.

Mary has a special place at Christmas, the birthday of Jesus. One week later, New Year's Day is celebrated as a holy day by Catholics under the title of Mary, Mother of God. The Solemnity of Mary's Assumption is observed as a holy day on August 15, as is the Solemnity of the Immaculate Conception on December 8. Many other liturgical celebrations bring Mary to mind at various times of the year.

There are nonliturgical prayers honoring Mary that are well known to most Catholics. The Hail Mary is one of the first prayers memorized by Catholic children. The first part is taken from the Bible and the second part asks Mary to "pray for us sinners now and at the hour of our death." The rosary recalls the great mysteries of our salvation, and through it Mary brings us closer to her Son. There are hymns, novenas, and litanies to Mary. Many Catholics wear medals, such as the "Miraculous Medal," to honor Mary and to remind themselves of Mary's loving care. May is observed as the month of Mary in many parishes with processions and May crownings. October is set aside as the month of the holy rosary. In these and many other ways, Catholics show their love to Mary and ask her to help us grow closer to her Son, Jesus.

What a Family!

Why honor the saints? Why pray to the saints? Why pray for the souls in purgatory? Because it's natural to remember our loved ones, to ask friends to pray for us, and to pray for our friends. Because it is a grand thing to belong to a good family, and Christ has called us to belong to the great family of believers, present and past. Because all of us — believers on earth, saints in heaven, souls in purgatory — are one in the communion of saints. "So then you are no longer strangers and sojourners, but you are fellow citizens with the holy ones and members of the household of God, built upon the foundation of the apostles and prophets, with Christ Jesus himself as the capstone" (Ephesians 2:19-20). Indeed, what a family!

Questions for Discussion or Reflection

In your own words answer the questions, "Why do Catholics pray to the saints? Why don't they pray directly to God?" Do you have a favorite saint? Why does that saint appeal to you?

Activities

At Baptism most Catholics are named after a saint. Write a brief description of your patron saint. Try to become more familiar with that saint's life. If you attend a Catholic Church named after a saint, try to discover why that saint was chosen. Look through a Catholic magazine such as the *Liguorian*. Search for articles on the lives of saints or for other references to saints.

CHAPTER FIFTEEN

Jesus Brings Us to Fullness of Life

Sunlight streamed through her window, and Annie wheeled her chair into its warmth. Bright yellow daffodils bouncing in the wind outside made her remember an Easter dream sixty years before. She had only two weeks to wait until the birth of her first child. She was sitting at a window admiring the flowers near her porch steps when she must have fallen asleep. She began to dream, and in her dream she spoke with the child in her womb...

Hello, Johnny. *What? Who are you?* I'm your mother. *Mother? What's a mother?* Johnny, I'm the one, along with your father, who brought you into this world. *Oh? Then where are you? Why can't I see you?* You can't see me because you're living inside me. But soon you'll be born, and then we'll see each other. *Born? What does that mean?* Well, Johnny, you've been growing, and there's not enough room for you there. The life-support system that's keeping you alive won't work much longer. *You mean I'm going to die?* No, you won't die, you'll just begin to live in a new way. *Why should I believe that? I can't see you. Maybe you're not even there. Maybe I'm all alone and just imagining this.* Johnny, you don't think you just came from nothing, do you? Where you're living is real, but the world is much bigger than you think. When you're out here you'll grow tall and strong; you'll run and play; you'll make friends; you'll go hiking in the woods; you'll have a puppy. You'll...*Wait a minute. What are friends? What are woods? What's a puppy?* Friends and woods and puppies are...Johnny, I can't explain them because there's nothing like them where you are. The more I try to explain, the more impossible they'll seem to you. You'll just have to wait and see. *Now I know I'm imagining this. I'm going to die, and I'm afraid.* Johnny, don't be afraid. I know this sounds hard to believe, and I can't really explain it to you, but it's real. Maybe this will help: do you know what your feet are? *Yes, and I have ten toes too!* That's right, Johnny. But what good are they to you in there? What can you use them for? *Nothing.* Right, Johnny, but you have them because there is an earth here for you to walk and run on. Your feet wouldn't make any sense if there weren't a world out here. Can you believe that? *I'd like to, really I would. But I'm afraid.* I know, and what you're afraid of, your birth, will have to come. There will be some pain and darkness. But then there will be light and life, more life than you can imagine. All I can say is that I've been through what you'll go through, and I'll be waiting here for you with open arms and a big smile. What you think of as death you'll find is really birth!

"That dream seemed so real," Annie thought. Two weeks later her son was born. He had grown into a man she'd always been proud of. He'd soon be coming at Easter to visit her at the nursing home....

Annie. A voice startled her out of her thoughts. An aide perhaps? She turned, but saw no one. Just the crucifix on the wall above her dresser. *Annie.* She heard the voice again, but this time it seemed to come from within. She understood. She closed her eyes and prayed, "Yes, Lord?"

Annie, it's almost time for you to come home. You mean I'm going to die? *No, Annie, you'll soon be born. You'll soon begin to live in a new way.* Lord, I'm afraid. Sometimes I doubt and wonder if you are really there. I wish I could see you face to face. *That's not possible now, Annie, because I'm on the other side of death. But you don't think you came from nowhere, do you?* No, but sometimes heaven seems like a fairy tale. *Well, I can't describe heaven any more than you could explain your world to Johnny before he was born.* I suppose so, Lord, but I'm still afraid. *I know, Annie, but think of your heart. Has it ever really been satisfied? Have you ever been completely happy?* No, because your heart is made for *God and for eternity. Johnny's feet were made for walking on earth, and your heart was made for heaven.* I'm still afraid, Lord. *Yes, Annie, and what you fear will have to come. There will be some pain and darkness. But then there will be light and life, more life than you can imagine. All I can say is that I've been through what you'll go through, and I'll be waiting here for you with open arms and a big smile. And what you think of as death you'll find is really birth!*

"Amen, Lord," Annie whispered. And she knew that her dream was real.

Death as Birth

We who are Catholic believe that death is not just an end but a new beginning. Perhaps the best way for us to understand this is to compare death with birth. We spent nine months in the womb of our mother. Then we outgrew our environment, and our life-support system could no longer sustain us. We "died" to life in the womb as everything keeping us alive seemed to fall apart. But "death" turned out to be birth, and we found ourselves suddenly in the light, living in a new way we could never have imagined. We found ourselves breathing and eating, using a new life-support system we could never have dreamed of in the womb. We found ourselves in a new world where there were opportunities for growth, knowledge, and love which far surpassed anything in the womb.

Death is really a second birth. Our life-support system, our body, will wear out because of age, illness, or accident. Everything that keeps us alive will seem to fall apart. But death will turn out to be birth once again, as darkness turns into day and we find ourselves suddenly in the Light, fully alive at last, face to face with Jesus Christ, in a new world with opportunities for growth, knowledge, and love which far surpass anything on earth.

How will this happen? We can't say for sure, although people who have had near-death experiences seem to have at least peeked into the doorway of the life to come. They tell of light, of peace, of being in touch with loved ones in ways unimaginable, of knowing they are loved, of being sure that God is, of having what they can only describe as a "spiritual body."

Saint Paul wrote: "What you sow is not brought to life unless it dies. And what you sow is not the body that is to be but a bare kernel of wheat, perhaps, or of some other kind....So also is the resurrection of the dead. It is sown corruptible; it is raised incorruptible. It is sown dishonorable; it is raised glorious. It is sown weak; it is raised powerful. It is sown a natural body; it is raised a spiritual body" (1 Corinthians 15:36, 42-44).

Because Christ died and rose, death will be birth. Because Christ rose, Saint Paul assures us, we too shall be "brought to life" (1 Corinthians 15:22). Our resurrection and the eternal life that will follow are essential doctrines of our faith. Trusting in Jesus, we can even look forward to the moment when we shall be born and say, not just with resignation but with joy and hope: "Father, into your hands I commend my spirit" (Luke 23:46).

The Particular Judgment

The Bible tells us that "it is appointed that human beings die once, and after this the judgment" (Hebrews 9:27). At the moment of our death we will stand in the presence of God, seeing our years on earth as God sees them. We will understand the evil of sin with complete clarity, and we will grasp the full extent of Christ's love for us. If our fundamental option has been toward God, we will be attracted to his love in an ecstasy of gratitude and peace. If our fundamental option has been away from God, if we have died in unrepented mortal sin, we will be repulsed by the very love which called us into existence. This is the particular judgment: To stand in God's presence as we really are, to be judged by our own conscience, to be judged by the God of holiness and justice and love.

Many people who have been through a near-death experience report that soon after they leave their physical body they see an "instantaneous playback" of the events of their lives. Time seems to be suspended, for even if it takes only a few moments for doctors to revive them, they have enough "time" to review their whole life. Many say that they return to this life with an appreciation of the importance of love and knowledge and with new insight into the value of other things. Whether this experience is the beginning of the particular judgment is uncertain, but it can help us understand how the judgment might take place.

Catholics believe that through the particular judgment we become aware of our eternal destiny. In referring to the world to come, Jesus speaks of those who will enter into "eternal life" and of those who will go off to "eternal punishment" (Matthew 25:46). Catholics call eternal life "heaven" and eternal punishment "hell" and believe that those who are free from sin will enter heaven after judgment, but that those who have rejected God through unrepented mortal sin will be in hell. Those individuals who are not guilty of grave sin but come into God's presence with attachments to venial sins will need to be purified before they enter heaven, and their state of purification is called "purgatory." The reality of judgment, heaven, hell, and purgatory is taught as official doctrine by the Catholic Church.

Heaven

Heaven is mentioned in Old Testament books like Wisdom, which mentions the "innocent souls' reward" (2:22), but not all Jews of Jesus' time believed in life after death. The Pharisees professed belief in eternal life; the Sadducees did not.

Jesus left no doubt about the reality of eternal life: "For this is the will of my Father, that everyone who sees the Son and believes in him may have eternal life" (John 6:40). This was no vague promise of reincarnation. Jesus said to the criminal who was crucified with him, "Today you will be with me in Paradise" (Luke 23:43). Just as the person who dies to life in the womb is the one born into this world, so the person who dies to this life is the one who enters eternal life.

We don't know exactly what heaven will be like. Saint Paul says that he was "caught up into Paradise and heard ineffable things, which no one may utter" (2 Corinthians 12:4). Saint John writes, "Beloved, we are God's children now; what we shall be has not yet been revealed. We do know that when it is revealed, we shall be like him, for we shall see him as he is" (1 John 3:2). As our life on earth surpasses life in the womb, so life in heaven will surpass this life. Certainly all that is good, beautiful, interesting, and exciting in this life will be more so in heaven, and what causes grief will pass away: "Then I saw a new heaven and a new earth....God himself will always be with them [as their God]. He will wipe every tear from their eyes, and there shall be no more death or mourning, wailing or pain, [for] the old order has passed away" (Revelation 21:1-4).

The greatest joy of heaven will be to see God "face to face." "Blessed are the clean of heart," promises Jesus, "for they will see God" (Matthew 5:8). Catholic tradition calls this vision of God the "beatific vision" because of the happiness it will bring us. And what an incredible experience it will be to stand in the presence of our Creator, to realize that what we have been longing for since the first moment of our existence is now ours forever, to feel completely loved and to love without limits. If we visualize great moments of joy in this life, such as time spent with a best friend, holidays with our family, arriving home after a long absence, presentation of a diploma, a safe landing after a perilous flight, word from the doctor that we are cured, and if we put all these moments together, then we can begin to imagine the happiness that will be ours when we arrive at our true home in heaven and stand in the presence of God!

Sometimes heaven is pictured as "up there" in the clouds, with saints and angels floating around strumming on harps. But heaven is the state of being joined to God and those who love God. Heaven is where God is, everywhere. It may be that God has created our vast universe because he wants us to have eternity to enjoy it. We will not be limited by space or time, and what an exciting prospect it is to have forever to explore all of creation in the company of our friends, the saints and angels, and to visit with these great ones forever!

Hell

Hell is not a pleasant subject, but the New Testament teaches that we can choose to be eternally separated from God, using imagery like fire, wailing, and gnashing of teeth to describe the pain of hell. How literally this imagery is to be taken is uncertain, but it is surely meant to alert us that the suffering of hell will be terrible. Jesus warned us of the chilling words which will be spoken to the condemned: "Depart from me, you accursed, into the eternal fire prepared for the devil and his angels. For I was hungry and you gave me no food, I was thirsty and you gave me no drink" (Matthew 25:41-42).

Sometimes people ask, "If God is merciful, how could he condemn someone to hell forever?" The answer is that God simply ratifies the decision of those who have rejected him by mortal sin. It is true to say that God does not create hell. People do, for hell is essentially the state of separation from God, and people cut themselves off from the love of God when they choose the hatred of sin. God never forces us, and if we choose to reject him, he will respect our choice.

Imagine this situation: Don and Susan fall in love and are married. Life is full of romance when they are near each other. Don hears music in the sound of Susan's voice. But as a few years go by, the excitement of romance begins to dim for Don. He starts to flirt at the office, and his love for Susan begins to cool. She notices and asks what's wrong, but he evades the question. Susan loves Don as much as ever and would do anything for him, but he continues to pull away. Eventually, he has an affair and reaches a point where he cannot stand to be near Susan. Her beauty now repulses him. The sound of her voice grates on his ears. Even though friends tell him that he is a fool, he leaves Susan for another woman.

Now suppose that the other woman and all else that entertains Don are taken away. He is alone in the universe with Susan. Where would he be? In hell, of course. The very person who once brought him such joy and ecstasy now brings him disgust and pain. And why? Not because Susan wants this, for she still loves him, but because he has made decisions that turn her love into something that repulses his whole being.

Hell may be something like that. God loves us, and when we accept and return God's love, we find happiness and joy. But if we turn to evil, God's presence and love seem unreal, even disgusting. As long as we are on this earth and have "playthings" to distract us, we can at least have "fun," if not happiness. When we die, however, and all our toys are taken way, we stand empty-handed before God. But God and his love are now repugnant to us because of the decisions we have made. The universe is full of God's presence, and the only way we can escape is to fall headlong into the hell of our own selfishness and find company with all those who have made the same awful choice. And why? Not because God wants this, for he still loves us. But because we have made decisions that turn God's love into something that repulses our whole being.

Hell is a dreadful fate. It is eternal misery. And the worst part of hell is that for all eternity the damned will know that the one thing which could bring them happiness, God's love, is what they have set themselves against forever.

Purgatory

Catholics also believe in a temporary state of purification after death called "purgatory." The Church bases its belief on the biblical teaching of prayer for the dead (2 Maccabees 12:38-46, quoted in chapter fourteen). If heaven and hell were the only possibilities after death, there would be no reason to pray for the dead. Those in heaven would not need prayers, and those in hell would be beyond the reach of prayer. As a result the Church reasoned to the existence of purgatory, an intermediate state where people can be helped by prayer.

Saint Paul's words in 1 Corinthians 3:13-15 have also been interpreted by some as referring to purgatory. "The work of each one will come to light, for the Day will disclose it. It will be revealed with fire, and the fire [itself] will test the quality of each one's work. If the work stands that someone built upon the foundation, that person will receive a wage. But if someone's work is burned up, that one will suffer loss; the person will be saved, but only as through fire." At the very least, Saint Paul's words seem to express a belief on his part that purification from sin is possible even beyond the grave, on the "Day of Judgment."

The Catholic Church teaches that there is a state of purification after death. It does not teach that purgatory is a place or that those in purgatory experience the pain of fire. Popular explanations of purgatory in the past have sometimes included graphic descriptions of the suffering of the "poor souls." However, those in purgatory are assured of heaven and are even closer to the love of God than we are on earth, and as a result they must experience profound joy. At the same time they have a clear realization of the evil of even the smallest sin, and they suffer the pain of knowing that they are not yet ready to enter the unlimited joys of heaven.

An illustration may be useful: Sarah and Jim plan to celebrate their first wedding anniversary. Sarah's anniversary gift to Jim will be to cook his favorite meal. Jim promises to be home from work by 6:30 that evening. Sarah prepares the meal with loving care and decorates the table with flowers, candles, and their best linen. But just as Jim leaves his office building, he is greeted by a high-school buddy he hasn't seen in years. They start talking about old times, so excited that neither notices the passing of the hours, until Jim glances at his watch. It's 7:15, and now he remembers Sarah and the dinner. As Jim hurries home, he knows that Sarah will understand; she has always been patient and forgiving. But he feels terrible because he realizes that he has let her down. He wants to tell her he is sorry, even though it will be painful to acknowledge his fault and forgetfulness. Sarah will do nothing to cause Jim's suffering. But there is pain in his standing before Sarah, in apologizing, and in receiving her love and forgiveness. It is a pain Jim wants to experience because he knows it will remove any barriers his thoughtlessness might have placed between them.

Purgatory might be like that. When we die we may find ourselves in a situation similar to Jim's. We will realize that we have been less responsive to God's great love than we should have been. We will want to go through the pain of standing in God's presence, acknowledging our failings, and expressing our sorrow so that all barriers we have placed between God's love and ourselves may be removed. It will be a painful process, but one we will gladly endure.

We do not know who might need purgatory, and since those in purgatory are beyond earth's space and time, it is not possible to know "how long" anyone might be there. We pray for those in purgatory because the Bible teaches that they can be helped by our prayers. We know that God is not limited by time, and he can take our prayers of a lifetime and apply them to the needs of a loved one at death. We may pray, then, as long as we wish for our beloved dead.

In teaching the doctrine of purgatory, the Catholic Church shows that God's mercy extends even beyond death. Perhaps most of us will die with some imperfections that would keep us from being "comfortable" in God's presence where "nothing unclean will enter" (Revelation 21:27). Purgatory means hope for us, a way we can walk to enter heaven in the life of the world to come.

The Second Coming of Christ and the General Judgment

We who are Catholic believe in life after death and in judgment. Christ will come to us when we die. We will see him face to face and be judged at that moment. But the full meaning of our lives will not be complete until the world ends. For example, we may bring someone into the Church; that person, in turn, may help others, resulting in much good down through the ages. An evil life, on the other hand, can have repercussions that last through many centuries. So, at the end of time, Jesus will bring human history to a close in a Final Judgment, which will not change the results of the particular judgment, but will bring the consequences of all our deeds to light.

The Bible and Church have given such names to this judgment

as the End Time, Parousia, General Judgment, Day of the Lord, and Second Coming of Christ. In describing these events, the Bible speaks vividly of angels, trumpets, fire, falling stars, and people being caught up in the air (Matthew 24:29-31; 25:31- 46, Mark 13:24-27, 1 Thessalonians 4:16-17). These terms may be poetic, and the Church has not made a dogmatic statement on their exact meaning or on exactly how the world will end. Science tells us that in time our sun will expand into a "red giant" and consume the planets before it dies out. But scientists are unsure about the ultimate fate of the universe as a whole. We simply do not know when or how the world will end. We leave this in God's hands and trust that in his own way he will transform the universe into a "new heaven and a new earth."

Nor does the Church define exactly what is meant by "gather his elect" at the end of time (Matthew 24:31). Artists paint pictures of bodies rising from graves in response to angelic trumpets, but the resurrection of the body on the last day does not mean the reassembly of the atoms which formed our mortal body on this earth. The essential meaning of the resurrection of the body may be that our risen bodies will have a new relationship to the universe, once time on earth is through. Before the last day, all things on earth are moving toward their completion. After the last day, when time has ended and all human beings have entered eternity, God's masterpiece will be seen in all its glory, and the elect will be living and active participants in it.

The Bible teaches that the end of the world will be preceded by signs such as the gospel being preached to all nations (Matthew 24:14) and the conversion of the Jews (Romans 11:25-32). Other signs spoken of in Mark 13, Matthew 24, Luke 21, and elsewhere include wars, confusion, suffering, wickedness, and the rise of an antichrist. These signs are general, and there is little official Catholic teaching about how to understand them because the Church wants us to avoid useless worry and, instead, to focus on the main truth that this world is passing away.

In fact, Jesus said that even he (as a human being) did not know the day or hour (Mark 13:32). Down through the centuries various groups have tried to predict the time of the end of the world. They've all, obviously, been wrong!

What is important is that we always be prepared to meet Jesus. Trusting in God's love and in the salvation won for us by Christ, we even dare to pray with the early believers: *"Marana tha!"* "Come, Lord Jesus!"

The Light Shines in the Darkness

Our story of the Catholic Church began with the vastness and beauty of the universe. It concludes with our prayer to Jesus asking him to bring us into the new creation. God wants us to be led through the great goodness of this world into the full light of his presence (John 1:5). There is sin and darkness on this earth, surely, but Christ our Light has turned the darkness into day. In every age members of the Catholic Church, with all their faults and failings, have tried to be faithful to the Lord. Now we have the great privilege of being part of that Church, the Body of Christ, as the Light continues to shine.

Questions for Discussion or Reflection

Have you ever thought of death as birth? As an exciting possibility? What are some great moments of earthly joy that foreshadow the beatific vision? Name some things you want to experience in heaven? What will purgatory be like? Could God do away with hell and still leave us free?

Activity

Picture yourself as Annie (our character to illustrate our birth/death in Christ) and talk with Jesus about death. Imagine yourself trying to explain this life to an unborn child and reflect on the difficulties you would encounter in doing so.

Bibliography

Adler, Mortimer. *How to Think About God*. Bantam Books.

Day, Edward, C.SS.R. *The Catholic Church Story*. Liguori Publications, 1978.

Greeley, Andrew. *The Great Mysteries: An Essential Catechism*. Harper and Row, rev. 1985.

_____ *The Jesus Myth*. Doubleday.

Handbook for Today's Catholic. Liguori Publications, 1978.

Kaler, Patrick, C.SS.R. *You and the Bible*. Liguori Publications, 1985.

Knight, David. *His Way: An Everyday Plan for Following Jesus*. St. Anthony Messenger Press, 1977.

Lewis, C.S. *Mere Christianity*. MacMillan, 1986.

Link, Mark, S.J. *Path Through Scripture*. Tabor Publisher, 1987.

Lowery, Daniel, C.SS.R. *A Basic Catholic Dictionary*. Liguori Publications, 1985.

_____ *Following Christ: A Handbook of Catholic Moral Teaching*. Liguori Publications, 1982.

McBrien, Richard P. *Catholicism Study Edition*. Harper and Row, 1981.

McGloin, Joseph. *How to Get More Out of the Mass*. Liguori Publications, 1974.

New American Bible: Revised New Testament. Catholic Book Publisher, 1988.

New American Bible — New Testament. Twelve cassette tape set. Hosanna, 2421 Aztec Road NE, Albuquerque, NM 87107. Phone 1-800-545-6552.

O'Rourke, David K. *The Holy Land as Jesus Knew It*. Liguori Publications, 1983.

Schreck, Alan. *Catholic and Christian*. Servant Publications, 1984.

Index